PEARSON CUSTOM
Education

EDUC 373
Principles of Instruction

Instructor: Jan Stivers, Ph.D.

PEARSON

ISBN 10: 1-269-68535-X
ISBN 13: 978-1-269-68535-1

Table of Contents

What Is Inclusion, and Why Is It Important?

What Is Inclusion, and Why Is It Important?

KEY TOPICS

After reading this chapter you will:

- Understand why inclusion is for all students.
- Know the concepts that support inclusive practices.
- Be aware of the characteristics of effective, inclusive programs.
- Describe the role of the teacher and other professionals in an inclusive school.
- Know the importance of being a good teacher for all students.

A VIEW FROM PARENTS

Is Inclusion Good for Grace?

In June 2007, Annette and Larry Jeffrey (pseudonyms are used for Grace and her parents) had their third child, Grace, a bubbly, active girl. Like the other two children, Grace was typical in every way, and for the first year of her life, she developed just as her siblings had. However, shortly after her first birthday, Grace contracted transverse myelitis (TM), a neurological disorder caused by inflammation on both sides of her spinal cord (for more information on transverse myelitis, see NIH, 2011). About one in three people who contract TM fully recover, but Grace was not so fortunate. Her lower body remains weak. She has very limited mobility from the waist down, and uses a wheel-chair to get around. Her parents report that difficulty exploring her environment has also contributed to somewhat delayed language development.

Annette and Larry both work outside the home and had to make a difficult decision about where to place Grace in day care. There was considerable pressure from some of their relatives who felt strongly that Grace should be placed with other students with disabilities because they felt that she needed to be protected from what might happen in a setting with typical children and "because the professionals in those settings know what to do with those children." Putting Grace in such a setting didn't feel right to Annette and Larry, however, and so they decided to place her in a day-care setting with students without disabilities, while she continued to receive services from specialists to support her physical and language development.

When they placed Grace in day care, Annette and Larry readily admitted, "We were pretty apprehensive. Are they paying enough attention to Grace?" They found that Grace enjoyed being around the other children in the day care and was able to play with them, but they were surprised to find that the teachers seemed to pay *too much attention* to her. "They weren't sure or confident whether it was going to be safe for her, so she was often secluded. When they would go outside to play, one of the day-care teachers would take Grace and sit on the mat while the other kids played on the slides and all that stuff." Annette and Larry didn't know how to react to this, as they, too, were apprehensive about Grace's safety. However, they knew that by overprotecting Grace, "they were restricting her; they weren't letting her grow."

Overall, Annette and Larry found that the day-care setting was good for Grace. She made many friends, and her language development began to accelerate. But as Grace's third birthday approached in June 2010, they had another decision to make regarding whether to try to find a local, inclusive school, or to accept a placement in a separate class with other students with disabilities. As Annette said, "We were apprehensive about putting her in school at a young age.

She's only three, and I thought, 'Hmmm, my baby in school!?'" Grace's parents also realized that many schools did not offer inclusive programs for preschool children with disabilities.

Fortunately for Annette and Larry, their decision would be made easier because they lived near a model inclusive school—Gilpin Manor Elementary—that had an excellent preschool teacher who valued inclusion for all students. In the fall of 2010, Grace began school at Gilpin Manor in Allison Meyer's inclusive preschool class for 3- and 4-year-old children. Annette and Larry had decided that inclusion was good for Grace, but what would the school year bring? Would the teachers provide too much protection for Grace, or would they treat her much like other students and encourage her to grow and flourish? You can read more about Gilpin Manor Elementary in the descriptions of our model schools, and we'll provide more information about Grace Jeffrey's first year at Gilpin Manor later in this chapter.

Introduction

What does being included in a community mean to you? For most people, being part of a community means that others care for and respect them for who they are, regardless of their particular strengths and shortcomings. It also means that people have a sense of belonging that brings satisfaction and comfort, and knowing that they can depend on others for support when it is needed. Many go to great lengths to achieve this sense of belonging by moving to certain neighborhoods, joining clubs, and participating in productive and meaningful group activities.

For those of us who work in education with students with disabilities, being part of the school community is often referred to as *inclusion*. In this chapter, we take the perspective that inclusion is not a place or a classroom setting but is a philosophy of education. *We define inclusion quite simply as including students with disabilities as valued members of the school community.* This suggests that students with disabilities *belong* to the school community and are accepted by others; that they actively *participate* in the academic and social community of the school; and that they are given supports that offer them the *opportunity* to succeed. In short, they participate in the school community in ways that we all want to participate in a community.

Pause & Reflect

What does it mean to you to be *included* as part of a community? Perhaps reflecting on instances of when you have been excluded will provide insight into why being included is so important.

Was Grace Jeffrey included in her day care based on this definition of inclusion? Although she seemed to be valued, she certainly didn't actively participate in all aspects of the day-care community, nor did she always receive the necessary supports to have an opportunity to succeed. Is it reasonable for Grace's parents to expect that Grace be valued and supported in the day-care setting? Were these expectations different from what other parents would want for their children?

We agree with Grace's parents that an inclusive setting is best for her, and that placing her in such a setting is well worth the effort and apprehension that may occur. Although most teachers want to provide an inclusive education for all students, we recognize that providing such programs can be challenging, time-consuming, and frustrating. In fact, the reality of how to address effectively the academic and behavioral challenges associated with students with special needs is often daunting to school personnel. Many questions remain regarding how to develop effective, inclusive programs, and provide support for teachers as these programs are implemented (McLeskey & Waldron, 2011a).

In this chapter, we present evidence-based practices with examples from real-world schools and classrooms. We do this because it is our view that information regarding effective, inclusive programs and practices

Students with disabilities are included in most general education classrooms.

is best presented in a practical and straightforward fashion. Consequently, throughout this book, you will notice that we explain a significant amount of content within the context of three effective, inclusive schools: Gilpin Manor Elementary School, West Hernando Middle School, and Heritage High School. These schools serve students of different age and grade levels and have diverse student bodies.

It is important to note that we do not present these schools as examples of ideal inclusive practices. Indeed, the work of developing an inclusive school is never done (McLeskey & Waldron, 2000), as school professionals must adapt to the ever-changing needs of students as each school year progresses. These three schools are no exception, as they continue to actively strive to meet the needs of all their students. You will hear from the teachers, administrators, parents, and students from these schools throughout this chapter, as they provide a real-world perspective on their continuing quest to provide effective, inclusive programs. We introduce you to these schools in the accompanying box, "Descriptions of Three Highly Effective, Inclusive Schools."

Inclusion Is for All Students

If you reflect on your experiences in K–12 general education classrooms, you'll readily recognize that many students have difficulty making academic and social progress in these settings or do not fit in well and need supports or accommodations to succeed. We say this because inclusion is not just about students with disabilities. Although much of our focus in this chapter is on students with disabilities, many of the interventions we describe are useful for a wide range of students who need support in general education classrooms.

Descriptions of Three Highly Effective, Inclusive Schools

Gilpin Manor Elementary School

Elkton, Maryland (population 14,842), is a small town located off of I-95, midway between Baltimore and Philadelphia, just north of the Chesapeake Bay. Many of the people who live in Elkton work in Baltimore or Philadelphia and choose to live in this rural community because of its more laid-back lifestyle. About six years ago, the schools in the Cecil County School District (in which Elkton is the county seat) adopted the philosophy and practice of inclusion for students with disabilities. Gilpin Manor Elementary School (GMES) was one these schools.

Built in 1952, Gilpin Manor was originally a "side-by-side" school. On one side was the "regular" elementary school for children without disabilities in grades K–5. On the other side (actually a back wing) was the "special school," in which students with disabilities spent their days separated from the other children by two heavy double doors that were always closed. According to Mrs. Jennifer Hammer, the current principal and former assistant principal at Gilpin Manor, the two groups of children lived completely separate lives during the school day.

Mrs. Hammer played a significant role in ending the separation and guiding Gilpin Manor toward becoming an inclusive school. Dr. Carolyn Teigland, Associate Superintendent in Cecil County, said, "Mrs. Hammer is an advocate for inclusion for *all* students. She has been at Gilpin throughout the change process and has provided her staff with the vision, training, and support necessary to transform the school into one that educates students with disabilities within inclusive settings along with their peers who are age appropriate."

Mrs. Hammer explained how Gilpin Manor moved from separate schools within a school to become a fully inclusive school. "Approximately seven years ago, I was assigned to Gilpin Manor as an assistant principal. I remember our associate superintendent meeting with my principal and me to discuss our plan to fully include all students in our school.

"We first established an Inclusive Practices Committee. This committee was supported with a representative from Maryland Inclusive Practices Coalition. The committee had several stakeholders, including regular education and special education teachers, paraprofessionals, parents, and community members. The committee first established a vision. One of our first tasks was to help our community understand the legal implications of least

(Continued)

restrictive environment (LRE). We scheduled meetings and began to identify our plan for including students in the regular setting.

"We began by integrating the Level 4 students (students with milder disabilities) into the regular classroom. We had to conduct individualized education program meetings to change the definition of *least restrictive environment* and deploy staff to provide support to the students. All Level 4 classrooms were fully integrated in the first year. Over the next three years, we integrated the students who were in the remaining Level 5 classrooms (students with more significant disabilities). At the same time, we stopped the 'pipeline' that brought students with special needs to GMES. After students completed their preschool experience, they transitioned to their home schools.

"The journey was not without tension, stress, and challenges. At the very beginning, we asked our county's attorney to make a presentation explaining LRE to our staff. Many members of our staff were resistant to this change and feared for their students' futures. They challenged our county vision and questioned the need for a continuum of services. However, in the end, all students successfully integrated into their home schools with appropriate support, including Gilpin Manor."

Today, Gilpin Manor is a school where a very diverse group of children learn together in inclusive classrooms throughout the day. Its mission statement says that its goal is to "support the academic, social, and behavioral development of every child" and it does so with a great deal of pride and success. It serves about 450 children, from preschool to fifth grade, from various backgrounds: 1% of the students are American Indian or Alaska Native, 1% are Asian Pacific Islanders, 31% are African American, and 62% are European American. Among these students, 25% are identified as students with special needs, 1% are English-language learners (ELLs), 2% are homeless, and 67% participate in the free or reduced lunch program.

How can a school like Gilpin Manor be successful with so many students with so many diverse needs and characteristics? Here is what Mrs. Hammer said: "I believe that our greatest strength is that everything that we do is based on what is best for children.... The culture in this building is positive and child centered. You can almost feel the warmth when you enter the building. Teachers support one another and are eager to fill their tool boxes with the strategies and techniques that will meet their students' needs."

Tucked away in the small town of Elkton, Gilpin Manor Elementary School offers an inclusive learning environment for students with a range of abilities. You can learn a lot about the real-world practices used in Gilpin Manor and the impact that these practices have on its students. Knowing about these practices will make educators more successful at including all students and creating effective, inclusive schools.

West Hernando Middle School

West Hernando Middle School (WHMS) is located outside the small town of Brooksville, FL, in rapidly growing Hernando County, a suburban area 50 miles north of Tampa. West Hernando enrolls approximately 1,050 students in grades 6–8, and is the county's cluster school for students with disabilities. About 75% of students in WHMS are Caucasian, and the remaining 25% are Hispanic, African American, American Indian/Alaska Native, multiethnic, or Asian. Over 19% of the students in WHMS have disabilities, and 76% qualify for free or reduced lunch.

Rick Markford has been the principal of West Hernando for the past two years. Prior to that time, he was an assistant principal at a high school and a K–8 school. It is noteworthy that most of his prior administrative experience has been in an inclusive high school that is next door to West Hernando. It was at this school that he learned first-hand about inclusion and the importance of a peer-support program for students with more substantial disabilities.

An inclusive philosophy pervades the West Hernando school community in all activities, and is reflected in the following belief statement that guides the work of the school improvement team and all school staff.

WHMS students soar with WINGS (W—Wise choices, I—Innovative learning, N—new challenges, G—Good citizenship, S—Strong positive attitudes). WHMS faculty and staff work to create an environment where all community stakeholders embrace innovative learning strategies and new challenges. We intend to accomplish this by encouraging strong positive attitudes, practicing good citizenship, and recognizing students' wise choices. We are dedicated to providing a rigorous curriculum delivered through research-based programs and practices with differentiated instruction to ensure that all student can and will learn.

The school community at West Hernando is close-knit and supportive of all students. This philosophy is obvious to a visitor when entering the school, as a quote by Booker T. Washington is prominently displayed on the building opposite the entry: "If you want to lift yourself up, lift up someone else." It is also obvious from observing students walking in halls, congregating in the large courtyard that the school building surrounds, or interacting in classrooms. Teachers and students at WHMS are a community of learners who support one another in a range of ways, formal and informal, large and small.

Mr. Markford discusses this emphasis on building relationships and supporting all students as part of West Hernando's culture. "At West Hernando, success is the only option, and the foundation of that success is relationship building. My mantra from my teaching days has always been 'discipline without relationships leads to rebellion.' If you don't have that relationship first, everything else will be impossible or at least a struggle." Mr. Markford goes on to note that at West Hernando, relationships are established with all students early in the school year to provide a foundation for behavioral and academic success.

We'll discuss many of the instructional approaches used at WHMS to support students with disabilities in general education classrooms and as part of the school community throughout the chapters that follow. These activities include co-teaching, peer buddies, differentiated instruction, grouping practices, collaborative teaming, and a range of other effective practices. However, the most powerful aspect of the education students receive at West Hernando Middle School is the dedication of the school staff and students to build a community that supports and includes all students, and the pride that staff and students feel in being part of this special community.

Mr. Markford also emphasizes the importance of teacher collaboration at West Hernando Middle School to support all students. This collaborative work ethic has been especially important as a response-to-intervention (RTI) model has been developed at West Hernando to identify students and provide them with high-quality, tiered instructional support in their classrooms. "Collaboration is one of the key components of RTI at West Hernando as we emphasize working together as a team to develop a system of student support," Mr. Markford states. He also emphasizes the importance of collaboration as part of the many co-taught classrooms at West Hernando. In these classrooms, general and special education teachers work as partners to differentiate instruction for all students. As Mr. Markford notes, "The basis of the inclusion model at West Hernando is the collaboration between co-teachers to develop lesson plans and deliver differentiated instruction."

The success of WHMS can be measured in several ways, including the awards the school has received (an "A" school in Florida for each of the last 5 years, and receiving an award from the Governor of Florida as one of the Top 50 Combination Schools for Making Progress in the state), the rates at which students with a range of disabilities are included in general education classrooms (well above the state average), or by student academic progress, as measured by several state and local tests. By any of these measures, WHMS excels. It also excels as an extraordinary middle school, where all students belong to a school community that provides academic and social support, and where teachers work collaboratively to ensure that success is the only option for every student.

Heritage High School

Heritage High School, a modern comprehensive high school of approximately 1,340 students, is located in Leesburg, Virginia. Leesburg, the county seat of Loudoun County, is a historic area, having once, during the War of 1812, been the temporary location for the U.S. government and its archives. The areas surrounding the town center are also known for their Civil War battlefields (e.g., Antietam). Located at the far end of the densely populated Washington, DC, and the northern Virginia corridor, Leesburg has experienced tremendous growth in population, particularly among Hispanic and Asian immigrant groups. Reflecting the influx of families from these cultures, Heritage High School is considerably diverse, with 17.8% of its students of Hispanic origin, 12.1% African American, 4.6% multiracial, and 10.2% of Asian descent. The remaining 55.1% are European American. Among all students enrolled, approximately 18% are eligible for free or reduced lunch, and 12.6% have identified disabilities.

Margaret Huckaby, the founding principal of Heritage, had the rare and challenging opportunity of developing the school's administrative structure, climate, and culture from the ground up. With an energetic, positive, and creative interactive style, she garnered considerable input from all the school's stakeholders—from cafeteria workers to psychologists—to develop student-centered approaches and procedures to provide sustained success for all students.

Visitors to Heritage can readily see the results of these efforts: Collaboration and empowerment pervade the school's administrative, instructional, and extracurricular policies and activities. Teams of administrators, teachers, and professional staff work together, ensuring that all students have opportunities to receive supportive instruction and caring related services. This teaming is not left to chance: Margaret and her administrative staff

(Continued)

are sensitive to interpersonal dynamics and form teams that build on how teachers' strengths can be combined to improve student outcomes.

Heritage High's efforts at collaborative teaming have resulted in a number of impressive outcomes. The school routinely scores well above the state average on Virginia State Report Card measures, resulting in the all-important designation of meeting adequate yearly progress (AYP). Numerous Advanced Placement courses are offered, and approximately one third of graduating students receive an Advanced Studies Diploma with the coveted Governor's Seal.

Perhaps the most notable element of teaming at Heritage is the day-to-day operation of its inclusive education philosophy. Monitored and nurtured by Dean Susan Hill, special education services are delivered in a variety of ways, depending on the unique needs of the student. Most students with disabilities at Heritage receive services within general education content classrooms. Depending on the instructional and behavioral profile of the student, special education teachers either consult or co-teach with general education content-area specialists. Teachers often use universally designed instructional techniques (adaptations and accommodations that are useful for students with and without disabilities) or curricular supports in lessons and unit plans. In many other cases, classes are actively co-taught by both highly qualified general and special education teachers. Because co-teaching has been a mainstay of the Heritage instructional delivery system since the school opened, it is not viewed as strange or unusual. It is just the way things are done at Heritage.

Some students at Heritage require supplemental supports in addition to what is provided in their general education classrooms. For these students, small-group sessions are arranged and delivered in a private area of the school (i.e., the library) or another classroom. Students with significant disabilities are included in general education classrooms for social, behavioral, and general knowledge exposure and also may spend time receiving direct instruction in separate class settings. Peer Teams are employed to support these students in their classrooms and during extracurricular activities. Based on the success of their programs, Heritage is embracing several new challenges. Students with challenging behaviors who had been placed in segregated day school placements have been returned to Heritage, their neighborhood school, and essential supports and accommodations are being provided. Not surprisingly, these students are achieving academically and socially at heretofore unseen levels of success. The school has also stepped up its efforts in the area of transition to the world of work. In particular, The SWEET (Student Work Experience Enabling Transition) Shop, staffed by students and job coaches, offers valuable job skills training to students while providing time-saving clerical services (e.g., copying, laminating) to teachers and staff.

As in any school, things are not perfect at Heritage. Situations arise that require swift action, creative problem solving, and sometimes difficult decision making. However, with a solid foundation of administrative support, substantive parent involvement, and collaborative teaming, staff feel empowered and supported in their attempts to address the many issues typical of teaching and managing large numbers of developing adolescents.

We provide information that illustrates the diversity of the general education classroom in the following sections. In addition to students with disabilities, students in general education classes who contribute to this diversity and may need accommodations include students who are at risk for difficulty in school, students from diverse cultural and linguistic backgrounds, and students identified as gifted and talented.

Students with Disabilities and Special Education

Special education consists primarily of services and supports that teachers provide to meet the needs of students who are identified with disabilities. Although the categories used to define disabilities vary across states, most use some variation of the federal definitions of disability categories. Table 1 includes brief descriptions of the disability categories used by the federal government in the Individuals with Disabilities Education Improvement Act, or PL 108-446 (IDEA, 2004).

As you will note, these disability categories include a broad range of students with abilities and disabilities related to cognitive, social, physical, and sensory skills. To simplify disability categories, some states use more general categories such as *mild-to-moderate*

Table 1 Disability Categories and Definitions adapted from PL 108-446, IDEA 2004

Disability Category	Brief Definition
Learning disability (called *specific learning disability* in IDEA, 2004)	Includes students who have difficulty making adequate academic progress in school, especially in basic skill areas such as reading, writing, and/or mathematics.
Speech or language impairment	Includes students with communication disorders (e.g., difficulty articulating certain speech sounds or difficulty using or understanding words) that affect educational performance.
Other health impairments	Includes a range of health impairments (e.g., epilepsy, diabetes) that adversely affect a student's educational performance. Attention-deficit/hyperactivity disorder (ADHD) is included as part of this category.
Intellectual disabilities (called *mental retardation* in IDEA, 2004)	Includes a broad range of students, from those with mild to significant impairments in intellectual and adaptive skills.
Emotional disturbance	Includes a broad range of students, including those who exhibit aggressive behavior as well as students who have more internalized emotional disorders (e.g., pervasive unhappiness or depression).
Autism (often referred to as *autism spectrum disorders*)	Includes students who exhibit a developmental disability that significantly affects verbal and nonverbal communication and social interaction.
Multiple disabilities	Includes students who have disabilities in more than one area (e.g., intellectual disability and blindness, intellectual disability and orthopedic impairment) that often result in substantial impairments and significant educational needs.
Developmental delay	Includes students who experience delays in physical, cognitive, communication, emotional, or adaptive development. This category is used at the discretion of states, and can be used for students ages 3 through 9.
Hearing impairments and deafness	Students with hearing impairments have some residual hearing that may be used to understand oral speech. In contrast, children who are deaf lack such residual hearing.
Orthopedic impairments	Includes students who have physical limitations and may use a wheelchair. These students have a full range of intellectual abilities but may have difficulty demonstrating this ability without specialized supports.
Visual impairments including blindness	Includes students who are blind and those with significant visual impairments.
Traumatic brain injury	Includes students who have an acquired injury to the brain caused by an external physical force, resulting in a disability that adversely affects educational performance. This is the only category limited to students who acquire a disability after birth.
Deaf-blindness	This is the smallest disability category, and includes only individuals with significant educational needs.

disabilities and *significant disabilities*. The mild-to-moderate category includes most students who are identified with learning disabilities and speech or language impairment and some students from other categories (e.g., autism, other health impairments, intellectual disabilities). About 90% of students with disabilities are included in the mild-to-moderate category. The significant disability category includes about 10% of all students, and most students who are identified with multiple disabilities and deaf-blindness fall into this category. In addition, some students in several other categories may be identified with significant disabilities (e.g., autism and intellectual disabilities).

About 11.2% of school-aged students in the United States are identified with disabilities (U.S. Department of Education, 2011). Special education services and supports are specially designed to meet the needs of these students. Several factors make special education "special," including the following (Kauffman & Hallahan, 2005):

- **Intensity.** Special education instruction may involve adjusting the intensity of instruction provided to a student. More time for direct instruction and practice are critical elements of more intensive instruction. This may involve a lower teacher–pupil ratio, using strategies such as class-wide peer tutoring, cooperative learning, or co-teaching.
- **Structure.** Students with disabilities are provided with learning conditions that are more organized, explicit, and predictable.
- **Curriculum.** Almost all students with disabilities learn based on the general education curriculum (i.e., the same curriculum as all other students), but many of these students require specialized supports and accommodations to access this material. Some students with significant disabilities require an alternative curriculum for some part of the school day that addresses basic life skills, alternative communication skills, or social skills.
- **Collaboration.** For a successful educational experience, professionals from general and special education must combine their expertise to address the needs of students with disabilities.
- **Monitoring/Assessment.** Teachers monitor the student's progress in an academic area, and adjust instructional methods based on this information. Thus, teachers may use a variety of approaches if a student with a disability has difficulty learning critical elements of the curriculum.

Other Students Who May Need Support in the General Education Classroom

Many teachers and other school professionals have noted that the effective practices used in inclusive classrooms are beneficial for many students who do not have disabilities but struggle academically or socially. As Cathy Dofka, Director of Special Education in Hernando County Florida (and for West Hernando Middle School), notes, "Inclusion benefits all students academically and socially. Effective teaching methods are good for all students who struggle, not just those with disabilities." Students who benefit from these practices may include students who are at risk for difficulty in school, students from diverse cultural and linguistic backgrounds, and students identified as gifted and talented.

Students at Risk for Difficulties in School

Students who grow up in poverty are at greater risk than other students for having academic or social difficulty in school. But as you will recognize, many students who have risk factors in their backgrounds do quite well in school; for others, however, these factors may

Many students with and without disabilities need supports to be successful in general education classrooms.

contribute to academic or social difficulties. At least five factors related to growing up in poverty influence student performance in school (Kauchak & Eggen, 2012):

1. Fulfillment of basic needs, including sufficient nutrition and medical care
2. Family stability, including marital stability, and parent frustration related to economic struggle
3. School-related experiences, including exposure to educational experiences (e.g., visits to museums, libraries) or educational activities (e.g., computer classes, dance lessons) outside of school
4. Interaction patterns in the home, including the use of less elaborate language, and the tendency to "tell" rather than to "explain"
5. Parental attitudes and values, including the value placed on getting a good education and reading in the home

Students who are at risk in school are placed in general education classrooms and are the responsibility of general education teachers. Effective practices that are designed to address the needs of all students in inclusive classrooms will often work with these students as well. For example, these practices may improve academic achievement levels, and ensure that many of these students achieve at levels that are similar to classroom peers (Torgesen, 2009).

Students from Diverse Cultural and Linguistic Backgrounds

Another major component of diversity in general education classrooms relates to students from culturally and linguistically diverse backgrounds. These students often come from backgrounds that are different from that of their teachers, who most often are European American. In 2008–2009 (National Center for Education Statistics, 2009), approximately 45% of all school-aged students in public schools in the United States were from non-European American backgrounds. This includes 21.5% of students who are of Hispanic or Latino origin, and 17.0% who are African American. Further adding to the diversity in classrooms across the United States is the range of languages that are spoken. The U.S. Census Bureau (2008) reported that in 2007, a language other than English was spoken in 20.5% of all homes.

Key considerations for teachers (Ross, Kamman, & Coady, 2011) in meeting the needs of individuals from diverse language and cultural backgrounds include (1) understanding the students' cultural and linguistic backgrounds and (2) learning to adapt teaching based on this information to ensure positive student outcomes.

Students Who Are Gifted and Talented

Children who are identified as gifted or talented are those who learn academic content in one or more areas much more rapidly than most other students, or have high levels of performance ability in visual or performing arts, creativity, or leadership. In some states, students who are identified as gifted or talented must meet a cutoff for IQ and/or achievement (e.g., an IQ cutoff of 130 or higher) that is significantly higher than average performance by peers (Rosenberg, Westling, & McLeskey, 2011).

Gifted and talented is not a category of disability, and thus is not addressed in IDEA 2004. Identification criteria and funding for programs for these students are typically addressed in state law. The level of support for gifted and talented programs across the United States varies widely. Many general education classrooms have students who achieve at a level that is much higher than most other peers in the class. Some of these students are assigned to separate classes (e.g., advanced mathematics) for part of the school day. Further, many schools have teachers who provide support for gifted and talented students in general education classrooms.

Concepts That Support Inclusive Practices

Two critical concepts provide the foundation on which inclusive practices are built. These concepts are *normalization* and the *least restrictive environment.*

Figure 1	An Example of the Principle of Normalization

Biklen (1985) describes one of Bengt Nirje's favorite illustrations of the principle of normalization. While Nirje was president of the Swedish Association for Retarded Children, he asked a group of adults with intellectual disabilities what requests they would make to change national policies that affect their lives. These individuals did not ask to be given special privileges (e.g., preference for housing during housing shortages that all Swedes faced at the time). Presumably, they already received enough treatment that they viewed as "special." Rather, they said that they wanted to go on outings (e.g., shopping) in groups of two or three rather than in large groups. Further, they did not want to go to camps for persons with intellectual disabilities, but rather wanted to vacation like everyone else, in vacation resorts in Europe. In short, persons with intellectual disabilities wanted to be treated like everyone else, and have the same opportunities as others, and did not want to receive special activities or privileges because of their disability. This is the crux of the principle of normalization.

Normalization

The concept of normalization originated in Scandinavia and was initially used to address individuals with intellectual disabilities. This concept has since been applied to all people with disabilities. Bengt Nirje defined *normalization* as making available to all persons with intellectual disabilities "patterns of life and conditions of everyday living, which are as close as possible to the regular circumstances and ways of life of society" (p. 6, cited in Biklen, 1985). This suggests that persons with disabilities should have the opportunity to live their lives as independently as possible, making their own life decisions regarding work, leisure, housing, and so forth. See Figure 1 for an example of this principle.

This concept sharply contrasts perspectives on people with disabilities that were previously held by many educators, and continue to be held by much of the general public. For example, people with intellectual disabilities were long held to be "eternal children" who needed to be protected and could not live independently or make their own life decisions. In contrast, the concept of normalization suggests that people with disabilities should be self-determined, making their own life decisions, and accorded the dignity of risk, rather than protection, in making decisions about their lives as they grow older, similar to other individuals. Furthermore, a goal of schooling for people with disabilities should be to provide them with the knowledge and skills needed to lead as typical a life as possible and to live as independently as possible, with a job, a place to live in the community, and leisure activities that result in a full, enjoyable, productive life. In short, persons with disabilities should be provided opportunities similar to those that are desired by everyone—to be treated with respect, to be independent, and to be given the opportunity to make their own decisions.

Cathy Dofka, Director of Special Education in Hernando County, Florida, emphasizes the importance of this perspective, when she states, "Students with disabilities have been too isolated in separate classes, where they only see other students with disabilities. They don't learn to get along with other people in these settings. You don't have (a special education) Wal-Mart or Publix. Students with disabilities need to learn to get along in a community with everyone else."

The wide acceptance of the concept of normalization has led to increased expectations for life outcomes and increased value for the lives of people with disabilities. Coupled with these changes, disability rights advocates

Inclusion is intended to provide students with disabilities a school experience that is as typical as possible.

Figure 2	People-First Language

People-first language emphasizes that persons with disabilities are just that: people who happen to have an intellectual, sensory, physical, or emotional disability. Language should be used that is respectful of people with disabilities. For example, language should not be used to express pity for persons with disabilities, nor should words that are used to describe people with disabilities be used in negative ways. For example, "He's a *retard*." Some terms have taken on such a negative connotation that they are no longer used to describe people with disabilities (e.g., retarded or handicapped, suggesting a person begging with "cap in hand"). A law that was passed in 2010 by the U.S. Congress that eliminates the use of the term *mental retardation* in federal laws, and replaces this term with *intellectual disability* illustrates this. Language describing a disability should be used only when it is necessary to communicate clearly with others. It often isn't necessary to point out that a person has a disability. Suggestions for using respectful, people-first language include:

People-First Language	Inappropriate Language
Disability	Handicap
Intellectual disability	Retarded or mental retardation
John has an intellectual disability.	John is retarded.
Nancy uses a wheelchair.	Nancy is wheel-chair bound.
	(*Or:* Nancy is confined to a wheel-chair.)
Dane has cerebral palsy.	Dane suffers from cerebral palsy.
Karson has Down syndrome.	She's Down's.
The boy with a learning disability	The learning disabled boy

Source: For more information on people-first language, see www.disabilityisnatural.com and www.r-word.org

have demanded the use of more respectful language when discussing persons with disabilities, including the use of **people-first language**. (For more information regarding people-first language, see Figure 2.) Inclusive practices in schools are built on the assumption that the principle of normalization should be applied in school settings; that is, students with disabilities should have school experiences that are as typical as possible, and student differences should be accommodated in as typical a manner as possible. Further, it is assumed that this type of school experience is more effective in preparing a person with a disability to live an independent, self-determined life as an adult.

Least Restrictive Environment

A second concept that provides support for inclusion in federal law is the **least restrictive environment (LRE)** mandate. This mandate was included in the Individuals with Disabilities Education Improvement Act when the U.S. Congress initially passed this law in 1975 (the law was then called the Education for All Handicapped Children Act). The LRE mandate states, "To the maximum extent appropriate, children with disabilities . . . are educated with children who are non-disabled; and special classes, separate schooling, or other removal of children with disabilities from the regular educational environment occurs only if the nature or severity of the disability is such that education in regular classes with the use of supplementary aids and services cannot be achieved satisfactorily" (PL 108-446, IDEA, 2004, Regulations Part 300, Sec. 300.114).

Although the term *inclusion* is not included in federal law, the LRE mandate creates a presumption in favor of educating students with disabilities in the general education classroom (McLeskey, Landers, Williamson, & Hoppey, 2011). The law is interpreted to mean that every student with a disability has a right to be educated in a classroom with peers without disabilities, if they can succeed in that setting with appropriate supports. Thus, students with

Pause & Reflect

Is people-first language important, or is it an overreaction to a minor concern? What language have you heard being used in schools to describe people with disabilities? In social settings outside of school? What does this language say about our attitudes toward people with disabilities?

Figure 3

Continuum of
Educational Services
for Students with
Disabilities

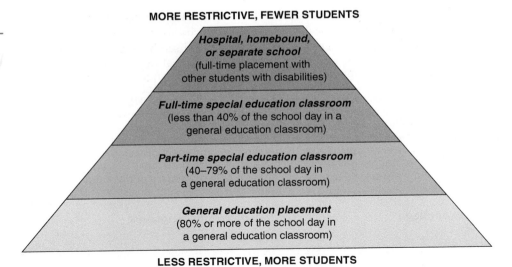

MORE RESTRICTIVE, FEWER STUDENTS

*Hospital, homebound,
or separate school*
(full-time placement with
other students with disabilities)

Full-time special education classroom
(less than 40% of the school day in a
general education classroom)

Part-time special education classroom
(40–79% of the school day in
a general education classroom)

General education placement
(80% or more of the school day in
a general education classroom)

LESS RESTRICTIVE, MORE STUDENTS

Figure 3

Continuum of Educational Services for Students with Disabilities

disabilities should be placed in more restrictive settings (i.e., a separate, special education class, or separate school) only if they do not succeed in the general education classroom with supports and if the separate class can lead to more success than the general education placement.

To ensure that the needs of all students with disabilities are met, IDEA 2004 requires provision of a continuum of services for students with disabilities. Figure 3 provides a description of the continuum of services as it exists in most school systems. As you will note in this figure, placement options differ based on the time students with disabilities spend in the general education classroom with peers without disabilities.

General Education Classroom

Approximately 62% of students with disabilities are provided services in a general education classroom for most of the school day (U.S. Department of Education, 2011). If separate special education services are provided, the student is in a separate classroom for no more than 20% of the school day. This placement includes students who are in a general education classroom full time, with only consultation services from a special education teacher; students who are served in a general education classroom that is co-taught by a general and a special education teacher; and students who are provided short-term, intensive instruction in particular content areas (e.g., reading, learning strategies) or instructional support in specific content areas (e.g., science, social studies) in separate, special education settings.

Part-Time Special Education Classroom

These settings are often referred to as *resource classes*. In these classes, a small number (e.g., three to eight) of students with disabilities are provided instruction for short periods of time in basic skills (i.e., reading, writing, mathematics), tutorial support in specific subjects, or instruction in the use of learning strategies. Students with disabilities who are in part-time special education classes spend from 40 to 79% of the school day in general education classrooms, and the remainder of the day in a special education classroom. A special education teacher and/or a paraeducator, under the supervision of a special education teacher, provide services in these part-time classes. Approximately 21% of all students with disabilities are served in these settings (U.S. Department of Education, 2011).

Full-Time Special Education Classroom

Approximately 16% of all students with disabilities are served in full-time special education classrooms on local school campuses (U.S. Department of Education, 2011). These students with disabilities spend most of the school day (60% or more) in a classroom with other students with similar disabilities. These classrooms typically include a small number of students (5 to 10 or more, depending on the severity of the disabilities and the number of professionals in the classroom), a special education teacher, and one or more paraeducators. Students most often served in these settings include those with intellectual disabilities, emotional disturbance, multiple disabilities, deaf-blindness, and autism.

Hospital, Homebound, Separate Residential Schools, and Separate Day Schools

Students who are educated in these settings attend school full time in a placement other than their neighborhood schools. These schools may be separate settings in the local school system, or residential schools in another city where students live full time during the school year. Separate schools are designed to provide highly specialized instruction and supports for students with disabilities and often include students from a single disability category (e.g., deaf or hearing impaired, blind or visually impaired, significant intellectual disabilities, serious emotional disturbance), or a limited number of disability categories. Approximately 1.5% of all students with disabilities are served in these settings (U.S. Department of Education, 2011).

What Are Effective Inclusive Programs?

You will note that none of the service-delivery settings we described are called "inclusive." This is because inclusion is not a place or a setting. As we noted previously, inclusion is a philosophy of education, and we define *inclusion* quite simply as including students with disabilities as valued members of the school community. This suggests that students with disabilities *belong* to the school community and are accepted by others; that they actively *participate* in the academic and social community of the school; and that they are given supports that offer them the *opportunity to succeed*. In short, they participate in the school community in ways that are much the same as other students. You will remember that this is just what Annette and Larry Jeffrey wanted for their daughter Grace in her day-care setting, and what most parents want for their children with disabilities. For more about Grace's first year in an inclusive preschool classroom at Gilpin Manor Elementary, see "A View from Her Parents and Teacher: Has Inclusion Been Good for Grace?"

A View from Her Parents and Teacher

Has Inclusion Been Good for Grace?

As you will recollect from the vignette that opened this chapter, during the summer of 2010, Grace Jeffrey's parents, Annette and Larry, had a difficult decision to make. Grace became eligible to attend a preschool class in a local elementary school. However, Annette and Larry remained apprehensive. For one thing, they were fearful "that not all children are as respectful as some, and she might be picked on." They also found it difficult to watch when their daughter was with other students who could walk around, given her inability to actively participate. As they pondered these feelings, they realized that they were having difficulty making a decision because they were overprotecting Grace, and that they had to overcome these feelings if she was going to be successful in school. After putting off the decision for several months, they decided to place Grace in Allison Meyer's inclusive preschool class at Gilpin Manor Elementary in the fall of 2010.

Allison Meyer collaborates with a co-teacher and paraeducator to provide inclusive services for students in her preschool classroom of 3- and 4-year-old children. She also works closely with an occupational therapist and a physical therapist to provide push-in services (i.e., professionals come into the general education classroom) for Grace and any other students who need support in the general education classroom, while occasionally pulling students out of the class for specialized services. Grace also receives occasional services from a speech–language pathologist.

(Continued)

The approach the teachers take in Grace's inclusive preschool differs dramatically from her experience in day care. The teachers expect Grace to participate in all class activities, and they treat her like every other student whenever possible. Her parents have appreciated this respectful and challenging perspective. "I really appreciate that they don't seclude her when activities occur and her disability comes into play. When children are playing on the playground, they always find a way to include her. They're there to help her participate."

Allison Meyer reports that Grace has flourished during her first year in an inclusive preschool program. "She wants to be mobile . . . she wants to do what the other children are doing. She can keep up with them in conversation and play, so it motivates her to be more independent, to do more on her own like her peers are." During the school day, Grace spends about half an hour in her wheelchair. For the remainder of the day "she's either on the floor crawling or sitting in a chair with the group during whole-group sessions. There are times when she just tells us no (she doesn't want help), and she wants to get herself across the room (by herself)." And she does that successfully.

According to Ms. Meyer, Grace has developed "fabulous social skills. It was difficult at the beginning of the year with her physical restrictions, because it's painful, the therapy she goes through. She gets very shaky." She went on to note that as the year progressed, Grace has gotten more comfortable and has made several friends. "The other kids love her. She had a couple that wanted to 'mommy' her at first, treating her like a baby. But now she's their buddy." Her parents concur that Grace has made many friends who have been "a big motivation for her. I've seen her try things that she wouldn't have tried before. Being with these other children has really just sparked her interest. It's given her that kind of attitude where she says 'I can do this!' She wants to do what the other kids are doing. She tries harder."

After one year in an inclusive preschool class, Annette and Larry Jeffrey feel that Grace has made significant progress in speech and language. "Her speech has come a long way. She did have speech therapy frequently, but now she doesn't need it much. She's been around the other kids and her communication has improved tremendously—and her awareness. Since she's been here I've noticed a lot more questions and interest in different things." They go on to say, "She loves to interact with the other kids. She really enjoys school!"

Perhaps the most important change in Grace that her parents have noticed is her level of motivation and confidence. Being in an inclusive classroom "is a huge motivational factor. She wants to do everything that everybody else is doing. It's almost like, at times, she doesn't realize that she has any limitations. She has those moments when she will get frustrated. But my biggest fear was her loss of confidence. (That hasn't happened as) she fully thinks that she can do everything the other children can do." Grace's parents believe that "if she was with other children (with disabilities) she would just accept her limitations." But in her inclusive classroom, she is "motivated to overcome her limitations" and continues to grow.

As Annette and Larry Jeffrey look to the future, they want to continue to have Grace attend Gilpin Manor and participate in inclusive settings. As their comments suggest, they want her to be a valued member and active participant in the school community, and they want her to receive supports that give her an opportunity to succeed. Such a setting will "give her the confidence to face her disability down the road." Just like any other parents, Annette and Larry want Grace to have as typical a childhood as possible, participating in T-ball and swimming alongside her peers. Annette notes that the children in her class will be her friends and peers in the future as she grows up. She then concludes, "I never saw inclusion when I was growing up, I never went to school with a child with a disability. That was why we were initially apprehensive about it. This is a change in society, and I think it's a good change. I think it will benefit children in the long run. Those with disabilities and those without will learn to understand and respect each other."

Not all educators define *inclusion* in the same way. It is important to seek clarification when discussing inclusion to ensure a clear understanding of the intended meaning of the term. For example, much controversy has surrounded the use of the term **full inclusion**, and the perspective taken by some that all students with disabilities should be included in general education classes for the entire school day (Fuchs & Fuchs, 1994; McLeskey, 2007; McLeskey & Waldron, 2011b). We find that this approach to inclusion is less likely to occur in today's schools, as most parents, teachers, and administrators emphasize that schools be both inclusive and effective in meeting student needs, and this may require occasional separate class instruction that is highly specialized for students with disabilities (McLeskey & Waldron, 2011a). However, there remain instances of inclusion that could be characterized as ineffective or irresponsible. To be successful, inclusion takes careful planning involving teachers, administrators, and parents. Irresponsible and ineffective inclusion occurs when students with disabilities are moved (often quickly)

Pause & Reflect

Does it surprise you that Annette and Larry Jeffrey want the same things from school for Grace that all parents want? Do you think that persons with disabilities want the same things from life that everyone else wants? What does this say about the importance of inclusive programs in schools?

into general education classrooms with limited planning and little support for general education teachers (e.g., Dymond & Russell, 2004). This results in poor outcomes for many students with and without disabilities, and much frustration on the part of their teachers.

When we discuss inclusive programs or classrooms in this text, we refer to well-designed, effective inclusive programs. We thus make the following assumptions regarding these programs:

1. All students with disabilities are part of the academic and social community of the school. They are valued members of the school, and participate in the school community in much the same way as all other students.

2. Most students with disabilities are educated for most of the school day in general education classrooms, but specialized, highly effective instruction is provided in separate settings as needed to improve student outcomes.

3. Student academic and social progress is monitored to ensure the effectiveness of instruction and improved student outcomes. Educational materials, instruction, and/or placement are changed as needed to improve student outcomes.

4. Resources, including both personnel and materials, are available to provide appropriate supports for students in general education classrooms or separate settings.

5. Time is available to allow general and special education teachers and other professionals to collaboratively plan the delivery of services and their instructional roles. This time is available to plan the inclusive program before it begins, as well as to conduct ongoing planning once the program is implemented.

6. Teachers are provided high-quality professional development to learn new skills needed to provide students with appropriate services.

7. Teachers adapt the general education curriculum to meet the needs of all students. This may include providing supports to ensure access to the general education curriculum or providing alternative curriculum for some students with highly specialized needs.

8. Teachers plan instruction so that most student needs are met as a natural part of the school day.

9. Teachers provide classroom supports in a manner that is natural and unobtrusive. These supports are used with a range of students, not just those with disabilities, and serve to make student differences a natural part of the school day.

10. The rhythm of the school day for students with disabilities is similar to the rhythm of the day for all students. The schedules of students with disabilities are similar to those of other students, and their school day is not readily identifiable because they have a disability.

Inclusive Programs: Research on Effectiveness

Much controversy has surrounded research on the effectiveness of inclusive programs (Fuchs & Fuchs, 1994; Kavale & Forness, 2000; McLeskey, 2007; McLeskey & Waldron, 2011b). This controversy largely relates to how *effectiveness* is defined. Some have argued that researchers, educators, and policy makers have placed too much emphasis on providing students with disabilities access to general education classrooms in neighborhood schools and too little emphasis on improving student outcomes (McLeskey & Waldron, 2011a). These criticisms have taken on added importance with the passage of the No Child Left Behind (NCLB) Act (2001), which mandates that schools must be held accountable for educational outcomes for all students, including those with disabilities.

Most of the needs of students with disabilities should be met as a natural part of the school day.

With the passage of the NCLB Act, local schools must provide access to the general education classroom for students with disabilities and also ensure improved student outcomes. As we're sure you would speculate based on the previous information in this chapter, as well as any previous experience you've had with inclusion, it is not a simple task to develop an effective, inclusive program. However, research evidence supports the effectiveness of well-designed inclusive programs (e.g., Cole, Waldron, & Madj, 2004; Salend & Garrick Duhaney, 2007). These programs allow students with disabilities to benefit from access to the general education curriculum, as well as to have intensive, focused instruction in critical skill areas (i.e., reading, writing, mathematics) as needed. They also provide a context for developing social skills, making friends, and so forth, that serve to prepare all students, including those with disabilities, for a successful, independent life beyond their school years. Key findings from research regarding the academic and social benefits of inclusive programs are included in Figure 4.

As Figure 4 reveals, many students with disabilities benefit from well-designed inclusive programs in a range of ways. However, three caveats should be noted regarding this research. First, several studies have revealed that students with disabilities do not make improved academic progress when inclusive programs are not well designed (e.g., Pivik, McComas, & Laflamme, 2002). In fact, these investigations reveal that poorly designed (or irresponsible) inclusive programs may have negative effects on academic outcomes for students with disabilities as well as their peers without disabilities.

A second caveat relates to the fact that no matter how well an inclusive program is designed, most research has revealed that some students with disabilities do not make as much academic progress as we'd like them to make (Lindsay, 2007; McLeskey & Waldron, 2011b). To improve outcomes of inclusive programs, some researchers have studied the use of well-designed, intensive, small-group instruction to support inclusive program placements (Fuchs, Fuchs, Craddock, et al., 2008; Rashotte, MacPhee, & Torgesen, 2001; Torgesen, 2009; Vellutino, Scanlon, Small, & Fanuele, 2006). Several of these programs

Figure 4	Research on Academic and Social Outcomes for Students in Inclusive Placements

- Students with disabilities do at least as well, and often better, on academics in inclusive programs than when they are educated in resource or self-contained classrooms (Cole, Waldron, & Madj, 2004; Freeman & Alkin, 2000; Rea, McLaughlin, & Walther-Thomas, 2002; Ryndak, Morrison & Sommerstein, 1999; Salend & Garrick Duhaney, 2007; Waldron & McLeskey, 1998; Waldron, McLeskey, & Pacchiano, 1999).
- Students with disabilities in inclusive programs benefit from improved work habits, increased self-confidence, increased willingness to take risks, and more on-task or attentive behavior (Dore, Dion, Wagner, & Brunet, 2002; Foreman, Arthur-Kelly, Pascoe, & King, 2004; Waldron, McLeskey, & Pacchiano, 1999).
- Students without disabilities do at least as well, and often better, academically when educated in a well-designed inclusive classroom (Cole, Waldron, & Madj, 2004; Salend & Garrick Duhaney, 2007).
- Given appropriate supports, inclusive placements have been shown to improve self-esteem, increase interactions with other students, improve social competence, develop richer and more long-lasting friendships, and improve social status of students with disabilities (Boutot & Bryant, 2005; Freeman & Alkin, 2000; Salend & Garrick Duhaney, 1999; 2007).
- Students without disabilities benefit socially from inclusion through increased personal growth, appreciation and acceptance of other children, feelings of accomplishment as they provide assistance to others, development of friendships with students with mild and significant disabilities, and improved understanding of disability-related issues (Boutot & Bryant, 2005; Burstein, Sears, Wilcoxen, Cabello, & Spagna, 2004; Carter & Hughes, 2006; Gun Han & Chadsey, 2004; Idol, 2006; Lee, Yoo, & Bak, 2003; Peck, Staub, Galucci, & Schwartz, 2004; Salend & Duhaney, 1999).

have resulted in improved student achievement outcomes. This instruction occurs for brief periods of time, includes small groups of students (e.g., two to five students) who have similar academic needs, focuses on the development of certain academic skills (e.g., phonemic awareness), and includes frequent assessment of student progress to ensure the effectiveness of the intervention (McLeskey & Waldron, 2011a).

Finally, research has revealed that simply placing students with disabilities in general education classrooms does not improve their social skills or social status (Carter, Sisco, Brown, Brickham, Al-Khabbaz, & MacLean, 2008). It is often necessary for teachers in inclusive classrooms to provide instruction and support to ensure that social interactions for these students are successful and beneficial. If this does not occur, placement of some students with disabilities in general education classrooms can result in limited social interactions (Rotheram-Fuller, Kasari, Chamberlain, & Locke, 2010) and may produce negative outcomes such as social isolation and negative interactions with peers that are characterized by teasing, negative comments, staring, and isolation (Meadan & Monda-Amaya, 2008; Pivik, McComas, & Laflamme, 2002).

> ## Pause & Reflect
>
> Why do you think students with disabilities often do better academically in general education classrooms? What is it about general education classes that often lead to higher achievement levels?

Teaching in an Inclusive School

Your Role as a Teacher

Similar to Allison Meyer at Gilpin Manor Elementary, if you work as a general education teacher in a well-developed inclusive school, you will very likely teach in an inclusive classroom with a range of students with disabilities and other students from diverse backgrounds (e.g., different language and cultural backgrounds) for much or all of the school day. Moreover, in any school, you will likely spend at least part of the day teaching in an inclusive setting. Let's look at the data for a moment to put this in perspective. In an average school with 1,000 students, about 112 students will be identified with disabilities (U.S. Department of Education, 2011). About 101 of these students will have mild disabilities (e.g., learning disabilities, speech and language impairments, and other health impairments such as ADHD), and about 11 will have significant disabilities (e.g., significant intellectual disability, multiple disability).

These data suggest that if you are a general education teacher, it is very likely that you will have one or more students with mild disabilities in your classroom each year. In addition, over a number of years, you will likely have a student with a significant disability in your class. Successfully meeting the needs of students with disabilities presents a range of challenges and requires that school professionals work collaboratively to meet these needs. In the following section, we look at different professionals within schools and see how they can contribute to successful inclusion as they work collaboratively with other professionals.

General Education Teachers

Whether an elementary or secondary educator, the general education teacher is expected to have knowledge of the curriculum content students are to learn and to design instruction with an expectation that all students will be successful learners. The practice of including students with disabilities in general education classrooms and having them participate in the general curriculum places the general education teacher in a critical role. To ensure that all students succeed, the general education teacher often works closely with the special education teacher and other professionals to develop accommodations and supports for students with special needs.

Although the special education teacher continues to play a central role as students with disabilities are included in general education classrooms, the general education teacher *shares* responsibility for providing instruction to these students. An important ingredient for the general education teacher to succeed in this role is an open mind and a willingness to collaborate. The general education teacher not only needs to help students with disabilities feel that they belong in an inclusive classroom but he also needs to be a catalyst for acceptance of these students among their classmates.

Special Education Teachers

When working with students with special needs in general education classrooms, special educators may provide direct support to students by working with the general education teacher as a co-teacher. When working as co-teachers, the general and special education teachers plan instruction collaboratively, and their roles in the classroom are often indistinguishable to students because both teach all of the students at different times.

Special education teachers may also provide indirect support by observing in the classroom and working with the general education teacher as a consultant to plan instruction and related supports for students with special needs. This may include collaborative supervision with a general educator of a paraeducator who works in the general education classroom to support students with special needs.

Related Services Professionals

Related services are special supports required by federal law for students in special education that are necessary to help the students benefit from other school services. For example, if a student needs physical therapy to participate in learning activities, then physical therapy must be provided. The result of this legal requirement is that public schools employ many professionals besides general education or special education teachers to serve students with special needs.

According to data from the U.S. Department of Education (2011), U.S. public schools employ approximately 30,800 school psychologists, over 18,000 social workers, about 60,600 speech–language pathologists, more than 7,900 physical therapists, and over 18,000 occupational therapists to work with students with disabilities. Additionally, educational administrators, counselors, rehabilitation specialists, and school psychologists play significant roles in the education of students with special needs. We can't fully describe all of these professionals, but Table 2 lists and briefly describes the roles of some who often work with students with special needs.

In many schools where students with special needs are included in general education classrooms, related services professionals work closely with general education teachers to support these students. They do this in several ways. For example, a speech–language pathologist might help the student work on communication skills that allow more participation in class activities; a physical therapist might help design the layout of a classroom so it will be accessible to students with physical disabilities. Similarly, a school psychologist might provide collaborative support to develop a behavior intervention plan to improve a student's challenging behavior.

Paraeducators

Teacher assistants, often referred to as *paraeducators, paraprofessionals, educational assistants,* or *teacher aides,* also play a major role in the education of students with special needs in general education classrooms (Giangreco, Suter, & Doyle, 2010). Paraeducators perform a range of instructional and noninstructional activities under the supervision of the special and general education teachers. These activities may include tutoring a student after a teacher provides primary instruction, preparing instructional materials and games, reading a story to students, and a range of other activities (Correa, Jones, Thomas, & Morsink, 2005). When paraeducators are assigned to work with students with disabilities included in general education classrooms, they are in a position

Paraeducators often provide support to students with disabilities in general education classrooms.

Table 2   Other Professionals Who Work with Students with Disabilities

Professional	Role
School psychologists	The primary roles of the school psychologist are to conduct assessments used to identify students with disabilities, and work with teachers and other professionals to plan academic and behavioral interventions.
Physical and occupational therapists (PTs and OTs)	The PT evaluates, plans, and develops interventions to improve posture and balance; to prevent bodily misformations; and to improve walking ability and other gross-motor skills. The PT works primarily with students who have significant disabilities. The OT has knowledge and skills similar to the PT, but has an orientation toward purposeful activities or tasks such as the use of fine-motor skills related to daily living activities.
Speech–language pathologists (SLPs)	The SLP evaluates a student's speech and language skills and develops appropriate goals in this area if necessary. SLPs also may work with students with more significant disabilities to develop alternate or augmentative communication systems.
Social workers	Social workers address many issues that occur outside of the school related to families. They often make home visits to help resolve conflicts or improve parent–child interactions, and also may arrange for support from community service agencies.
School guidance counselors	Guidance counselors provide support for students in the areas of academic achievement, personal/social adjustment, and career development.
Art, music, and recreational therapists	These professionals use their particular specialties to help improve students' functioning in several areas, such as communication or social skills.

to have a very positive influence, as they help students to learn successfully and adapt to an inclusive setting.

Teacher Attitudes toward Inclusion

One of the most important issues in determining whether an inclusive program will be effective and sustained over time is support for the program by teachers who are involved in implementing inclusive practices in their classrooms. Working in an inclusive setting can be challenging for a teacher, but many teachers find this work very rewarding.

Consider the perspective of Vicki Eng, a seventh-grade special education teacher at West Hernando Middle School.

Teaching in an inclusive classroom can be frustrating at times, but it's not what's best for me, it's what's best for the child. I can make a difference in their lives during the 7 1/2 hours a day they're in school. And that's what I tell myself; that's what keeps me going. And you know what, we make progress, and it's exciting to make progress, and to know that you've helped somebody by including them and helping them learn. And inclusion is more like real life. You're going to meet people with all types of abilities and disabilities, no matter where you are. That's what we're preparing them for. We're not just teaching them academics; we're preparing them for life.

Figure 5	Questions Teachers Ask Regarding Inclusive Programs

1. Do students with disabilities benefit from inclusion?
2. Do students without disabilities benefit from inclusion?
3. Do students with disabilities have a negative effect on the classroom environment, especially related to disruptive behavior?
4. Do teachers have enough time to effectively teach all students?
5. Do teachers have sufficient knowledge and skills to address the needs of all students?
6. Is sufficient professional development available to ensure teachers are well prepared for inclusive classrooms?
7. Do teachers have sufficient instructional materials?
8. Do teachers have sufficient personnel support in the classroom?
9. Do teachers have consultative support for highly specialized student needs from a team of professionals?
10. Do teachers have sufficient time to collaborate with other professionals?

Sources: Carter & Hughes, 2006; McLeskey, Waldron, So, Swanson, & Loveland, 2001; Scruggs & Mastropieri, 1996; Waldron, 2007; Werts, Wolery, Snyder, & Caldwell, 1996.

In the well-developed inclusive schools that we described previously, most teachers are strongly supportive of inclusive programs. But how did they get to this point? What were their concerns as they began discussing the development of inclusive programs? When such major changes occur, teachers are often anxious about these changes, and have many questions that need to be answered. This area has been extensively researched, providing insight into the nature of teacher attitudes toward inclusion and factors that influence these attitudes.

Although some have contended that teachers are not supportive of inclusion, most research has not supported this perspective, instead indicating that most teachers support the concept of inclusion and find it a desirable practice (Scruggs & Mastropieri, 1996; Waldron, 2007). However, although most teachers tend to support the concept of inclusion, many have concerns regarding how these programs are implemented. These concerns do not relate to social prejudice or negative attitudes toward students with disabilities, but rather are related to whether general education teachers could make inclusion work in their classrooms and to concerns regarding the substantial changes necessary to make these efforts succeed (Waldron, 2007). These concerns must be addressed if inclusive programs are to succeed and be sustainable. The primary questions teachers express regarding inclusive programs are included in Figure 5.

As you can see from reviewing the questions teachers have regarding inclusion, all of the concerns that are raised are justified and reflect teacher concerns regarding whether they will be effective in an inclusive classroom. Indeed, these are questions any responsible teacher should ask when major changes are occurring in classroom practices (Waldron, 2007). For example, teacher concerns regarding whether they are well prepared for teaching students with disabilities and have the resources and support to ensure that the inclusive program succeeds are basic questions that must be addressed when any change occurs in classroom practice. Similarly, when teachers express concern regarding the need for support in addressing highly specialized student needs, it is reasonable to assume that professionals with this knowledge will be available to provide support to the teacher. Indeed, given the diversity of the needs of students with disabilities, it is not possible for any single teacher to have all the knowledge and skills that are needed to meet every student's needs.

As this research suggests, teachers' attitudes toward inclusion provide insight into issues that arise when inclusive programs are developed. When inclusive programs are poorly designed, as has been the case in some settings (e.g., Fox & Ysseldyke, 1997), teachers express justifiable concerns regarding these programs, and raise questions

Pause & Reflect

Are you surprised that teachers are generally supportive of the concept of inclusion? As you review the questions teachers ask about inclusion in Figure 5, do these questions seem reasonable and appropriate? What other questions do you think teachers may ask about inclusion?

about whether students benefit from such programs. However, when these programs are well developed, teachers tend to be very supportive of having students with disabilities in general education classrooms.

Being a Good Teacher of All Students

There is no doubt that the success of inclusion for students with special needs rests largely on the collaborative efforts of general education and special education teachers. We can state it no more simply than to say that without teachers of high quality who are committed to teaching *all* students, inclusion will not succeed.

So what does it take to be a good teacher for all students? What personal qualities are important? What areas of knowledge and sets of skills must teachers learn? The following attributes and characteristics are necessary for teachers who wish to be effective for *all* their students.

Appropriate Dispositions

The most effective teachers have a **disposition** that values human differences and recognizes the importance of being a good teacher for *all* students. Teacher dispositions are just as important as having appropriate content knowledge and pedagogical skills. If you plan to be a professional educator, it is critically important that you accept the responsibility to teach all students regardless of their different challenges or special needs.

Having an appropriate disposition means having an outlook that maintains that all students are important and should be valued as members of the learning community. Without such a disposition, the quality of a teacher is likely to be diminished. Effective, inclusive schools, such as those we described at the beginning of this chapter, have a philosophy that supports teachers who have these types of dispositions.

Positive Teacher Qualities

It is important that teachers reflect on their own qualities to see how those qualities might influence their teaching. Here we examine some critical characteristics that are necessary for an effective teacher. These qualities are important for teaching all students, but are especially important for teaching students with disabilities in inclusive settings.

Caring, fairness, and respect are not just good qualities for teachers to have; they are essential. A teacher who cares about her students is more likely to have a positive impact because most students will be more responsive to a caring teacher (Gay, 2010). Fairness and respect are also important qualities for teachers. Fairness means that teachers provide, without bias, the instruction and support that individual students need. This doesn't mean providing every student the same instruction; rather, it means providing each student with the instruction that particular child needs. Respect means that a teacher interacts with students in ways that acknowledge their humanity and strengths. Stronge (2002) reports that students feel most strongly about the following:

- They expect teachers to treat them as people.
- They view effective teachers as those who do not ridicule students or allow them to be embarrassed in front of their peers.
- They believe effective teachers are fair with regard to gender and ethnicity.
- They see teachers who are consistent and allow students to have input into the classroom as fair and respectful.
- They believe effective teachers offer all students opportunities to participate and to succeed.

Students' interest in what is being taught is affected by the teacher's interest. Teachers who are excited about what they are doing tend to increase the excitement and interest of their students (Stronge, 2002). If you are enthusiastic about teaching, you will likely also be motivated to be an effective teacher. Your enthusiasm and motivation can sustain you through challenging times and improve your students' motivation and interest in what is being taught.

Effective teachers are highly interested and invested in their students' learning as well as their own learning. They constantly search for better ways to teach and more effective ways to support the learning of their students. They collaborate with other professionals, share and receive ideas, and improve their practice by actively seeking and participating in opportunities to learn new teaching strategies. Effective teachers also continue to increase their expectations for student success, and provide students with high-quality instruction to meet these expectations.

Finally, a critically important quality of effective teachers is "personal teaching efficacy," or how teachers view their potential for success. This quality suggests that a teacher can have a positive impact on students, *regardless* of the nature or degree of the students' needs. Teachers with high levels of personal teaching efficacy believe that they can positively influence student achievement and motivation. These beliefs correlate positively with student achievement and with a teacher's willingness to learn to use innovative strategies to be a more effective teacher (Bruce, Esmonde, Ross, Dookie, & Beatty, 2010; Carlson, Lee, & Schroll, 2004). Think for a moment about the importance of these qualities when a teacher searches for ways to successfully include Grace Jeffrey on the school playground, especially when "her disability comes into play" and her wheelchair can become a hindrance to participation.

Using Evidence-Based Teaching Approaches

Although we cannot underestimate the importance of appropriate dispositions and positive qualities for teachers, this is not enough to be a highly effective teacher. Successful teachers use the most effective teaching strategies. This is especially true when students have learning difficulties or special needs.

To be highly effective, teachers must seek and use strategies that have been proven effective, including evidence-based instructional approaches, whenever possible. Evidence-based practices are those that are supported by scientific research and have been shown to demonstrate a high degree of success in terms of student learning outcomes. It is important to note that although some strategies are much more effective than others, no strategy works for *all* students *all* the time. Thus, coupled with the use of effective, evidence-based instructional practices, highly effective teachers monitor the progress their students are making, to make sure that instructional strategies are effective and meet the needs of each student. In short, to be a successful teacher, it is important to learn about the most effective ways to teach your students, while monitoring student learning to ensure that instructional strategies are effective.

Differentiated Instruction: Making Instruction Work for All Students

Inclusive schools and classrooms work because teachers create instructional settings in which the needs of all students can be met. A term that is widely used and that provides a perspective on assuring that this occurs is differentiated instruction, which has been defined as "shaking up what goes on in the classroom so that students have multiple options for taking in information, making sense of ideas, and expressing what they learn" (Tomlinson, 2001, p. 1). In a general sense, all of the methods we discuss in this text relate to differentiated instruction. These are methods that result in significant benefits for all students, but especially those with special needs. For a perspective on how students with disabilities (and others) benefit from these supports as they are educated in inclusive settings, see the following comments from teachers at West Hernando Middle School.

How Students Benefit from Being Taught in Inclusive Settings

We interviewed several teachers and staff at West Hernando Middle School regarding how students benefit from inclusion. Here's what they had to say.

The school counselor, Susan Dean, said, "All students benefit from inclusion. Students who have difficulty with academics have the opportunity to work with their same-age peers, and they are challenged more to be the best that they can be." Vicki Eng, a seventh-grade special education teacher, added, "Inclusion teaches all students tolerance and sensitivity. They learn that everybody has something they're good at, and some things they're not so good at. Everybody has strengths and weaknesses. And we try to help them recognize what their strengths and weaknesses are." Susan Dean continued by stating, "Including students with more significant disabilities benefits all students even more. The general education students who volunteer in our peer program, for example, gain by learning about these students, knowing these students, understanding these students. They gain as much as the students with disabilities."

Several teachers noted benefits of placement in general education classrooms that would not occur if students with disabilities were educated in a separate setting. For example, a sixth-grade teacher, Lisa Grover, stated that inclusion helps "kids realize that everyone is different. When they are all in general education classrooms, they tend not to make fun of one another. Kids can be very cruel to one another. When the kids with disabilities are separated, that's when the kids tend to pick on them. When they're included in their classrooms, you see those kids trying to help them out a lot."

Several teachers noted that the quality of the instruction in the general education classroom is often better. For example, behavior specialist Eileen Walls stated, "Even the best special education teacher can never reproduce the richness of what happens in [the general education] classroom in terms of class discussion and student interaction, the stuff that naturally occurs. You have more teachable moments that occur in a class discussion in a regular class, when the kid finally gets it."

Finally, everyone we talked with mentioned the importance of being in a class with models for good academic and social behavior. For example, many teachers at West Hernando Middle School noted the importance of providing students with the opportunity to model appropriate strategies to gain knowledge and improve outcomes. Eileen Walls eloquently illustrated this point, as she said,

> When you take a group of kids and put them with others with similar types of problems, they think that's what normal is. Kids with disabilities in separate settings learn from other kids in that setting. Take a kid who's not a desk thrower and put him in a class with desk throwers, he's going to become a desk thrower. When that's the only thing you know in the separate environment, you don't have a chance to practice more appropriate behaviors to behave or learn, or know more appropriate behaviors. You develop a self-fulfilling prophecy that is so destructive in preventing kids from reaching their potential. That's a very strong casualty of separate classes, and an argument for more inclusion.

Summary

This chapter addressed the following topics:

Inclusion is for all students

- Inclusion is for all students with disabilities, including those in all 13 categories of disability in IDEA 2004, ranging from mild-to-moderate disabilities, such as learning disabilities and speech and language impairments, to significant disabilities, such as deaf-blindness and multiple disabilities. Some categories include students with disabilities that range from mild-to-moderate to significant disabilities, including intellectual disabilities and autism.

- Other students may need accommodations or supports in a general education classroom, including students who are at risk for difficulties in school related to growing up in high poverty backgrounds, and students from culturally and linguistically diverse backgrounds.
- Students who are gifted or talented may achieve at a level that is much higher than most of their peers and may need accommodations in the general education classroom.

Concepts that support inclusive practices

- The key concept underlying inclusion in federal law is the least restrictive environment (LRE), which requires that all students be educated with typical peers to the maximum extent appropriate.
- *Normalization* is a concept that has influenced inclusion. This concept suggests that all persons with disabilities should have the opportunity to live their lives in as typical a manner as possible.

What are effective inclusive programs?

- Not all educators define *inclusion* the same way. Some educators have developed programs that were called "inclusive" that did not meet student needs.
- Effective inclusive programs are designed to ensure that all students with disabilities are part of the academic and social community of the school.
- Effective inclusive schools are designed to ensure that teachers receive needed support and all students benefit.
- Research reveals that the academic outcomes for students with disabilities are at least as good, and sometimes better, in well-designed, effective, inclusive settings.
- Simply placing a student in an inclusive setting does not improve social outcomes. Teacher instruction and support are needed to improve social outcomes.
- Students without disabilities often benefit socially from inclusive placements, and do at least as well, and often better, academically in well-designed inclusive classrooms.

Teaching in an inclusive school

- Most general education teachers will have one or more students with disabilities included in their classes.
- General education teachers share responsibility with special education teachers for educating students with disabilities in their classes.
- Special education teachers are responsible for providing intensive, specialized instruction to students with disabilities to improve performance in basic skill areas.
- Related services professionals (e.g., school psychologists, speech–language pathologists, physical therapists) are available to provide support to students with disabilities who are educated in inclusive settings.
- Paraeducators often work with students with disabilities and general education teachers in inclusive settings.
- Most general education teachers support the concept of inclusion but have concerns regarding how these programs are implemented.
- Concerns of general education teachers relate to the need for appropriate levels of support to meet student needs and to ensure that all students benefit from inclusion.

Being a good teacher of all students

- Good teachers' classroom practice reflects qualities such as caring, fairness, respect, enthusiasm, motivation, and dedication.
- Good teachers have high expectations regarding their ability to teach all students.
- Good teachers use effective, evidence-based teaching approaches.

Addressing Professional Standards

At the end of this chapter we will include professional standards that are addressed in the chapter. These standards are used to design teacher education programs, and are widely viewed as necessary for effective teaching. Standards are taken from the Council for Exceptional Children (CEC), the largest organization for special education teachers and other professionals in the United States.

Standards addressed in this chapter include:

MyEducationLab

Go to the topic Inclusive Practices in the **MyEducationLab** (www.myeducationlab. com) for *Inclusion*, where you can:

- Find learning outcomes for Inclusive Practices, along with the national standards that connect to these outcomes.
- Complete Assignments and Activities that can help you more deeply understand the chapter content.
- Apply and practice your understanding of the core teaching skills identified in the chapter with the Building Teaching Skills and Dispositions learning units.
- Examine challenging situtations and cases presented in the IRIS Center Resources.
- Check your comprehension on the content covered in the chapter with the Study Plan. Here you will be able to take a chapter quiz, receive feedback on your answers, and then access Review, Practice, and Enrichment activities to enhance your understanding of chapter content.

Glossary

Accommodations: Changes in curriculum, instruction, and/or grouping arrangements to meet the needs of students with disabilities in general education classrooms.

Continuum of services: A requirement of IDEA 2004; students with disabilities must be offered a continuum of placement options for service delivery, including both general education and special class placements.

Cooperative learning: Involves a range of strategies in which students work together to learn and to ensure that others in their group learn.

Co-teaching: When used in inclusive classrooms, co-teaching is defined as a general and special-education teacher working collaboratively to share responsibility for instructing a diverse group of students in a single classroom.

Differentiated instruction: An approach to instruction that includes proactive planning to meet diverse students' needs. Differentiated instruction is student centered, based on student assessment data, and includes multiple approaches to content, process, and product to ensure that all students learn.

Direct instruction (DI): "A model that uses teacher demonstration and explanation combined with student practice and feedback to help learners acquire well-defined knowledge and skills needed for later learning" (Eggen & Kauchak, 2012, p. 266).

Dispositions: One's temperament or tendency, generally learned over time, to act or respond in a certain way, given a certain situation.

Evidence-based practices: Teaching approaches that have been repeatedly demonstrated through research to result in improved student learning.

Full inclusion: The perspective taken by some disability advocates that all students with disabilities should be educated in general education classrooms for the full school day.

Inclusion: Students with disabilities are included as valued members of the school community. This suggests that they belong to the school community and are accepted by others; that they actively participate in the academic and social community of the school; and that they receive supports that offer them the opportunity to succeed.

Least restrictive environment (LRE): A mandate of IDEA that requires that students with special needs are educated with children without disabilities to the maximum extent appropriate.

Normalization: Suggests that persons with disabilities should have the opportunity to live their lives as independently as possible, making their own life decisions regarding work, leisure, housing, etc.

Paraeducator: A person who assists a teacher in a special education or general education classroom. Also called a paraprofessional, teacher assistant, or teacher's aide.

Peer-assisted strategies: Engage peers in supporting students using activities such as peer tutoring or peer buddy systems.

Peer tutoring: A series of grouping alternatives that allow same-age or cross-age peers to assist classmates who are struggling with specific academic content.

People-first language: Emphasizes that persons with disabilities are just that: people who happen to have a disability. This language is respectful of people with disabilities, puts the person first (*person with a disability,* and not *disabled person*), and avoids the use of negative terms (*handicapped, wheelchair bound, retard*) to describe people with disabilities.

Phonemic awareness: The ability to hear, identify, and manipulate sounds (phonemes) in words. Phonemic awareness is a basic prerequisite skill needed to use phonics in learning to read.

Phonics: The relationship between the sounds of oral language and the symbols (letters) of written language.

Physical therapy: Provided by a physical therapist who evaluates, plans, and develops interventions to improve posture and balance; to prevent bodily misformations; and to improve walking ability and other gross-motor skills. The physical therapist works primarily with students who have significant disabilities.

Self-determination: Assumes that persons with disabilities will act as the primary decision makers in their lives and make choices free from undue influence.

References

Biklen, D. (1985). *Achieving the complete school: Strategies for effective mainstreaming.* New York: Teachers College Press.

Boutot, E., & Bryant, D. (2005). Social integration of students with autism in inclusive settings. *Education and Training in Developmental Disabilities, 40*(1), 14–24.

Bruce, C. D., Esmonde, I., Ross, J., Dookie, L., & Beatty, R. (2010). The effects of sustained classroom-embedded professional learning on teacher efficacy and related student achievement. *Teaching and Teacher Education, 26*(8), 1598–1608.

Burstein, N., Sears, S., Wilcoxen, A., Cabello, B., & Spagna, M. (2004). Moving toward inclusive practices. *Remedial and Special Education, 25*(2), 104–116.

Carlson, E., Lee, H., & Schroll, K. (2004). Identifying attributes of high quality special education teachers. *Teacher Education and Special Education, 27,* 350–359.

Carter, E., & Hughes, C. (2006). Including high school students with severe disabilities in general education classes: Perspectives of general and special educators, paraprofessionals, and administrators. *Research & Practice for Persons with Severe Disabilities, 31*(2), 174–185.

Carter, E., Sisco, L., Brown, L., Brickham, D., Al-Khabbaz, Z., & MacLean, W. (2008). Peer interactions and academic engagement of youth with developmental disabilities in inclusive middle and high school classrooms. *American Journal on Mental Retardation, 113,* 479–494.

Cole, C., Waldron, N., & Madj, M. (2004). Academic progress of students across inclusive and traditional settings. *Mental Retardation, 42*(2), 136–144.

Correa, V., Jones, H., Thomas, C., & Morsink, C. (2005). *Interactive teaming: Enhancing programs for students with special needs.* Upper Saddle River, NJ: Merrill/Pearson Education.

Dore, R., Dion, E., Wagner, S., & Brunet, J. (2002). High school inclusion of adolescents with mental retardation: A multiple case study. *Education and Training in Mental Retardation and Developmental Disabilities, 37*(3), 253–261.

Dymond, S., & Russell, D. (2004). Impact of grade and disability on the instructional context of inclusive classrooms. *Education and Training in Developmental Disabilities, 39*(2), 127–140.

Eggen, P., & Kauchak, D. (2012). *Strategies and models for teachers: Teaching content and thinking skills* (6th ed.). Upper Saddle River, NJ: Pearson Education.

Foreman, P., Arthur-Kelly, M., Pascoe, S., & King, B. S. (2004). Evaluating the educational experiences of children with profound and multiple disabilities in inclusive and segregated classroom setting: An Australian perspective. *Research and Practice for Persons with Severe Disabilities, 29,* 183–193.

Freeman, S., & Alkin, M. (2000). Academic and social attainments of children with mental retardation in general education and special education settings. *Remedial and Special Education, 21*(1), 3–18.

Fox, N., & Ysseldyke, J. (1997). Implementing inclusion at the middle school level: Lessons from a negative example. *Exceptional Children, 64*(1), 81–98.

Fuchs, D., & Fuchs, L. (1994). Inclusive schools movement and the radicalization of special education reform. *Exceptional Children, 60*(4), 294–309.

Fuchs, L., Fuchs, D., Craddock, C., Hollenbeck, K., Hamlett, C., & Schatschneider, C. (2008). Effects of small-group tutoring with and without validated classroom instruction on at-risk student's math problem solving: Are the two tiers of prevention better than one? *Journal of Educational Psychology, 100*(3), 491–509.

Gay, G. (2010). *Culturally responsive teaching: Theory, research, & practice.* New York: Teachers College Press.

Giangreco, M. F., Suter, J., & Doyle, M. (2010). Paraprofessionals in inclusive schools: A review of recent research. *Journal of Educational and Psychological Consultation, 20,* 41–57.

Gun Han, K., & Chadsey, J. (2004). The influence of gender patterns and grade level on friendship expectations of middle school students toward peers with severe disabilities. *Focus on Autism and Other Developmental Disabilities, 19*(4), 205–214.

Idol, L. (2006). Toward inclusion of special education students in general education. *Remedial and Special Education, 27*(2), 77–94.

Individuals with Disabilities Education Improvement Act (IDEA) of 2004, Public Law 108-446 (2004). Retrieved November 24, 2008, from http://frwebgate.access.gpo.gov/cgi-bin/getdoc.cgi?dbname108_cong_publiclaws&docidf:publ446.108

Kauchak, D., & Eggen, P. (2012). *Learning and teaching: Research-based methods* (6th ed.). Upper Saddle River, NJ: Pearson Education.

Kauffman, J., & Hallahan, D. (2005). *Special education: What is it and why we need it?* Boston: Pearson Education.

Kavale, K., & Forness, S. (2000). History, rhetoric, and reality: Analysis of the inclusion debate. *Remedial and Special Education, 21*(5), 279–296.

Lee, S., Yoo, S., & Bak, S. (2003). Characteristics of friendships between children with and without disabilities. *Education and Training in Developmental Disabilities, 38*(2), 157–166.

Lindsay, G. (2007). Educational psychology and the effectiveness of inclusive education/mainstreaming. *British Journal of Educational Psychology, 77,* 1–24.

McLeskey, J. (Ed.). (2007). *Reflections on inclusion: Classic articles that shaped our thinking.* Arlington, VA: Council for Exceptional Children.

McLeskey, J., Landers, E., Williamson, P., & Hoppey, D. (2011). The Least Restrictive Environment mandate of IDEA: Are we moving toward educating students with disabilities in less restrictive settings? *The Journal of Special Education,* first published online as doi:10.1177/0022466910376670

McLeskey, J., & Waldron, N. (2000). *Inclusive schools in action: Making differences ordinary.* Alexandria, VA: Association for Supervision and Curriculum Development.

McLeskey, J., & Waldron, N. (2011a). Educational programs for elementary students with learning disabilities: Can they be both effective and inclusive? *Learning Disabilities Research and Practice, 26*(1), 48–57.

McLeskey, J., & Waldron, N. (2011b). *Are full inclusion programs for elementary students with LD justifiable?* Paper presented at the Council for Exceptional Children Convention, National Harbor, MD.

McLeskey, J., Waldron, N., So, T. H., Swanson, K., & Loveland, T. (2001). Perspectives of teachers toward inclusive school programs. *Teacher Education and Special Education, 24,* 108–115.

Meadan, H., & Monda-Amaya, L. (2008). Collaboration to promote social competence for students with mild disabilities in the general classroom: A structure for providing social support. *Intervention in School and Clinic, 43*(3), 158–167.

National Center for Education Statistics. (2009). *Digest of Education Statistics: 2009.* Retrieved November 29, 2010, from nces.ed.gov/programs/digest/d09/tables_1.asp

National Institutes of Health (NIH). (2011). *Transverse myelitis fact sheet.* National Institutes of Health, retrieved June 6, 2011, from www.ninds.nih.gov/disorders/transversemyelitis/detail_transversemyelitis.htm

National Reading Panel. (2000). *Teaching children to read: An evidence-based assessment of the scientific research literature on reading and its implications for reading instruction.* Washington, DC: National Institute of Child Health and Human Development.

No Child Left Behind Act. (2001). 20 U.S.C. 6301 et seq.

Peck, C., Staub, D., Galucci, C., & Schwartz, I. (2004). Parent perception of the impacts of inclusion on their nondisabled child. Research & Practice for Persons with Severe Disabilities, 29(2), 135–143.

Pivik, J., McComas, J., & Laflamme, M. (2002). Barriers and facilitators to inclusive education. *Exceptional Children, 69*(1), 97–107.

Rashotte, C., MacPhee, K., & Torgesen, J. (2001). The effectiveness of a group reading instruction program with poor readers in multiple grades. *Learning Disability Quarterly, 24*(2), 119–134.

Rea, P., McLaughlin, V., & Walther-Thomas, C. (2002). Outcomes for students with learning disabilities in inclusive and pullout programs. *Exceptional Children, 68*(2), 203–222.

Rosenberg, M. S., Westling, D. L., & McLeskey, J. (2011). *Special education for today's teachers* (2nd ed.). Upper Saddle River, NJ: Merrill/Pearson Education.

Ross, D., Kamman, M., & Coady, M. (2011). Accepting responsibility for the learning of all students: What does it mean? In M. Rosenberg, D. Westling, & J. McLeskey (Eds.), *Special education for today's teachers: An introduction* (2nd ed., pp. 50–77). Upper Saddle River, NJ: Merrill/Pearson Education.

Rotheram-Fuller, E., Kasari, C., Chamberlain, B., & Locke, J. (2010). Social involvement of children with autisj spectrum disorders in elementary classrooms. *The Journal of Child Psychology and Psychiatry, 51,* 1227–1234.

Ryndak, D. L., Morrison, A. P., & Sommerstein, L. (1999). Literacy before and after inclusion in general education settings: A case study. *Journal of the Association for Persons with Severe Handicaps, 24,* 5–22.

Salend, S., & Duhaney, L. (1999). The impact of inclusion on students with and without disabilities and their educators. *Remedial and Special Education, 20*(2), 114–126.

Salend, S., & Garrick Duhaney, L. (2007). Research related to inclusion and program effectiveness. In J. McLeskey (Ed.), *Reflections on inclusion: Classic articles than shaped our thinking* (pp. 127–159). Arlington, VA: Council for Exceptional Children.

Scruggs, T., & Mastropieri, M. (1996). Teacher perceptions of mainstreaming/inclusion, 1958–1995: A research synthesis. *Exceptional Children, 63,* 59–74.

Stronge, J. H. (2002). *Qualities of effective teachers.* Alexandria, VA: Association for Supervision and Curriculum Development.

Tomlinson, C. A. (2001). *How to differentiate instruction in mixed- ability classrooms* (2nd ed.). Alexandria, VA: Association for Supervision and Curriculum Development.

Torgesen, J. (2009). The response to intervention instructional model: Some outcomes from a large-scale implementation in reading first schools. *Child Development Perspectives, 3*(1), 38–40.

U.S. Census Bureau. (2008). *Population: Ancestry, language spoken at home.* Retrieved November 29, 2010, from www.census.gov/compendia/statab/cats/population/ancestry_language_spoken_at_home.html

U.S. Department of Education. (2011). *Individuals with Disabilities Education Improvement Act (IDEA) data: Data Accountability Center.* Retrieved January 10, 12, and 25, 2011, from www.ideadata.org

Vellutino, F., Scanlon, D., Small, S., & Fanuele, D. (2006). Response to intervention as a vehicle for distinguishing between children with and without reading disabilities. *Journal of Learning Disabilities, 39*(2), 157–169.

Waldron, N., & McLeskey, J. (1998). The impact of a full-time inclusive school program (ISP) on the academic achievement of students with mild and severe learning disabilities. *Exceptional Children, 64*(2), 395–405.

Waldron, N. (2007). Teacher attitudes toward inclusion. In J. McLeskey (Ed.), *Reflections on inclusion: Classic articles that shaped our thinking* (pp. 161–187). Arlington, VA: Council for Exceptional Children.

Waldron, N., McLeskey, J., & Pacchiano, D. (1999). Giving teachers a voice: Teachers' perspectives regarding elementary inclusive school programs (ISPs). *Teacher Education and Special Education, 22,* 141–153.

Werts, M., Wolery, M., Snyder, E., & Caldwell, N. (1996). Teachers' perceptions of the supports critical to the success of inclusion programs. *Journal of the Association for Persons with Severe Handicaps, 21,* 9–21.

Photo Credits

Credits are listed in order of appearance.
Creatas; Richard Hutchings/Digital Light/Newscom; Scott Cunningham/Merrill; © Robin Nelson/PhotoEdit; © Bob Daemmrich/PhotoEdit.

Introduction to Inclusive Teaching

Light in the Canyon

PAUL ADAMS   Paul Adams, after many years in teaching, developed muscular dystrophy, which led to his retirement and taking up photography as a hobby. His lack of mobility means that most of his photographs are taken from a wheelchair or from a vehicle. This does limit his ability to photograph some subjects, but has a benefit in that he finds himself seeking different and often lower viewpoints. Paul says, "Somehow the opportunities for developing one's photography are more focused when you are disabled, as you have to work out ways to do things that able-bodied photographers find easy. I enjoy street photography and I find that the photographer becomes less prominent when shooting from a wheelchair. Other areas that I find are more manageable are still life, table-top, and studio photography. Photography is a real therapy for the disabled, as there are images around us all the time and wherever we go."

Introduction to Inclusive Teaching

Objectives

After studying this chapter, you should be able to:

- Understand federal laws protecting the educational services for students with disabilities.

- Analyze several important court cases relating to students with disabilities, presenting a progression of increasing rights for students with disabilities.

- Identify the disability categories served under IDEA (Individuals with Disabilities Education Act).

- Summarize and describe the legal foundations, litigation, and legislation concerning students with disabilities, such as IDEA, Section 504 (Vocational Rehabilitation Act), and ADA (Americans with Disabilities Act).

- Describe the continuum of services available to students with special needs and the "least restrictive environment" concept.

- Compare and contrast the issues surrounding inclusive instruction for students with disabilities.

In 1975, Congress passed a law that would change the face of public education in the United States. The Education for All Handicapped Children Act (now known as the Individuals with Disabilities Education Act, or IDEA) specified that all children—including those with disabilities formerly excluded from school—were entitled to a free, appropriate public education. This law went far beyond any previous legislation in specifying that, to the greatest extent possible, this "special" education was to be provided in the least restrictive environment. In other words, students with disabilities were to be educated to the greatest extent possible in the general education classroom. This text is dedicated to describing the means by which this "least restrictive environment" can become a reality.

The passage of IDEA, and its subsequent amendments, has largely achieved its purpose. More than ever, students with disabilities now receive free, appropriate public education. Furthermore, this education is being provided more often in the general education classroom.

Before the passage of IDEA, students with disabilities were often denied access to public education (Yell, 2012). In some cases, they were placed in institutions. In other cases, the parents were forced to pay for private schools, often in inappropriate settings. Today, all students with disabilities are legally entitled to a free, appropriate education suited to their needs. The following scenarios compare a case from many years ago with a similar case from today. As a result of IDEA and related legislation, society has an increased understanding of individuals with disabilities and is much better able to accommodate individual differences in schools, in workplaces, and in social settings.

HISTORICAL SCENARIOS

Mr. and Mrs. Patterson

In 1960, Mr. and Mrs. Patterson had a brand-new baby girl, Hope. The initial excitement about the successful pregnancy and delivery was soon shrouded by a dark cloud. They were informed by the doctors that their precious infant was "retarded." Mrs. Patterson tells their story:

"We felt horrible when the physician informed us that our beautiful baby girl was retarded. I can still hear his words: 'You probably don't want to keep her. The state institution is the best place for infants like her. The staff at the institution will be able to take care of her better than you.' I immediately hated the doctor. How could he be saying this to me about my brand-new baby girl? I felt as if I was having a nightmare and that at any moment I would awake and find that everything was okay.

"At first we were so angry and couldn't help thinking thoughts like: Why did this happen to us? We didn't do anything wrong; this is unfair! We looked for someone to blame. We blamed the doctors and the staff at the hospital. It must be their fault—it couldn't be ours! Then, gradually, we both felt so guilty. We racked our brains for things that we might have done incorrectly during pregnancy. Did I fall? Was I exposed to any harmful substances? We didn't know whom to turn to for help. We felt overwhelmed and lost. The only individuals we knew we could speak with were the doctors and staff at the hospital, who had already expressed their opinions to us.

"We loved our baby and decided to keep her. She was very slow at developing. We were always searching for effective ways to help her. Everything was so hard. Each little thing we did seemed like an enormous journey. When Hope reached kindergarten age she had passed some important developmental milestones. We knew she wasn't developmentally the same as other children her age, but we hoped that she might begin to catch up once she was in school.

"Unfortunately, however, within the first week of kindergarten we were contacted by the school and asked to remove Hope from the school. We were told that she wasn't ready for school and that she took too much time away from the other children in the class. If we wanted Hope exposed to any educational program, the only solution available to us was to place Hope in the state institution's school.

"We were again devastated with this horrible decision. We felt as if we had no educational option. We went through the same grieving process as we did when Hope was born. We were angry and felt guilty for sending her away, but we sincerely believed we had no other options available to us. Although we made the best decision for us at the time, we still feel guilty."

Mr. and Mrs. Baxter

Now imagine a family in circumstances similar to that of the Pattersons over 55 years later. Mr. and Mrs. Baxter have a brand-new baby girl, Holly. The excitement turns to dismay when they are informed by the doctors that their precious infant is severely developmentally delayed. This time, however, the Baxters have additional legal guarantees in place that will provide a free and appropriate education for their child in the least restrictive environment, beginning with early intervention services and continuing through supported employment options into adulthood. Some early intervention programs are available in their own community. Some of the program options are center-based, in which the intervention occurs at the school, some are home-based, in which the intervention takes place in the home, and others are a combination of center- and home-based programs. This means that Holly can participate daily in relevant educational programs in a variety of setting options.

Additionally, established networks of organizations provide support to parents and families of children with disabilities. Although the Baxters will still have some of the same painful experiences that the Pattersons had, at least the federal government has mandated services for families with children with severe special needs. Mrs. Baxter tells her story:

MyEducationLab™
Visit the MyEducationLab™ for this text to enhance your understanding of chapter concepts with a personalized Study Plan. You'll also have the opportunity to hone your teaching skills through video- and case-based Assignments and Activities, IRIS Center Resources, and *Building Teaching Skills and Disposition* lessons.

"We felt horrible when the physician informed us that our beautiful baby girl was developmentally delayed. Her words still ring in my ears: 'Your baby has a serious disability.' We barely heard the rest of her statement: 'We have a staff of early childhood specialists and nurses who will be in contact with you later today.' We couldn't believe our ears. The doctor must have us mixed up with someone else. There must be a horrible mistake. How could anything be wrong with our brand-new baby girl? I felt as if I was having a nightmare and that at any moment I would wake up and find that everything was okay."

The Baxters, like the Pattersons, went through the same questions of "Why us?" and "What happened?" and the associated feelings of denial, anger, guilt, and aloneness. Later on the same day, however, the Baxters felt the support from an early childhood specialist and a nurse. As Mrs. Baxter reported:

"They explained the types of intervention services that were available for our baby and for us. At first everything seemed like a blur, but then as reality sank in we realized that we had hope for Holly again. Specialized services were available, she would receive assistance, and we would receive educational support. Although we still felt the anger and wanted to blame someone, we began to realize there were individuals and support services that would help us begin to adapt and provide appropriate services for our baby with special needs."

QUESTIONS FOR REFLECTION

1. Describe the various feelings experienced by the Pattersons. In what way were they similar to the feelings expressed by the Baxters? How do you think you would feel as a parent facing these issues?
2. Which of the Baxters' program options do you think you would have chosen? Why?

What Are the Educational Rights for Individuals with Disabilities?

Before the passage of federal legislation mandating services for students with disabilities, these individuals were routinely and legally excluded from school. Johnson (1986, pp. 1–2) documented several instances across the United States, including the following examples:

- In Massachusetts in 1893, a child with disabilities was excluded by a school committee because "he was so weak in mind as to not derive any marked benefit from instruction and further, that he is troublesome to other children . . ." (*Watson v. City of Cambridge*, 1893).

- In Wisconsin in 1919, a 13-year-old with normal intelligence but physical disabilities was excluded for the following reasons:

    His physical condition and ailment produces a depressing and nauseating effect upon the teachers and school children; . . . he takes up an undue proportion of the teacher's time and attention, distracts attention of other pupils, and interferes generally with discipline and progress of the school. (*Beattie v. Board of Education of City of Antigo*, 1919).

- In 1963, Nevada excluded any student whose "physical or mental conditions or attitude is such as to prevent or render inadvisable his attendance at school or his application to study" (Nevada Revised Statutes, 1963).

- In 1971, Alaska excluded students with "bodily or mental conditions rendering attendance inadvisable" from school (Alaska Statutes, 1971).

Parents of children with disabilities face awesome responsibilities and challenges, including the need to advocate for the rights of their children.

TABLE 1 Percentage of Students Ages 6 Through 21 with Disabilities Receiving Services in Different Educational Environments

	Served Outside the Regular Class			
Disabilities	**<21% of the Day**	**21–60% of the Day**	**>60% of the Day**	**Separate Environments (e.g., Residential, Separate Facilities, and Home-Bound/ Hospital Environments)**
Specific learning disabilities	54.8	31.4	11.8	2.0
Speech or language impairments	84.2	6.1	6.8	2.8
Intellectual disabilities	16.0	28.7	48.4	6.9
Emotional disturbance	35.1	20.8	26.6	17.5
Multiple disabilities	13.4	16.7	44.5	25.4
Hearing impairments	48.4	17.8	19.8	13.6
Orthopedic impairments	47.1	19.0	26.3	7.6
Other health impairments	54.8	26.5	14.9	3.8
Visual impairments	57.2	14.7	15.9	12.2
Autism	32.3	18.4	38.7	10.5
Deaf-blindness	20.8	13.4	35.4	30.3
Traumatic brain injury	41.7	26.1	23.7	8.5
Developmental delay	58.9	21.2	18.4	1.5
All disabilities	**53.7**	**23.7**	**17.6**	**5.1**

Source: *Thirtieth Annual Report to Congress on the Implementation of Individuals with Disabilities Act* (Section I, p. 59), 2011, Washington, DC: U.S. Department of Education.

- Virginia law in 1973 allowed school exclusion for "children physically or mentally incapacitated for school work" (Code of Virginia, 1973).

Today, these laws are no longer applicable. According to federal law, all students, regardless of disability, are entitled to a free and appropriate public education, including access to the general education curriculum. Since 1975, public education has truly become "education for all."

Along with increased rights of individuals with disabilities from legislation such as IDEA come increased responsibilities for teachers. General education teachers today have more students with disabilities in their classrooms than ever. In fact, only a small proportion of students with disabilities currently receives more than 60% of their education outside the general education classroom (see Table 1). Today, therefore, teachers must be especially aware of their responsibilities in providing appropriate instruction for students with disabilities.

Although more responsibilities are placed on the general education teacher, they should not be considered a burden. On the contrary, classroom diversity—whether in the form of gender, race, ethnicity, or ability—is something to be valued in its own right. Diversity provides a more exciting, dynamic classroom and the opportunity for students to learn that all people are not the same. Diversity provides opportunities for students to understand, respect, and value others for their differences. Finally, diversity provides the opportunity for you to use all of your imagination, skills, and resources, to be the best teacher you can be. In the end, effective inclusive teaching is about being the most effective teacher possible and supporting all students to learn in the least restrictive environment.

The Least Restrictive Environment

WHERE ARE STUDENTS WITH DISABILITIES SERVED?

Critical to IDEA legislation is the concept of *least restrictive environment* (Rozalski, Miller, & Stewart, 2011). This phrase means that students with disabilities must be educated in the setting least removed from the general education classroom. To the greatest extent possible, students with disabilities are not to be restricted to education in special schools or special classrooms but rather should have access to the same settings to which students without disabilities have access. When students with disabilities are educated, to any extent, in a different setting, there must be a compelling reason that this setting is in the student's best interest.

MAINSTREAMING AND INCLUSION

Mainstreaming was the first movement devoted to placement of students with disabilities within the general education classroom. Advocates of **mainstreaming** three or four decades ago did not necessarily want to see students with disabilities placed in special classes for the entire school day, but argued that more exposure to the general classroom would be in everyone's best interest (e.g., Blankenship, 1981). Often, mainstreaming was thought to be something individual special education students could "earn" by demonstrating that their skills were adequate to function independently in general education settings. Since then, the term **inclusion** has been used to describe the education of students with disabilities in general education settings. Although many definitions have been used to describe *inclusion*, the term is generally taken to mean that students with disabilities are served primarily in the general education classroom, under the responsibility of the general classroom teacher. When necessary and justifiable, students with disabilities may also receive some of their instruction in another setting, such as a resource room. Additional support can also be provided within the general education classroom by paraprofessionals or special education teachers. Although this is a similar concept to mainstreaming, a critical difference of inclusion is the view of the general classroom as the primary placement for the student with disabilities, with other special services regarded as ancillary (Lipsky & Gartner, 1997).

Effective inclusive teaching is about being the most effective teacher possible.

In addition to mainstreaming and inclusion, the term *full inclusion* is also used, referring to the practice of serving students with disabilities and other special needs entirely within the general classroom. In full-inclusion settings, all students with disabilities are served the entire day in the general classroom, although special education teachers and other personnel may also be present in the general classroom at times (Kauffman, Nelson, Simpson, & Mock, 2011).

WHO IS SERVED UNDER IDEA?

IDEA is intended to provide necessary support services to students with disabilities. To accomplish this goal, students with disabilities are categorized in particular disability groups. It is important to remember, however, that all students served by IDEA are first human beings and individuals, capable of achievement, accomplishment, friendship, affection, and all other attributes of any other individual. Disability status may not be a permanent characteristic of all individuals; in fact, most people can expect to be considered "disabled" at one time or another in their lives. This in no way detracts from their fundamental worth as human beings. In fact, it is this principle of individual worth that has inspired much of today's special education legislation.

In short, although students served under IDEA have been given a disability "label," it is important to consider the individual first, and then consider the label as a secondary factor, along with other characteristics that help identify the unique aspects of the individual. For this reason, it has been recommended that "person-first" language be adopted (Russell, 2008). For example, we speak of "students with hearing impairments," rather than "hearing-impaired students." It is also important to remember that we use these descriptions only when it is directly relevant to a situation. When it is not relevant to list hearing impairment as a characteristic, for example, we speak simply of "Amy," or "Richard," or "Ana." For example, Margo, as a high school student, was best friends with Carol, a student 1 year older. They played on the basketball team

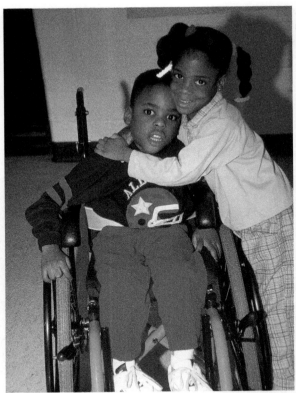

All individuals with disabilities are, first and foremost, individuals.

together and spent much of their after-school time together. After several years of close friendship, Margo expressed surprise that Carol had not gotten her driver's license, even a year after her 16th birthday. Further, Carol went to a separate setting to take the SAT. When she asked Carol about these things, Carol revealed that she was legally blind. Margo was astonished to hear this—and this situation demonstrated clearly to her that many characteristics of individuals, such as warmth, caring, sincerity, and understanding, can be much more important than disability status. It also demonstrated that important relationships can be developed and maintained that have little or nothing to do with disability status.

GENERAL CHARACTERISTICS   Students served by IDEA are distributed among 13 disability categories. Following is a brief description of each category (see IDEA, 2007; U.S. Department of Education, 2011, pp. 46756–46757). Individual states may use different terminology.

- *Autism:* Autism is a developmental disability generally manifested within the first 3 years of life. Major characteristics can include impairments in communication and reciprocal social interaction, resistance to change, engagement in repetitive activities, and unusual responses to sensory stimuli.

- *Deaf-blindness:* Individuals in this category have moderate to severe impairments in both vision and hearing, causing such severe communication and educational needs that programming solely for children with deafness or children with blindness is not appropriate.

- *Deafness:* Individuals with deafness have hearing impairments so severe that processing linguistic information through hearing is severely limited, with or without amplification, and educational performance is negatively impacted.

- *Emotional disturbance (or serious emotional disturbance):* This category includes individuals with a condition in one or more of the following areas during an extended period of time: (a) inability to learn, not due to intellectual, sensory, or health problems; (b) inability to build and maintain social relationships with peers and teachers; (c) inappropriate behavior and affect; (d) general pervasive depression or unhappiness; (e) tendency to develop fears or physical symptoms associated with school and personal problems; and (f) schizophrenia (a disorder in perception of reality). According to the federal definition, emotional disturbance is not intended to apply to socially maladjusted children unless they are also characterized as having serious emotional disturbance.

- *Hearing impairments:* Hearing impairments, with or without amplification, affect educational performance and developmental progress. The impairment may be permanent or fluctuating, mild to profound, unilateral or bilateral, but includes impairments not included under the definition of deafness.

- *Intellectual disabilities:* Intellectual disabilities (referred to as mental retardation in IDEA) describes significantly below-average intellectual functioning, as well as concurrent deficits in "adaptive behavior" (age-appropriate personal independence and social responsibility). It is manifested between birth and age 18 and negatively affects educational performance.

- *Multiple disabilities:* This category includes any individuals with two or more disabling conditions. However, this category often includes intellectual disability as one of the categories and is usually used when disorders are serious and interrelated to such an extent that it is difficult to identify the primary area of disability. It does not include deaf-blindness.

- *Orthopedic impairments:* Orthopedic impairments are associated with physical conditions that seriously impair mobility or motor activity. This category includes individuals with cerebral palsy, diseases of the skeleton or muscles (such as poliomyelitis), and accident victims.

- *Other health impairments:* This category includes chronic or acute health-related difficulties that adversely affect educational performance and are manifested by limited strength, vitality, or alertness. It can include such health problems as heart conditions, sickle-cell anemia, lead poisoning, diabetes, and epilepsy. It can also include attention deficit hyperactivity disorder (ADHD).

- *Specific learning disabilities:* This category refers to a disorder in one or more of the basic psychological processes involved in understanding or using spoken or written language, which can result in difficulties in reading, writing, listening, speaking, thinking, spelling, or mathematics. The term *learning disabilities* does not apply to children with learning problems that are primarily the result of visual, hearing, or physical disabilities; intellectual disability; emotional disturbance; or environmental, cultural, or economic disadvantage.

- *Speech or language impairments:* A disorder of articulation, fluency, voice, or language that adversely affects educational performance.

- *Traumatic brain injury:* Traumatic brain injury is an acquired injury to the brain due to external force resulting in a total or partial disability or psychosocial impairment, or both, which negatively affects educational performance (does not apply to congenital or degenerative injuries, or to brain injuries acquired during birth).

- *Visual impairments including blindness:* A visual impairment is a loss of vision that, even when corrected, affects educational performance. It may be mild to moderate to severe in nature. Students who are blind are unable to read print and usually learn to read and write using Braille. Students with low vision can usually read when the print is enlarged sufficiently.

In addition, children aged 3 to 9 can be classified as experiencing developmental delay if they have developmental delays in one or more of the following areas: physical, cognitive, communication, social or emotional, or adaptive development; such children may need special education and related services (IDEA, 2007).

OTHER INSTANCES OF CLASSROOM DIVERSITY

IDEA provides service to most of the recognized disability areas. However, there are other sources of classroom diversity, not associated with disabilities, that you need to consider when planning and implementing classroom instruction. These areas include the following:

- *Culturally and linguistically diverse groups:* These students are culturally or linguistically different from the majority U.S. culture or different from the teacher. Teachers should plan and implement instruction that is considerate of and sensitive to students' linguistic or cultural differences (Gollnick & Chinn, 2009).

- *At-risk:* Students characterized as "at-risk" exhibit characteristics, live in an environment, or have experiences that make them more likely to fail in school, drop out, or experience lack of success in future life. These factors are many and varied, but they include "slow learners" not served by IDEA categories and individuals who have sociocultural disadvantages, are at risk for suicide, or come from dysfunctional home environments (e.g., marred by drug or alcohol abuse, domestic violence, or child abuse). Such learners may require any of a variety of adaptations to help them succeed in school and later life (Frieman, 2001).

- *Gifted and talented:* These students exhibit skills or abilities substantially above those of their age in areas such as academic achievement in one or more subject areas, visual or performing arts, or athletics. If the abilities of such students greatly exceed classroom standards or curriculum, special adaptations or accommodations may be appropriate. Although many states have passed laws providing for the identification and education of gifted and talented students, in many cases funding for gifted programs is not provided (Davis & Rimm, 2004).

Legal Foundations

In the years following World War II, political change, litigation, and resulting legislation began to emerge that increased the inclusion of all groups of people in U.S. society. Most significant was the civil rights movement, which primarily addressed the rights of African Americans in U.S. society. This movement influenced the ideas on which much litigation and legislation involving individuals with disabilities are based. In the *Brown v. Board of Education* (1954) decision, the Supreme Court ruled that it was unlawful to discriminate against any group of people. With respect to school children, the Court ruled that the concept of "separate-but-equal" educational facilities for children of different races was inherently unequal. The justification for this ruling was found in the 14th Amendment to the U.S. Constitution, which states that individuals cannot be deprived of life, liberty, or property without due process of law.

LEGAL PROCEEDINGS AND LEGISLATION

People with disabilities also began to be identified as a group whose rights had been denied. In the years following *Brown v. Board of Education*, court cases were decided that underlined the rights of individuals with disabilities to a free, appropriate education. Other cases supported nondiscriminatory special education placement of individuals from minority groups in the United States. Some of the important court cases relating to individuals with disabilities demonstrate a progression of increasing rights for individuals with disabilities (see also Murdick, Gartin, & Crabtree, 2006; Wright & Wright, 2007; Yell, 2012):

- *1954: Brown v. Board of Education* (Kansas). The Supreme Court determined that "separate-but-equal" education is illegal.
- *1970: Diana v. State Board of Education* (California). The court ruled that children cannot be placed in special education based on culturally biased tests.
- *1972: Pennsylvania Association for Retarded Children (PARC) v. Commonwealth of Pennsylvania* and *Mills v. Board of Education* (District of Columbia) established the right to education for students with disabilities and found that denial of education violates the 14th Amendment.
- *1977: Larry P. v. Riles* (California). A court ruled that the use of standardized IQ tests for placement into special education classes for students with "educable mental retardation" was discriminatory.
- *1982: Board of Education v. Rowley* (New York). The Supreme Court defined "free and appropriate education" (FAPE), and directed that public schools must provide appropriate special education services.
- *1988: Honig v. Doe* (California). This decision was concerned with extensive suspensions of students with emotional disturbances from school for aggressive behavior that the court determined was disability related. The court ruled that a suspension of longer than 10 days was effectively a change in placement, requiring all the necessary procedures governing a change in placement.
- *1992: Oberti v. Board of Education of the Borough of Clementon School District* (New Jersey). A federal district court ruled that a self-contained special education class was not the least restrictive environment for a student with Down syndrome. The court ruled that school districts were obligated to first consider regular class placement, with supplementary aids and services, before considering alternative placements.

Along with this litigation, laws began to be passed that provided further support for the rights of students with disabilities. Some of these laws are summarized in Figure 1. In the following text, some of the most significant legislation involving individuals with disabilities is described (see also Murdick et al., 2006; Rothstein, 1999; Yell, 2012). This legislation includes Section 504 of the Vocational Rehabilitation Act, the Americans with Disabilities Act, and the most significant law for special education, the Individuals with Disabilities Education Act (PL 94-142).

SECTION 504

Section 504 of the Vocational Rehabilitation Act of 1973 (reauthorized as the Carl D. Perkins Career and Technical Education Act of 2006; U.S. Department of Education, 2006) is a civil rights law that prevents discrimination against individuals with disabilities by any institution that receives federal funds and provides for a free, appropriate public education (FAPE). Some private schools that do not receive federal funding may be exempt from

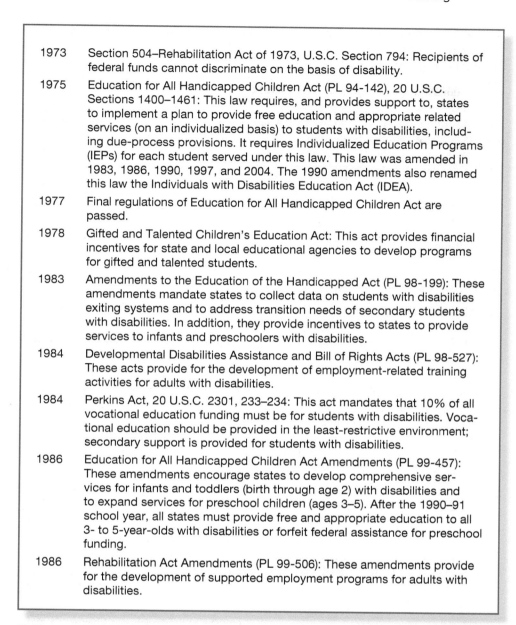

1973	Section 504–Rehabilitation Act of 1973, U.S.C. Section 794: Recipients of federal funds cannot discriminate on the basis of disability.
1975	Education for All Handicapped Children Act (PL 94-142), 20 U.S.C. Sections 1400–1461: This law requires, and provides support to, states to implement a plan to provide free education and appropriate related services (on an individualized basis) to students with disabilities, including due-process provisions. It requires Individualized Education Programs (IEPs) for each student served under this law. This law was amended in 1983, 1986, 1990, 1997, and 2004. The 1990 amendments also renamed this law the Individuals with Disabilities Education Act (IDEA).
1977	Final regulations of Education for All Handicapped Children Act are passed.
1978	Gifted and Talented Children's Education Act: This act provides financial incentives for state and local educational agencies to develop programs for gifted and talented students.
1983	Amendments to the Education of the Handicapped Act (PL 98-199): These amendments mandate states to collect data on students with disabilities exiting systems and to address transition needs of secondary students with disabilities. In addition, they provide incentives to states to provide services to infants and preschoolers with disabilities.
1984	Developmental Disabilities Assistance and Bill of Rights Acts (PL 98-527): These acts provide for the development of employment-related training activities for adults with disabilities.
1984	Perkins Act, 20 U.S.C. 2301, 233–234: This act mandates that 10% of all vocational education funding must be for students with disabilities. Vocational education should be provided in the least-restrictive environment; secondary support is provided for students with disabilities.
1986	Education for All Handicapped Children Act Amendments (PL 99-457): These amendments encourage states to develop comprehensive services for infants and toddlers (birth through age 2) with disabilities and to expand services for preschool children (ages 3–5). After the 1990–91 school year, all states must provide free and appropriate education to all 3- to 5-year-olds with disabilities or forfeit federal assistance for preschool funding.
1986	Rehabilitation Act Amendments (PL 99-506): These amendments provide for the development of supported employment programs for adults with disabilities.

Figure 1   History of Relevant Legislation

Section 504. This law applies both to schools and to the workforce. Section 504 provides for equal opportunities in all aspects of education. Students may not be classified as disabled according to the IDEA guidelines, but they must demonstrate a significant learning problem that affects their ability to function in school. Under Section 504, disability is considered to be an impairment, physical or mental, that substantially limits a major life activity (Lazarus, Thurlow, Lail, & Christensen, 2009; U.S. Department of Education, Office of Special Education and Rehabilitative Services, 2006). Some students who may not be served under IDEA, because they do not meet the definitional requirements of one of the IDEA disability categories, can still obtain services under Section 504 (deBettencourt, 2002). For example, some students with attention deficit hyperactivity disorder (ADHD), as well as some students who require modifications for their severe allergies or asthma, may be covered under this law. Other types of disabilities likely covered under Section 504, but not IDEA, might include the following (Smith, 2002):

- Students who had been placed in special education programs but have transitioned out;

- Students thought to be socially maladjusted, or who have a history of alcohol or drug abuse; and
- Students who carry infectious diseases such as AIDS.

Students can be referred for Section 504 services by anyone but are usually referred by teachers or parents. If a group of knowledgeable school personnel believes the child is eligible, the school must then conduct an evaluation to determine eligibility and the nature of services needed to ensure a free, appropriate public education. The decision is based on professional judgment rather than test scores and numerical indicators. If a student is considered eligible, the law does not provide funding; however, it does require that school personnel create a written plan that will help accommodate these special needs and provide an accessible environment. Accommodation plans can include a statement of student strengths and weaknesses, a list of accommodations to be implemented, and designation of the person(s) responsible for implementation. Accommodations are usually inexpensive, commonsense modifications intended to provide nondiscrimination and free, appropriate public education (Smith, 2002).

AMERICANS WITH DISABILITIES ACT

The Americans with Disabilities Act (ADA) was signed into law in 1990, and mandated that individuals with disabilities should be provided with "reasonable accommodations" in the workplace, and that such individuals could not be discriminated against. ADA also included protections for individuals enrolled in colleges and universities. Adults with disabilities attending universities are also entitled to appropriate modifications in classes. These modifications, in many ways, parallel those made in public schools in compliance with IDEA. Major components of the ADA are given in Figure 2.

The ADA is of particular significance because of its aim to maximize the employment potential of millions of Americans with disabilities. It can be considered an important extension of IDEA, in that it provides for reasonable accommodations and nondiscriminatory treatment of individuals with disabilities beyond the high school years.

INDIVIDUALS WITH DISABILITIES EDUCATION ACT (IDEA)

This act is the major special education law. Originally signed in 1975 as the Education for All Handicapped Children Act, IDEA has been amended several times since then, most recently in 2004 (IDEA, 2007), as summarized in Figure 3. The most important provision in IDEA is that all children, from 3 through 21 years of age, regardless of type or severity of disability, are entitled to a free, appropriate public education (see Yell & Crockett, 2011). Discretionary assistance is also provided to develop interagency programs for all young children with disabilities, from birth to 3 years of age. This provision overrides previous legislation and decisions that limit the attendance of students with disabilities in public schools. Overall, six major

- Employers may not discriminate on the basis of disability.
- Employers may not ask if applicant has a disability.
- "Reasonable accommodations" must be provided in the workplace.
- New buses must be made accessible.
- Most communities must provide transportation.
- Rail service must accommodate individuals with disabilities within 20 years.
- Public locations—hotels, stores, and restaurants—are accessible.
- State and local governments may not discriminate.
- Telephone companies must provide adapted communication options for the deaf.

Figure 2 Major Components of ADA
Note: From *U.S. Department of Justice, 1990.*

Content of IEPs
- Present level of performance must include the "child's academic achievement and functional performance."
- Annual goals must be measurable.
- Short-term objectives are required only for children who take alternative assessments.
- IEPs must describe how progress will be measured and when reports will be issued.

Research-based practice
- Statements supporting special education services must be based on peer-reviewed research.

Accommodations and alternative assessments
- Statements indicating the need for individual accommodations for testing and alternative state-wide assessments must be provided.
- Justification for participation in alternative assessments must be provided.

IEP meetings
- The teacher's attendance may be waived (1) if the teacher's curriculum area is not addressed, or (2) if a report based on the curriculum area is submitted prior to the meeting and is approved by the student's parents and the local education agency (LEA).
- Fifteen states may apply for an optional multi-year IEP pilot program. This means that, in some cases, annual IEP meetings may not be required and may be conducted no less than every 3 years.

Discipline
- If students violate a code of conduct at school, they may be suspended for up to 10 days.
- If the behavior was related to the disability, a functional behavior assessment and behavior intervention plan must be completed for the child.
- If the behavior was unrelated to the disability, students may be suspended for more than 10 days, like any other student in the school.
- If students are suspended for more than 10 days, they must be provided with a free and appropriate education, and the IEP team must identify alternative placements.

Identification of learning disabilities
- Schools can use a *Response to Intervention* model to determine eligibility for learning disabilities.

Early intervention funding
- LEAs may apply some of its special education funding to develop coordinated early intervention services, which may include students not identified for special education, but in need of academic or behavioral support.

Special education teacher licensure
- A highly qualified teacher is one who holds full teaching credentials required by state in conformance with *No Child Left Behind Act*. Special education teachers who teach in core subject areas must also hold the full teaching credentials in those subject areas.

Figure 3   IDEA 2004 Amendments
Source: IDEA 2004 (2007), Mandlawitz (2006), and Wright and Wright (2005).

principles have remained in the law throughout its amendments (Murdick et al., 2006; Yell, Katsiyannis, & Bradley, 2011). These principles are as follows:

1. *Zero reject.* This principle requires that no child with a disability can be excluded from public education.

2. *Nondiscriminatory testing.* Schools are required to use a variety of nondiscriminatory methods to determine whether a student has a disability, and, if so, whether special education is required. Testing must not discriminate on the basis of race, culture, or ethnicity, and must be administered in the student's native language. A variety of measures is required so that placement decisions are not made on the basis of a single test score. Further, the law is intended to address multicultural issues, as described in the *Diversity in the Classroom* feature.

Originally called the Education for All Handicapped Children Act (PL 94-142), Individuals with Disabilities Education Act (IDEA) mandates that all the children between the ages of 3 and 21, regardless of disability, are entitled to a free, appropriate public education.

3. *Free and appropriate education.* Students who have been referred to special education must have an individualized education program (IEP) that details their special learning needs and mandates appropriate services. Short- and long-term goals and objectives for students are listed explicitly on IEPs.

4. *Least restrictive environment.* Students with disabilities are entitled to be educated with their nondisabled peers to the greatest extent possible.

5. *Due process.* Due process must be followed in all placement decisions and changes in placement. Records are to be kept confidential, and parents are to be involved in all aspects of the planning and placement process.

6. *Parent participation.* Schools must collaborate with parents in the design and implementation of special education services (see also Staples & Dilberto, 2010).

Along with these six common principles, several additions have been made to the original law:

1. *Transition services.* All 16-year-old students with disabilities must be provided with a statement of transition-services needs on their IEP. These services, which must be included in the IEP by age 16, are intended to facilitate the student's transition from school to community, vocational programs, college, or employment. The transition plan can involve professionals from other agencies, such as social or vocational services. Transition planning conferences are also specified for transition from infant and toddler programs to preschool programs.

2. *Early childhood education.* Amendments to the Education for All Handicapped Children Act (now IDEA) in 1986 and 1990 provided for services to infants, toddlers, and preschoolers with disabilities. Very young children (younger than 3) are entitled to an individualized family service plan (IFSP, which replaces the IEP), which takes family needs and responsibilities into account. Necessary components of the IFSP are provided in Table 2. States are required to take action to locate as many young children as possible who may require special education services.

3. *Assessments.* Students with disabilities must participate in general state- and district-wide assessment programs. If students cannot participate in state- and district-wide assessments, justification must be provided, and they must participate in alternative assessments.

4. *Early intervention services.* The 2004 amendments to IDEA specify that not more than 15% of the funding the local education authority receives from the

TABLE 2	Necessary Components of the Individualized Family Service Plan

1. A current statement of child's functioning levels.
2. A current statement of the family's needs and strengths in relation to the child with special needs.
3. A statement of the major expected outcomes, including a timeline.
4. A statement of the specific services to be provided to meet the special needs of the child and the family.
5. The initiation and anticipated duration dates for services.
6. Designation of a case manager.
7. A statement of the transition steps from infant early intervention services to preschool services.

Diversity in the Classroom

Multicultural Considerations for the Identification of Individuals with Disabilities

Legal Assistance

 Federal legislation has provided protections and guidance for the proper identification of individuals with disabilities. These assurances are to guarantee that only the correct individuals become identified as having disabilities. It is especially important that individuals from culturally and linguistically diverse backgrounds are not overrepresented in special education programs. The following protections are part of the Individuals with Disabilities Education Act (IDEA):

- *Disproportionality requirement:* States must devise plans to prevent overidentification and provide data to document whether disproportionality by race is happening with respect to identification and placement of individuals with disabilities.
- *Development, review, and revisions of IEPs:* Consider the language needs as related to the IEP

for individuals with limited English proficiency.

- *Evaluation procedures:*
  - Test materials are not to be discriminatory against races or cultures.
  - Tests must be administered in the individual's native language.
  - Test materials for individuals with limited English proficiency must be used to measure a disability and not the individual's English skills.
  - Tests must be valid and reliable and administered by trained professionals.
  - No single procedure can be used as a sole criterion for determining whether a disability exists.
- *Eligibility determination:* An individual may not be eligible if the only difficulty appears to be limited English proficiency.

The U.S. Office of Civil Rights also provides guidance and protections and

is the compliance monitor for prereferral practices that may also influence overrepresentation of individuals from culturally and linguistically diverse backgrounds. These protections include the following:

- *Section 504 of the Rehabilitation Act of 1973 and Title II of the Americans with Disabilities Act:* Provide protection against discrimination for individuals with disabilities and those perceived as having disabilities or those who have been misclassified.
- *Title VI of the Civil Rights Act:* Provides protection from discrimination based on national origin, color, or race.

When districts are out of compliance with these federal laws and have an overrepresentation of individuals from culturally or linguistically diverse backgrounds, they may become involved in legal actions and asked to provide a plan to correct the problems.

---

federal government can be allocated to programming for students (K–12, with an emphasis on K–3) not currently identified for special education, but who need additional academic and behavioral support to succeed in the general education environment (U.S. Department of Education, 2006). These services can include those referred to as response-to-intervention (RTI) tiered services.

NO CHILD LEFT BEHIND ACT OF 2001

The No Child Left Behind Act (NCLB), also known as the Elementary and Secondary Education Act, was not written specifically for students with disabilities. However, many aspects of the legislation have important implications for students with disabilities (Chrismer, Hodge, & Saintil, 2006).

The law requires that all children be tested in grades 3 through 8, in reading and math, by tests developed by the states. Schools must demonstrate adequate yearly progress (AYP) toward the goal of 100% proficiency in reading, math, and science for all students within 12 years. Schools must demonstrate that students make progress in equal increments toward this goal, that is, that they are making steady, equivalent gains from year to year. Schools that fail to make AYP for two consecutive years must offer parents of the students the option to transfer to another public school, and the districts must pay the cost of transportation (if allowed under state law). The school district must provide technical assistance to the school. If

Apps for Education

Federal Government Updates

 One way to keep abreast of the changes in federal legislation is to check regularly the U.S. Department of Education website (*www.ed.gov*). This website contains a wealth of frequently updated information as well as links to relevant research and legislation sites. For example, a link to the Elementary and Secondary Education Act (No Child Left Behind Act) (*www2.ed.gov/nclb/landing.jhtml*) provides an overview of the act that was signed in January 2002, as well as commonly asked questions and answers that are presented in an easy-to-understand format, links to specific state-level contacts, information on how states can apply for waivers in the law, links for parents and for educators and policymakers, newsletters, and even slide presentations that emphasize key points.

Additional helpful websites linked to the U.S. Department of Education

(U.S. DOE) page are directly relevant to special education initiatives. These sites are the Office of Special Education and Rehabilitative Services website (*www.ed.gov/about/offices/list/OSERS/index.html*) and the office of Special Education Programs website (*www.ed.gov/about/offices/list/osers/osep/index.html*). These sites contain information such as current special education initiatives, including the recent IDEA legislation; possible changes in the procedures for identification of learning disabilities; recent research findings from projects funded by the U.S. DOE; model programs and personnel preparation; and the annual reports to Congress indicating the status of special education programs across the country with respect to numbers of children served, aged birth through 21. The Library of Congress website (*http://thomas.loc.gov/home/thomas.php*) allows individuals to research federal legislative information such as the

Congressional Record, bills, and congressional activities. Information about sponsored special education research can also be found on the website the Institute of Education Sciences (*http://ies.ed.gov*).

The Council for Exceptional Children (CEC) website (*www.cec.sped.org*) has numerous updates and interpretations of federal legislation relevant to special education. Check the CEC website for updates to this information.

Two apps are available that describe relevant legislation. The *Americans with Disabilities Act Reference* app (Connecting People Software) provides the actual bill in sections, and is easy to use. The *DLAWS* app (Connecting People Software) provides easy access to disability-related laws. Another app, the *Federal Register* (Allogy Interactive), provides regular listings of all federal funding opportunities and notices.

---

schools fail to make AYP for more than two consecutive years, more corrective measures must be taken, including replacing staff, implementing different curricula, or, ultimately, a state take-over, hiring a private management contractor, or converting to a charter school (Council for Exceptional Children, 2002). Other aspects of the law include compensatory education grants (Title I), bilingual and immigrant education programs, and standards and provisions for teacher training and recruitment (Wright, Wright, & Heath, 2004).

The NCLB Act has several important implications for special education (Crockett, 2011). If students with disabilities receive accommodations for statewide tests, and those accommodations result in the scores being deemed unreliable or invalid, the students will not be considered to have participated in the assessment. If the overall participation rate does not meet the minimum requirement (possibly as high as 95%), the state can be considered out of compliance and subject to sanctions (Council for Exceptional Children, 2002). Finally, NCLB requires that all teachers be "highly qualified" and hold full state certification or licensure. Meeting all these requirements may represent an important challenge in some cases (Sindelar, McCray, Kiely, & Kamman, 2008). Recently, the Department of Education (2012) has offered states to apply for waivers to these standards in some cases.

One important feature of federal legislation is that it is constantly changing. Some technological approaches for keeping abreast of federal legislation are described in the *Apps for Education* feature.

Models of Service Delivery

THE CONTINUUM OF SERVICES

The initial emphasis of legal actions was to provide access to educational services for students with disabilities. Once access was obtained, the focus shifted to the setting and placement of students with disabilities during education. Most placement guidelines emphasized availability of a range of services and programs, commonly referred to as a **continuum of services**, within the least restrictive environment for students with disabilities. *Least restrictive environment* (LRE) is defined in IDEA as meaning that students with disabilities should be educated in a setting that as closely as possible resembles the general education program, while simultaneously meeting the unique special needs for each individual with disabilities (Rozalski et al., 2011). The basic model of a continuum of services ranges from full-time placement in the general education classroom to full-time placement in a nonpublic school facility, on a day or residential basis, based on student need. As the needs of the individual with a disability increase, the LRE may be further removed from the general education class on the continuum of services. Figure 4 presents a sample of the range of placement options.

Watch this video for an example of the various types of services offered in special education.

WHERE ARE MOST STUDENTS WITH DISABILITIES SERVED?

Most students with disabilities are served in the public school with their nondisabled peers in Levels 1 through 5. In other words, these students receive their education in their local public school. Most students with mild disabilities, including those with learning disabilities, mild intellectual disabilities, speech and language disabilities, and serious emotional disturbance, are currently served in Levels 1 through 4. That is, these students spend some, if not all, of the day in the general education classroom along with students without disabilities. The general education teacher is responsible for their education for some, if not all, of the day, depending on the amount of time spent in that general education class. Table 1 provides a listing of disability categories and the corresponding proportion of students currently served outside general education classrooms.

In this video, the Least Restrictive Environment is discussed. Watch carefully to see what the LRE looks like in the classroom.

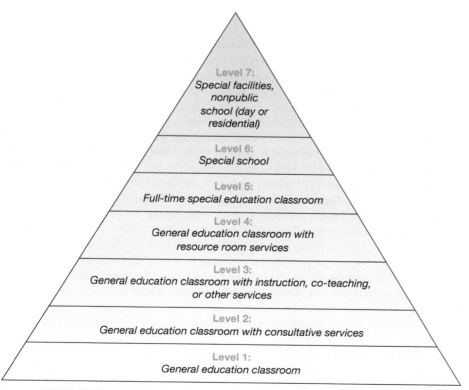

Figure 4 Sample Continuum of Services, from Least Restrictive to Most Restrictive

WHAT ARE GENERAL EDUCATION CLASSROOM AND CONSULTATION SERVICES?

In some cases, students may be served in general education classes by general education teachers. Some special services may be provided by a **consultant** who works with individuals as needed. Special education teachers frequently provide consultative services to general education teachers. This consultation is intended to provide assistance and ideas for how to teach and work with the students with disabilities who are placed in general education classes. Although special education teachers may not work directly with identified students, they may meet regularly with general education teachers, review assessment and progress data, and make specific recommendations for addressing special learning needs. These students would be receiving services at Levels 1 or 2 of the continuum-of-services model.

In other cases, special education teachers and classroom assistants (or paraprofessionals) may deliver instruction to students with special needs in the general education classroom. In these cases, students with disabilities still receive all their instruction in the general education classroom, but it may be delivered by different teachers or paraprofessionals. Teachers collaborate and share instructional responsibilities in one of several **co-teaching** models (Dettmer, Thurston, & Dyck, 2005). For example, a special education teacher may lead instruction for small groups of elementary students with special needs during classroom reading instruction. At the secondary level, the special education teacher may co-teach with a general education teacher in a high school biology class. The two teachers share teaching responsibilities, with the special education teacher focusing on strategies for addressing special learning needs. These students would be receiving services at Level 3 of the continuum-of-services model.

WHAT ARE RESOURCE AND SELF-CONTAINED SERVICES?

Special education teachers also provide instruction in resource and self-contained classrooms within the public schools. In a resource-room model, students with disabilities leave the general education class for a designated time period to visit the resource room and receive specialized instruction in areas such as language, reading, and math. For example, Kathi is a sixth-grader who has been classified as having learning disabilities. Kathi is functioning intellectually within the average ability range, but she has reading, spelling, and written language skills at an upper-third-grade level. The multidisciplinary team recommended that Kathi receive specialized instruction in reading, written communication, and spelling with a special education teacher for 1.5 hours per day in her school's resource room. This means that Kathi would be receiving services at Level 4 of the continuum-of-services model.

Most of her school day will be spent in the least restrictive environment of her general education class with Mrs. Gomez. Mrs. Gomez will be responsible for Kathi's instruction for the entire time that she is in the general education class. This might even include making some adaptations in instructional procedures and assignments to accommodate Kathi's special learning needs in the general education sixth-grade classroom. For example, during content-area classes, Mrs. Gomez will need to provide adapted reading and study materials appropriate to Kathi's skill levels. During her 1.5 hours in the resource room, Kathi will receive instruction from Mr. Halleran, the special education teacher in the same school. This resource-room arrangement represents the least restrictive environment to meet Kathi's special needs in reading, written communication, and mathematics, while maintaining her placement in her general education class for the majority of the school day.

The resource model is often referred to as a *pull-out* model, indicating that students with disabilities are pulled out of the general education class for special education instruction. In a self-contained model of instruction (Level 5 of the continuum-of-services model), students with disabilities receive all or most of their classroom instruction from special education teachers. Even in these models, however, students with disabilities usually have opportunities to interact with their nondisabled peers during such activities as art, music, physical education, recess, lunch, and assemblies.

SPECIAL SCHOOLS AND SPECIAL FACILITIES

In some cases, the need for specialized instruction is considered so significant that a special school or other facility is considered necessary. In some cases, special public schools are established to focus specifically on the special needs of the students. In other cases, students are sent to nonpublic schools, either as special day schools or as residential schools. These students would be receiving services at Level 6 or 7 of the continuum-of-services model. The numbers of special schools or other facilities have declined since the early years of IDEA, as traditional public schools have accommodated more students with disabilities and other special needs within their educational programs.

WHAT OTHER RELATED SERVICES ARE AVAILABLE?

Students with disabilities are also eligible to receive related services, if it is determined that the students require these services to benefit from special education. According to IDEA, related services may include parent counseling and training, physical therapy, occupational therapy, school health services, or special transportation. This means that in addition to receiving special services along the continuum of services for a primary disability area, some students may also be eligible to receive additional related services. Related services may be delivered to individuals with disabilities in any of the setting options. Although described as "related" services, in many cases these services may be of critical importance in attending to the special needs of individual students (Downing, 2004). For example, Michael, a student with intellectual disabilities, receives physical therapy in addition to his educational program to meet his special needs. Janice requires special transportation services to accommodate her wheelchair and adaptive PE, which are provided as related services.

The continuum-of-services and related-services models have been effectively applied throughout the history of IDEA. However, over this same time period, there have been recommendations regarding how all or most students with disabilities could be more easily served entirely within the general education classroom. These movements have been referred to as the Regular Education Initiative and the full-inclusion movement.

FULL INCLUSION

Over the past decades, the full-inclusion movement came to the forefront (Fuchs & Fuchs, 1994). Full inclusion has been referred to as placing and serving all students with disabilities, regardless of severity or type of disability, entirely within the general education classroom for the entire school day.

Consider the case of Kathi, our sixth-grader with learning disabilities. If Kathi were placed in a full-inclusion classroom, Mrs. Gomez, her general education teacher, would have Kathi in her room all day, every day with all of the other sixth-grade students. Mrs. Gomez would be primarily responsible for all of Kathi's instruction and for making adaptations appropriate for addressing Kathi's learning disabilities. In some full-inclusion models, Mr. Halleran, the special education teacher, would consult with Mrs. Gomez and provide ideas for her to use in teaching Kathi in her IEP need areas. In other full-inclusion models, Mr. Halleran might go into Mrs. Gomez's room and teach Kathi reading, spelling, and writing in that room. In this model, instruction with Mr. Halleran and Kathi may occur at a small table, perhaps with other students with special needs, while other groups of students meet for literacy activities. In still other full-inclusion models, Mr. Halleran may co-teach with Mrs. Gomez for part or all of the school day. During co-teaching, Mr. Halleran and Mrs. Gomez would work collaboratively on planning and implementing instruction for the entire class. In any of these full-inclusion models, however, Kathi remains in the general education class with her nondisabled peers all day.

As might be expected, debate surrounds the issue of full inclusion. It is important to remember that virtually all educational professionals recommend placement in general education classes for students with disabilities and other special needs; the disagreement usually centers on the extent to which students should be placed in general education settings. Both proponents of full inclusion and proponents of a continuum of services have articulated their positions, which are summarized in Figure 5 (see also Fuchs & Fuchs, 1994; Kauffman et al., 2011; Lipsky & Gartner, 1997, 2008; Zigmond & Kloo, 2011).

As can be seen, the issue of full inclusion versus a continuum of services is still debated. Professional organizations and advocates do not always agree on the best

In full-inclusion classrooms, students with disabilities may spend the entire school day in regular classroom settings.

Proponents of Full Inclusion	Proponents of a Continuum of Services
1. *Full inclusion is a civil right.* Students with disabilities have a right to be educated alongside their nondisabled peers. Separate educational settings are inherently not equal.	1. *A continuum of service options is necessary.* Many services needed by students with disabilities are not usually available in the general education classroom. Court decisions have usually placed more emphasis on "appropriate education" than "least-restrictive" components.
2. *Full inclusion reduces stigma.* Harmful stigmatizing effects may be associated with students attending special schools or special classrooms.	2. *The regular classrooms may also be stigmatizing.* Special services, such as speech therapy, physical therapy, or specialized reading instruction may be stigmatizing when undertaken in the company of general education peers.
3. *Full inclusion is beneficial.* Students in full-inclusion classrooms improve their interactions with others, learn to communicate better, develop better social skills, and increase their friendships.	3. *General education teachers are not prepared for full inclusion.* Many general education teachers lack the necessary time and training to make full inclusion a success.
4. *Full inclusion is more efficient.* Fully included students avoid the disruptive and time-consuming effects of being "pulled out" of the general education class to receive special services. Full inclusion guarantees access to the general education curriculum.	4. *General education classrooms may lack appropriate resources.* Students with special needs may require materials at lower reading levels, braillers, speech synthesizers, specialized computers, or specialized training materials that general education classrooms lack.
5. *Full inclusion promotes equality.* Including all students in the same classroom is simply the most fair and equitable solution to the problem of placement. Including all students in the same classroom actively promotes the idea of equality.	5. *Research evidence does not support the superiority of full inclusion.* Although research data are to some extent equivocal, clear evidence of the superiority of full-inclusion placements is presently lacking.

Figure 5 Arguments of Proponents of Full Inclusion and Proponents of a Continuum of Services

service options (e.g., Andrews, Shaw, & Lomas, 2011). General education students have expressed various opinions (e.g., Siperstein, Parker, Norns Bardon, & Widerman, 2007); parents also seem to be divided between those who favor specialized placement and services and those who favor integration in the general education class (Palmer, Fuller, Arora, & Nelson, 2001).

WHAT DOES THIS DEBATE MEAN FOR TEACHERS?

Teachers need to be aware of the arguments for and against full inclusion. As a teacher, you also must become familiar with your own legal responsibilities. For example, what are general education classroom teachers' legal responsibilities with respect to the IEP when all instruction is implemented in the general education classroom? Other questions, although not necessarily legal in nature, may be relevant to the spirit of the law.

Teachers should approach the issue in a practical way, with respect to their own school and district. Specific questions to ask about full inclusion include the following:

- What are the school- and district-wide policies and procedures regarding full inclusion?
- What are my obligations as a general educator with respect to the IEP, IEP meetings, case conferences, assessment procedures, annual review meetings, and meetings with parents?

- What types of modifications are expected, and is there a "reasonableness" standard associated with the number and types of modifications expected?
- Is this the best placement option for the student with special needs?
- How will we evaluate whether or not this placement and this set of accommodations are successful?
- What resources are available to assist me in working with the student with special needs?
- How can I receive necessary training for working with students in specific disability areas?
- What kinds of records and documentation should I maintain?

Answers to questions such as these can help determine the best placement options for students with disabilities and other special needs.

TEACHER ATTITUDES

One of the most important determinants of inclusion success is the attitude of the general education teacher toward accommodating students with disabilities. Although most teachers are positive about inclusion, general education teachers report a need for additional planning time, additional training for inclusive teaching, and additional resources, in the form of personnel and specialized instructional materials (Cook, Tankersley, Cook, & Landrum, 2000; see also the *Research Highlight*). Teacher and administrator support for collaborative efforts in schools can also affect attitudes. The two scenarios that follow help illustrate the initial implementation of inclusion in two different schools under very different circumstances.

 Listen to the teacher in this **video** describe what needs to be present for effective inclusive practices to occur.

CLASSROOM SCENARIOS

Volunteerism

In a small rural school, Mrs. Ghardisi, the fourth-grade teacher, volunteered to take all the fourth-grade students with disabilities into her classroom. Because she worked well with Mrs. Rana, the special education teacher, she went to her principal and said, "Next year, I would like to have all five of the fourth-graders who have disabilities in my room. They can still go to the resource room for part of the day, but during science class and other content classes, I would like to have all of them. Also, Mrs. Rana and I would like to team-teach during science class when all five children are included."

That summer, Mrs. Ghardisi and Mrs. Rana met and discussed curriculum and planning issues for their science class. Mrs. Ghardisi was considered the "content expert," whereas Mrs. Rana was the "adaptation expert." When the school year began, they met at least one day a week after school to co-plan the activities for each science class. Mrs. Ghardisi and Mrs. Rana had a good working relationship that enabled them to solve problems as they arose. Because they planned together, they took turns presenting information and monitoring students during class. They were both enthusiastic and worked hard to design adaptations so the five students with disabilities could be active participants. They viewed science as an opportunity to have fun, and their students appeared to really enjoy science.

Mandated Inclusion

In a suburban middle school, Ms. Irby, the special education teacher, was told by her building principal 2 days before school began that she was going to implement inclusive instruction for one period per day during the coming year. She was told she would be working with six students with learning disabilities in Mrs. Toro's sixth-period, seventh-grade history class on a daily basis.

Unfortunately, Mrs. Toro, the history teacher, had not been informed by the principal that Ms. Irby was going to be team-teaching with her. When Ms. Irby went to see Mrs. Toro, and explained the situation, Mrs. Toro appeared visibly shaken.

Now both teachers, who had never discussed the possibility of working together, felt awkward. Neither had previously thought about team-teaching, although neither was

Research Highlight

Teacher Attitudes Toward Inclusion

 Teacher attitudes have been considered fundamental to successful inclusion (Cullen, Gregory, & Noto, 2010). But what are teacher attitudes, and have they changed over time? Scruggs, Leins, and Mastropieri (2011) summarized the results of 61 survey, comparative, and qualitative investigations of teacher attitudes published between 1996 and 2010, and compared these with the results of a previous investigation (Scruggs & Mastropieri, 1996), which studied attitudes from 1958 through 1995. For the survey research, it was reported that 62.8% of teachers (vs. 65.0% from the 1996 investigation) overall supported the concept of inclusion, while 61.4% (vs. 54.4%, 1996) expressed willingness to teach students with disabilities. These numbers were remarkably similar over the years. Further, it was found that there was higher agreement for more generally worded items of less intensity. That is, whereas 70.8% voiced general support for inclusion, only 40.5% supported inclusion for all students with disabilities, for most or all of the school day. Again, these percentages were very similar to data from earlier decades. Across all years of surveys, teachers generally expressed a wish for additional time and training, as well as personnel and administrative support for implementing inclusion in their classrooms. Analysis of comparative studies revealed that, similar to previous years, more positive attitudes were reported by elementary teachers (vs. secondary teachers), special education teachers (vs. general education teachers), female teachers (vs. male teachers), and by teachers who had taken more (vs. less) coursework relevant to inclusion. Qualitative studies generally confirmed other types of research, especially with reference to both the benefits and challenges of inclusion. Reported benefits include social benefits, support from the special education teacher, and the general enrichment provided by a more diverse classroom. Reported challenges included class size, student skill levels, and making accomodations.

Scruggs et al. (2011) concluded that teacher attitudes are generally positive, and have changed very little over the past several decades. Teacher attitudes seemed to be less influenced by prejudice toward students with disabilities, and more oriented to practical classroom concerns, including sufficient class size, time to prepare for inclusive instruction, and training appropriate to teaching inclusive classes. Appropriately supported teachers are more likely to have positive attitudes toward including students with disabilities.

QUESTIONS FOR REFLECTION

1. Why do you think attitudes toward inclusion have changed so little over the years?
2. How might overall attitudes toward inclusion be improved?
3. Why do you think elementary-grade teachers report more positive attitudes than secondary-grade teachers?

particularly opposed to the idea. Perhaps more important, the teachers did not have the same preparation periods free, which meant that any co-planning would have to take place before or after school. This would mean that Ms. Irby and Mrs. Toro now had additional responsibilities they had not requested.

Neither teacher had a good understanding of the principal's expectations. They were also unsure of how to execute the co-teaching. Ms. Irby had expertise in special education and in making accommodations, and Mrs. Toro had content expertise in history, but now they had to figure out a way to blend their strengths during one period of instruction per day.

Although both teachers tried to be optimistic, there were so many ambiguities regarding their roles and expectations that they both initially experienced some discomfort with the situation. Mrs. Toro said she would continue to prepare and present information from the social studies textbook to the class and requested that Ms. Irby circulate around the room during independent activities to provide assistance to anyone who needed it. Ms. Irby agreed to this arrangement but felt uncomfortable during class presentations, as she was unsure of what to do with herself. Both teachers tried to meet and plan, but something else always seemed to take priority.

QUESTIONS FOR REFLECTION

1. Compare and contrast the two teaching situations. What differences seem most likely to affect the success of inclusive instruction? What changes can you recommend?

2. In the second case, neither teacher had been given adequate notice, nor had they volunteered for team-teaching. What options are available to Ms. Irby and Mrs. Toro? How can they begin to monitor and evaluate their team-teaching? How can they overcome the barriers and make the experience successful for them and their students?

It is clear that many aspects must be considered in order for inclusive placements to be successful. These involve careful planning and attention to the multiple perspectives of general education teachers, special education teachers, parents of students with and without disabilities, and, of course, the students themselves. However, with careful planning and appropriate programming, inclusive instruction can prove to be a successful and rewarding experience for everyone.

Summary

- In 1975, Public Law 94-142 (IDEA) was passed. This law, and its subsequent amendments, established the rights of students with disabilities to a free, appropriate public education. It further provided that this education would take place, to the maximum extent possible, in the least restrictive environment. Before the passage of this law, students with special needs were routinely excluded from public school.

- IDEA provides for special services for disability areas, including autism, deafness, hearing impairments, intellectual disability, multiple disabilities, orthopedic impairments, other health impairments, emotional disturbance, specific learning disabilities, speech or language impairments, traumatic brain injury, visual impairments, and deaf-blindness. However, other groups of students may also require special adaptations by general education teachers, including students who are culturally or linguistically diverse, students at-risk for school failure, and students with gifts or talents.

- Other court rulings and federal laws, such as Section 504 and the Americans with Disabilities Act, have provided for nondiscriminatory treatment of individuals with disabilities.

- Six important principles in IDEA are (1) zero reject, (2) nondiscriminatory testing, (3) free and appropriate education, (4) least restrictive environment, (5) due process, and (6) parent participation.

- Current educational practice provides for a continuum of services for students with disabilities, from full-time placement in the regular education classroom to special residential schools. Currently, most students with disabilities are served in regular education classrooms.

- "Full inclusion" is the full-time placement of students with disabilities in regular classrooms. Important points have been raised by concerned individuals on both sides of this issue.

- Most teachers favor some form of inclusion for their own classes. However, teachers report a need for sufficient time, training, and resources to teach effectively in inclusive classrooms. When these supports are provided, attitudes toward inclusive teaching improve.

PROFESSIONAL STANDARDS LINK:
Introduction to Inclusive Teaching

Information in this chapter links most directly to:

- CEC Standards: 1 (Foundations), 2 (Development and Characteristics of Learners), 3 (Individual Learning Differences)
- INTASC Standards: 2 (Learning Differences), 3 (Learning Environments), 4 (Content Knowledge)

Note: **CEC** is the Council for Exceptional Children, an organization dedicated to improving educational outcomes for students with disabilities and gifted students. **INTASC** is the Interstate New Teacher Assessment and Support Consortium, which created standards for licensing new teachers to be compatible with the National Board for Professional Teaching Standards.

References

Alaska Statutes, Title 14, Chapter 30, 1971.

Andrews, J.F., Shaw, P.C., & Lomas, G. (2011). Deaf and hard of hearing students. In J.M. Kauffman & D.P. Hallahan (Eds.), *Handbook of special education* (pp. 233–246). New York: Routledge.

Beattie v. Board of Education of City of Antigo, 172 N.W. 153, 154 (1919).

Russell, C. (2008). How are your person first skills? A self-assessment. *Teaching Exceptional Children, 40*(5), 40–43.

Brown v. Board of Education, 347 U.S. 483 (1954).

Blankenship, C. (1981). *Mainstreaming students with learning and behavior problems.* Orlando, FL: Harcourt School.

Chrismer, S., Hodge, S., & Saintil, D. (Eds.)(2006). Assessing NCLB: Perspectives and prescriptions. *Harvard Educational Review, 76* (4).

Code of Virginia, Section, 22.275.3 (1973).

Cook, B. G., Tankersley, M., Cook, L., & Landrum, T. J. (2000). Teachers' attitudes toward their included students with disabilities. *Exceptional Children, 67,* 115–135.

Council for Exceptional Children. (2002). No Child Left Behind has major implications for special education. *CEC Today, 9*(4), 4.

Crockett, J. (2011). Conceptional models for leading and administrating special education. In J.M. Kauffman & D.P. Hallahan (Eds.), *Handbook of special education* (pp. 351–362). New York: Routledge.

Cullen, J. P., Gregory, J. P., & Noto, L. A. (2010, February). *The Teacher Attitudes Toward Inclusion Scale (TATIS): Technical report.* Paper presented at the Annual Meeting of the Eastern Educational Research Association, Savannah, GA. (ERIC Document Reproduction Service No. ED509930)

Davis, G. A., & Rimm, S. B. (2004). *Education of the gifted and talented* (5th ed.). Boston: Allyn & Bacon.

deBettencourt, L. U. (2002). Understanding the differences between IDEA and Section 504. *Teaching Exceptional Children, 34*(3), 16–23.

Department of Education (2012). *ESEA flexibility.* Washington, DC: Author. Retrieved February 27, 2012, from http://www.ed.gov/esea/flexibility

Dettmer, P., Thurston, L., & Dyck, N. (2005). *Consultation, collaboration, and teamwork for students with special needs.* Boston: Allyn & Bacon.

Diana v. State Board of Education, Civ. No. C-70-37 RFP (N.D. Cal. 1970, 1973).

Downing, J. A. (2004). Related services for students with disabilities: Introduction to the special issue. *Intervention in School and Clinic, 39,* 195–208.

Educational Testing Service. (2002). *Special education: Core knowledge study guide.* Princeton, NJ: Author.

Frieman, B. B. (2001). *What teachers need to know about children at-risk.* New York: Allyn & Bacon.

Fuchs, D., & Fuchs, L. S. (1994). Inclusive schools movement and the radicalization of special education reform. *Exceptional Children, 60,* 294–309.

Gollnick, D. M., & Chinn, P. C. (2009). *Multicultural education in a pluralistic society* (8th ed.). Upper Saddle River, NJ: Merrill/Pearson.

Honig v. Doe, 484 U.S. 305 S.Ct. 592, 98 L.Ed.2d 686, 43 Ed. Law Rep. 857 (1988).

Individuals with Disabilities Education Improvement Act of 2004. Public Law 108-446. (2007). Washington, DC: U.S. Government Printing Office.

Johnson, T. P. (1986). *The principal's guide to the educational rights of handicapped students.* Reston, VA: National Association of Secondary School Principals.

Kauffman, J.M., Nelson, C.M., Simpson, R.L., & Mock, D.R. (2011). Contemporary issues. In J.M. Kauffman & D.P. Hallahan (Eds.), *Handbook of special education* (pp. 15–26). New York: Routledge.

Larry P. v. Riles, 343 F. Supp. 1306 (N. D. Cal. 1972, *aff'd* 502 F.2d 963 (9th Cir. 1974), *further action* 495 F. Supp. 926 N. D. Cal. 1979), *aff'd* 793 F. 2d 969 (9th Cir. 1984).

Lazarus, D., Thurlow, M., Lail, K., & Christensen, L. (2009). A longitudinal analysis of state accommodation policies. *Journal of Special Education, 43,* 67–80.

Lipsky, D. K., & Gartner, A. (1997). *Inclusion and school reform: Transforming America's classrooms.* Baltimore, MD: Paul H. Brookes.

Lipsky, D. K., & Gartner, A. (2008). *Inclusion: A service, not a place.* Port Chester, NY: Dude.

Mandlawitz, M. (2006). *What every teacher should know about IDEA 2004.* Boston: Pearson Education.

Mills v. Board of Education, 348 F. Supp. 866 (D.D.C. 1972).

Murdick, N. L., Gartin, B. C., & Crabtree, T. L. (2006). *Special education law* (2nd ed). Upper Saddle River, NJ: Merrill/Prentice Hall.

Nevada Revised Statutes, Section 39.050 (1963).

Oberti v. Board of Education of the Borough of Clementon School District, 995 F. 2d 1204 (3rd Cir. 1993).

Palmer, D. S., Fuller, K., Arora, T., & Nelson, M. (2001). Taking sides: Parent views on inclusion for their children with severe disabilities. *Exceptional Children, 67,* 467–484.

Pennsylvania Association for Retarded Children v. Commonwealth of Pennsylvania (PARC), 334 F. Supp. 1257 (E.D. Pa. 1972).

Rothstein, L. F. (1999). *Special education law* (3rd ed.). New York: Longman.

Rozalski, M., Miller, J., & Stewart, A. (2011). Least restrictive environment. In J. M. Kauffman & D. P. Hallahan (Eds.), *Handbook of special education* (pp. 107–120). New York: Routledge.

Russell, C.L. (2008). How are your person-first skills? A self-assessment. *Teaching Exceptional Children, 40*(5), 40–43.

Scruggs, T. E., Leins, P., & Mastropieri, M. A. (2011, April). *Teacher attitudes towards inclusion: A synthesis of survey, comparative, and qualitative research, 1958 – 2010.* Paper presented at the annual meeting of the Council for Exceptional Children, Washington, DC.

Scruggs, T. E., & Mastropieri, M. A. (1996). Teacher perceptions of mainstreaming/inclusion, 1958–1995: A research synthesis. *Exceptional Children, 63,* 59–74.

Sindelar, P. T., McCray, E. D., Kiely, M. T., & Kamman, M. (2008). The impact of No Child Left Behind on special education teacher supply and the preparation of the workforce. In T. E. Scruggs & M. A. Mastropieri (Eds.), *Personnel preparation: Advances in learning and behavioral disabilities* (Vol. 21, pp. 89–123). Bingley, UK: Emerald.

Siperstein, G., Parker, R., Norns Bardon, J., & Widerman, K. (2007). A national study of youth attitudes toward the inclusion of students with intellectual disabilities. *Exceptional Children, 73,* 435–455.

Smith, T.E.C. (2002). Section 504: What teachers need to know. *Intervention in School and Clinic, 37,* 259–266.

Staples, K., & Diliberto, J. (2010). Guidelines for successful parental involvement. *Teaching Exceptional Children, 42*(6), 58–63.

U.S. Department of Education. (2006). *Carl D. Perkins Career and Technical Education Act of 2006: Reauthorization of Perkins.* Washington, DC: Author. Retrieved April 10, 2008, from http://www.ed.gov/policy/sectech/leg/perkins/index.html

U.S. Department of Education, Office of Special Education and Rehabilitative Services. (2006a). *Assistance to states for the education of children with disabilities and preschool grants for children with disabilities*. Final Regulations. 71 Fed. Reg. 46540 (30 C.F.R. Parts 300 and 301). Washington, DC: Author.

U.S. Department of Education (2011). *Thirtieth Annual Report to Congress on the Implementation of Individuals with Disabilities Education Act*. Washington, DC: Author.

Watson v. City of Cambridge, 32 N.E. 864, 864 (1893).

Will, M. (1986). Educating students with learning problems: A shared responsibility. *Exceptional Children, 52,* 411–415.

Wright, P. W. D., & Wright, P. D. (2005). *Wright's law IDEA 2004: Parts A & B.* Hartfield, VA: Harbor House Law Press.

Wright, P. W. D., & Wright, P. D. (2007). *Wrightslaw: Special education law* (2nd ed.). Hartfield, VA: Harbor House Law Press.

Wright, P. W. D., Wright, P. D., & Heath, S. W. (2004). *Wright's law: No child left behind.* Hartfield, VA: Harbor House Law Press.

Yell, M. (2012). *The law and special education* (3rd ed.). Upper Saddle River, NJ: Merill/Prentice-Hall.

Yell, M.L., & Crockett, J.B. (2011). Free Appropriate Public Education. In J.M. Kauffman & D.P. Hallahan (Eds.), *Handbook of special education* (pp. 77–90). New York: Routledge.

Yell, M.L., Katsiyannis, A. & Bradley, R. (2011). The Individuals with Disabilities Education Act: The evolution of special education law. In J. M. Kauffman & D.P. Hallahan (Eds.) *The handbook of special education* (pp. 61–76). New York: Routledge.

Zigmond, N., & Kloo, A., (2008). General and special education are (and should be) different. In J.M. Kauffman & D.P. Hallahan (Eds.), *Handbook of special education* (pp. 160–172). New York: Routledge.

Photo Credits

Credits are listed in order of appearance.

Paul Adams © Tony Freeman/PhotoEdit; Anthony Magnacca/Merrill; Scott Cunningham/Merrill; © Jonathan Nourok/PhotoEdit; © Bob Daemmrich/Photo Edit.

CHAPTER 1

What Is Explicit Instruction?

Over the past 25 years, competing educational philosophies and instructional models have often been described as "at war." The "reading wars" are a prominent example of how disagreements over different teaching approaches have characterized the instructional landscape of schools. Teacher-directed instructional approaches have been the particular target of disdain among educators. Often, when working with a group of teachers or teacher education students, I will ask them to play a game of free association: "When I say the words *explicit instruction*, what words come immediately to mind?" Almost unanimously, they will say *boring, rote, mechanistic, robotic*—sometimes even *cruel* and *harmful*. I then ask them to examine the reasons why explicit instruction has garnered such a negative reputation, especially in light of the fact that it has been strongly supported by research in a variety of settings, for different types of learners. After all, many less well documented strategies have very positive reputations among educators.

Critical examination of this issue reveals that the misapplication and misunderstanding of the strategy rather than the strategy itself may have led to its demise among many educators. Problems result when any one teaching method is uniformly applied without regard for students' individual instructional needs. In the case of explicit instruction, classrooms are sharply criticized (and rightly so) in which students are passive learners, their voices rarely heard, in submission to large, uninterrupted swaths of teacher talk. Many new teachers, themselves victims of this type of indifferent instruction, enter the profession determined to do things differently. As a result, approaches to explicit instruction have been labeled "traditional"—what Rosenshine (1997) has called "politically and romantically incorrect."

As teacher-directed approaches fell out of favor among educators, more student-centered, constructivist methods gained popularity. According to these approaches, the teacher should not function as a disseminator of knowledge; rather, students must actively construct their own learning. The teacher serves as a facilitator or guide, arranging the environment in ways that maximize students' learning. A central tenet of constructivist approaches is the "minilesson." Teachers conduct brief periods of explanation in response to student questioning or "teachable moments." Labeling any direct teaching as "mini" might be interpreted as a response to the overwhelming amount of teacher talk that could be found in more traditional classrooms. It's as if educators wanted to say, "You can't accuse me of being one of those boring windbags! I don't spend much time directly teaching at *all*!"

3

The rise of constructivist methods meant that once again, many teachers (myself included) uniformly applied these approaches without regard to the consequences for some students. It takes a fairly bright, engaged student to think to ask the right question at precisely the right moment. What about those students who are so lost that they don't know what question to ask? "Mini" instruction may not be sufficient for them. In addition, teaching that happens only in response to teachable moments demands that teachers are prepared to provide any explanation in response to any question at any time. While many experienced teachers may feel comfortable and competent teaching "on the fly," less experienced teachers may need more careful planning in order to provide students with clear, accurate explanations. Although many teachers may feel more comfortable as a "guide" than as a "director," it is important to acknowledge that even in general education classrooms, many students actually *need* instruction that is explicit, directive, and intense, especially as they work to acquire basic skills and strategies. As Mrs. N, a fifth-grade resource teacher, wrote about her struggle to meet her students' needs,

> A great deal of content I must teach is based on the assumption that my students have certain skills, which they do not possess. When students are given strategies for accomplishing a task, they perform with greater success. One of the greatest issues of concern to me is that many of my colleagues do not want to spend time teaching something they feel students should have learned prior to entering their class. What difference does it make who teaches the student as long as the student is taught? If they do not learn skills and strategies they need, they cannot possibly move forward and access the content of any curriculum. Often my colleagues assume that a student can do the work, but chooses not to. This is difficult to assess. How do I know when a student is choosing not to work? If they are making that choice, why are they making it? Are they frustrated? I think most often the student is not taught strategies for how to react when they do not understand something. Also, they may not be taught how to generalize a strategy—that a strategy that was helpful in sixth grade may also be helpful in seventh.

Mrs. N's comments reflect a common tension between educators in inclusive settings. Mrs. N believes in the merits of providing explicit instruction across the curriculum—even to the extent of teaching her students affective strategies, such as how to express frustration appropriately. Others view themselves as grade-level or content-area specialists; bringing students "up to speed" is outside their realm of responsibility or expertise. Mrs. N's frustration highlights the need for inclusive educators to reconceptualize effective teaching across grade levels, content areas, and settings.

This book is called *Explicit Instruction* because it provides a contemporary middle ground for teachers who are wary of traditional direct instruction approaches but who acknowledge that many students—particularly in today's inclusive classrooms—need something *more*. The framework presented here is teacher led, but with a greater emphasis on the teacher–student transaction. In order to create a successful explicit instruction lesson, the teacher and students are joined in the instructional encounter; each has an important role to play in constructing learning. The purpose of this book is to challenge the view of explicit instruction as an outdated, mechanistic instructional strategy and to present it as timely, proven, and accessible. The explicit instruction framework is flexible and holds wide applicability for teachers across grade levels (elementary, middle, and secondary), settings (whole group, small group, general education, and special education), and content areas.

In this chapter, we examine the history and research behind teacher-directed instructional models. This historical perspective will provide the background and rationale for the explicit instruction framework. Contradictions of explicit instruction are discussed along with four assumptions that guided construction of the explicit instruction framework.

Skip ———→

DIRECT INSTRUCTION (D.I.) VERSUS DIRECT INSTRUCTION (d.i.)

Teacher-directed instructional approaches have their roots in the behaviorist tradition of direct instruction. Direct instruction (D.I.), sometimes called expository, didactic, teacher-centered instruction or "active teaching," is a teacher-directed strategy in which the teacher transmits information directly to students. In a D.I. model, the teacher's role is to pass facts, skills, or strategies on to students in the most explicit way possible. This most often takes the form of a structured presentation that includes specific events of instruction, such as explanations, examples, and opportunities for practice and feedback. The D.I. format is a multifaceted presentation that requires verbal lecture and teacher–student interactions involving explanations, questions and answers, review and practice, and checking student understanding. The degree of student learning that occurs is directly related to the time a student is actively engaged in the learning process. Thus, efficient, effective use of instructional time and active student practice of content are key ingredients in D.I. strategies.

Two conceptions of D.I. are present in the literature. D.I. refers to a highly structured, ritualized, and scripted instructional model in the behaviorist learning tradition (Becker, Englemann, Carnine, & Rhine, 1981). The term "direct instruction" (d.i.) refers to the type of explicit, structured teaching outlined in the teacher-effectiveness literature (Rosenshine & Stevens, 1984). It is important to distinguish between these models of instruction since many scholars and practitioners have blurred the lines between them, and their differences have often become unclear. Research findings regarding these models cannot conveniently be taken together, as they espouse very different approaches to teaching.

D.I.

D.I. originated from two distinct lines of research. The first line of research focused on a set of models labeled *Direct Instruction*. D.I. models are based on the premise that through a teacher-directed instructional process, students can be trained to succeed. Behavioral theorists believe that it is not useful to speculate about internal cognitive processes since they cannot be directly observed or controlled. The curriculum and practice of D.I. are based on Skinner's (1968) operant conditioning theory, which stated that a behavior must be reinforced to bring about its regular occurrence. The "Direct Instructor," therefore, would conceive of teaching as a process of producing changes in students' observable behavior. These changes take the form of adding new responses to the student's educational repertoire.

Several key principles underlie D.I. approaches to teaching and learning. The central task of D.I. is to present students with the appropriate material on which to focus their attention and mental effort so that they will learn particular information, skills, and concepts. Skills and student performances of those skills are broken down into small units so that behavior and learning can be shaped incrementally. Initial teaching of any skill involves explicit, often scripted instruction on each step in the sequence. The teacher models behaviors before expecting students to perform them. The likelihood that students will generalize their learning to new situations is increased through engagement in practice consisting of real-life application and many examples from different contexts. Immediate feedback is provided on each step of a task. During demonstration and guided practice, the teacher provides redundant explanations, gives many examples, and provides sufficient instruction so that students can do the work with minimal difficulty. As student errors are minimized, the probability, frequency, and persistence of desired behavior are increased. A high frequency of student errors gives the teacher an indication that the presentation was inadequate and that reteaching is necessary.

The notion that a high percentage of correct, automatic responses plays a role in successful learning resulted from research by Samuels (1981) and others (Anderson, Evertson, & Brophy, 1979; Gersten, Carnine, & Williams, 1982; Good & Grouws, 1977). Teachers can minimize student errors by breaking instruction down into smaller steps and giving students instruction and practice to mastery on each step before proceeding. Students are provided with explicit demonstration of skills interspersed with checks of student understanding and teacher-monitored practice. In this way, the teacher can correct errors before they become part of the student's repertoire. A high frequency of correct responses is particularly important in the elementary grades. Research in D.I. indicates that the most effective teachers continue practice beyond the point where students are accurate, until overlearning has occurred (Engelmann & Carnine, 1982). When student responses are quick, accurate, and firm, the teacher moves on to a new question or topic, thereby maintaining the momentum of the lesson. Thus, D.I. constitutes a teacher-controlled method of instruction in which the learner is viewed as the recipient of information.

In addition to teacher presentation, D.I. is concerned with rigorous analysis of exactly how curricular materials are constructed. The key principle in the design of D.I. programs is that for student learning to occur, both materials and teacher presentation of those materials must be clear and unambiguous (Engelmann & Carnine, 1982). D.I. advocates argue that while commonly used teacher guides attempt to facilitate student interest and motivation, they fail to teach anything systematically. Different teachers will interpret directions such as "give an explanation" or "generate student definitions" in different ways. That is, how concepts and relationships will be taught is often left open to teacher preference or interpretation. Deviations in the way material is presented may result in confusion for low-performing students. According to D.I., instructional sequences must be detailed, precisely crafted, and implemented with fidelity in order to be effective.

D.I., then, is a teaching approach in which the level of teacher control is *high*. In fact, it has been criticized for being overly rigid and routinized and for ignoring individual differences among learners. For example, one of the most well known of the D.I. lesson formats is Reading Mastery (Distar Reading; Engelmann & Bruner, 1998). A highly ritualized, scripted, and phonics-based system of reading instruction, Reading Mastery calls for the use of tightly controlled vocabulary and complete mastery of each skill by each student in the group before proceeding to a new skill. Although many educators (especially those in general education) may feel uncomfortable with the level of teacher control imparted by strict D.I. programs, they have been shown to be effective for particular learners and contexts, including those with mild to moderate disabilities (e.g., Engelmann, 1980; Fabre, 1984; Gersten, 1985; Stebbins, St. Pierre, Proper, Anderson, & Cerva, 1977).

d.i.

A second line of research generated the term *direct instruction* (d.i.) to refer to the systematic, explicit teaching of skills and strategies. Many correlational studies found a relationship between student achievement and teachers' use of specific instructional strategies, such as teaching in small steps with student practice after each step, guiding students during initial practice, and ensuring that all students experienced a high level of successful practice (e.g., Gage & Needels, 1989; Good & Grouws, 1979; Weinert & Helmke, 1995). These techniques were intended to emphasize the teacher's role in maximizing the time that students are actively engaged in learning, thereby resulting in higher student achievement (Rosenshine & Stevens, 1984). This research was conducted primarily in basic reading and mathematics in the elementary grades.

Experimental studies also compared the achievement of students whose teachers were trained in d.i. strategies and students whose teachers were not. In other words, teachers were trained in the methods used by effective teachers, and their students' achievement was compared to that of students whose teachers did not receive such training (Slavin, 2000). These studies showed more mixed results. Some findings suggest that this is due to the fact that the recommendations from d.i. research make so much sense. That is, when studies have found no differences between teachers trained in d.i. models and other teachers, it may be because both groups of teachers already had many of the skills before the training took place.

Out of the teacher-effects research of the 1970s and 1980s, common teaching "functions" were abstracted that were associated with improved student learning. These were combined into a set of models labeled *direct instruction* (Rosenshine, 1995). These models developed as scholars examined the same research literature and generated similar but different models of d.i. (see, e.g., Gagne and Briggs, 1979; Good and Grouws, 1979; Hunter, 1982; Rosenshine, 1995). In general, all d.i. models share a common set of principles. These include teacher direction (rather than student self-direction or seat work); active presentation of information; clear organization of presentation, usually in the form of specific steps; step-by-step progression of instruction based on task analysis; use of examples, prompts, and demonstration; constant assessment of student understanding; effective use of time; and maintaining student attention. Guided practice, which follows the demonstration, allows the teacher to ask questions of students, check for understanding, and give feedback. Finally, students work on activities directly related to the new material during independent practice.

The general structure of a d.i. lesson takes on vastly different forms in different subject areas and at different grade levels. Teachers of older students may take several days to complete the steps of the process, ending with a formal test or evaluation. Teachers of younger students may go through the entire cycle in a class period, using informal assessments at the end. The sequence of a d.i. lesson flows along a logical path, from eliciting student attention and interest to presenting new information to allowing students to practice their new knowledge or skills to assessment (Slavin, 2000). This orderly progression is what characterizes d.i. at any grade level and in any subject, although the various components and how they are implemented will look different for different subjects and grades.

In comparison with D.I., d.i. is a generic teaching model rather than a scripted, fully elaborated program for teaching reading or mathematics. Unlike D.I., d.i. does not directly address issues of curriculum. Rather, d.i. is based on all available naturalistic research on classroom processes—research conducted primarily in general education classrooms, often with at-risk students. Low-performing students repeatedly show higher academic achievement when their teachers follow a consistent pattern of d.i. that includes demonstration, practice, and feedback (Tarver, 1992). The differences between D.I. and d.i. are summarized in Table 1.1.

Out of the history and background described previously, a set of contradictions emerged regarding d.i.:

1. Although many students across educational settings need some form of teacher-directed instruction, many teachers are reluctant to deliver it.

TABLE 1.1   D.I. Versus d.i.

D.I.	d.i.
"Specific" teaching program	"Generic" teaching model
Based on operant conditioning theory. Teacher direction is very high	Based on research on classroom processes
Highly structured, scripted, and ritualized	Teacher direction is high
Targeted at adding new responses to the student's repertoire	Structured, explicit, clear, and controlled
Skills broken into small units	Emphasizes teacher's role in maximizing academic learning time
Behavior and learning are shaped gradually	Step-by-step presentation
High percentage of correct responses	Includes demonstration, practice, and corrective feedback
Skills are practiced to overlearning	Does not directly address issues of curriculum
Concerned with design of curricular materials	

2. Although d.i. has a strong research base, it is often degraded.
3. Contemporary views of learning hold that students must actively construct their own learning, yet many lack the prerequisite skills to do so.

These contradictions highlight the need for an alternative to traditional D.I. and d.i. models. In the current educational climate, instructional models are needed that are attentive to teachers' desires to actively engage students in the learning process and that can be adapted to the learning needs of diverse learners, across contexts, in response to different types of cognitive demands.

Continue ———→

EXPLICIT INSTRUCTION: A MEANINGFUL ALTERNATIVE

Explicit instruction (e.i.) represents a research-based alternative to D.I. or d.i. approaches. The e.i. framework differs from these models because it is based on the teacher-effects literature as well as research in learning strategies and cognitive processes. Whereas D.I. and d.i. approaches focus on how presentation of material influences behavior, e.i. seeks to understand and capitalize on how incoming information is processed and organized by the learner. Interest in students' cognitive processes occurred as a natural outgrowth of a shift in orientation from teacher-controlled, behaviorist theories of instruction to theories of learning that attempt to teach students *how* to learn. Along with this change in emphasis, a shift occurred in the way educators viewed learners. Current theories hold that the educational process is based on building the cognitive structures of the learner's mind (Brown, 1994).

This change in approach modified our conception of the teaching and learning process in important ways. Learning is seen as an active process that occurs within the learner and that can be directly influenced by the learner. Although d.i. models (e.g., Hunter, 1982; Rosenshine, 1983) are teacher directed and share an emphasis on teaching that is structured, explicit, and clear, they emphasize the teacher's role in maximizing academic learning time. Learner-centered, inquiry-oriented approaches emphasize the learner's role in constructing learning. Since learning occurs *within* the learner, the teacher serves as a facilitator (rather than a director) of that learning. The

TABLE 1.2   Explicit Instruction (e.i.) as an Alternative

d.i.	Learner-Centered Approaches	e.i.
Teacher directed	Learner centered	Teacher structures and directs the learning process
Structured, explicit, clear	Discovery oriented	Structured, clear, explicit
Emphasizes teacher's role in maximizing academic learning time	Emphasizes learner's role in constructing learning	Emphasizes teacher's role in maximizing academic learning time *and* learner's role in actively constructing learning
	Teacher as *facilitator* or *guide*	Conceived for use in inclusive classrooms
	Tailored toward learners who are independent and self-directed	"Instruction as usual" = planning for and teaching *all* students
		Accommodations for diverse learners are integrated into the framework

e.i. framework merges these two viewpoints: the outcome of learning is not believed to depend mainly on what the teacher presents or what is going on cognitively inside the learner. Rather, the outcome of learning depends *jointly* on what information is presented and how the learner processes that information. From this perspective, e.i. is teacher led but with a greater emphasis on the ways in which students actively construct and process knowledge (see Table 1.2).

Previous approaches to d.i. were conceptualized before inclusive classrooms became widespread. Delivering whole-group and small-group instruction in an academically diverse classroom poses a particular set of challenges. As a result, teachers often continue to plan and deliver "instruction as usual." Modifications or accommodations for less capable students can become an afterthought and may include the same few options every time. These accommodations may or may not do much to help students with learning difficulties, but their teachers may not know of more meaningful ways to modify their instruction. The e.i. framework was conceptualized specifically for use in inclusive classrooms. It includes elements that have been identified by research as providing access to the general education curriculum for diverse learners, such as a high level of active engagement, use of strategies and prompts, activating background knowledge, explicit review/preview of new material and/or vocabulary, and cognitive modeling. The e.i. framework reframes "instruction as usual" as giving conscious consideration to planning for and teaching *all* students. The need for additional tacked-on accommodations can be significantly reduced because strategies that promote success among diverse learners have already been incorporated into the lesson.

Some readers may be thinking, "If components such as generating prior knowledge, thinking aloud, and formative assessment for and of learning are all components of lessons, how is e.i. different from learner-centered, constructivist approaches? Certainly, a skilled teacher can take any concept and teach it through specific steps, think-alouds, conducting an inquiry-based teaching method, and emerging student discussion." In many cases, that is true. However, it is important to consider that there are many students in general education classrooms with highly gifted teachers who still fail to progress at the same rate as their peers. These students often continue to languish and ultimately end up in special education. Such students cannot wait for certain skills, strategies, or content to take hold incidentally. In order to accelerate their progress, structured, intentional, and sustained efforts must be made to help them achieve, including the use of e.i.

Four underlying assumptions guided the content and organization of this book. First, *the way teachers think about e.i. influences the way they teach.* Research has documented that teachers will not adopt teaching practices that do not fit with their personal beliefs about teaching and learning (Richardson, 1996). If teachers believe that e.i. is boring, rote, meaningless, and wrong, they will either dismiss it or implement it halfheartedly. Therefore, e.i. allows teachers to preserve their value for teaching that is holistic and meaningful and that promotes the active engagement of students in the learning encounter while providing the structure and control needed by many students (see Table 1.3).

Second, *a teacher's preference for certain teaching approaches should not supersede individual students' instructional needs.* It is commonly held that teachers are autonomous decision makers, capable of making well-informed instructional decisions for their students. Certainly, teachers are in the best position (as opposed to administrators, policymakers, or researchers who are far

TABLE 1.3   What Is Explicit Instruction (e.i.)?

e.i. shares similar goals with other approaches to teaching (e.g., constructivist, holistic, or student centered)	These goals include teaching students to enjoy and be competent at reading, writing, and math; to understand what they read and how math works; and to apply their skills in meaningful ways.
e.i. is holistic	For example, teachers can use e.i. to teach everything that is included in "literacy" (i.e., decoding, comprehension, spelling, and the writing process).
e.i. integrates smaller learning units into meaningful wholes	e.i. does not teach basic skills in isolation from meaningful contexts.
e.i. is developmentally appropriate	Instruction is tailored specifically to students' learning and attentional needs.
e.i. is not skill and drill	e.i. is skill based, but students are *active* participants in the learning process.
e.i. is not rote	The teacher constantly monitors understanding to make sure students are deriving meaning from instruction.
e.i. is not basic skills only	e.i. is used in diverse contexts and curricular areas.
e.i. is not boring and alienating	Students like it because they are *learning*!
e.i. is not all teacher directed	Students are cognitively engaged throughout the learning encounter. They have opportunities throughout the lesson to self-monitor and direct their own learning and participation.

removed from the classroom context) to know what their students need. It is important to acknowledge, however, that there are times when we hold fast to our instructional preferences out of anxiety, fear of change, lack of expertise, or entrenched ideological beliefs. A goal of this book is to challenge teachers who have rejected e.i. in the past to expand their instructional repertoires to meet the needs of *all* students.

Similarly, a third guiding assumption is that *teaching is student centered to the extent that it meets each student's instructional needs.* Definitions of student-centered teaching typically hinge "student centeredness" on the extent to which learning is directed by students. However, student-centered teaching that fails to produce learning in many students cannot be considered effective. This book conceptualizes student centeredness as providing the kind of instruction most likely to maximize individual students' learning.

Finally, *e.i. is flexible and purposeful.* Here, the word *explicit* refers to the careful structuring of the learning *process* by the teacher (see Table 1.4). The e.i. framework combines elements drawn from behavioral theory (e.g., gaining students' attention, explicit modeling, guided practice, and checking students' understanding). Also included are elements gleaned from cognitive-behavioral and constructivist theories of learning (e.g., informing students of the learning objective, activating prior knowledge, preteaching key vocabulary, and think-aloud).

TABLE 1.4   What Is Explicit in Explicit Instruction (e.i.)?

What Is Explicit?	Why?
The teacher knows precisely what she wants students to learn (be able to do) at the end of the lesson.	Unclear learning objectives result in vague teaching and learning.
The teacher tells students what they will be learning.	Students are given a sense of predictability and control. They are joined with the teacher in the instructional encounter.
The teacher focuses her attention and students' attention on the task at hand.	Students know where to direct their attention so that learning is maximized.
The teacher explains, models, gives examples and nonexamples, restates when necessary, and helps students to state and restate goals and strategies.	Knowledge that is usually covert is made overt and explicit; students are "let in" on the secret of how independent learners learn.
The curriculum is arranged so that students are taught prerequisite skills ahead of time.	Students are set up for success!
The learning is meaningful and purposeful.	Students are not taught useless facts and concepts; what students are taught now they use now and in the future; explicit connections are made between prior and current learning.
The instructional transaction follows a structured framework.	The e.i. framework combines elements that maximize achievement for many students.
The teacher provides corrective feedback.	Particularly in the acquisition stage, the teacher corrects *all* errors. Otherwise, students will practice errors and have difficulty learning more complex skills later on.

As such, e.i. is a flexible, multidimensional model. Student achievement is increased when instructional decisions are made on the basis of sound pedagogical theory and appropriate understanding of students and the learning context. The components contained in this book constitute a pharmacy of alternatives from which you can create an effective e.i. prescription for your students. As you learn these components, you will see that the decision to include *every* one of them in *every* lesson may not be instructionally sound. The use of an effective preinstructional set, for example, may serve the dual purpose of organizing student learning *and* reviewing prerequisite skills. You can manipulate the components of e.i. to form highly behavioral, tightly controlled lessons when necessary; e.i. components can also be combined with other approaches (e.g., peer learning strategies) to craft lessons that are well structured but partly student directed. Knowing these components, having categories and labels for the instructional decisions you make, knowing the research that supports them, and deliberately and expertly combining them to meet students' instructional needs are the hallmarks of the master teacher.

PLAN OF THE BOOK

This book is intended to speak to teachers about the necessity of becoming effective explicit instructors while explaining the e.i. framework in a clear, user-friendly manner. Although the theoretical underpinnings of e.i. are presented, the primary focus is on the "how" of becoming an effective instructor. Readers will be able to gain expertise a by mastering small chunks of the e.i. framework at a time—mirroring the process of teaching young students to master new skills and strategies.

Explicit instruction focuses first on getting ready to use e.i. The first order of business is to understand who exactly needs e.i. In order to avoid the mistakes of the past, e.i. must be used for appropriate purposes and in response to identified student needs. Following this discussion, we then move on to describe variables that overarch and interact with the teacher's ability to implement e.i. *Teacher presentation variables* have been identified as fundamental behaviors for communicating effectively with all students and promoting student achievement (Mastropieri & Scruggs, 1997). These variables are viewed as necessary to any teacher presentation *regardless of the model of instruction being implemented*. An explanation of three key teacher presentation variables is included in Chapter 3: teacher clarity, enthusiasm, and appropriate rate of presentation.

Another key consideration in the effectiveness of an e.i. lesson is the incorporation of *student engagement variables*. These are strategies that have been identified by cognitive research as promoting students' ability to acquire new skills and strategies through more effective storage, retrieval, and generalization (King, 1990; Pressley et al., 1995; Scardamalia & Bereiter, 1985). Strategies that actively engage students in the construction of their own learning are a distinguishing feature of high-quality e.i. Therefore, a discussion of student engagement variables is presented in Chapter 4.

Chapters 5 through 8 present the components of the e.i. framework (see Figure 1.1). Three components of an e.i. lesson—(a) preinstructional set, (b) preparing the knowledge base for instruction, and (c) instruction—have been broken down into smaller, more digestible "chunks." For example, preinstructional set has been organized into three discrete teaching skills: (a) gain students' attention, (b) inform students of the learning objectives, and (c) use informed instruction. Taken together, these three bite-size chunks constitute the skills teachers need to implement an effective preinstructional set. Although the components of e.i.

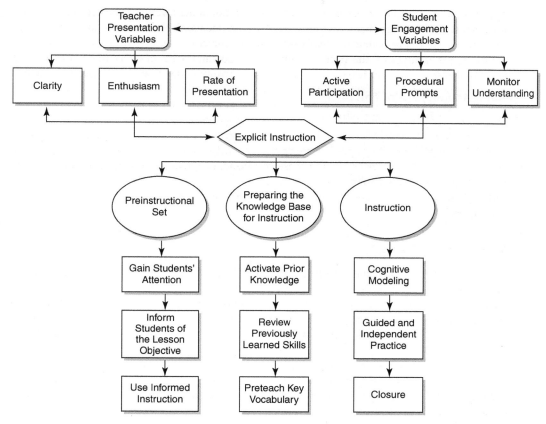

FIGURE 1.1   The e.i. Framework.

have been broken down to promote mastery of the lesson format, they are intended to be combined into seamless, smoothly paced lessons.

The final section of this book provides specific examples of how e.i. can be applied across the curriculum. Research findings regarding the effectiveness of e.i. in specific curricular areas are provided, along with lesson examples that will help you visualize what e.i. looks like in practice.

Summary

In this chapter, we examined the background and research related to e.i. As noted previously, the principles of e.i. were gleaned from the teacher-effects research as well as research on learning strategies and students' cognitive processes. Contradictions of e.i. were explained, guiding assumptions of this book were described, and characteristics of e.i. were presented.

Contradictions of e.i.

• Many students across educational settings need e.i., but many teachers are reluctant to deliver it.

- Explicit instruction has a strong research base, yet it is often degraded.
- Students are urged to construct their own learning, yet many lack the prerequisite skills to do so.

Guiding Assumptions of This Book

- The way teachers think about e.i. influences the way they teach.
- A teacher's preference for certain teaching approaches should not supersede students' individual instructional needs.

- Teaching is student centered to the extent that it meets each student's instructional needs.
- Explicit instruction is effective, meaningful, and engaging.

Characteristics of e.i.

- It is flexible and purposeful.
- It promotes active engagement of all students.
- It structures the learning process.

Effective Differentiated Instruction for All Students

Variegated Rose

JOHN W. GREEN   John W. Green is 86 and has studied and been interested in photography since the age of 9. Two heart attacks, two strokes, type II diabetes, and arthritis in his shoulders, spine, and feet prevent him from walking far. Having to use a walking stick for support hinders his picture taking. Despite his disabilities, between 2003 and 2009, he has attained many distinctions for his photography, and in 2007 he and several friends founded a photographic group (http://e-voice.org.uk/brelubreluphotogroup/) that now has 23 members. His other passion, and once his career, is engineering. Since retiring, he has set up a small engineering workshop for making parts for his cameras, such as lens adaptor rings and tripod mounts. As John notes, "I haven't let my disability hold me back; in fact, the two interests keep me reasonably fit and active."

Effective Differentiated Instruction for All Students

OBJECTIVES

After studying this chapter, you should be able to:

- Describe the PASS variables and their application to effective instruction in inclusive settings.
- Describe how to **p**rioritize instruction.
  - —Describe planning for content coverage and curriculum decisions.
- Describe how to **a**dapt instruction.
- Identify the different types and levels of learning to be considered in instruction.
- Describe how to **s**ystematically teach in inclusive settings.
  - —Describe the teacher presentation (SCREAM) variables.
  - —Identify strategies for maximizing academic engagement (time-on-task).
  - —Compare and contrast higher-level and lower-level questioning.
- Describe how to **s**ystematically evaluate the outcomes of inclusive instruction.
  - —Describe the use of practice activities to reinforce recall and comprehension.

To be an effective inclusive classroom teacher, you must first be an effective teacher. You must employ the skills that enable you to expect, and receive, the very best in learning and achievement from your students. This chapter describes the variables most important for maximizing student learning, and ways you can implement these variables in your classroom. As you learn to apply these strategies consistently and systematically, you will see the learning, achievement, and attitudes of all of your students increase dramatically.

Research over the past several decades, known as *teacher effectiveness research,* has identified the variables most strongly associated with student achievement (e.g., Archer & Hughes, 2011; Danielson, 2010; Good & Brophy, 2007; Mastropieri & Scruggs, 2004; Rosenshine & Stevens, 1986). Some of this research also has shown that teachers who are most effective at including students with disabilities and other diverse learning needs are also effective classroom teachers in general (Larrivee, 1985; Scruggs & Mastropieri, 1994b). Overall, this research has been critically important in identifying the things teachers should do and not do to maximize learning for all students. In this chapter, we summarize much of what has been learned from this research.

Promoting Effective Differentiated Instruction: The PASS Variables

To maximize the success of students with special needs in inclusive settings, we recommend using the **PASS** variables (Mastropieri & Scruggs, 2002; Scruggs & Mastropieri, 1995). PASS represents a way of thinking and approaching differentiated, inclusive instruction. PASS stands for:

1. **P**rioritize instruction.
2. **A**dapt instruction, materials, or the environment.
3. **S**ystematically teach with the "SCREAM" variables.
4. **S**ystematically evaluate the outcomes of your instruction.

The PASS variables can be used as a guideline for planning, delivering, and evaluating effective inclusive instruction for specific students with special needs. Using these variables and other information from this chapter, you can deliver effective instruction to all your students.

P: Prioritize Instruction

When planning instruction, it is very important that you determine the relative importance of what you will teach. There are elements of your instruction that are very important for every student to learn; others are of less importance. For example, a teacher found that some students spent a lot of time staining slides of onion cells; there was a lot of mess to clean up, and poorly stained slides could not be viewed easily. She determined that understanding cell structure was the most important element of this unit, and that staining slides was less important, and adjusted her instruction accordingly to spend the most time on the content with the highest priority.

Prioritizing instruction should not be thought of as something teachers can only apply to individual lessons; you should prioritize all of your instruction, by planning for content coverage, basing your instruction on prioritized objectives, considering scope and sequence, selecting appropriate curriculum, and pacing instruction to maximize coverage of your prioritized objectives.

STRATEGIES FOR
PLANNING FOR CONTENT COVERAGE

The importance of content coverage is obvious, in that students almost certainly will not learn content that has not been covered. However, the amount of content covered must be appropriate to the skills and abilities of the students learning the content, and must reflect your instructional priorities. Careful planning of content coverage can help ensure that learning will be maximized for all students. Several important considerations to make when planning content coverage include objectives, scope and sequence, curriculum, and pacing.

BASE INSTRUCTION ON SPECIFIC PRIORITIZED OBJECTIVES All content to be covered should be based on specific instructional objectives. Objectives state the outcomes of instruction in ways that allow you to find out whether your instruction was successful. Objectives specify (1) the content of the objective (what is being taught), (2) the conditions under which a student's performance will be assessed (e.g., in writing, oral responding), and (3) the criteria for acceptable performance (level of achievement). For example, consider the following objective: "The student will write five precipitating causes of the Civil War with 100% accuracy." The content of the objective is the causes of the Civil War; the conditions specify that students will write; and the criterion for acceptable performance five causes written with 100% accuracy. Another example of an objective is as follows: "The student will read 3 pages from the grade-level reading materials at a rate of 120 words per minute with 95% of words read correctly." This objective also specifies the content, the conditions, and the criteria to be achieved. Another objective could state, "After silent reading of a grade-level narrative reading assignment, the student will verbally restate the setting, main characters, problem, and resolution with 100% accuracy."

Because the content of instruction is based on objectives, it is important to include as many objectives as necessary to maximize content coverage. This is particularly important for students who receive special education services, because their individualized education

MyEducationLab™

Visit the MyEducationLab™ for this text to enhance your understanding of chapter concepts with a personalized Study Plan. You'll also have the opportunity to hone your teaching skills through video- and case-based Assignments and Activities, IRIS Center Resources, and *Building Teaching Skills and Disposition* lessons.

programs (IEPs) are based on objectives. An effective inclusive teacher specifies objectives and translates IEP objectives into relevant methods and materials, with the assistance of the special education teacher.

In order to ensure that all students are learning and engaged with the curriculum, teachers may need to select and prioritize objectives for some students with disabilities. This means examining all instructional objectives, determining which are the most important for students with disabilities who are included in general education classes, and eliminating objectives that are unnecessary for those students. For example, Cliff has severe arthritis and has a great deal of difficulty using a pencil and completing tasks that require much fine motor control. He uses canes to assist with mobility. His fifth-grade teacher, Mr. Masoodi, employs a hands-on approach to science instruction. To accommodate Cliff's needs, Mr. Masoodi prioritized his class objectives. He examined the content and selected the most important objectives for Cliff. He determined that understanding of critical scientific concepts and a positive attitude toward science had the highest priority as objectives. Handwriting and physical manipulation of instructional materials had a lower priority, and were not always required in Cliff's case. By first examining all the class objectives and then reviewing Cliff's instructional needs, Mr. Masoodi was able to prioritize objectives for Cliff.

PLAN INSTRUCTION BASED ON SCOPE AND SEQUENCE Scope and sequence refer to the breadth and depth of content that will be presented in school (scope) and the order in which the content will be presented (sequence). All areas of instruction should be presented with respect to an overriding scope and sequence of prioritized instructional objectives. Scope and sequence allow for long-term planning and evaluation of instruction, provide implications for time allocations, and set the overall pace of instruction. Most states have published their curriculum guidelines that contain scope and sequence for all subject areas across grade levels. Prioritized content should receive substantial attention within the scope and sequence of instruction.

The **Common Core State Standards Initiative** introduced in 2011 is a state-led effort to provide a clear and consistent framework in order to prepare students for college and the workforce by the time they graduate high school. Nearly all states are participating in this initiative. Teachers in participating states should determine what these standards are, and how these standards will be implemented in inclusive classrooms in their own schools (Scruggs, Brigham, & Mastropieri, in press).

SELECT APPROPRIATE CURRICULUM The curriculum not only includes the instructional materials used for learning, but also refers to the course of study for each discipline and the scope and sequence within each grade level necessary to build conceptual understanding. Curriculum serves as an interface between the student and the learning objectives, and has been described as the overall experience provided to a student by the school (Gartin, Murdick, Imbeau, & Perner, 2002; Moore, 2011).

Curriculum decisions can play an important role in inclusive schooling. The accompanying *In the Classroom* feature shows a checklist of curriculum materials being considered to maximize learning for all students. When serving on curriculum adoption committees, or making a choice from existing school materials, be certain to consider the points noted to maximize learning for all students. Curriculum materials that feature many of these characteristics should be given a higher priority than those with fewer of these characteristics.

Curriculum need not be the same for every student. In fact, curriculum can be carefully selected to address specific learner needs, and individual curriculum decisions are an important component of differentiated instruction.

PACE INSTRUCTION EFFECTIVELY Pacing refers to the rate at which teachers and students proceed through the curriculum, and is another way of prioritizing instruction. For example, Mr. Isaac teaches American history, but has only gotten to World War II by the end of the school year. He has determined (intentionally or not) that events in American history from 1945 to the present have a lower priority, as he did not cover this content. Unless the content at the beginning of the text has a higher priority, and content at the end of the text is judged to be of less value, however, more efficient planning would have produced a pace of instruction that better reflected instructional priorities.

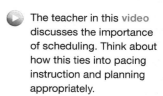

The teacher in this **video** discusses the importance of scheduling. Think about how this ties into pacing instruction and planning appropriately.

In the Classroom

Checklist for Curriculum Materials for Inclusive Environments

- ☐ Do the materials provide sufficient opportunity for active student involvement, or do they simply provide verbal information to be recalled?

- ☐ Are the materials written on a level that is most comprehensible to all students, or do they include unnecessary complexity or an overabundance of unnecessary vocabulary?

- ☐ Do the materials lend themselves to use by cooperative learning groups or other peer-interactive activities?

- ☐ Do the materials allow for sufficient practice of key concepts before moving on to other content?

- ☐ Do the materials provide simple means for frequent evaluation of learner progress toward prespecified goals and objectives?

- ☐ Do the materials include examples of individuals from culturally diverse backgrounds and people of diverse learning abilities?

- ☐ Do the materials provide recommendations for modifications for students with disabilities or other special needs?

- ☐ Do the materials provide evidence-based practice data that demonstrate that positive learning gains can be realized from use of the materials?

One of the most significant problems teachers encounter in inclusive settings is adjusting the pace of instruction to diverse learning needs. Whereas some students appear to master new content almost as soon as they are exposed to it, other students require substantially more instructional time to learn the same content. Students who have learned certain concepts should not be held back, but could be engaged in learning more in-depth knowledge about a concept, or learning about related concepts, while other students receive additional practice.

A: Adapt Instruction, Materials, or the Environment

Once the instructional objectives have been prioritized, the instruction, materials, and/or the environment can be adapted to accommodate more completely the needs of the students with disabilities. These adaptations carefully link the characteristics of the curriculum with the characteristics of the learner, and are at the heart of differentiated instruction. For example, students in Cliff's group often recorded Cliff's notes for him or carried out experiments according to Cliff's directions, when needed. Mr. Masoodi provided extra time for Cliff to work on the science activities if necessary. Mr. Masoodi also adapted materials, for example, by acquiring hand-lenses that were larger and easier to handle. Mr. Masoodi also adapted the environment by rearranging desks to create more aisle space for Cliff and his two canes. Similar adaptations for differentiated instruction, for a wide variety of objectives, are described throughout this chapter.

Appropriately developed adaptations allow students of different abilities to succeed within the same curriculum, and constitute the core of differentiated instruction. When planning adaptations to improve student learning, consider specifically *what* will be taught, and to *what level of proficiency*. These considerations have been referred to as **types and levels of learning** (Mastropieri & Scruggs, 2002). Knowing what types and levels of learning are desired provides guidelines for planning instructional adaptations.

STRATEGIES FOR
MAKING ADAPTATIONS

BASE ADAPTATIONS ON STUDENT CHARACTERISTICS   All instruction is concerned with the interaction of characteristics of the learner with the characteristics of the instructional methods, materials, and environment. Appropriately adapted methods or materials take this interaction into account. Table 1 lists some examples of possible adaptations based on specific learning characteristics.

TABLE 1 Adaptations Based on Student Characteristics	
Learner Characteristics	**Possible Adaptations**
Physical	• Optimal location of student in classroom (preferential seating) • Rearrange classroom layout to promote mobility, accessibility for wheelchairs or braces • Adaptations to promote grasping (e.g., pencil grips, alligator clips, Velcro) • Peer assistance to support physical manipulation • Technological adaptations for computer use
Sensory	• Physical adaptations to accommodate low vision (e.g., clear routes through the classroom) or hearing ability (e.g., carpets to reduce extraneous noise) • Adaptations to promote access to text (e.g., Braillers, Kurzweil readers) • Peer assistance to support access to visual or auditory stimuli • Sign language support for hearing impairments • FM systems to promote hearing
Language	• Language cards for specific vocabulary • Boardmaker or teacher-made communication boards • Targeted language instruction • Hands-on/activity-oriented instruction • Peer models/peer assistance • Peer tutoring/cooperative learning • Sign language instruction • Performance assessment
Literacy	• Direct teaching of literacy skills • Literacy strategy instruction • Books on tape • Reading and writing software (e.g., Kurzweil readers) • Software for reading text • Peer reading/writing assistance • Adapted worksheets to reduce literacy demands • Hands-on/activity-oriented instruction • Peer tutoring/cooperative learning
Emotional/Behavioral	• "Safe" areas of classroom for target student to use when needed • Reduced interaction with peers if needed • Recording chart for monitoring target behaviors with token systems • Posted list of positive behaviors • Peer support • Class rewards for target student behavior • Self-monitoring systems • Parent involvement for social behavior

This **video** describes the different types of learning that may occur in the classroom. Pay attention to the differentiation that is occurring.

BASE INSTRUCTIONAL ADAPTATIONS ON TYPES OF LEARNING Different types of learning occur in school, across all different subject areas. These types include learning of discriminations, facts, rules, procedures, and concepts, as well as problem solving/critical thinking. Although there can be much overlap on school tasks, it is helpful to examine some of the distinctions among the categories. Teachers who understand the different types of learning required of students are more able to plan effective instruction. They are also more able to plan effective instructional adaptations, focused specifically on the nature of the learning task. That is, when a student is demonstrating difficulty with a learning task, it is helpful to determine the type of learning the task represents (e.g., factual learning rather than math or social studies or English) when planning adaptations.

Discrimination Learning Discrimination often occurs early in learning and involves determining how one stimulus is either the same or different from another stimulus. Making discriminations is important in early learning of such things as the alphabet, numbers, colors, shapes, or math concepts. For example, learning to discriminate between a triangle and a square may be difficult at first for students with disabilities. Careful attention to the relevant and irrelevant distinctions between various stimuli can help improve **discrimination learning**. For example, the critical feature that distinguishes "p" from "q" is the relative placement of the round part of the letter. The critical feature that distinguishes squares from triangles is the number of sides (and not, for example, size). For students exhibiting difficulty in discrimination learning tasks, additional repeated practice that emphasizes comprehension of the critical distinctions can be beneficial.

Factual Learning **Factual learning** is a common aspect of school learning and includes vocabulary words and their definitions, names of famous people and their accomplishments, dates and causes of historical events, addition facts, and names of rivers. Some factual learning is in the form of **paired associates**, where one thing is paired with another (e.g., Ulan Bator = Capital of Mongolia; or the Italian word *mela* = "apple"). Other factual learning is in the form of a **serial list** (e.g., "a–b–c–d–e–f–g . . ."; or, "2–4–6–8–10 . . ."), where information is learned with respect to a specific sequence. Appropriate strategies include redundancy, drill and practice, enhancing meaningfulness, and use of elaborations or other memory-enhancing techniques; all of these strategies can be useful in adapting instruction for special needs.

Rule Learning Rules are also pervasive in school, and many students with disabilities and other special needs have difficulties learning these rules. Examples of **rule learning** include social behavior rules (e.g., "Always raise your hand before speaking in class") and math rules (e.g., "When dividing fractions, invert the divisor and multiply"). Rules often include discriminations and facts, and appropriate circumstances for use of those rules. For example, students might need to know that the rules for speaking in class are different in Mr. Halleran's class than they are in Ms. Butcher's class, and that they need to learn to apply the rules appropriately in each class. Some individual students may have more difficulty assimilating these differences.

Procedural Learning **Procedural learning** involves the sequential execution of multiple steps, and is found frequently in school tasks. Remembering and executing the steps involved in going through the cafeteria lunch line (e.g., take your place at the end of the line, take your tray, pick up your silverware) is an example of procedural learning. Academic examples include reading comprehension strategies (e.g., determine the purpose, survey the material, read, recite, review), math algorithms (e.g., learning to execute the steps in solving long-division problems), and study strategies. This can involve describing or listing the steps in the procedure, modeling or demonstrating the application of the procedure, or prompting

Learning factual information can be difficult for some students with disabilities.

students to execute the steps of the procedure. Procedural learning requires that students (1) *recognize* when a specific procedure is called for (e.g., a strategy for learning a list of spelling words), (2) *retrieve* the steps in the procedure (e.g., C–C–C, or cover, copy, and compare), and (3) correctly *execute* the procedure (e.g., use the strategy correctly to learn the list). When students exhibit difficulty with procedural learning tasks, consider which of these three steps they have not mastered.

Conceptual Learning   Most tasks involve some conceptual learning, which can be taught using procedures similar to those for discrimination, factual, and rule-learning paradigms. **Concepts** are completely learned only when the concept can be applied to a new instance. For example, students do not know the concept of "dog" if they can only identify their own household pet as a dog—they must be able to identify dogs they have never seen before.

Concepts can range from simple ("red") to more complex ("radial symmetry," "nonpolar covalent bonding"). Conceptual learning can be enhanced by the use of examples (e.g., of radial symmetry, or of the color red), provision of noninstances ("this is *not* an example of a carnivore"), and statement and application of rules ("insects have six legs; how many legs does this specimen have?"). These enhancements can be helpful for any students who do not immediately master relevant concepts.

Problem Solving/Critical Thinking   **Problem solving** refers to determining solutions when no specific strategy for solving the problem is known. Similarly, **critical thinking** skills refers using active reasoning to acquire novel concepts, ideas, or solutions, or to evaluate or analyze information to reach a justifiable conclusion. These types of learning are commonly found in science and mathematics curriculum (e.g., geometric proofs), but could also be found in any other area (e.g., understanding or solving a social problem in social studies). Problem solving and critical thinking are important goals in education, but also present some of the greatest challenges for students with disabilities. They can be enhanced by the use of teacher "think-alouds" ("Here's how I think as I try to solve this problem . . ."), and careful questioning or coaching techniques, described elsewhere in this chapter.

BASE INSTRUCTIONAL ADAPTATIONS ON THE APPROPRIATE LEVEL OF LEARNING   Another important consideration for teachers when planning instructional adaptations is the level of proficiency to be attained by the student for any of the previously described types of learning. Levels of learning address *how well* something will be learned, and it may be possible to isolate learning problems within these parameters. For example, if we say that a student "has not learned" something, it may be that the student *has* learned at one level (e.g., initial acquisition), but not on the level necessary for success (e.g., fluency or application). These levels include—in order of complexity—initial acquisition, fluency, application, and generalization. Consideration of the appropriate level of learning can help when planning adaptations.

Acquisition and Fluency   **Acquisition** refers to a simple accuracy level criteria, such as 9 out of 10 correct responses to listing 10 letters of the alphabet. Accuracy criteria are important in the initial stages of learning. **Fluency** combines the accuracy criteria with a specified amount of time. For example, 90% accuracy within 2 minutes, or 90 out of 100 letters correct in 5 minutes. Fluency is particularly important when tasks need to become automatic, such as in basic literacy, math, and letter-formation skills. Many students, for example, have acquired the skills needed to read individual words, but are not sufficiently fluent to comprehend what they are reading. Such students would benefit from fluency instruction.

Application and Generalization   **Application** refers to applying learned skills or content to relevant contexts, and **generalization** is the ability to transfer

Concrete experiences can help students develop an understanding of concepts.

Students who thoroughly understand concepts are more likely to apply them to new situations.

previous learning to novel situations. For example, applying a social skill learned in a lesson in the special education setting to a role-play activity is an example of the application level. An example of generalization is employing appropriately, in an inclusive classroom setting, a social skill previously learned in the special education classroom.

Application and generalization levels of learning can be difficult for some students with disabilities to attain (Sabornie & deBettencourt, 2009). Simply because a student has learned a particular skill (e.g., telling time, or a social skill for greeting new people) in one situation, you should not assume the student will now apply or generalize that skill to every appropriate situation. In many cases, specific strategies to promote application and generalization are needed.

Application and generalization levels of learning can be promoted by training "loosely" and allowing flexibility in responding; by using "indiscriminable contingencies" (rewarding students when they do not know they are being observed); by using modeling and role-play; by employing classroom peers; by encouraging self-monitoring, where students evaluate their own performance; and by retraining the desired behavior in a variety of different circumstances (see also Alberto & Troutman, 2012; Scruggs & Mastropieri, 1994a).

Identification Versus Production   For any of the levels of learning, students can be asked to identify or produce relevant responses. **Identification** includes such responses as pointing to the correct answer (for example, on a communication board) and responding to matching, multiple-choice, or true/false test formats, and is usually learned more readily. **Production** is more difficult and includes such responses as writing, saying, computing, orally spelling, and exhibiting appropriate behavior. When planning instruction, consider whether students will be required to identify or produce correct responses. For example, if students are required to produce correct responses (such as spelling words), it is important that they practice producing, rather than simply identifying, correctly spelled words during instruction.

Consider Types and Levels of Learning to Address Specific Learning Problems
To best address special learning needs, first determine where the problems lie. For example, Janine cannot remember the correct sequence of steps in multiplying an algebraic expression. Mario can identify but not produce correctly spelled words from his weekly list. Shawna can control her impulsivity in the classroom but not the cafeteria. Once these are identified as problems of procedural learning, identification/production, and generalization, respectively, they can be specifically addressed. As such, your instruction can be much more precise (and much more effective) than if these problems are simply considered to be problems with math, spelling, or social behavior. Tables 2 and Table 3 present some suggested instructional strategies to accompany specific levels and types of learning. Remember that many different strategies may be successful, and that in teaching, identification and production formats can be considered with any of the other levels and types of learning.

USE PRINCIPLES OF UNIVERSAL DESIGN   Universal Design for Learning (UDL) principles involve developing materials or the environment to improve accessibility for all learners (CAST, 2012; Hall, Meyer, & Rose, 2012). The three guiding principles for UDL proposed by CAST and the National Center for UDL are (1) multiple means of representation (e.g., perception, language, expressions, symbols); (2) multiple means of action and expression (e.g., physical action, expression and communication); and (3) multiple means of engagement (e.g., recruiting interest, sustaining effort and persistence), in order to address the needs of all types of learners. CAST provides specific guidelines for the development of new materials to promote accessibility for diverse learners, rather than adapting existing materials. Those guidelines provide options for the representation (e.g., options that vary the size of font or

TABLE 2	Instructional Strategies for Specific Types of Learning
Type of Learning	**Instructional Strategies**
Discrimination	Present examples and nonexamples (e.g., "This is purple. This is not purple. Is this purple?"); use models, prompts, and feedback; provide instruction on the relevant dimensions (e.g., "This is the letter 'b.' Notice that the bubble at the bottom faces toward the right"); use mnemonics.
Factual	Repetition, rehearsal, and practice using drill procedures (e.g., "*Dorado* is a kind of fish. What does *dorado* mean?"); chunking pieces of information together; elaborating on information to enhance meaningfulness (e.g., with labeled pictures of dorado fish); using mnemonic strategies ("*Dorado* means fish. *Dorado* sounds like *door*. Think of a fish on a door").
Rule	Practice using the rules; repetition; making up meaningful "sayings" using the rules; drill and practice with the rules; modeling applications of the rules (e.g., "Remember, '*i* before *e* except after *c*' is the rule to use to check your spelling." "Everyone, repeat the rule for recess: 'stay in the playground area.'").
Procedure	Clearly explain and model use of procedures (e.g., "First we get our materials. Second, we write our names on the papers. And third, we complete the task."); use cue cards with steps of procedures written out as reminders; drill and practice; practice with applications using the procedures; provide mnemonics involving acronyms (e.g., "Remember that SQ3R stands for Survey, Question, Read, Recite, and Review"); provide feedback on recall of steps and accurate use of steps.
Concept	Use procedures for teaching rules and discriminations; use examples and nonexamples; model; prompt; give feedback; use "if–then" scenarios to demonstrate instances and noninstances of concepts (e.g., "if an insect has six legs and three body parts, then is this [show picture] an insect?"); use coaching, questioning procedures, application activities, and elaborations to enhance meaningfulness.
Problem solving	Use modeling, coaching, and prompting; demonstrate examples of successful problem solving; show how to activate prior knowledge and use that to solve problems (e.g., "Why do anteaters have long front claws? I don't know, but what else do I know about anteaters? What do they eat? Where do they live? Now do I know why they might have long front claws?").

amplitude of sound), the expression (e.g., options for interacting with hand, switch, or adapted keyboard), and the engagement (e.g., options in level of perceived challenge, type of rewards or recognition, level of novelty) of materials. CAST's guidelines (CAST, 2011) involve using multiple options for language, symbols, and expression, and options for comprehension and self-regulation. One example of a curriculum material designed with UDL principles is WiggleWorks (produced and distributed by Scholastic), which provides a blend of technology, literature, and teacher support to help students develop reading and writing skills. However, because many materials were developed without the principles of UDL, those existing materials may be adapted or differentiated more successfully by using the UDL guidelines.

S: Systematically Teach with the SCREAM Variables

Systematic teaching is the third component of the PASS variables and builds on the previous ones; indeed, in order to systematically teach you need to incorporate planning for content and prioritizing objectives as well as adapting instruction, materials, and/or the environment.

TABLE 3 Instructional Strategies for Specific Levels of Learning

Levels of Learning	Instructional Strategies
Acquisition	Slower pace of instruction, modeling, demonstrations, lots of reinforcement for accurate responding, examples and nonexamples, direct questions (both lower-level and higher-level questions depending upon the nature of the content: e.g., "An ecosystem is a place where living and nonliving things affect and depend on each other. Look at our terrarium; here are some examples of living and nonliving things . . . How do they affect and depend upon each other? . . . So what is the definition of an *ecosystem*?").
Fluency	Faster pace of instruction; reinforce more rapid, accurate responding (e.g., "Let's see how quickly and accurately we can complete our math problem solving today . . . I'll set the clock . . . ready . . . go."); graph performance and goal-setting; vary schedules of reinforcement; vary types of reinforcers.
Application	Provide several instances and application problems; model procedures and directions; provide demonstrations; make examples concrete and meaningful; use active coaching with questioning to prompt correct responding (e.g., "Remember how we did . . ., This is just like it, only now. . .").
Generalization	Ensure students have mastered relevant skills; train and retrain in "real-world" settings and situations; train loosely, using multiple examples of stimuli; use peer assistance; use indiscriminable contingencies; train self-monitoring; use modeling and role-play; reinforce generalization; practice skills ("When we go to the store, we are going to use the *polite behaviors* that we practiced in class. What are we going to do? If you need help, how will you ask? Is this a good way?").

Systematic teaching refers to the use of effective teaching techniques for content coverage and teacher presentations, known as the SCREAM variables: **s**tructure, **c**larity, **r**edundancy, **e**nthusiasm, **a**ppropriate rate, and **m**aximized engagement through questioning and feedback (Mastropieri & Scruggs, 2002, 2004; Scruggs & Mastropieri, 1995). If you implement these techniques and consider the specific needs of students with disabilities, all students may be more successfully included, and overall classroom achievement will improve.

STRATEGIES FOR IMPLEMENTING THE SCREAM VARIABLES

STRUCTURE YOUR LESSONS Structure refers to the organization of the components of the lesson. Structure does not necessarily mean that the content of your lesson will be teacher-driven or that your students sit in rows doing worksheets. Rather, lessons are structured when you (1) communicate to students the overall organization and purpose of the lesson, (2) display outlines of the lesson and indicate transition points, (3) emphasize the critical points of the lesson, and (4) summarize and review throughout the lesson. Following is an example of structure in teacher dialogue, taken from a fourth-grade science lesson on ecosystems:

> The first thing—and Mrs. (name of special education teacher), if you would like to write this on the board—the first thing you're going to do is get your supplies and aquarium. . . . The second thing that I want you to do is put your gravel in, which is step number 2 . . . [repeats]. . . . The third thing that's going to happen is that you are going to fill out parts of your activity sheet. . . . (Mastropieri et al., 1998, p. 18)

Structure is particularly helpful for students who have difficulty sustaining attention, or who exhibit difficulties in language comprehension. Structure refers not only to providing an overall organizational framework for the lesson, but also to ensuring that students understand this organization.

Communicate Lesson Structure to Your Students Carefully design your lessons with a clear idea of the structure, including stating the purpose, reviewing the main ideas, and making clear transitions between lesson elements (Good & Brophy, 2007). You will communicate structure best to your students if you yourself are very familiar with the structure and organization of your lessons.

Tell students the structure of the lesson. This can be done by announcing the components of the lesson directly, by writing the outline on the board or on an overhead projector, and by using illustrations or handouts to indicate the lesson's sequence.

Remind students about the structure throughout the lesson. Say, for example, "Remember, when you finish your group work, we are going to meet again as a class to review what we have learned about bird migration."

PROMOTE CLARITY IN YOUR PRESENTATIONS

A teacher exhibits clarity when he or she speaks clearly and directly to the point of the objective, avoids unclear or vague language or terminology, and provides concrete, explicit examples of the content being covered. Clear presentations address only one objective at a time, and are directed explicitly to the lesson objective.

Select Vocabulary and Syntax That Are Familiar to All Students in the Class If you use a word that is unfamiliar to some or all students, take a minute to practice the word meaning. If English language learners are included in the class, use illustrations, physical modeling, or hand gestures to support verbally provided directions. These procedures are also beneficial for communicating with students with hearing impairments who have language difficulties, and students with learning disabilities who have language comprehension difficulties. When employing co-teaching, the special education teacher can assume the role of promoting clarity and understanding where needed.

Eliminate Vague Language in Your Presentations Smith and Land (1981) reported that vague terms added to teacher presentations consistently lowered achievement. Vague terms are in italics in the following teacher presentation:

> This mathematics lesson *might* enable you to understand *a little more* about *some things* we *usually call* number patterns. *Maybe* before we get to *probably* the main idea of the lesson, you should review *a few* prerequisite concepts. *Actually,* the first concept you need to review is positive integers. *As you know,* a positive integer is any whole number greater than zero. (Smith & Land, 1981, p. 38)

Clarity is also impeded by *mazes,* which include confusing word patterns ("we don't know it can't be done without . . ."), false starts ("facilit . . . I mean, make it better to . . ."), and unnecessary or irrelevant repetition ("This is, this is . . . it's true that this is the most important . . ."). Smith (1977) reported that lower student achievement was found in classrooms where teachers said "uh" frequently. Also avoid vague language such as "kind of," "you know," "sort of," and "pretty much." Avoid *negated intensifiers* ("not a lot," "not much," "not very"), *indeterminate quantification* ("a number," "a few of," "several"), and *ambiguous designation* ("some kind of," "somewhere"). Instead, use clear, direct, and precise language (Good & Brophy, 2007; Smith & Land, 1981). Clarity can be particularly important when restating comments made by individual students, so that they will be more understandable to all students.

EMPLOY REDUNDANCY EFFECTIVELY

Redundancy increases learning by emphasizing and reinforcing the most important aspects of lessons. Unlike unnecessary and irrelevant repetition of words, continued re-emphasis of key concepts, procedures, and rules is critical to the success of the lesson. Many students with disabilities require additional opportunities to hear, see, and practice lessons before mastering the objectives. It is unnecessary for components of the lesson to be identical to provide redundancy for students (Archer & Hughes, 2011).

Embed redundancy in your presentations. Discuss the main points of the lesson, and then be sure to refer to the key concepts throughout the lesson. Question students directly on these key concepts to reinforce their learning.

Create opportunities for extra practice to help provide redundancy for selected students. For example, supplemental practice times can be arranged for students either before or after school, or during lunch and study hall periods. Peers who have mastered the topics can be asked to provide assistance during these additional practice periods. Focus on the most important content and provide many opportunities for responding.

Create opportunities to apply and generalize learned information to novel situations. For example, prompt students to use newly learned arithmetic to compute the cost of a single slice of a whole pizza, or to use a reading comprehension strategy to study a social studies book.

TEACH WITH ENTHUSIASM! Students consistently learn more and appreciate the content more when teachers display enthusiasm in their teaching. Enthusiasm also creates higher levels of student engagement with the lesson, increasing academic learning time. Enthusiastic teachers create exciting learning environments, in which students perceive that learning is fun, challenges are great, curiosity is enhanced, and thinking is encouraged (Good & Brophy, 2007). Enthusiastic teaching can be especially helpful for students who have histories of academic failure and are poorly motivated to succeed in school. For example, some students with disabilities are used to performing poorly in classes and have little motivation to attempt to succeed; however, an enthusiastic teaching style can provide the necessary excitement and encouragement to motivate such students to be successful (Brigham, Scruggs, & Mastropieri, 1992; Brophy, 2010).

Speak enthusiastically, using an upbeat tone of voice, a rapid (but not too fast) presentation rate, and a varied inflection. Use some variation in choice of words. Be physically enthusiastic: use physical gestures and movement to emphasize your points and convey interest in the topic. Use eye movements and facial gestures to animate your presentations. Openly accept student contributions, and demonstrate a high overall interest and energy level.

USE AN APPROPRIATE RATE OF PRESENTATION Effective teachers deliver instruction at the optimal rate. Generally, a brisk rate of presentation throughout the lesson, and a brisk rate of interacting with students, works well with enthusiasm variables and helps keep lessons interesting and motivating. During basic skills instruction, a fast pace may be important in increasing learning (Carnine, 1976; Gleason, Carnine, & Vala, 1991). However, an excessively rapid rate of presentation may not be related to increased learning. When learning outcomes are not being met, changing the overall rate of presentation may allow information to be better understood by all students.

Begin with a brisk presentation rate, and frequently question students. Students' answers to your questions will tell you whether you are proceeding too rapidly. Record yourself, and evaluate your rate of presentation. Perhaps your rate of presentation is good, but other presentation elements (speaking directly and clearly, and with sufficient volume) are inhibiting understanding and need to be modified.

Some teachers begin lessons with a brisk rate of presentation, but later slow down, and lose student attention by overly focusing on minor issues, or by questioning some students repetitively while the rest of the class waits. If some individual students, but not others, need additional practice, work with them individually, in small groups, or with peer tutors (Brophy & Good, 2007).

MAXIMIZE ACADEMIC ENGAGEMENT Research has consistently supported the idea that the more time students devote to a particular subject or skill, the more likely they are to master it. This is true whether the area is reading, science, creative writing, archery, music, or debate: more time effectively engaged in learning leads to more (and better) learning outcomes. Maximizing student engagement and time-on-task is the best single way of increasing your students' learning. Research has shown that teachers who maximize student engagement are also effective in many other ways, as described in the **Research Highlight**.

It seems clear that Jimmy's learning will not improve until he can increase the amount of time spent on his work. Although most teachers **allocate** appropriate time for learning a certain subject (by, for example, scheduling a specific amount of time per day to reading instruction), a far smaller number of teachers will ensure that students are actually **engaged** in learning, to the greatest extent possible, during this allocated time. This distinction between allocated and engaged academic time is critical for student learning. In some cases, teachers may be able to greatly increase classroom learning simply by increasing student engagement rates.

Characteristics of Highly Engaging Teachers

Seo, Brownell, Bishop, and Dingel (2008) studied the classroom reading practices of beginning special education teachers, with particular reference to their ability to promote student engagement. Although academic engagement is often thought of as time spent on-task, it is better conceptualized as a broader construct, referring to "the intensity and emotional quality of children's involvement in initiating and carrying out learning activities" (Skinner & Belmont, 1993, p. 572). Viewed this way, academic engagement includes classroom behaviors and emotional responses, such as active participation in learning activities, volunteering to read aloud, asking or answering questions, asking for assistance when needed, volunteering, using specific learning strategies, and demonstrating interest and enthusiasm in learning (see also Greenwood, Horton, & Utley, 2002). Teachers who are able to elicit these behaviors can be considered highly skilled in engaging students.

These researchers used a rating scale to identify 14 beginning special education teachers as most engaging, highly engaging, moderately engaging, or low engaging. They then observed these teachers over a 6-month period. Using qualitative data analysis techniques, Seo et al. (2008) identified four themes related to instructional engagement that differentiated these teachers: (a) instructional quality, (b) responsiveness to student needs, (c) socio-emotional climate of the classroom, and (d) student autonomy. The most highly engaging teachers were relatively consistent in demonstrating these themes; however, most other teachers were not. For example, the most engaging teacher, "Kayla," also used high-quality and well-integrated reading instruction. She was consistently responsive to student needs—immediately correcting errors and providing feedback, anticipating academic and behavioral problems, and dealing with them proactively. She created an open, accepting, and positive classroom environment, providing frequent positive comments and encouraging positive interactions among students. Finally, she promoted student autonomy by encouraging student choice and self-regulated learning. In contrast, teachers who were not rated as high in student engagement were found to be less effective in other areas of instruction. These findings suggest that teachers who promote high rates of engagement in their students are also found to be highly skilled in many other areas of teaching.

QUESTIONS FOR REFLECTION

1. Why do you think a teacher's ability to promote student engagement would play such an important role in other areas of instruction?
2. What could teachers do to become better at promoting student engagement?
3. Would strategies for promoting engagement differ between elementary and secondary grade levels?

CLASSROOM SCENARIO

Jimmy

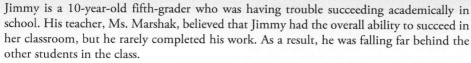

Jimmy is a 10-year-old fifth-grader who was having trouble succeeding academically in school. His teacher, Ms. Marshak, believed that Jimmy had the overall ability to succeed in her classroom, but he rarely completed his work. As a result, he was falling far behind the other students in the class.

Ms. Marshak began to pay more attention to how Jimmy was spending his time. She found that he was often the last student to take his books, paper, and pencil from his desk and begin working. During this period, he also spent more time than other students going to the pencil sharpener, asking to get a drink of water, daydreaming, or playing with pencils or rulers in his desk. When Ms. Marshak recorded his behavior at the end of every minute over a 30-minute period, she found that Jimmy was actually working on his assignment only 10 of the 30 times she sampled his behavior. Clearly, Jimmy needed to increase the amount of time he put into his schoolwork.

QUESTIONS FOR REFLECTION

1. Why is Jimmy off-task so often? How could you find out?
2. Why doesn't concern about poor grades motivate Jimmy to work harder?
3. What are some simple things Ms. Marshak could do to help Jimmy?

But what are the specific techniques you can use to maximize academic engaged time? In a broad sense, teachers need to maximize student learning by maximizing student engagement with instruction and instructional materials. Selecting materials that are at the correct level of difficulty and that are motivating and interesting for students will help with this. Additionally, teachers need to carefully plan, monitor, and reward high rates of engagement, such as in the scenario about Jimmy, and carefully implement questioning, praise, and feedback. However, the first step is to understand what is meant by academic engaged time, or "on-task" behavior.

On-task behaviors of students vary depending on the grade level of the students, the curriculum, the type of lesson, the learning activities, and the behavior of the teacher. However, in general, students are considered on-task when they are doing such things as actively looking at or otherwise attending to the teacher, instructional materials, or other students who are actively engaged. Giving direct answers to relevant teacher questions or asking relevant questions are also considered on-task behaviors. During teacher presentations, examples of on-task student behavior include actively listening, taking notes, outlining, and asking for clarification. Likewise, being appropriately engaged in science experiments or math manipulatives and engaging in relevant debate in social studies can also be considered on-task behaviors. Overall, student behavior is usually considered on-task if it is logically related to instructional activities.

Some students with disabilities may be engaged in different ways. For example, some students, including students with visual impairments, with emotional handicaps, or with autism, may not be actively watching the teacher, but nonetheless provide other signs that they are attending. Students with physical disabilities may interact differently with educational materials, but nonetheless can be observed to be interacting. Students with hearing impairments may need to watch the interpreter rather than the teacher. Some students with learning disabilities are unable to listen and take notes simultaneously, but may be on-task. Careful consideration of the special needs and abilities of different learners will reveal how different students may display appropriate on-task behavior.

On the other hand, off-task behavior is not logically related to academic learning. Off-task behavior can include tardiness, daydreaming, attending to inappropriate material, asking irrelevant questions or making irrelevant statements, or interacting inappropriately with peers or instructional materials. These activities are negatively related to learning; in other words, the more off-task behavior that occurs in a classroom, the less learning takes place.

STRATEGIES FOR MAXIMIZING ON-TASK BEHAVIOR

Your on-task behaviors as a teacher influence how much students learn. These include statements directly relevant to the lesson, questioning and feedback directly relevant to the lesson, and demonstrations and modeling directly relevant to the lesson.

USE EFFECTIVE QUESTIONING TECHNIQUES   Teachers must be effective at questioning students. Generally, the more questions asked that are directly relevant to the lesson, the more students learn from the lesson. Questioning has several purposes. First, questioning allows teachers to monitor students' understanding of the content being presented. In inclusive classrooms, questioning can be particularly helpful in determining whether all students understand the content being presented. When breakdowns in understanding are revealed through questioning, teachers can modify and adjust their instruction (considering such things as rate of presentation, choice of vocabulary, and use of examples) to address students' learning needs more effectively.

Second, questioning allows students to actively practice the information being covered. In this way, repeated questioning related to the same concept can provide the redundancy necessary for information to be learned and remembered:

TEACHER: In Boston, in 1770, what was one of the major concerns of the colonists, Marcia?

MARCIA: Taxation without representation.

TEACHER: Taxation without representation. What's another way of saying that, Dan?

DAN: That, uh, you have to pay taxes, but you don't have someone to represent you in the government.

TEACHER: You pay taxes, but don't have a representative, good!

Questioning can be delivered to individuals or groups. When addressed to individuals, state the question first, before calling on a particular student. If you give a student's name first, other students may be less likely to carefully consider an answer. For example, ask, "Why do you think Germany would strengthen its relation to Mexico during the first years of World War I? Frederick, why do you think this happened?" Rather than, "Frederick, why do you think Germany . . .?"

Be certain the question is clearly stated, so that students will know what type of response is expected, and that instructional time will not be lost in subsequent clarification. For example, referring to a passage in a text, a teacher might ask, "What problem do you see with this statement?" Although the teacher may be expecting an answer regarding verb tense, students might not know what the teacher means by "problem." Instead, she might ask, "Is there a problem with verb tense in this statement?" or, more generally, "Is there a grammatical problem in this sentence?" (Good & Brophy, 2007).

When addressing the question to groups, it may be possible to promote "covert" responding on the part of all students, which will maximize student engagement. For example, "Now I want everyone to think about this problem, and make a prediction: If I add weight to this pendulum, will it swing more rapidly? Everyone think (pause), now, thumbs up for yes, thumbs down for no." Alternatively, ask students to write down answers to questions individually, to be read back later. For example, "Everybody, write down a definition of *metonomy,* and give an example. When you're done, we'll compare answers."

There are also different types of questioning, including lower-level questioning and higher-level questioning. Lower-level questioning usually involves repetition or restatement of previously covered information, and is often used in basic skills instruction or in early stages of learning. For basic skills and basic facts, questioning should be fast paced and require simple, direct answers (examples: "What is the silent-*e* rule?"; "What is the Pythagorean theorem?"; "What are the three branches of government?"). For this type of questioning, teachers should aim for 80% to 100% correct responding. This type of questioning is frequently used when building fluency with responding, such as when practicing math facts or vocabulary definitions using flashcards.

Higher-level questioning requires more in-depth thinking. For higher-level responses requiring thinking and reflection, questioning should proceed at a slower rate and may not require simple, direct answers. For example, "Why do you think a type of moss is often found on the north side of trees? Would this be true all over the world?" In this example, students could consider the general position of the sun in the northern hemisphere, and conclude that the south side of trees may often be drier. Considering the characteristics of moss, students may conclude that it may more frequently—but not always—grow on the north side of trees. This, of course, would not be generally true in the southern hemisphere. With such questioning, you should consider that students

Effective questioning in inclusive classrooms means providing students with extra time to answer.

will need more time for reflection, and may need additional questioning to direct their thinking (e.g., "What conditions are favorable for moss growth? When would moss not grow on the north side of a tree in the northern hemisphere? Is there a rule that would better predict where moss would grow on a tree?").

Research has documented that when students with mild disabilities have been "coached" to answer higher-level questions, they can be successful (Scruggs, Mastropieri, & Sullivan, 1994; Sullivan, Mastropieri, & Scruggs, 1995). For example, consider the coaching dialogue in Figure 1 used with students with learning disabilities and mild intellectual disabilities to promote thinking about animals. This type of explicit coaching provides the structure and support students need to promote reasoning, but still allows them to come up with their own answers.

Some questions—some may say the most important questions—do not have simple answers with which everyone would agree. These include such questions as, "Who was the United States' most important president?"; "Should the Ten Commandments be displayed in schools?"; and "Does life exist on other planets?" Some students may have difficulty answering questions like this. When presenting this type of question, inform students that a specific answer is not required, but rather an answer that reflects both knowledge of the subject and careful thought about the answer. Give students models of good possible answers. Ask students to consider subquestions, such as, "What qualities are considered important in a president?"; "What is the relevance of the 'establishment of religion' clause in the 1st Amendment?"; or "What conditions appear necessary for life to develop? What is the likelihood that these conditions exist elsewhere in the universe?"

Good and Brophy (2007) suggested that teachers generally should avoid four types of questions:

1. Questions that require yes-or-no answers

2. "Tugging" questions ("What else?"; "Yes . . ."; Tell me more . . .")

3. "Guessing" questions, that is, asking students to guess when they do not have relevant information

4. Leading questions ("Isn't that so?")

Overall, the best questions are clear, purposeful, brief, phrased in simple language, sequenced, and thought provoking.

PROVIDE HELPFUL FEEDBACK   How teachers respond to student answers is as important as how the questions are asked. Appropriate feedback can be helpful in informing students of their level of understanding, providing redundancy, and encouraging students to continue to learn (Burnett, 2003). Feedback should be clear and overt, so that there is no

Figure 1   Coaching Dialogue

Note: From "L'instruzione Mnemonica e L'interrogazione Elaborativa: Strategie per Ricordarsie per Pensare," by M. A. Mastropieri, 1995, in C. Cornoldi & R. Vianello (Eds.), *Handicap e Apprendimento: Ricerche e Proposte di Intervento* (pp. 117–124), Bergamo, Italy: Juvenilia. Copyright 1995 by Juvenilia. Reprinted with permission.

Experimenter: Anteaters have long claws on their front feet. Why does this make sense?

Student: I don't know.

Experimenter: Well, let's think. What do you know about anteaters? For example, what do they eat?

Student: Anteaters eat ants.

Experimenter: Good. And where do ants live?

Student: They live in holes in the ground.

Experimenter: Now, if anteaters eat ants, and ants live in holes in the ground, why do you think that anteaters have long claws on their front feet?

Student: To dig for ants.

Experimenter: Good. To dig for ants.

ambiguity about the teacher's evaluation of the answer. When appropriate, it should provide the entire class with information on the correctness of the response of an individual student.

During rapid questioning, drill and practice of skills, or review of previously learned material, feedback may be simple and brief. In some cases, the fact that the teacher has continued with the lesson imparts the information that the previous answer was correct (e.g., multiplication facts prompted by flashcards). At other times, feedback may be more substantive.

The type of feedback delivered depends to some extent on the response that has been given. If a student does not respond right away, you should try to elicit some type of response to determine the level of student understanding. It is important to consider whether the question is a lower-level question that should require only a short "wait time" (the amount of time the teacher waits for a response) or a higher-level question that may require a longer wait time for the student to develop a more thoughtful answer. Research has shown that longer wait times (when appropriate to the question) are associated with better and longer student responses, and an increase in voluntary student contributions (Good & Brophy, 2007).

When students do not respond correctly, it is important to determine whether the answer is unknown, the question was unclear, or whether the student simply did not hear the question. You should also determine whether students can answer the question with additional coaching or prompting. Teachers should not appear to "badger" students who clearly do not know how to respond. However, it is important to retest students later in the lesson.

For completely incorrect responses, a simple, tactful statement that the answer was incorrect may be sufficient. Simply state the correct answer, provide the student with a prompt or additional information and restate the question, or call on another student for the answer.

If an answer is partially correct, first acknowledge the part of the answer that was correct, then provide additional prompts or restate the question to elicit the rest of the answer, or call on another student. For any question that was incorrectly answered, partially or completely, teachers should make an effort to return to the question with individual students later in the lesson to ensure that the material was learned.

If the question was correctly answered, acknowledge the correctness of the answer and move on in the lesson:

> TEACHER: Now, which astronomer first determined that the planets travel in an elliptical pattern? Juanita?
>
> JUANITA: Kepler.
>
> TEACHER: Kepler, correct.

PRAISE STUDENTS FREQUENTLY   Praise can be an important motivator for students. When the situation warrants it, actively praise your students for paying attention to the lesson, carefully considering teacher questions, and providing answers that are correct, or at least reasonable and thoughtful. Effusive or overly elaborate praise may not be helpful in many instances, because it may interrupt the flow of the lesson or embarrass students (particularly students at the secondary level). However, most teachers deliver too little praise to students. Praise may be particularly important to help students with disabilities or special learning needs persist in their efforts to learn.

STRATEGIES FOR
MAXIMIZING TIME FOR LEARNING

MAXIMIZE ON-TASK TEACHER BEHAVIOR   Teachers also may be off-task, and this behavior can impede student achievement. One example of off-task behavior is making unnecessary digressions, such as talking about personal experiences or current events that are irrelevant to the lesson. Students with special learning needs may find it especially difficult to follow teachers when they are making irrelevant digressions. During practice activities, teachers can be off-task by being unprepared with student materials, or by speaking loudly to an individual student and disrupting other students. Teachers can also be off-task by not returning promptly after breaks, allowing longer-than-necessary transition times, and by being unprepared for teacher presentations. The *Apps for Education* feature describes a helpful timer for class use.

Apps for Education

Managing Time with the Time Timer™

Many students have difficulties with understanding the concept of time, especially when told they need to keep working for a specified amount of time. Other students have difficulties with transition periods and changing from one activity to the next. A technological device called the Time Timer may help students visually see the amount of time left as they work and help them comprehend in a more concrete fashion the amount of time left for work or the amount of time left for one activity before moving to the next activity. The visual timer is a clock that comes in various sizes. One standard version is approximately 8 inches square and has a 60-minute timer. A smaller, 3-inch-square version is also available that can be clipped to a student's belt. When setting a specified amount of time, say

15 minutes, that amount of time appears in red. A red disk actually shows on the timer when a time is set. As the time passes, the red disk disappears bit by bit, such that when time is up, the red disk is gone. As this happens, students can visually see the red disk disappearing as time passes and obtain a better picture of the amount of time left. Such a device may help students feel more comfortable with the concept of time because it makes the concept more concrete for them.

An app version of Time Timer, the iPad Edition (Time Timer LLC), is available that functions similarly but is designed for use with an iPad. Again, the visual counting down of the minutes provides students with immediate cues about remaining time. Many additional timer apps are also available including Timer+ (Minima Software LLC) and Easy Stop Watch&Timer (BND Co, Ltd.), which

From Time Timer LLC. Reprinted with permission.

include similar features in counting down time, and some also include stopwatch features.

Other apps help teachers track student behaviors. For example, Teacher's Assistant: Track Student Behavior (Lesson Portal, LLC) and TeacherKit (ITWorx Egypt) organize students by class, enable note taking for comments, allow storage of grades, and interface with e-mail for contacting parents as well as *Dropbox* for backing up files.

Class composition may also influence classroom interactions. The *Diversity in the Classroom* feature describes the differences in attitudes and classroom interactions between same- and mixed-gender classes.

Research suggests that much **academic engaged time** is lost for a number of reasons, including inefficient transition activities, inappropriate verbalizations, and inappropriate social behavior.

This **video** shows a teacher using transition. Pay attention to the type of strategies used.

STREAMLINE TRANSITION ACTIVITIES   **Transition activities** involve students moving from one location, subject, or group to another. Academic engaged time can be lost during transitions through such activities as going to the restroom, sharpening pencils, and unnecessary socializing. Students with disabilities can lose time going between the regular classroom and the resource room.

One way to maximize transition efficiency is to set time limits and reinforce adherence to those limits. For example, if classes begin at the sound of a bell, let students know exactly what is expected of them when the bell rings. Typically, students should be in their places and prepared with their materials at this time. Any time lost after the bell—for example, sharpening pencils or finding workbooks or other materials—takes away from instructional time. Likewise, at the end of the class, if materials are not put away before students leave, time may be lost at some other point in the day. If your students are transitioning to a resource room, you should document the time they left the classroom and report the time to the resource teacher. Similarly, the resource teacher should inform you when students have left the resource room to return to your class.

One obvious way to promote efficient transitions is to inform students that time lost in transition will be made up during free time, in after-school detention, or during other student activities. However, teachers can also reinforce prompt transitioning more positively

Diversity in the Classroom

Student Interactions and Attitudes in Single-Gender Versus Mixed-Gender Classrooms

 Researchers have speculated whether differences between same-gender and mixed-gender school settings influence students' education. Some previous findings have suggested that females are less likely to be called on and less likely to volunteer in mixed-gender settings (American Association of University Women, 1998). Special education research has not typically addressed this issue (see Coutinho & Oswald, 2011). It is well known that males outnumber females in special education settings. However, little is known about interactions and attitudes of students in same- versus mixed-gender special education settings. Madigan (2003) addressed this issue by conducting an observation and interview study with females with learning disabilities who were either Latino or African American. All students attended either a same- or mixed-gender special education class in the same high school.

Students were observed during classes and interviewed in small groups and alone. The mixed-gender class was taught by a male teacher with 15 years of experience, and the all-female class was taught by a female teacher with 2 years of experience. Behaviors measured included independent hand-raising, answering teacher questions, interacting in class discussions, on-task behavior, and assignment completion. Overall, females in the single-gender class exhibited more of these behaviors, with the exception of hand-raising. This difference, however, was attributed to the fact that the teacher of the mixed-gender class required hand-raising, whereas the teacher of the single-gender class did not.

Overall patterns from interviews supported observational findings, in that students in single-gender classes participated more during class and felt more comfortable. Females in mixed-gender classes reported feeling frustrated frequently with the male students. Furthermore, interview data revealed that although all of the females found special education settings supportive, regardless of single- or mixed-gender setting, they also felt some stigma associated with special education. These feelings emerged when they were asked about the views of general education students. Results thus provided some interesting information for gender and classroom configurations for students with disabilities. Although the results cannot be considered evidence that same-gender classes are generally superior, they do provide information for teachers to consider when teaching mixed-gender classes.

by awarding points, stickers, or tokens, or simply by responding positively to students when they make smooth transitions.

As the teacher, you can facilitate efficient transitions by being prepared ahead of time with materials for the next activity, and not losing time looking for instructional materials, organizing supplies, or inefficiently passing out student materials. By setting a good model for transitions, you can promote good transitions in your students.

REDUCE INAPPROPRIATE VERBALIZATIONS Academic engaged time is lost when class discussions drift away from the point of the lesson. Teachers may find themselves wandering off-topic, and students may also wander by raising irrelevant issues. Some students deliberately attempt to keep teachers off-task to avoid getting to homework, tests, or other undesired activities. Monitor inappropriate verbalizations with video or audio recordings of individual lessons, and review them in reference to the purpose of the lesson and the appropriateness of teacher and student verbalizations.

At times, however, digressions may reflect genuine curiosity or interest on the part of students, or a developing understanding of the concepts. When this happens, acknowledge that the lesson objective has changed, and evaluate it with respect to the changes that were made. Alternatively, you can inform students that the class can talk about those other important ideas after finishing the present activity.

REDUCE INAPPROPRIATE SOCIAL BEHAVIOR Inappropriate social behavior—including passing notes or electronic messages, teasing, arguing, and fighting—is one of the greatest threats to academic engaged time. Handle inappropriate social behavior quickly and efficiently, so that as little instructional time as possible is lost. Punitive classroom environments that include long-winded lectures on social behavior are not as effective (or as time efficient) as positive learning environments where good behavior is expected and rewarded, and misbehavior is dealt with efficiently.

USE STRATEGIES FOR INDIVIDUAL CASES   Many classrooms contain one or more students who seem to spend far less time on schoolwork than other students. Frequently, these are the very students who need to spend more time on their schoolwork, such as Jimmy in the earlier scenario. In such cases, try to increase the students' amount of engaged on-task time. Following are some procedures that may be helpful:

1. *Be certain the student can do the work.* Many students become off-task if they cannot (or believe they cannot) do the assigned work. If you find the work is too difficult, assign more appropriate work or modify assignments. Also, consider enlisting support from special education teachers, paraprofessionals, or classroom peers.

2. *Try simple strategies, such as direct appeal and proximity.* Tell individual students you would like to see them working harder on schoolwork. Tell them that you will send a signal when they are getting off-task by approaching their desks. When students return to work, walk away.

3. *Provide simple rewards or consequences.* Students can be offered stickers, free time for a preferred activity, or other rewards for completing all work in a specified time period. Alternately, students can be required to make up work they have not completed.

4. *Notify parents or guardians.* Contact parents or guardians to elicit their suggestions or support for increasing on-task behavior. Perhaps arrangements can be made to link home privileges or rewards to assignment completion in school. In some cases, simply communicating the idea that parents and teachers are interested in the student's academic progress can make an important difference.

S: Systematically Evaluate the Outcomes of Your Instruction

The last S in PASS stands for *systematic evaluation.* Systematic evaluation means frequently measuring students' progress toward meeting the instructional objectives of the class, as well as IEP objectives, using formative evaluation procedures. Teachers should continuously monitor and adjust instruction based on student progress as documented by formative evaluation measures.

FORMATIVE EVALUATION   Formative evaluation refers to the frequent and systematic monitoring of learner progress toward prespecified goals and objectives. It is different from summative evaluation, in which, for example, tests are given at the end of a school year to determine how much was learned during the year. Teachers who use formative evaluation monitor student progress continuously throughout the school year, and do not wait until the end of the year to determine whether learning took place. Formative evaluation techniques are reviewed briefly here.

Research has suggested that formative evaluation works best when it is used at least twice a week. In some cases, student learning (for example, words read correctly per minute) can be recorded on a chart or graph, so that rate of learning can be assessed. In other cases, student progress may be more difficult to place on a chart, but progress can still be monitored. For example, for handwriting, weekly samples can be collected in student folders.

Systematic evaluation of student performance or products over time can provide teachers with important information regarding the adequacy of students' progress. This information is used, in turn, to make further adaptations in instruction to ensure learning is maximized for all students. When progress for one or more students is not acceptable, teachers can consider how to modify and adapt instruction to help students meet learning goals. For example, using the information from this chapter, a teacher could decide to increase academic engagement, to increase review activities, to improve teacher presentations, or to make further adaptations in instructional materials. The Inclusion Checklist at the end of this chapter provides suggestions for improving instruction in specific areas, in response to outcomes of systematic evaluation of student performance.

Formative evaluation can be conducted on a variety of student outcomes, including regular "probes" of student skills and knowledge, evaluations of regularly implemented practice activities, and homework products, as described in the following section.

STRATEGIES FOR
PROMOTING SYSTEMATIC EVALUATION OF INSTRUCTION

IMPLEMENT CURRICULUM-BASED MEASUREMENT *Curriculum-based measurement* refers to regular assessment of student progress toward prespecified goals and objectives using frequently administered "probes" of student performance. For example, in reading instruction, Ms. Sánchez assigned Billy regular 1-minute timed readings of grade-appropriate text. For each timed reading, Ms. Sánchez calculated correct and incorrect words read per minute, and placed the results on a chart that demonstrated Billy's progress over time. Teachers can evaluate progress on these measures to determine whether instructional modifications are necessary for the student to meet long-term goals (. Curriculum-based measurement can also be used with a variety of student activities, as described next.

MONITOR AND EVALUATE PRACTICE ACTIVITIES Practice activities are intended to reinforce memory and comprehension of information that was gained in the lesson. If the lesson involves the teaching of skills, such as how to write the letters "p," "d," and "q" in cursive, practice activities are used to promote application and skill development and to ensure the skills learned will be remembered. If the lesson involves the acquisition of content information, such as the causes of the War of 1812, practice activities promote recall, comprehension, and application objectives. The products of practice activities can provide teachers with formative evaluation of student understandings of and progress within the curriculum.

Practice activities are particularly helpful for students with special needs, as they provide more engaged time to ensure relevant concepts are fully understood. Often, practice activities are taken from worksheets or workbooks, but practice activities can take other forms as well, such as practice with tutors or classroom peers, flashcards, computer programs or apps, group problem solving, or application tasks using relevant materials. Table 4 provides examples of appropriate practice activities.

Practice activities can be divided into *guided* and *independent* practice (Archer & Hughes, 2011; Rosenshine & Stevens, 1986). Guided practice takes place under teacher supervision, and is most appropriate immediately after presentation of the initial concept. Students' rates of correct responding may be lower in this type of practice, and more teacher supervision is needed than when students practice independently. Independent practice uses indirect teacher supervision (some activities can be done as homework), and is undertaken when students' rates of correct responding are very high and students can correct themselves by proofreading and checking their work.

TABLE 4 Appropriate Practice Activities	
Lesson	**Practice Activity**
Writing words in cursive for handwriting practice	*Guided:* Teacher provides dictation; work is checked after every sentence.
	Independent: Students write from manuscript models, then check each other's work at the end of the period.
Solving quadratic equations from a formula	*Guided:* Students solve problems one at a time, while the teacher monitors their execution of each step.
	Independent: Students solve a set of problems independently, corrected by the teacher at the end of the activity.

Reviewing information—opportunities for overlearning—promotes application and generalization of concepts.

Both types of practice are necessary to ensure that concepts are mastered and remembered, and that learning is complete for all students. Request assistance from special educators for devising supplemental practice activities and determine when and where the extra practice can occur—for example, study hall, other school periods, or homeroom. Any successful practice activity must meet several criteria. First, it must be directly relevant to the objective of the lesson. Second, practice activities must be used to enhance learning that occurred during the earlier part of the lesson; practice activities usually are not intended to introduce new information or skills. Students with disabilities or other special learning needs are particularly unlikely to learn new information from worksheet-type activities. Therefore, select practice activities that enhance and augment learning that has already occurred.

Practice activities also must be at an appropriate level of difficulty. If they are too difficult, students will not be able to work on them independently. If they are too easy, student learning will not be enhanced. Finally, it must be remembered that students soon tire of repetitive, worksheet-type activities. Keep the pace and enthusiasm level as high as possible during guided practice (e.g., "Everyone who thinks they have the answer, put your thumbs up!"). During independent practice, teachers should reinforce prompt, accurate, and neat responding, and should keep the activity moving at an efficient pace.

Homework can often be considered a type of independent practice activity, undertaken outside the classroom. Because teachers are less likely to be available to answer questions when homework assignments are being completed, it is necessary that students completely understand assignments before taking them home. It may be helpful to complete the first part of the homework assignment in class, as a guided practice activity, to be certain every student knows how to complete the assignment. Homework completion can be facilitated by having students meet in groups at the beginning of class, under the direction of rotating group leaders, to record and provide peer feedback on homework assignments (Jakulski & Mastropieri, 2004; Sheridan, 2009).

When using guided and independent practice activities, in the form of classroom and homework activities, evaluate student products carefully, and use this information as formative evaluation to determine whether students are making adequate progress, and if not, how instruction will be modified and adjusted to meet student goals and objectives. For example, satisfactory performance on independent practice and homework activities indicates that students have learned the material and are functioning satisfactorily. Difficulties in independent practice and homework activities suggest that students need further examples, explanation, and guided practice.

FREQUENTLY REVIEW IMPORTANT MATERIAL AND EVALUATE STUDENT PERFORMANCE Near the end of a lesson, it is important to summarize what has been learned and review this information with students. It is also important to review information weekly and monthly, to ensure that previously learned information is not forgotten and that students understand the relation between previous and current learning. Information gained from regular review can provide formative data on student learning and retention over time, as well as important information for possible instructional modifications.

Although frequent review is helpful for all students, it is particularly so for students with disabilities, who are more likely to forget or not understand the relevance of previously learned material. This extra review and evaluation may be especially helpful before exams. As discussed in the redundancy section, students with disabilities not only benefit from review, but may require more review to be successful. Additional review of successfully learned content can be helpful in "overlearning" information, which can help promote long-term retention, application, and generalization.

Special education teachers can assist in providing additional review for students with disabilities or brainstorming ideas for review. For example, you could make videotapes of the class engaged

Daily Review
- Begins with a review of previous learning.
- Provides teacher with information on how much was learned and retained from previous lessons.
- An example of daily review:
  "We have been studying ecosystems. Hold up your hand if you can tell me what an ecosystem is [calls on individual students]. Yesterday, we said that ecosystems have nonliving and living parts. We listed several nonliving parts of ecosystems. Write down on your paper three nonliving parts of an ecosystem. [The teacher waits for a minute or two, walking around the classroom to encourage students to think and write answers.] Now, who can tell me what you wrote . . ."

Statement of Purpose
- State the main objective of the current lesson in language meaningful to students.
- An example stated clearly and simply is the following:
  "Today we are going to learn about the living parts of ecosystems, and how they may interact with the nonliving parts."

Presentation of Information
- Present the content of the lesson using a variety of instructional materials, depending on the purpose and objectives of the lesson.
- Use the teacher presentation or SCREAM variables. That is, deliver content or procedures with structure, clarity, redundancy, enthusiasm, appropriate rate, and maximized engagement using questioning, feedback, and praise.

Guided Practice
1. Practice newly acquired content, skills, or concepts with teacher guidance.
2. Carefully monitor students and provide corrective feedback, as necessary.

Independent Practice
- Provide opportunities for students to repeat, apply, and extend information from the lesson more independently.

Formative Evaluation
- Evaluate students' independent performance.
- An example could take the form of a brief quiz: "See if you can solve the following problems independently."
- Results provide the basis for decisions about the adequacy of student progress and can be considered in planning future lessons.

Figure 2 Putting the Components into a Model Lesson

in activities during the instructional unit, and then show them to students who may benefit from extra review of the information. Students can make "descriptive video scripts" (narrations describing everything in the video) to accompany the videos, either on paper or using a tape recorder. Students with visual impairments may benefit from these descriptions. Photographs, student journals (including photo and vocabulary journals), and daily logs can also provide material for review.

Using a digital camera and scanner, you and your students can create websites that contain their journals and portfolios. Sunburst's school version of Web Workshop, for example, contains many easy-to-use templates to help students create websites. Student performance on these activities can also provide the basis for formative evaluation.

Putting the PASS Variables to Work: Including Model Lesson Components in Instruction

The teacher effectiveness variables most closely related to high achievement have been described. But how do these variables appear in a real lesson? As you review the structure of a model lesson, observe how teacher effectiveness variables fit into a lesson sequence, as indicated in Figure 2.

MyEducationLab™

Go to the MyEducationLab™ (www.myeducationlab.com) for *The Inclusive Classroom*, where you'll find multiple opportunities to more deeply understand the content in this chapter, including learning outcomes and relevant national standards, activities, assignments, learning units, and practical information about licensure and certification.

Summary

- The PASS variables stand for: **p**rioritize instruction; **a**dapt instruction, materials, or the environment; **s**ystematically teach; and **s**ystematically evaluate the outcomes of instruction. The PASS variables provide a model for planning and delivering effective differentiated instruction in inclusive settings.

- *Prioritize* instruction to ensure that students are working on the most important objectives, and that individual objectives reflect the characteristics of the student.

  — Planning for content coverage involves prioritizing instruction, and is a critical component of teacher effectiveness. Teachers must consider carefully the role of prioritized objectives, scope and sequence, curriculum, and pacing of instruction over time.

- *Adapt* instruction, materials, and/or the environment to meet the specific characteristics of the student. Appropriately adapted instruction is a significant component of *differentiated instruction*.

  — Types of learning include discrimination, factual, procedural, rule, conceptual, and problem solving/critical thinking.

  — Levels of learning include acquisition, fluency, application, and generalization. Students can provide either identification or production responses. Consideration of types and levels of learning can be beneficial when planning appropriate differentiated instructional strategies.

- *Systematic teaching* refers to maximizing the effectiveness of your instruction, and includes effective teacher presentations using the SCREAM variables.

  — Effective teaching strategies include maximizing academic time-on-task, making effective teacher presentations, monitoring practice activities, review, and formative evaluation. All are critical components of effective teaching for all students.

  — Effective teacher presentations use the SCREAM variables: **s**tructure, **c**larity, **r**edundancy, **e**nthusiasm, **a**ppropriate rate, and **m**aximized engagement. Additionally, effectively used questioning, feedback, and praise are all important contributors to student learning.

- *Systematic evaluation* refers to continuous measuring of student progress toward meeting the specific objectives. Teachers should continuously monitor and adjust instruction based on their students' progress on formative evaluation measures.

  — Curriculum-based measurement provides the basis for evaluating student progress in learning and determining whether student goals and objectives are being met.

  — Practice activities provide opportunities for students to solidify and apply their learning, and provide more opportunities for formative evaluation of student progress over time. Practice activities can include guided practice, in which teachers closely monitor student responding, and independent practice, in which students work more independently. Homework can be considered a type of independent practice activity.

  — Frequent review promotes retention and long-term learning, and provides teachers with opportunities to evaluate student learning. Students with disabilities may especially require frequent review of previously learned material.

PROFESSIONAL STANDARDS LINK:
Effective Differentiated Instruction for All Students

Information in this chapter links most directly to:

- CEC Standards: 4 (Instructional Strategies), 7 (Instructional Planning)
- INTASC Standards: 2 (Learning Differences, 3 (Learning Environments), 6 (Assessment), 7 (Planning for Instruction), 8 (Instructional Strategies)

EFFECTIVE DIFFERENTIATED INSTRUCTION FOR ALL STUDENTS

If you are having problems with classroom or individual academic achievement, have you examined the following? If not, see the relevant sections of this chapter.

STRATEGIES FOR PLANNING FOR CONTENT COVERAGE

- ☐ Base instruction on specific prioritized objectives
- ☐ Plan instruction based on scope and sequence
- ☐ Select appropriate curriculum
- ☐ Pace instruction effectively

STRATEGIES FOR MAKING ADAPTATIONS

- ☐ Base adaptations on student characteristics
- ☐ Base instructional adaptations on types of learning
- ☐ Base instructional adaptations on the appropriate level of learning
- ☐ Use principles of universal design

STRATEGIES FOR IMPLEMENTING THE SCREAM VARIABLES

- ☐ Structure your lessons
- ☐ Promote clarity in your presentations
- ☐ Employ redundancy effectively
- ☐ Teach with enthusiasm!
- ☐ Use an appropriate rate of presentation
- ☐ Maximize academic engagement

STRATEGIES FOR MAXIMIZING ON-TASK BEHAVIOR

- ☐ Use effective questioning techniques
- ☐ Provide helpful feedback
- ☐ Praise students frequently

STRATEGIES FOR MAXIMIZING TIME FOR LEARNING

- ☐ Maximize on-task teacher behavior
- ☐ Streamline transition activities
- ☐ Reduce inappropriate verbalizations
- ☐ Reduce inappropriate social behavior
- ☐ Use strategies for individual cases

STRATEGIES FOR PROMOTING SYSTEMATIC EVALUATION OF INSTRUCTION

- ☐ Implement curriculum-based measurement
- ☐ Monitor and evaluate practice activities
- ☐ Frequently review important material and evaluate student performance

Inclusion Checklist

References

Alberto, P. A., & Troutman, A. C. (2012). *Applied behavior analysis for teachers* (9th ed.). Upper Saddle River, NJ: Merrill/Prentice Hall.

American Association of University Women. (1998). *Gender gaps: Where schools still fail our children.* New York: Marlowe & Company.

Archer, A., & Hughes, C.A. (2011). *Explicit instruction: Effective and efficient teaching.* New York: Guilford.

Brigham, F. J., Scruggs, T. E., & Mastropieri, M. A. (1992). The effect of teacher enthusiasm on the learning and behavior of learning disabled students. *Learning Disabilities Research & Practice, 7,* 68–73.

Brophy, J. (2010). *Motivating students to learn* (3rd ed.). New York: Routledge.

Burnett, P. C. (2003). The impact of teacher feedback on student self-talk and self-concept in reading and mathematics. *Journal of Classroom Interaction, 38,* 11–16.

Carnine, D. (1976). Effects of two teacher presentation rates on off-task behavior, answering correctly, and participation. *Journal of Applied Behavior Analysis, 9,* 199–206.

CAST (2011). *Universal Design for Learning Guidelines, version 2.0.* Wakefield, MA: Author.

CAST (2012). *About UDL.* Cambridge, MA: Author. Retrieved from http://www.cast.org/udl/index.html

Clare, S. K., Jenson, W. R., Kehle, T. J., & Bray, M. A. (2000). Self-modeling as a treatment for increasing on task behavior. *Psychology in the School, 37,* 517–523.

Coutinho, M., & Oswald, D. P. (2011). Gender and exceptionality. In J. M. Kauffman & D. P. Hallahan (Eds.), *Handbook of special education* (pp. 759–772). New York: Routledge.

Danielson, C. (2010). *Implementing the framework for teaching in enhancing professional practice.* Alexandria, VA: Association for Supervision and Curriculum Development.

Gartin, B. C., Murdick, N. L., Imbeau, M., & Perner, D. E. (2002). *How to use differentiated instruction with students with developmental disabilities in the general education classroom.* Reston, VA: Council for Exceptional Children.

Gleason, M., Carnine, D., & Vala, N. (1991). Cumulative versus rapid introduction of new information. *Exceptional Children, 57,* 353–358.

Good, T. L., & Brophy, J. E. (2007). *Looking in classrooms* (10th ed.). Boston: Allyn & Bacon.

Greenwood, C. R., Horton, B. T., & Utley, C. A. (2002). Academic engagement: Current perspectives on research and practice. *School Psychology Review, 31,* 328–349.

Hall, T. E., Meyer, A., & Rose, D. H. (Eds.). (2012). *Universal design for learning in the classroom: Practical applications.* New York: Guilford.

Jakulski, J., & Mastropieri, M. A. (2004). Homework for students with disabilities. In T. E. Scruggs & M. A. Mastropieri (Eds.), *Advances in learning and behavioral disabilities: Research in secondary settings* (Vol. 18, pp. 77–122).

Larrivee, B. (1985). *Effective teaching for successful mainstreaming.* New York: Longman.

Madigan, J. C. (2003). Female students of color in special education: Classroom behaviors and perceptions in single-gender and coeducational classrooms. *E-journal of Teaching and Learning in Diverse Settings, 1,* 75–93.

Mastropieri, M. A. (1995). L' instruzione mnemonica e l' interrogazione elaborativa: Strategie per ricordarsi e per pensare. In C. Cornoldi & R. Vianello (Eds.), *Handicap e apprendimento: Ricerche e proposte di intervento* (pp. 117–124). Bergamo, Italy: Juvenilia.

Mastropieri, M. A., & Scruggs, T. E. (2002). *Effective instruction for special education* (3rd ed.). Columbus, OH: Merrill.

Mastropieri, M. A., & Scruggs, T. E. (2004). Effective classroom instruction. In C. Spielberger (Ed.), *Encyclopedia of applied psychology* (pp. 687–691). Oxford, UK: Elsevier.

Mastropieri, M. A., Scruggs, T. E., Mantzicopoulos, P. Y., Sturgeon, A., Goodwin, L., & Chung, S. (1998). "A place where living things affect and depend on each other": Qualitative and quantitative outcomes associated with inclusive science teaching. *Science Education, 82,* 163–179.

Moore, K. D. (2011). *Effective instructional strategies: From theory to practice.* Thousand Oaks, CA: Sage.

Rosenshine, B., & Stevens, R. (1986). Teaching functions. In M. C. Wittrock (Ed.), *Handbook of research on teaching* (3rd ed., pp. 376–391). New York: MacMillan.

Sabornie, E. J., & deBettencourt, L. U. (2009). *Teaching students with mild and high-incidence disabilities at the secondary level* (3rd ed.). Upper Saddle River, NJ: Merrill/Prentice Hall.

Scruggs, T. E., & Mastropieri, M. A. (1994a). The effectiveness of generalization training: A quantitative synthesis of single subject research. In T. E. Scruggs & M. A. Mastropieri (Eds.), *Advances in learning and behavioral disabilities* (Vol. 8, pp. 259–280). Greenwich, CT: JAI Press.

Scruggs, T. E., & Mastropieri, M. A. (1994b). Successful mainstreaming in elementary science classes: A qualitative investigation of three reputational cases. *American Educational Research Journal, 31,* 785–811.

Scruggs, T. E., & Mastropieri, M. A. (1995). What makes special education special? An analysis of the PASS variables in inclusion settings. *Journal of Special Education, 29,* 224–233.

Scruggs, T. E., Mastropieri, M. A., & Sullivan, G. S. (1994). Promoting relational thinking skills: Elaborative interrogation for mildly handicapped students. *Exceptional Children, 60,* 450–457.

Seo, S., Brownell, M. T., Bishop, A. G., & Dingle, M. (2008). An examination of beginning special education teachers' classroom practices that engage elementary students with learning disabilities in reading instruction. *Exceptional Children, 75,* 97–122.

Sheridan, S. M. (2009). Homework interventions for children with attention and learning problems: Where is the "home" in "homework"? *School Psychology Review, 38,* 334–337.

Skinner, E., & Belmont, M. (1993). Motivation in the classroom: Reciprocal effects of teacher behavior and student engagement across the school year. *Journal of Educational Psychology, 85,* 571–581.

Smith, L. (1977). Aspects of teacher discourse and student achievement in mathematics. *Journal for Research in Mathematics Education, 8,* 195–204.

Smith, L., & Land, M. (1981). Low-inference verbal behaviors related to teacher clarity. *Journal of Classroom Interaction, 17,* 37–42.

Sullivan, G. S., Mastropieri, M. A., & Scruggs, T. E. (1995). Reasoning and remembering: Coaching thinking with students with learning disabilities. *Journal of Special Education, 29,* 310–322.

Photo Credits

CHAPTER 3

The Engaging Teacher: Dispelling the Boring Myth

Most veteran teachers will tell you that teaching is, at least in part, a performance. After all, few other professions (other than acting itself) require an individual to be "on" for so many hours of the day. We have all had the experience of sitting in a classroom in which the teacher was less than entertaining. Although he or she may have been an expert in their content area, their bland delivery meant that the urge to sleep often overpowered our will to learn. Hopefully, we have also had the experience of sitting in front of a teacher who was captivating, funny, and a born storyteller. That teacher could have been reading us her grocery list, but we could not look away.

The most effective teachers are those who can combine their expertise in learning and teaching with a riveting performance. Learning to teach can be likened to a jazz conservatory where aspiring musicians practice scales and play exercises to hone their technical chops. Learning to play jazz involves deep discipline and the study of classical technique: mastering everything "inside the box" before artfully stepping outside it. The science of explicit instruction (e.i.) involves the events of instruction and strategies for engaging the learner. The art comes into play in how the lesson is delivered. Ask any experienced teacher, and she will tell you what it feels like when she is at the top of her game. It's the same feeling a musician gets after a great performance or an athlete has after winning a race; you know when you've delivered a brilliant lesson and your students "got it." Effective e.i. involves implementing a scientific understanding of teaching and learning in the most creative and inspiring way possible.

DISPELLING THE BORING MYTH

As previously discussed, teacher-led instruction has fallen prey to negative associations. As a result, teachers often resist engaging in e.i. out of fear that their students will be bored or that they themselves will be labeled *boring*. However, you might consider the notion that teaching methods are not inherently boring; only teachers are. One of the goals of this book is to challenge teachers' conceptions about what it means to be an effective instructor. If teachers have formed

29

a negative association with a particular teaching method (e.g., that it is undesirable, frowned on, or even harmful), it is highly unlikely that even when called on to do so, they will do an effective job of delivering that instruction. In their heads, they may be saying things to themselves like, "This is taking too long! I'm talking too much! I need to hurry up and get through this!" If a teacher's primary goal in delivering e.i. is that it be *brief*, what are the chances that his or her instruction is going to be *effective* for students?

Instead, teachers should be concerned with delivering clear, dynamic instruction that is appropriate to their students' needs, no matter what the format. Of course, teaching does not always have to be a grand performance. At times, it can be understated—as with small groups or individuals—and still be highly effective. The purpose of this chapter is to describe teacher presentation variables that can be stage-managed to make e.i. lessons more dynamic and engaging.

TEACHER PRESENTATION VARIABLES

Teacher presentation variables describe how you can best interact and communicate with students (Mastropieri & Scruggs, 1997). Although researchers have described these variables primarily in the context of teacher-led models of instruction, effective teacher presentation skills are critical for *any* model of instruction. They take on increased importance in inclusive settings, where students with learning difficulties may vary in their ability to comprehend spoken language and/or their level of interest and motivation. A teaching style that incorporates teacher presentation variables can provide the necessary excitement and encouragement to motivate such students to succeed (Brigham, Scruggs, & Mastropieri, 1992). More effective communication with all students in the classroom can be fostered through consideration of these three variables: clarity, enthusiasm, and appropriate rate of presentation.

Researchers (Brigham, Scruggs, & Mastropieri, 1992) have described teacher presentation variables as "alterable" because they include things that teachers can alter in themselves to become more effective, as opposed to static, "nonalterable" variables, such as age or gender. Such descriptions underscore the fact that clarity, enthusiasm, and appropriate rate are things that teachers *do*, not things that teachers *are*.

It is important to note the interrelationship of the teacher presentation variables outlined here (see Figure 3.1). Both rate of presentation and teacher enthusiasm are integrally related to teacher clarity. For example, if the rate of presentation is too rapid for the teacher to be understood or if the teacher's efforts at enthusiasm cloud the instructional objective, clarity is undermined. Overall, it is important to remember that these techniques should *support* and *enhance* the pursuit of instructional objectives.

Teacher Clarity

The teacher effectiveness literature of the 1980s identified teacher clarity as a crucial communication variable (Brophy & Good, 1986; Smith & Land, 1981). As such, it is worthy of renewed attention given the prevalence of inclusive classrooms, where students may be present who have difficulty comprehending spoken language or who may not be native English speakers. A teacher demonstrates clarity when she or he speaks clearly and directly to the point of the objective, avoids unclear or vague language or terminology, and provides concrete, explicit examples of the content being covered (Mastropieri & Scruggs, 2000). As discussed in the previous chapter, learning objectives are closely linked to teacher clarity. Clear presentations focus on one objective at a time and are explicitly directed toward the

Goal: Appropriate Rate of Presentation →	**Goal:** Teacher Enthusiasm ← →	**Goal:** Teacher Clarity ←
Actions	**Actions**	**Actions**
• Distribute chances to participate • Stimulate and maintain interest • Challenge students to think • Incorporate physical activity • Affirm briefly; make simple corrections • Require overt responses that involve individual participation • Adjust according to student understanding	• Speak rapidly (but clearly and deliberately) • Use varied inflection • Use animated facial expressions • Vary word choice • Use dramatic and varied body movements • Actively and openly accept student ideas • Keep overall energy level high	• Speak clearly • Focus on one objective at a time • Avoid unclear language or terminology • Avoid vagueness terms (e.g., *maybe, might, sort of,* and *like*) • Give concrete examples • Avoid confusing word patterns, false starts, and irrelevant repetitions
↓	↓	↓

Results

- Higher levels of student engagement with the lesson
- Increased academic learning time
- Fun and exciting learning environment
- Learning is made concrete for learners
- Students become more motivated to learn
- Provide the necessary excitement and encouragement to motivate students with histories of school failure to be successful

FIGURE 3.1   Interaction Frame: Teacher Presentation Variables.

learning objective. Extraneous information that is not central to the learning objective is eliminated, and needless digressions are avoided.

To teach with clarity, it is important to eliminate vagueness from presentations (Brophy & Good, 1986). When vague terms (e.g., *might, some, usually, maybe,* or *probably*) are included in teacher presentations, student achievement is decreased (Smith & Land, 1981). Here is an example:

> This mathematics lesson *might* enable you to understand a *little more* about *some things* we *usually* call number patterns. *Maybe* before we get to *sort of* the main idea of the lesson, you should review a *few* prerequisite concepts.

It is also important to eliminate confusing word patterns, false starts, and unnecessary or irrelevant repetition. For example, Smith (1985) found lower student achievement in classrooms where teachers said "uh" frequently:

> This mathematics lesson *will enab* . . . will get you to understand *number, uh,* number patterns. Before we get to the main idea of the, main idea of the lesson, you need to review *four cond* . . . four prerequisite concepts. The first *idea, I mean, uh,* concept you need to review is positive integers.

Here is a comparative example of teacher clarity:

> This math lesson will help you to understand more about number patterns. Before we get to the main focus of the lesson, we will review four things that we've already learned.

Appropriate Rate of Presentation

Highly effective teachers deliver instruction at an appropriate rate. Teachers often mistakenly believe that in order to be *clear*, their instruction must be *slow*. This is a common misconception, especially when there are students with disabilities included in a group. In fact, a brisk rate of presentation throughout the lesson and a brisk rate of interaction with students keeps the lesson interesting and motivating (Mastropieri & Scruggs, 2000). An excessively rapid rate of presentation, on the other hand, may not be related to increased learning when learning outcomes are not being met.

Rate of presentation, therefore, is governed and balanced by students' degree of understanding. Often, I ask teachers to identify an appropriate rate of presentation for students with learning disabilities. Almost unanimously, they respond that such students need a *slow* instructional pace. A common concern about inclusive teaching is that the students with disabilities will hold back the other students in a general education classroom. Since students with disabilities are less likely to understand, instruction must proceed at a restricted rate. While it is certainly true that students with disabilities (or any students) profit from *clear* instruction, it need not be excessively slow. If instruction is targeted toward students' instructional level (rather than their frustration level), they will be able to keep up with a brisk pace of instruction and interaction. It is the strategies teachers use to facilitate understanding that promote student learning. A teacher who delivers unclear instruction *very slowly* is not doing her students any favors. Appropriate rate, then, is closely tied to effective assessment. It is important to determine students' instructional level so that they can derive the most benefit from your instruction.

Thus, pacing a lesson appropriately can pose a formidable challenge, especially to beginning teachers. It involves balancing many seemingly irreconcilable forces: learning to respond to each student's learning needs while maintaining the attention and interest of the group, distributing participation widely without dampening the enthusiasm of those who are eager to participate, assessing students' understanding, and allowing them to contribute to the interaction while keeping the lesson on course. These problems can be particularly acute in inclusive settings, where the teacher must attempt to adjust the pace of instruction to accommodate a range of diverse learning needs. While some students will master new content very quickly, other students will require substantially more instructional time to master the same content.

Lessons are less likely to be slowed down if the teacher has established a set of verbal or nonverbal signals that communicate important information about expected behavior to students, such as when they are to raise their hands, when they are to respond chorally, and so on. Without clear signals, students are likely to call out when the teacher wants them to raise hands or engage in other undesired behavior. Similarly, lessons become sluggish because of ambiguity in the teacher's questions or presentation. If students are clear as to what information they are expected to deliver, it is easier for them to respond.

The elements of e.i. are meant to be combined to create fluid, seamless lessons of appropriate length. A common mistake when teachers begin to implement e.i. is that their lessons drag on for protracted periods of time. Teachers should target an appropriate time period that is consistent with students' attentional skills and developmental stage. For example, 5 or 10 minutes is probably long enough to expect very young students to attend to an e.i. lesson. In elementary school, teachers might set a target of 15 to 20 minutes *maximum*. It is natural and predictable that things will often take longer than we expect. However, it is important to resist the urge to pack your lessons with every activity you can think of related to the topic. As you become more experienced with e.i., you will become adept at streamlining and pacing your lessons appropriately.

Strategies for meeting pacing challenges:

- Distribute chances to participate
- Provide think time without losing the pace
- Stimulate and maintain interest—inject mystery, suspense, humor, and novelty
- Challenge students to think
- Streamline: include only what will most effectively convey your intent; save those other fun activities for practice opportunities later
- Incorporate physical activity
- Provide feedback—affirm briefly, make simple corrections, prompt, or backtrack to a simpler question without belaboring the issue
- Require overt responses that involve individual participation, such as having students hold up fingers or response cards, physically display answers using manipulatives or whiteboards, or respond in chorus

Teacher Enthusiasm

Students are likely to learn more and appreciate the content more when teachers display enthusiasm in their teaching. Enthusiasm creates higher levels of student engagement with the lesson, thereby increasing academic learning time (Bettencourt, Gillett, Gall, & Hull, 1983; Brigham, Scruggs, & Mastropieri, 1992). Enthusiastic teaching can be particularly meaningful for students who have histories of school failure and are poorly motivated to succeed academically. Some students with learning difficulties, for example, are accustomed to performing poorly in classes and have little motivation to attempt to succeed. An enthusiastic teaching style can provide the necessary excitement and encouragement to motivate such students to attempt to be successful.

It is important to keep in mind that enthusiasm can be overdone. An essential element of enthusiasm is that it be genuine. If students view teachers' enthusiasm as sincere, they will probably welcome and enjoy very high levels of enthusiasm. If the enthusiasm seems forced or insincere, however, students will be less likely to appreciate it.

Enthusiastic teachers motivate their students to learn by doing the following:

- Creating fun and exciting learning environments
- Presenting challenges
- Fostering curiosity
- Encouraging thinking
- Making learning meaningful and concrete for learners
- Modeling interest in the subject being learned and the amount of enjoyment that can be achieved when learning occurs

Examples of teacher enthusiasm variables:

- Rapid (but not too rapid) speaking rate, varied inflection, and uplifting vocal delivery
- Physical gestures that emphasize what is being said and provide cues for when to pay particular attention
- Dramatic and varied body movements that attract student attention
- Emotive, animated facial expressions that model a state of alertness and interest
- Varied choice of words that prevents dialogue from sounding boring and predictable
- Active and open acceptance of ideas or suggestions made by students that conveys that teachers are secure with their own knowledge and anxious to hear other ideas
- General demonstration of a high energy level—enthusiasm conveyed through the teacher's overall manner

CASE EXAMPLE: MELINDA

A beginning first-grade teacher named Melinda called her students to the carpet for an introductory math lesson on coins and their values. First, Melinda read a story called *Alexander, Who Use to Be Rich Last Sunday* by Viorst (1987). Although the theme of the story related to money, it was long; students had been sitting for 10 minutes by the time Melinda finished reading. Next, she asked students what it means to be rich. A few students volunteered examples of what they would buy if they were rich (e.g., an iPod, a sports car, or a new house). Melinda reacted enthusiastically to their wishes. Then students watched as Melinda filled in an extensive graphic organizer about characteristics of different coins. By the time students were released from the carpet to engage in independent practice, they had been sitting for more than 40 minutes. At their seats, students colored and cut out coins from a worksheet. They then glued them on a graphic organizer under columns labeled with each coin name and value. Students needed a lot of assistance during seat work because their graphic organizers were different than the one Melinda had modeled. In total, Melinda's math lesson went on for an hour and a half.

Explicit instruction is meant to be clear, briskly paced, and streamlined. This example illustrates how teacher decisions about how to achieve the learning objective can affect the clarity and pacing of a e.i. lesson. As stated in the previous chapter, every event of instruction in an e.i. lesson should contribute directly to the learning objective; otherwise, it should not be included. When reflecting on her lesson, I challenged Melinda to consider whether reading the story and engaging in the discussion about what it means to be rich really contributed to her students' achievement of the learning objective, which was to be able to identify coins and their values. Melinda felt it was important to include the story and the discussion because it made using e.i. more "acceptable." Her belief was that if children's literature is included and students are asked their opinions, it makes the lesson more student centered. When asked why she gave students a different graphic organizer than the one she had modeled, Melinda said it would have been unfair if they had the same one because they could just copy from hers.

Inclusion of particular elements in a lesson does not make it inherently student centered. In this case, it could be argued that including the story and the discussion actually did Melinda's students a disservice by extending the length and pace of the lesson and taking them in a totally different direction than what she had intended. Her intent was that students learn coin names and their values, not muse about what it might be like to be rich. Rather than introducing and building toward this goal with each subsequent lesson event, Melinda led students down a mental path in which they were now focused on what fantasy items they could buy with their millions. Melinda's enthusiastic response to their ideas probably led some students to believe that this was the most important part of the lesson. Whereas some students will adeptly switch gears back to the intended focus of the lesson, others will not. Developing students' conceptions of wealth may be a valuable activity when there is extended time for discussion-based exposition of students' ideas, not as part of an e.i. lesson on coins and their values. When her lesson had already gone on for more than 40 minutes, Melinda then asked students to return to their seats to spend time cutting, coloring, and gluing. Although these are fun and age-appropriate activities at times, were they the best use of Melinda's instructional time in this math lesson? Melinda claimed to be concerned with the student centeredness of her teaching, yet she unwittingly put her students at a significant disadvantage by requiring them to complete a task she had not modeled. Their level of frustration with the task added undue time to an already overlong lesson.

This example illustrates how Melinda's instructional decisions strongly impacted the pace of her lesson and created a lack of clarity in her presentation. Although she attempted to show enthusiasm, it was not entirely useful in this situation because it had little meaningful relation to the learning objective; enthusiasm for an unclear lesson does not make it any clearer. This example also illustrates how teacher presentation variables interact. For these young students, the longer the lesson went on without a clearly defined focus, the less clear and more frustrating it became.

These may seem like trivial issues. If teachers believe strongly in the use of children's literature across the curriculum or in the fine motor benefits of cutting, is there really any harm in including these activities? The point is not that it is *never* appropriate to include these activities in your teaching. The point is to consider the impact of the clarity, rate, and enthusiasm of your presentation on students' ability to achieve the learning objective during e.i. Most teachers make instructional mistakes despite the best of intentions. Like Melinda, they may have inaccurate beliefs about what actually constitutes an effective e.i. lesson. Here are some important points to remember about teacher presentation variables:

- The clearest e.i. lessons are those in which each subsequent element of the lesson builds toward the ultimate achievement of the learning objective. If an element has the potential to obscure the objective, leave it for another time.
- Strive for clarity combined with a developmentally appropriate rate of presentation.

- Understand that enthusiasm cannot compensate for ineffective teaching.
- Rate of presentation is governed by degree of student understanding; assess and monitor student understanding to adjust the rate accordingly.

Summary

In this chapter, we discussed three teacher presentation variables: clarity, rate, and enthusiasm. These variables were framed as aspects of e.i. that can be powerfully controlled in order to stimulate student interest and engagement and to promote student achievement of learning objectives.

CHAPTER 4

The Active Learner: Dispelling the Passive Myth

Previous models of explicit instruction (e.i.) focused primarily on the teacher's behavior during instruction. Although the elements of instruction used and the way in which they are presented are critically important, the teacher's presentation creates only one-half of a balanced instructional encounter. Just as teachers need not deliver e.i. that is boring, students need not be passive receptors of information. If we frame e.i. as a transaction that occurs between the teacher and student(s), then both parties play an important role in creating an advantageous learning process. For teacher presentations to be effective, students must be encouraged to provide the second, complementary half of the transaction: active engagement. An optimal e.i. lesson involves an effective, dynamic teacher and an active, engaged learner.

If asked, we could all create a portrait of the active learner: the student who sits up, makes eye contact, and nods his or her head to indicate understanding of the topic. This student participates actively, asks questions for clarification, and strategizes effectively about how to complete tasks and assignments. Some students (typically the more capable ones) are naturally active learners; they will display these behaviors without prompting and, at times, even in response to less-than-satisfactory teaching. It may be a struggle, however, for less capable learners to become engaged and remain active during *any* kind of instruction. Therefore, it is critical that teachers routinely use variables that require all students to become actively involved with their learning. These variables take on increased significance in inclusive settings where students with learning difficulties may vary in their level of interest, confidence, and motivation.

Learning is an active process during which students create meaning by connecting new skills, strategies, and concepts to prior knowledge and ideas. Since e.i. is teacher directed, the extent to which all students actively participate depends largely on the ways in which the teacher choreographs their involvement in each lesson. Explicit instruction is an ideal time for the teacher to actively involve students and to closely monitor their understanding. It is important, therefore, that teachers help students to participate actively—to look at or handle objects, tell stories, answer questions, complete graphic organizers, refer to their own

37

experiences, or imagine particular scenes. A key advantage of requiring active participation by all students is that misunderstandings are often revealed and can be corrected promptly.

DISPELLING THE PASSIVE MYTH

At one time or another, most teachers have been cautioned against the dangers of student passivity. All of us have heard the ugly metaphor of students as passive receptacles, waiting to be filled by a curriculum-dispensing teacher. Nonetheless, in the current environment of high-stakes testing and accountability, many teachers feel the squeeze of competing pressures: delivering the curriculum in a timely fashion versus actively involving students in the learning process. As one teacher remarked in frustration, "We are constantly told that students need to be active learners, but there are times when they need to sit and listen and I need to impart information!"

The message of this chapter is that teachers can do both. It is possible to provide e.i. *and* to actively involve students with their learning. Here is a notion to consider: students are passive *to the extent that the teacher allows their passivity.* If teachers have resigned themselves to the fact that their students will not participate, that will be the outcome. If, on the other hand, teachers create the expectation that all students will actively participate and use strategies that promote participation in every lesson, this will be the outcome. Teachers are sometimes rankled by this notion. They will say, "That's not true! I've tried everything! Some students will never participate no matter how much I try to involve them!" My response to this is usually twofold. First, you have not tried *everything.* Undoubtedly, there are strategies you have not uncovered that may work quite well. Teaching is a process of trial and error. If you continue trying and the implementation is effective, eventually you will hit on a strategy that works. Second, there are always exceptions. Classrooms are diverse and unpredictable. Individual students have particular needs and some students are more reticent than others. Nonetheless, the key is to set the expectation from the beginning that all students will participate. You will not be content to call on the same seven students time after time while everyone else sits idly staring at their hands. Clear expectations that are consistently and positively reinforced will be more successful than a "let's try this every now and then and see if it works" approach.

Teachers should be concerned, then, with incorporating elements into their instruction that require active engagement by all students. This chapter describes student engagement variables that can be used to involve students with the learning process.

WHAT IS ACTIVE ENGAGEMENT?

Early studies of student engagement focused on the time students were engaged in on-task behavior (Brophy, 1983; Fisher et al., 1980). Other definitions have since emerged that consider the more subtle cognitive, behavioral, and affective indicators of student engagement (Skinner & Belmont, 1993). Students who are actively engaged demonstrate sustained involvement in learning activities combined with a positive affect. They display behaviors such as choosing challenging activities, initiating action when given the opportunity, exerting effort and concentration, and showing enthusiasm, interest, and curiosity. Taking it a step further, active engagement has also been associated with deeper, metacognitive, and self-regulatory strategies during the learning process (Pintrich & DeGroot, 1990). According to this view, student engagement is purposeful behavior chosen by students to direct their learning process. Students engaged in simple or surface participation (e.g., answering simple recall questions) are not engaged to the same extent as those who use deeper, more elaborative strategies (e.g., paraphrasing, summarization, and compare/contrast). Use of meaningful strategies, then, is taken as the indicator of active engagement.

STUDENT ENGAGEMENT VARIABLES

A key consideration for inclusive teaching is that you cannot assume that all students have the prerequisite skills to engage on a deeper, more elaborative level. In order for all students to participate actively and meaningfully, teachers must explicitly teach and reinforce strategies that promote a deep level of cognitive engagement. In other words, active engagement is not something that all students naturally *do*; rather, it is a mental state that skillful teachers *create* in their students. Students participate actively when they do the following:

- Try to understand and make sense of new materials
- Relate ideas and information to prior knowledge and experience
- Use organizing tools (e.g., graphic organizers) or principles to integrate ideas
- Relate supporting details and evidence to conclusions
- Look for principles or patterns

The following sections discuss three student engagement variables that can be used to help all students become active and engaged during e.i.: active participation, procedural prompts, and monitoring student understanding.

Active Participation

In order to actively engage students, teachers must do more than stand up and lecture. When students are actively engaged, they focus on what is being taught and process information more meaningfully. Active engagement helps students store and retrieve information more effectively and promotes student accountability for their learning. Rather than just assuming that students who are not participating are cognitively engaged in the lesson, teachers must provide ways for students to actively and overtly demonstrate their learning by posing and answering questions, manipulating new information, and relating it to what they already know.

In most classrooms, there is a typical pattern of how student participation is distributed. During an e.i. lesson or teacher explanation, the teacher will ask a question and wait for a few students to raise their hands to respond (e.g., "Can *anyone* share an experience they've had with spiders?" or "Can *someone* summarize the paragraph we just read?"). Usually, the same students raise their hands time after time; these are typically bright, engaged learners who participate routinely. The teacher will eventually call on one of these more capable learners to answer as the rest of the students sit passively; maybe the rest of the students heard and processed the answer, maybe not.

While this pattern may be widely used and accepted, it leaves many students out of the instructional transaction. For example, when the teacher calls on a student and *then* asks a question (e.g., "*Nancy*, can you tell me the capital of Idaho?"), the rest of the students immediately know that they are unaccountable for the question and can cognitively disengage from the encounter. Even when the teacher asks a question and *then* calls on a student (e.g., "*Who* can tell me the capital of Arkansas? *Joseph*?"), the rest of the class knows they are unaccountable for providing a response. This may seem like splitting hairs; however, the ways in which teachers ask questions and promote accountability for the answers raise questions about access and accountability in inclusive classrooms: Who is responsible for posing and responding to questions? Why are some learners held accountable while others are not? Would other students be more likely to participate if given different options for participation? Are there ways of promoting active participation that do not produce undue anxiety for diverse learners?

Using an appropriate questioning technique can be particularly challenging in an inclusive setting. Managing student participation involves striking a delicate balance between keeping eager students engaged and not leaving other students behind. Occasionally, teachers will make a conscious effort to break out of their accepted routine and randomly call on students whose hands are not raised. Recently, for example, a principal commented on the "excellent" questioning technique she observed during a fourth-grade teacher's social studies lesson: "He was peppering the students with questions, rapid fire—bam! bam! bam!—very quickly, with no lag in between. He kept that lesson on track!" I asked, "What were the students doing whose hands weren't raised?" She replied, "I don't know. I wasn't focused on those students." Often, the teacher conducting the lesson isn't focused on those students either. He or she is usually preoccupied (as was this principal) with content coverage and keeping the lesson "on track."

This type of effort can be problematic, however, because when students do not know the answer or need additional think time, the pace of the lesson can be thrown off. Students may also interpret this type of random questioning as a *high-threat* instructional technique: consistently calling on students in order to "catch" them not paying attention can erode the teacher–student relationship. Implicitly, this method conveys, "I value learners who can answer my questions quickly and correctly." In fact, other students may be able to answer the question correctly if given an alternative strategy. They quickly get the message, however, that sitting passively is preferable to getting in the "line of fire."

Alternatively, teachers can create a classroom culture in which all students are involved and accountable. Particularly during e.i., it is important to involve all students. Research has shown, for example, that when students are required to give overt responses using response cards or other mechanisms for simultaneously signaling their responses, participation and learning are increased as compared to the "one student answering at a time" method (Gardner, Heward, & Grossi, 1994; Heward, 1994). Teachers, in turn, gain important data about the effectiveness of their instruction and can respond accordingly. Table 4.1 presents different types of strategies for promoting active participation and examples of each.

You will notice in the examples in Table 4.1 that some of these strategies require simple or surface-level responding (e.g., recall). Others can be used for deeper processing using higher-order thinking skills (e.g., formulating questions, making judgments, and summarizing). Teachers can use these techniques strategically, depending on the students, the topic, and the lesson context. Sometimes, for example, you are just interested in involving students in a quick review of facts or procedures. Other times, you want all students to reflect and integrate what has just been learned. Having a repertoire of strategies for active participation allows you to apply the appropriate strategy to the particular learning moment.

You will also notice that these examples involve a particular teaching vocabulary. The teacher uses words like *everyone*, *class*, and *boys and girls*. One of the best ways to integrate active participation strategies into your teaching is to consciously remove the words *who*, *anyone*, *someone*, and *anybody* from your teaching. If you are using these words, it is a signal that you are falling back on the default method of student participation (i.e., the "one student answering at a time" method). Also notice that the examples involve statements such as "This is a learning moment," "Listen and think," and "Take a moment and think." Consider how these statements

TABLE 4.1 Active Participation Strategies

Strategy	Example
Choral response	"Class, let's review the sight words we learned yesterday. As I hold up the cards, let's all read together."
Signaled response (e.g., thumbs up/thumbs down, hold up the correct number of fingers, etc.)	"Boys and girls, raise your thumbs. I will say a series of statements about spiders and insects. Thumbs up for true; thumbs down for false; thumbs sideways for not sure."
Random questioning: 1. Pose a question to the whole group 2. Provide think time for all 3. Give a time limit or allow students to signal when ready to answer 4. Randomly choose a student to respond (e.g., choose a popsicle stick)	"This is a learning moment so listen and think. [Students put their heads down and listen.] What is one reason that the first amendment is so important? When you've thought of your answer, raise your hand. [Students keep heads down and raise hands. When all students have raised hands, the teacher chooses a student at random.] Raise your heads. Jason, tell us your answer."
Written individual private response (e.g., on chalkboards, whiteboards, index cards, ticket out the door, personal digital assistants, etc.)	"Everyone, on your whiteboards, write the stages in the life cycle of a butterfly. Then hold them up so I can check."
Wireless individual private response using Turning Point student response software and wireless hardware	The teacher presents a question in PowerPoint and allows participants to submit a response by using a ResponseCard keypad; responses are sent to the computer and displayed in PowerPoint according to the instructor's preference (bar graph, pie chart, etc.).
Verbal individual private response (e.g., turn to the person next to you and whisper, classroom whip-around, think–pair–share; verbal ticket out the door, etc.)	"Everyone, take a moment and think of one question you have about how the main character changed from the beginning of the story to the end. Now turn to the person next to you and share your question. When both partners have shared, raise your hands."

differ from the rapid-fire question-and-answer technique in the previous example. These kinds of statements not only provide cues to learners about when key moments in the lesson are occurring but also signal to students that you prioritize think time and value thoughtful rather than impulsive responding. There may be times when you want students to respond quickly as a measure of student fluency (e.g., "Let's see how quickly we can read through these sight words! If you can read them quickly and correctly, I can tell that you really know them."). At such times, it is equally important to provide students with the appropriate cue.

Finally, some of the examples involve having students cover their eyes while responding. The purpose for this is twofold. First, although our goal is to promote student accountability and active participation, our intention is never to humiliate anyone. Many students who remain passive during the default method of questioning do so out of fear of being embarrassed for giving incorrect answers. Covert signaled responses (i.e., with eyes covered) allow the teacher to gauge student understanding and students to "safe face" because their peers do not see their answers. Similarly, teachers are occasionally concerned that active participation strategies promote "cheating" because less capable students can see their peers' responses. Again, teachers may want to vary students' opportunities to give covert versus overt signaled responses. For example, when a skill or topic is brand new to students, they may initially benefit from being able to see their peers' responses in order to gauge their own understanding. When the goal is to review content that students should already know, the teacher may require covert responses as a measure of individual student mastery.

In summary, when students actively participate, they are more likely to process and retain information and to engage in higher-order thinking. When teachers use strategies that promote active participation, they facilitate student learning, keep students interested and on task, foster student accountability, and make learning active and fun.

Procedural Prompts

One of the reasons some students have difficulty acquiring new knowledge and skills is that teachers do not use strategies that promote independence and transfer to other settings. Procedural prompts (or procedural facilitators; Rosenshine, Meister, & Chapman, 1996) are cues that provide students with specific step-by-step procedures or suggestions. Because they reduce the demand on working memory, prompts facilitate students' ability to use newly acquired skills or strategies independently. Students can temporarily rely on procedural prompts until they have built their own internal structures for completing the task. In other words, prompts are concrete, skill-specific references on which students can rely for support until they become independent.

Prompts are often recommended for teaching students with learning disabilities because of their utility for reducing memory demands and promoting independent strategy use (Swanson, 1999). Research indicates that procedural prompts have been used successfully to teach skills and strategies in a variety of areas, including summarization (Alverman, 1981; Bauman, 1984), writing (Englert & Raphael, 1989; Scardamalia & Bereiter, 1985), and generating questions (Billingsley & Wildman, 1984; Singer & Donlan, 1982; Wong, 1986). In a summary of research on cognitive strategy instruction by Pressley et al. (1995), strategy learning in reading, writing, math, vocabulary, and science was almost exclusively mediated through the use of prompts.

Table 4.2 presents a procedural prompt that might be provided when teaching a lesson on identifying the main idea in a paragraph (Wong, 1996). This prompt is simply a set of steps that can be written on an index card (for an individual student) or chart (for the whole class) that reminds students how to use the newly acquired skill or strategy. For any new skill or strategy taught (or a skill or strategy that students are having difficulty mastering), the teacher should consider whether a prompt might be useful.

Procedural prompts are a powerful instructional tool because simply through their use, straightforward lessons are transformed into strategy instruction. Let's consider the differences between two teachers' lessons on rounding numbers to the nearest 10. In Ms. D's lesson on rounding, she introduces the concept of rounding, explains the rules for rounding, completes multiple examples on the board, and then gives students a worksheet to complete

TABLE 4.2 Procedural Prompt for Main Idea

Finding the Main Idea in a Paragraph

1. The main idea sentence is the most important sentence in the paragraph. It tells you clearly about the topic in the paragraph.
2. All the other sentences in the paragraph talk about it (refer to it).
3. All the other sentences in the paragraph give you more details about it.
4. Take away the main idea sentence in the paragraph, and the paragraph won't make sense.
   a. Try it. Use this step to check if you have picked out the correct sentence as the main idea.

independently. The rounding lesson of Mr. N, her colleague, consists largely of the same elements, with one important difference: as he explains the rules for rounding, he provides students with this procedural prompt:

> *5 and above, give it a shove.*
>
> *4 and below, keep it low.*

In other words, numbers with a 5 or above in the ones column can be rounded up to the nearest 10; numbers with a 4 or below in the ones column can be rounded down to the nearest 10. Not only is this a concrete reminder of the rules for rounding, but it is also a catchy rhyme—increasing the likelihood that students will remember it after the prompt has been removed. The difference between these two lessons is that Ms. D taught rounding with the assumption that given her usual instruction, all students would be able to learn this skill. Mr. N, on the other hand, anticipated that some students would need more in order to achieve independence with this skill. Through the use of the prompt, Mr. N gave his students a useful *strategy* for remembering how to round.

The following are suggestions for using procedural prompts effectively:

- Break the task (procedure, strategy, or concept) down into manageable steps (e.g., using a task analysis).
- Provide students with a suitable procedural prompt (e.g., clearly written, large enough for students to see, etc.).
- Model appropriate use of the prompt and leave it in view for students to refer to.
- Do not abruptly remove the prompt without notifying students that you will be doing so. Instead, gradually fade students' reliance on the prompt and provide appropriate scaffolding for independent strategy use.
- Permit students to put their name on the prompt and keep it in their folder to promote student ownership and responsibility.

Monitoring Student Understanding

Throughout e.i., teacher monitoring of student understanding is critical. Monitoring understanding allows the teacher to observe students' performance to make sure they exhibit the skills necessary to complete the instructional objective. It also allows the teacher to keep student engagement high by determining if it is appropriate to proceed; if more practice or elaboration is needed; if the skill, strategy, or concept should be retaught; or if it is appropriate to abandon instruction and return to it at a later time. In addition, it serves as additional "input" for some students because corrective feedback allows them to hear information one more time or in a different way. Monitoring student understanding involves two complementary skills: checking understanding and providing corrective feedback.

Rather than viewing assessment as something that is only done at the *end*, the teacher checks understanding throughout an e.i. lesson. It is particularly critical before moving on to independent practice, during which students will need to perform with minimal, if any, teacher support. The teacher needs to check for students' possession of the necessary information to work on their own and complete the instructional objective. Many teachers make the mistake of simply asking, "Does everyone understand?" or "Are there any questions?" Students who do not understand are unlikely to identify themselves under such circumstances. In addition, the use of such a strategy does not provide the teacher with any diagnostic information regarding the learners' skills. Therefore, use of an effective strategy is essential for gauging students' understanding appropriately.

The following types of strategies can be used from the outset and repeated throughout the lesson as the teacher monitors student progress. You will notice that some of these strategies are similar to those discussed previously in the section on active participation. Indeed, some of the same strategies that maintain student engagement throughout e.i. provide important data to the teacher about how well students understand. These strategies are meant to be employed as quick and easy forms of assessment, giving the teacher a large amount of diagnostic information in the quickest possible time frame.

Examples of Strategies for Checking Student Understanding

- Sampling
  - a. Pose questions to the whole group in order to focus all students on the problem and develop readiness to hear the answer
    - i. "Everyone, raise your hand when you know the answer to this question."
  - b. Get answers from representative members of the group (e.g. high, average, low)
- Signaled responses from each individual group member
  - a. Students select answers by showing a certain number of fingers
    - i. "Signal me whether you would 1) add or 2) subtract by holding up that number of fingers."
  - b. Thumbs up or down for "agree" or "disagree," to the side for "not sure"
    - i. "Thumbs up if the word I say has the -**at** word family, thumbs down if it doesn't, thumbs to the side if you're not sure." (signaled response)
  - c. Raise hands when examples are correct
- Individual private response
  - a. Written (e.g. on a slate or dry erase board, index card, PDA, etc.)
    - i. "Write the names of the three important parts of a story we have discussed on your slate. Then hold it up."
  - b. Whispered to the teacher so each student is accountable for demonstrating possession of, or progress toward, achievement of the required skill

    c. Students whisper to one another, followed by the teacher's use of sampling
       i. "Whisper to your buddy two rhyming words. Then raise your hand and tell me."

Nonexamples of Strategies for Checking Student Understanding

- "Does everyone understand?"
- "Are there any questions?"
- "Let's move on."

An important corollary to monitoring student understanding is providing appropriate corrective feedback. Giving effective feedback requires considerable *anticipatory teaching*. This means that the teacher anticipates obstacles or barriers to a particular student's understanding and responds to the student at his or her current level of understanding. In this way, the teacher helps the student work toward a response that advances his or her understanding on the way to achieving the instructional objective. In other words, the extent to which the teacher anticipates barriers to student understanding and provides useful corrective feedback can either help or hinder a student from moving along the continuum toward independent, self-directed learning.

At times, teachers fail to respond appropriately to student answers because of inattentiveness or distraction. Beginning teachers, in particular, are often self-conscious and so focused on their own behavior during the lesson that they fail to effectively process students' responses. Failure to give appropriate corrective feedback implicitly signals students that paying attention, responding correctly, and mastering the subject are not to be taken seriously.

Table 4.3 presents examples of corrective feedback that can be given in response to particular types of student answers. When checking students' understanding, potential responses to incorrect answers include reviewing key facts or rules, reexplaining the steps needed to reach a correct solution (preferably by modeling the use of a procedural prompt), or scaffolding with clues or hints. When these types of corrective feedback are used with individual students, they also benefit others in the group by clarifying information that may have been unclear or partially learned.

TABLE 4.3   Student Answers and Corrective Feedback

Type of Answer	Teacher Response
Quick, correct answer	Move on to new question; maintain pace of lesson
Correct but hesitant	Provide brief feedback on why the answer is correct
Careless mistake; incorrect answer	Correct student error and move on to maintain pacing
Inaccurate answer due to facts or processing	Restate question in simpler form; provide clues/prompts; reteach if necessary

Summary

This chapter examined the importance of incorporating student engagement variables into e.i.. Effective use of e.i. requires creating a deep level of engagement for all students throughout the lesson, including those with diverse learning needs. Teachers can combine student engagement variables to create active participation in the learning process, to promote the use of learning strategies, and to consistently monitor student progress toward achievement of the learning objective.

This chapter concludes Part I of this book. As discussed throughout Chapters 1 through 4, e.i. draws from best practices that include strong assessment strategies; development of instructional objectives based on assessment; clear, dynamic teacher presentations; and a high level of learner engagement. This discussion sets the stage for Part II: learning the e.i. framework.

CHAPTER 5

Preinstructional Set

Now that we have discussed the necessary background for implementing explicit instruction (e.i.), we move on to the nuts and bolts—the components of an e.i. lesson. In the next three chapters, individual elements of e.i. are presented. Although discussed separately, these elements are meant to be combined to form a fluid, effective e.i. lesson. For example, you might think of an e.i. lesson as a play with several acts. Each new act (lesson element) can be thought of as a specific kind of activity that takes place within the larger play. The teacher's role is to choreograph each act so that students can work successfully across the entire performance—the e.i. lesson.

In the following chapters, presentation of each e.i. element begins with a graphic organizer that lists essential characteristics of the element, examples, and nonexamples. These are intended to function as an advance organizer for each new lesson element as well as a quick-reference lesson planning tool. You can easily refer to these graphic organizers as you begin to incorporate e.i. elements into your teaching. At the top left of each graphic organizer, you will also see a clock icon. This icon indicates the amount of time that should be devoted to that particular lesson element. Keep in mind that the time indicated is a rough estimate; individual teachers will vary in the amount of time they devote to each lesson element. Beginning teachers, for example, often have difficulty keeping their lessons brief until they have had a lot of practice delivering e.i. Secondary teachers may be able to devote extended time to independent practice across several class periods. However you decide to combine these elements, the ultimate goal is to create seamless, streamlined, well-paced lessons.

This chapter presents the three e.i. elements that are combined to create an effective preinstructional set:

- Gain students' attention
- Inform students of the learning objectives
- Use informed instruction

WHAT IS PREINSTRUCTIONAL SET?

The first "act" in a successful e.i. lesson is the preinstructional set. Based on the work of Hunter (1982) and others (Ausubel, 1960; DeCecco, 1968; Gage & Berliner, 1988; Gagne, Briggs, & Wager, 1992; Gagne & Medsker, 1996), preinstructional set (sometimes called *anticipatory set*,

49

preset, advance organizer, or *set induction*) is a statement that prepares students for the instruction to follow. As the name connotes, it is intended to create a mental "set" in students so that they are in a receptive frame of mind for the lesson.

Lesson introductions are among the most frequently researched teaching skills. Much of this research promotes the ability of lesson introductions to be useful in improving levels of understanding and recall, especially when students lack well-developed prior knowledge. Gage and Berliner (1988) indicated that providing an advance organizer (i.e., telling students in advance what will happen during the lesson) facilitates student comprehension and recall. Similarly, DeCecco (1968) cited the *expectancy function* of teachers: teachers are in the best position to shape student understanding and behavior when they have prepared students in advance for what is expected.

Preinstructional set serves at least four primary purposes, depending on the students, the topic, and the lesson context. First, it is intended to focus student attention on the lesson. Second, it creates a cognitive framework for organizing the skills, strategies, or concepts to follow. In this way, storage and retrieval of new information is facilitated. Third, it can extend understanding and application of new ideas. This is often accomplished through the use of examples and nonexamples. Finally, it can stimulate student interest and involvement in the lesson. Active involvement at the beginning of the lesson can increase curiosity and sustain student interest in the lesson.

In accordance with these purposes, preinstructional set consists of three discrete teaching skills: gain students' attention, inform students of the learning objective, and use informed instruction. The following sections describe each of these elements in detail.

Gain Students' Attention

An effective attention-gaining strategy is the first step to an effective e.i. lesson (see Figure 5.1). At the start, the teacher should focus students' attention. Some teachers fail to do this and purposely start the lesson in a loud voice in an effort to get students to pay attention. This type of behavior constitutes talking *at* rather than *to* students and causes many learners to miss the beginnings of lessons. Once you have begun teaching without fully gaining student attention, you have implicitly conveyed, "I don't really care if you listen to this lesson or not. What I have to say isn't that important." Once this message is conveyed, subsequent efforts to regain student attention can be difficult. Rather than launching into lessons without first gaining full attention, teachers should develop effective strategies for helping students create a mental focus on what is about to be learned.

Explicit instruction often occurs soon after a transition. Students may be physically arriving at a new spot (e.g. from desks to carpet) and in the process of mentally "shifting gears" away from the activity just concluded. Because transitions can be chaotic, gaining students' attention is crucial for eliciting attending behavior and a deliberate readiness for the content of the ensuing lesson. Obviously, if students' attention is not gained, you cannot be confident that they are focused on the learning about to take place. Therefore, teachers should establish that they expect full attention to lessons at all times.

Routines for introducing lessons tell students that the transition between activities is over and a new one is about to begin. Thus, each e.i. lesson begins with an instructional event that engages students' attention, interest, and/or curiosity. At times, this will involve stimulating students' attention from a state of total disengagement to one in which they are listening and looking attentively. Alternatively, this may involve raising their attention from an already receptive state to a higher level of curiosity, interest, and engagement.

30 seconds

Essential Characteristics

- Done at beginning of lesson.
- Focuses students' attention and interest on the learning about to take place.
- Can be a focusing statement, a standard signal, or a question that elicits curiosity.
- Brief and effective (a few seconds to 2 minutes).
- Intensity will vary with characteristics of the instructional group.

Examples	Nonexamples
• "Right now you should be sitting silently, pretzel-legged, looking at me. Great job! Let's begin our lesson." • "Have you ever wondered why some animals come out only at night?" • Teach and practice a signal such as clapping a rhythm and having students respond.	• "Okay." • "Open your books to page 47." • "Now we're going to do math." • Begin the lesson in a loud voice.

FIGURE 5.1 Gain Students' Attention.

After giving the signal or using the intended focusing strategy, the teacher should pause momentarily and allow it to take effect. Once attention has been gained, the teacher should begin briskly by describing the learning objective for the lesson. The pause between giving the signal and beginning the lesson should be brief, just long enough for students to focus their attention. If the pause is too long, students will lose the sharp focus that has been created. It is important, then, that the teacher act quickly if a few students do not respond. Facial expressions and gestures can be used to indicate that they should pay attention, or their names can be called. If this is not enough, a brief focusing statement can be added, such as, "Josh, look over here."

Characteristics of a Good Attention-Gaining Strategy

- Attention-gaining activities should be brief and effective, lasting only long enough to get students ready so that the major portion of instructional time is available for accomplishment of the learning objective.
- A standard signal that tells the group that "we are now ready to begin a lesson" is useful. However, the signal must be taught ahead of time and practiced repeatedly in different contexts to ensure that it is recognized by all students as a sign that they should attend to the teacher.
- The intensity of an attention-gaining strategy will depend on the group of students. For example, a less capable fourth-grade group that meets after lunch may require a more dramatic attention-gaining strategy than will a self-directed, eager group meeting first

thing in the morning. Familiarity with your students will help with selection of the right strategy for gaining their attention.

Examples of Attention-Gaining Strategies

- Teach and use a signal such as holding up two fingers or placing a finger over the lips to signal quiet. For signals to be successful, it is essential to use your e.i. skills to explicitly teach the signal, role play the signal repeatedly, and practice it in multiple contexts.
- Review expectations for behavior before beginning an e.i. lesson. For example,

  "At this time you should be sitting up straight, pretzel-legged, looking at me. Hands are still and in your lap. Great job! Let's begin."

  "SLANT!" (Sit up, Lean forward, Ask questions, Nod your head, Track the speaker)

- Affirm students for their good attending behavior. For example,

  "It's wonderful when I come to the carpet to begin a lesson and you are already quiet, sitting up straight, keeping your hands still in your laps, ready to listen. Terrific job! Let's begin."

- Relate the content of your lesson to students' interests or use questions to arouse their curiosity. These questions, called "openers," are not intended to have a single right answer or even to reflect the fine details of what will follow but rather are meant to *amuse, stimulate,* or even *bewilder* students so that they become interested and receptive to the content that follows. For example,

  "Have you ever wondered why some animals only come out at night?"

  "Can you guess what I have in this box?"

Nonexamples of Attention-Gaining Strategies

- "Okay."
- "Open your books to page 47."
- "Now we're going to do math."
- Being the lesson in a loud voice.

In order for attention-gaining strategies to be effective, they must be explicitly taught using multiple examples and nonexamples, role-played, practiced in multiple contexts, and consistently reinforced. For example, at the beginning of the school year, the teacher decides which attention-gaining signals she wants to use (e.g., hand claps and response or call-and-response). During the first few days of school, the teacher explains and explicitly models the signal for students. The teacher and students role-play responding to the signal. The teacher randomly uses the signal in multiple contexts and then positively reinforces students for responding to it.

Ideally, once students have learned the signal or focusing statement and you have positively reinforced it over time, they will respond with minimal effort on your part. For example, a few weeks into the school year, students become familiar with the routine. They know that explicit instruction takes place on the carpet at a particular time each day. You have given a signal for students to sit quietly on the carpet. When you come to the carpet and sit in the teacher's chair, students automatically give you their attention. They have internalized the focusing signal and become independent; they give you their full attention without your having to do more.

An important notion for all teachers to consider is what good attention looks like. This is significant because having criteria for acceptable attending behavior helps you know when full student attention has been gained. In addition, you can more easily convey your expectations to students when you have clearly defined them for yourself. Research in learning strategies, for example, has attempted to teach students with attention problems a metacognitive strategy for monitoring their own attending behavior. The SLANT strategy (Ellis, 1989) includes very specific criteria for giving someone your attention. The intent behind SLANT is to help students develop the same kinds of attending behavior used by independent, successful learners. If it were okay for students to lie on the floor, this strategy would look very different: lie down, look around, daydream, and think your own thoughts. Individual teachers may have different criteria for what student attention looks like. What is irritating and off limits to one teacher may not be a big deal to another. One teacher may be comfortable allowing students to lounge in beanbag chairs during e.i., while another may not. Whatever good attending behavior looks like to you, it is important to clearly convey and reinforce your expectations to students.

What can you do if your attention-gaining strategy doesn't work? Telling students to simply open their books or making a broad statement about your next activity (e.g., "Now we're going to do spelling.") are not effective strategies for gaining attention. These statements do not provide any information about the lesson to follow or its value. In fact, they implicitly convey that school is about accomplishing a series of activities rather than learning. Similarly, there is a difference between gaining student attention and maintaining it. Maintaining student interest and engagement can be difficult for some teachers to establish. Do not continue to teach if students are not paying attention.

If you consistently have difficulty gaining and/or maintaining student attention, there could be several explanations. Perhaps you have not clearly established your expectations for student attention; somehow they have gotten the idea that you are not absolutely serious about their learning. You may not have taught your expectations explicitly enough, or your implementation may not be effective. Overused, tired strategies will eventually lose their effectiveness. Even effective signals can lose their power if the teacher has not used them recently or positively reinforced students for responding. In this case, reteaching and more consistent reinforcement is necessary.

A useful way to frame student attention is as a tacit, mutual agreement: in return for their attention, you provide students with instruction that is engaging, meaningful, clear, and appropriate. Some teachers mistakenly believe that they can simply demand students' attention to meaningless lectures or tasks for inordinate lengths of time. If students refuse to give you their attention, it may be because you have violated the agreement. Therefore, it is always important to ask yourself why you have lost or failed to sustain students' attention. Is the lesson too difficult? Are students talking to each other to figure out what to do because your teaching is unclear? Have you droned on for 40 minutes when your students' attention span is only 10 minutes? If so, they are giving *you* a signal to wrap it up.

Finally, commanding student attention is a skill that new teachers often find difficult. Unresolved feelings about authority can sometimes be the cause. Most teachers want to be liked by their students. Others hold strong personal beliefs about student-centered classrooms. Fears about seeming too authoritarian or "mean" can be tied in with those beliefs. One important thing to remember is that discipline is a form of caring. It is not mean or authoritarian to teach students to attend and hold high expectations for their attending behavior. Being able to give and sustain attention and to listen and respond effectively are important life skills that will help students become successful independent learners. Failure to teach such skills would be doing students a grave disservice.

Inform Students of the Learning Objective

There are at least four kinds of information that will help prepare students for any given instructional event: learning objective, learner activities, teacher activities, and evaluation activities (see Figure 5.2). Research has commonly advised teachers to introduce lessons by stating the learning objective in language that is meaningful to students. This lets students know what to expect and helps them to prepare to learn efficiently (Ausubel, Novak, & Hanesian, 1978; Mayer, 1979).

When instructional objectives are properly phrased as intended learning outcomes (i.e., as the types of student performance we are willing to accept as evidence of learning), they serve a number of useful purposes. A clear statement of instructional objectives provides a focus that results in more effective learning and teaching. Instructional theorists have shown that goal-directed learning is central to self-regulated learning processes (Schunk, 2003). In the hands of students, objectives promote self-direction by eliminating the ambiguity and waste that come from forcing them to guess at what the important outcomes of instruction might be.

Students are much more likely to find out what they need to know if they know what they are looking for. Likewise, teachers teach more effectively when they have this same information.

☐ 30 seconds

Essential Characteristics

- Research advises teachers to introduce activities by stating the learning objective in language meaningful to students.
- Phrased in terms of what students will be able to *do* on completion of the lesson.
- Provides a focus that results in more effective, goal-directed learning and teaching.
- * Learners know what to expect.

Examples	Nonexamples
• "At the end of today's lesson, you will be able to read and spell words with the -*ell* word family." • "At the end of today's lesson, you will be able to write three detailed sentences about Martin Luther King Jr." • "When we finish our lesson, you will be able to make a correct introduction of a friend to your teacher."	• "Today we will study Chapter 1 and answer questions about it." • "Now we are going to do social studies." • "Given five single-digit math addition problems, you will be able to solve them correctly 80% of the time." • "I am going to go over . . ." • * "I will teach you . . ."

FIGURE 5.2 Inform Students of the Learning Objective.

Clearly stated instructional objectives also result in effective planning. Too often, instructional planning focuses on the methods and materials of instruction without a clear idea of how students are to demonstrate what they have learned. Appropriately phrased instructional objectives provide a basis for selecting the methods and materials of instruction that are most likely to bring about the desired learning. It is valuable to determine what kind of learning activities students will carry out, but such decisions can be made only *after* it has been determined what students will accomplish. Once learning outcomes are identified and described, activities that are appropriate for attaining those outcomes can be chosen.

Some teaching models advocate *against* informing students of the learning objective at the outset of the lesson. These models (e.g., inquiry- or discovery-oriented approaches; Bruner, 1961; Papert, 1980; Steffe & Gale, 1995) view learning as a process of independent knowledge construction by the learner or collaborative knowledge construction among small groups of learners. If the teacher dictates the objective from the outset, students are not free to make their own hypotheses or draw their own conclusions. Teachers who prefer inquiry-oriented approaches may feel conflicted about directing students toward a predetermined learning objective. However, it is important to remember that e.i., like other instructional approaches, is most effective for teaching specific kinds of skills, strategies, and content. Even when used at the appropriate time, some students will need more structure and direction than inquiry-oriented approaches typically provide in order to draw appropriate conclusions.

A distinction can be drawn between how teachers phrase instructional objectives for use in their own lesson planning and for use in informing students of the same objectives. A more formal approach is necessary for teacher planning, which includes the three key characteristics discussed in Chapter 2:

1. *Performance.* An objective always says what a learner is expected to be able to *do*. A performance must be visible, like *write, add, solve,* or *recite*. Words such as *understand, apply,* or *know* are open to too many interpretations to be useful in an objective.
2. *Conditions.* Wherever necessary, an objective describes the important conditions under which the performance is to occur.
3. *Criterion.* An objective describes the criterion of acceptable performance by describing how well the learner must perform in order to be considered acceptable.

Examples of Usefully Stated Instructional Objectives for Teacher Planning

- Given 10 minutes of instruction and a lab exercise, students will identify and label a plant's roots, stem, leaves, flower, and seeds. Criterion: 80%.
- Given a bar graph and a list of statements, students will correctly identify four out of five statements that are supported or unsupported by the graph.
- Given a group of 10 objects, students will select one object that represents a circle and one object that represents a square with no more than two incorrect tries.

Presenting the objective to students in the formal way described previously will not be meaningful for their purposes. In order to be effective when informing students of the learning objectives, teachers should follow the following guidelines:

- Be concrete and specific; avoid describing in general terms what the task is about.
- Phrase objectives in terms of what the students will be able to *do* when they complete the lesson.

- Rate of presentation is short and sweet. Consider stating objectives both orally and in writing and repeating them during the lesson to remind students what they are learning.
- It is the learning outcome that is *most* important, not the learning activities that lead to that outcome. For example, if a teacher says, "This week we are studying Chapter 3 and will take the chapter test at the end of the week," she is not specifying instructional objectives but merely specifying the instructional activities and materials that will be used.

Examples of Usefully Stated Student-Oriented Objectives

- Today we are going to learn to identify and label the parts of a plant.
- At the end of today's lesson, you will be able to "read" a bar graph to get information about our class.
- Today we are going to learn to pick out objects that are two different shapes: circle and square.

Nonexamples of Student-Oriented Objectives

- "Today we will study Chapter 1 and answer questions about it." (These are activities or items on your agenda, not learning objectives.)
- "Now we are going to do social studies." (This is a meaningless statement that gives students no information about what they are about to learn.)
- "Given five single-digit math addition problems, you will be able to solve them correctly 80% of the time." (This is a teacher-oriented objective.)

Use Informed Instruction

Informing students of the learning objective gives them an overall framework for the instruction to follow (see Figure 5.3). For some students, however, knowing only the expected learning outcome may not be enough information to help them get the most out of a lesson. When preparing students for instruction, it can be helpful to tell them the learning objective as well as the activities and evaluation that will be required for them to achieve the objective successfully.

Students need explicit details about the lesson. Communication that informs students *how* a skill will be taught (i.e., what activities or procedures will be involved in the lesson), *what* they will be able to do by the end of the lesson, and *why* that accomplishment is important, useful, and relevant to present and future life situations is important for both learning and motivational reasons.

The teacher has a definite role in most instructional activities. Students can benefit from knowing, from the outset of the lesson, exactly what the role of the teacher will be and exactly how much guidance can be expected. How will students know if they have accomplished an expected learning outcome? How will the teacher judge their performance of that outcome? It is also helpful for students to be alerted to potential difficulties they may encounter and informed of ways to identify, anticipate, avoid, and address these difficulties should they arise. Providing answers to these questions helps prepare students for instruction and increases the efficiency of their learning.

In order for instruction to be "informed," teachers preview the lesson by providing details and information that convey specific teacher expectations. Informed instruction is provided at the beginning of the lesson, but like the learning objective, key features of informed instruction can be repeated throughout the lesson as teachers monitor student progress.

□ 30 seconds to 1 minute

Essential Characteristics

- Students need explicit details about the lesson.
- In addition to stating *what* the current skill/strategy is, it is important to inform students *why* it is important, *how* it is to be done, and *when* (and when not) it can be utilized.
- Meaningful to students' learning and motivation.

Examples	Nonexamples
• "Today we are going to learn . . ." • "This is important to know because . . ." • "We can use this skill when . . ." • "We will know we have learned this when . . ."	• "Today we are going to do math." • "Today we will learn to play a game. This is important to know because then I won't have to explain the rules to you next time." • Speed up and state details quickly and matter-of-factly.

FIGURE 5.3   Use Informed Instruction.

Teachers can also use this information to review before the following day's lesson or over the course of the unit.

Characteristics of Effective Informed Instruction

- Lesson details need to be communicated with the same deliberateness as the lesson content. It is common for beginning teachers to speed up and speak less distinctly when giving details about what to do, how the lesson will proceed, or when the skill can be used, and then slow down again when actually teaching the lesson. When students cannot follow your directives about how or why you want them to become engaged in the learning process, they usually will silently proceed, missing the intent of the lesson.
   a. Slow down when conveying lesson details.
   b. Divide the information into steps.
   c. Be sure each step is understood.
- Avoid overwhelming students with too much information at once.
   a. One of the most common criticisms of beginning teachers from students is that "we didn't understand what to do" (Good & Brophy, 2007). Students often won't admit that they could not follow the lesson or that it was said so quickly and matter-of-factly that they just missed it.
- Specific lesson details can be organized visually for students by posting them in sentence strips on the board or on a chart. For example,

   "Today we are going to learn . . ."
   "This is important to know because . . ."

"We can use this skill when . . ."
"We will know we have learned this when . . ."
"Sources of help available to you are . . ."

- Alert students to potential barriers they may encounter and share ways to identify, anticipate, avoid, and address these difficulties should they arise.
- Teachers can review this information over the course of the lesson or use it to review before the following day's lesson.

Nonexamples of Using Informed Instruction

- "Today we are going to do math." (Again, this is a meaningless statement that doesn't give students any meaningful details about the learning.)
- "Today we will learn to play a game. This is important to know because then I won't have to explain the rules to you next time." (Learning to play a game is not a learning objective. Saving yourself time is not a detail that holds meaning for students' learning.)
- Speed up and state details quickly and matter-of-factly. (Lesson details should be clearly stated.)

Summary

This chapter discussed the three elements of an effective preinstructional set: gain students' attention, inform students of the learning objective, and use informed instruction. Now let's put it all together. Here is an example of a preinstructional set for a secondary chemistry lesson:

The teacher gives the attention signal and waits until there is quiet. Once attention has been gained, the teacher says, "Everyone pick up the Periodic Table of Elements and raise your hand when you have found the first element on the table. At the end of today's lesson, you will be able to use the Periodic Table of Elements to identify the atomic number of an element and its symbol. This is important to know because the atomic number tells us how many protons and electrons the element has. This is also important because we use element identification when we study chemistry. You will know you have learned this when you can identify the atomic number and symbol of any element from the Periodic Table of Elements."

Review

1. Why is it important to gain students' attention before beginning a lesson?
2. What are some examples of effective attention-gaining strategies?
3. What can you do if your strategy to gain students' attention doesn't work?
4. Describe two purposes of clearly stated instructional objectives.
5. How do student-oriented objectives differ from teacher-oriented objectives?
6. What lesson details are most important for students to know?

Apply

1. Imagine that you have spent the last 15 minutes in your classroom having a snack. Students have been eating and freely chatting with one another. You have instructed them to put their snacks away, clean up their area, and come to the carpet to begin a lesson. (FYI: Joe always takes a very long time to clean up and finds straightening the Lego shelf much more interesting than coming to the carpet for your lesson.) Script the first few moments of the lesson, in which you attempt to use a focusing strategy to gain students' attention.

2. For each of the following objectives, decide whether it has a single, clear meaning by marking it with a C or an ambiguous meaning (i.e., it could mean more than one thing) by marking it with an A.

   _____ Students will know the presidents of the United States.

   _____ Students will list the presidents of the United States.

   _____ Given his picture, students will call by name each president of the United States.

3. You need to explain the use of imagery in written English to a group of sixth-grade students who have not yet been introduced to this concept. Script the explanation of lesson details you would deliver to your students. Write answers to the following four questions students need answered as they begin to learn:

   a. What do I need to know or be able to do on completion of this lesson?
   b. What do I need to do to learn that?
   c. What are you going to do to help me?
   d. How will we know when I have learned what was expected?

CHAPTER 6

Preparing the Knowledge Base for Instruction

As discussed in Chapter 1, teacher effects research studied how teachers or instructional practices affected student achievement. In contrast, research on students' cognitive processes examines how teaching or teachers influence what students think, believe, feel, say, or do that affects their achievement. Interest in students' cognitive processes has shaped our conception of the teaching and learning process in meaningful ways. For example, academic learning time has often been found to correlate with student achievement (Fisher & Berliner, 1985). The study of cognitive processes, however, would emphasize that it is the students' constructive use of that time rather than simply the time itself that affects learning and achievement. In other words, variables such as learning, memory, comprehension, learning strategies, and metacognitive processes mediate the effects of teaching on student achievement.

Explicit instruction (e.i.) proposes that the effectiveness of teaching depends partly on the teacher's presentation and partly on the learner's prior knowledge and active thought processes during learning (Anderson, Spiro, & Montague, 1984; Cook & Mayer, 1983; Weinstein & Underwood, 1985; Wittrock, 1978). This chapter presents three elements of e.i. that cognitively prepare students for instruction: activate prior knowledge, review previously learned skills, and preteach key vocabulary. After the lesson has been introduced through an effective preinstructional set, the teacher can use these elements to engage the learner and facilitate storage and retrieval of new skills, strategies, or content.

Note that you probably will *not* use all three of these strategies in a single lesson but rather choose the most effective alternative for that particular lesson. For example, activating prior knowledge is probably most useful for expanding students' knowledge of a particular content area or concept (e.g., electricity, plants, or the cardiovascular system) and can be beneficial when beginning a new unit or topic of study. Reviewing previously learned skills is most beneficial for linking component skills—skills that build one on the next (e.g., in math computation or reading); before teaching the next skill in a sequence, it is important to explicitly review what has already been learned. Preteaching key vocabulary lends itself to

61

vocabulary instruction in content areas such as social studies, science, and English and to building fluency during literacy instruction. Choosing appropriately among these elements can help students organize and relate information to foster active and efficient cognitive connections.

ACTIVATE PRIOR KNOWLEDGE

Prior knowledge provides the storehouse of experiences that are the basis for meaningful learning (see Figure 6.1). Not surprisingly, one of the most universal findings to emerge from educational research is the marked degree to which a learner's prior knowledge of a topic facilitates future comprehension (Anderson, Corbett, Koedinger, & Pelletier, 1995; Anderson, Reder, & Simon, 1996). Learning is the result of the interaction between existing knowledge and new information gained through experience with the real world (e.g., teachers, peers, and instructional materials). Learning is not a process of passive absorption. Students come to new tasks with previous knowledge, expectations, and beliefs, out of which they integrate new information by connecting old meanings to new. It is crucial, therefore, for teachers to assess what students know and believe about a topic, skill, or strategy before it is taught. Strategic teachers emphasize conscious connections to previous and future learning.

Activating prior knowledge is one of the most widely used instructional strategies; most teachers have been taught the importance of fostering active connections between new information and students' background knowledge and experience. Despite widespread belief in the value of this instructional strategy, teachers often fail to implement it in a way that garners the most cognitive benefits for students. This is due to several issues already discussed in this book. For example, perhaps the most common prior knowledge activation strategy is to pose

---

☐ 2 to 10 minutes

Essential Characteristics

- Done before the current concept is taught.
- Facilitates comprehension and learning.
- Reveals student beliefs/knowledge.
- Teacher responds by making connections or fostering predictions.
- Facilitates comprehension and learning.

Examples	**Nonexamples**
• Direct questioning or paper and pencil activity.	• Ask students, "What do you already know about . . .?" but do not give students the opportunity to respond.
• Ask students, "What do you already know about . . .?"	• Access to prior knowledge after the current concept is taught.
• Make a list with a buddy.	
• K-W-L.	
• Have students interview each other.	

FIGURE 6.1 Activate Prior Knowledge.

a question to the entire group and then call on a few students to respond. This strategy is effective for the handful of students who respond; however, you cannot be assured that the rest of the group has had their prior knowledge activated. In addition, teachers will sometimes activate prior knowledge around a theme that is not central enough to the lesson content.

For example, when teaching a language arts lesson on writing similes, a teacher might activate students' prior knowledge of what clouds are like: fluffy, wispy, white, wind swept, and so on. Although the teacher's intent is to use students' descriptions as a segue to an explanation of similes (e.g., "the clouds were as fluffy as pillows"), this constitutes little more than taking students down a meandering cognitive path *away* from the core focus of the lesson. Students are now thinking about *clouds* when the true focus of the lesson is on similes. Most students will quickly regroup and follow your lesson trajectory wherever it leads; others will find it more difficult to attain the learning objective in a meaningful way.

Teachers should make it a habit to ask students to share what they already know about a given subject, skill, or strategy so that they can actively link *relevant* background knowledge with the lesson goals. This practice can also reveal certain inaccurate beliefs that may inhibit students from engaging fully in the task and lead them to quick abandonment of the task at the first sign of frustration. It is important that students' prior knowledge is activated before a new concept or skill is taught so that they can readily make connections between their background knowledge and the learning that is about to take place. This information can be obtained by means of pencil-and-paper tasks that indicate what students know and what they need to be taught. A second approach is to use direct questions. Whatever strategy is used, it should foster active participation by all students.

Characteristics of an Effective Strategy for Activating Prior Knowledge

- A strategy that fosters active participation by *all* students is ideal.
  - a. Quick pencil-and-paper tasks
    - i. Make a list
    - ii. Fill out a questionnaire
    - iii. Take a brief quiz
    - iv. K-W-L
    - v. Peers interview each other
  - b. Brainstorming or direct questioning that gives all students the opportunity to respond (use active participation strategies)
    - i. "What do we already know about . . .?"
    - ii. "Have you seen something like this before? When? Please think of an example. Then raise your hand."
    - iii. "Everyone, have we done this before? How is this like . . .?"
- Since students may not consciously or actively draw connections between their background knowledge and the current learning, it is vital that the teacher respond strategically to student contributions.
  - a. Statements that explicitly connect students' prior knowledge to the current objective or that foster predictions about the current learning will help students to organize and integrate new information with what they already know.
- Teachers may also organize students' prior knowledge graphically by means of a chart, web, or diagram.
- Rate of presentation should be deliberate while keeping students' active participation high.

Examples of Strategies for Accessing/Activating Prior Knowledge

- Before students begin a science unit on weather, ask, "What do you already know about weather? Get together with a buddy and list three things you already know on your index card. In 5 minutes, I will call you back to the circle." After the initial brainstorm session, work with the whole group to categorize or classify information into some kind of logical visual structure (e.g., a web, chart, or semantic feature analysis).
- Before reading *The Seashore Book* by Charlotte Zolotow, ask students, "How many of you have ever been to the beach? What kinds of things did you see and do? Whisper one thing to the person next to you, then raise your hand." Fill in the "K" portion of a K-W-L chart together.
- Based on the title of a book, chapter, or unit, have students brainstorm possible words that might be encountered in the text and list them on a chart. Discuss the reasons behind certain choices that may appear strange in order to reveal covert misunderstandings.

Nonexamples of Activating Students' Prior Knowledge

- Ask students, "How many of you already know something about . . .?" but do not give students the opportunity to respond.
- Access prior knowledge of an unrelated or tangentially related topic.
- Use the "one student answers at a time" approach, then fail to draw explicit connections between students' answers and the current objective.

REVIEW PREVIOUSLY LEARNED SKILLS

You may think that beginning a lesson by reviewing or practicing previously learned, prerequisite content is a common practice. However, few teachers begin lessons in this way. This is an unfortunate fact because research has shown that teacher-led reviews are an important part of the active teaching process that is associated with strong student achievement (see Figure 6.2).

Reviews are valuable to students for several reasons. They facilitate storage of skills, strategies, and content in long-term memory and stimulate students to see relationships between their background knowledge and new information or skills. Daily review emphasizes the relationships between lessons so that students remember previous knowledge and see new knowledge as a logical extension of content already learned. It also provides students with a sense of wholeness and continuity, assuring them that what is to follow is not isolated knowledge unrelated to past lessons. This is especially important for gaining the attention and engagement of less capable learners who may lack appropriate levels of relevant prior knowledge or who may be anxious about having to master yet another piece of unfamiliar content. Review and practice at the beginning of a lesson is also the most efficient way of finding out if your students have relevant prior knowledge sufficient to begin a new lesson. If not, the relevant background knowledge can be explicitly taught (or retaught).

After conducting the preinstructional set, the teacher can provide a brief review or practice of previously achieved, related learning (i.e., review the main points of yesterday's lesson that will be extended today). In this way, the teacher can be sure that students have mastered prerequisite skills and link information that is already in their minds to the information you are about to present. Daily review and practice at the beginning of a lesson is easy to accomplish. If today's lesson is a continuation of yesterday's lesson, then the review may just remind

☐ 2 to 10 minutes

Essential Characteristics

- Before beginning a lesson, conduct a very brief review of previously achieved, related learning.
- Facilitates storage of information in long-term memory.
- Helps connect old learning to new.
- Indicates when reteaching is necessary.

Examples	Nonexamples
• Sample the understanding of a "steering group." • Lead an overt review/practice.	• Ask students, "Do you remember last week when we learned how to use a ruler?" and move on. • State, "On Friday we learned the sound the letter *b* makes" and move on.

FIGURE 6.2 Review Previously Learned Skills.

students about key points from the earlier lesson and ask students to complete a few quick examples before beginning the new one. However, if a new skill or concept is being introduced that depends on skills learned much earlier, more elaborate review and assessment of prerequisite skills may be needed. Consider the following examples of daily review strategies:

- If today's lesson is a direct continuation of yesterday's and you are reasonably sure that students understood yesterday's lesson, begin with a quick reminder about the earlier lesson by asking a few quick questions:

  "Yesterday we learned how to add the suffix -ed to a word ending in y*. Think for a moment about how this is done. Then raise your hand and be prepared to explain."*

- If a new skill is being introduced that depends on skills learned much earlier, a more elaborate discussion and explicit review of the task-relevant information is necessary before the day's lesson:

  "Let's review subtraction when we have enough ones." Put on the chalkboard and have all students solve:

$$\begin{array}{ccc} 47 & 56 & 89 \\ -3 & -4 & -8 \\ \hline \end{array}$$

  Give answers, discuss all items missed by many students.

- Sample the understanding of a steering group: a few low-, average-, and high-performing students who are probably good indicators of the range of knowledge possessed by the entire class. When high performers miss a large proportion of answers at the start of the class, this is a warning that extensive reteaching for the entire class is necessary. When high performers answer correctly but average performers do not, some reteaching should be done. Finally, if most of the high and average performers answer correctly but most of the low performers do not, then individualized reteaching is needed for low performers. This ensures that large amounts of large-group instructional time are not devoted to review and reteaching that may benefit only a small number of students.

PRETEACH KEY VOCABULARY

As teachers, we want students to understand a wide range of words. A key to successful learning is quick, fluent access to word meanings. Brief preteaching of new vocabulary can set students up for success by fostering fluency and prevent them from faltering over unknown words or terms during reading or instruction (Marzano & Pickering, 2005) (see Figure 6.3).

Vocabulary acquisition is fostered not by one approach but by a combination of approaches. Research suggests that e.i. is more effective than incidental learning for the acquisition of new vocabulary (Reutzel & Hollingsworth, 1988), but the combination of both incidental learning from context and e.i. is likely to be more effective than either strategy alone (Nagy & Herman, 1987). This means that teachers need to encourage students to continue to expand their concepts of words on their own as well as providing instruction that helps students process new words more deeply.

New words can be introduced prior to the first-time reading of trade books or basal stories. Words that should be pretaught are those that are relatively high in frequency, that are

---

☐ 2 to 10 minutes

Essential Characteristics

- Prevents students from puzzling over difficult words during instruction.
- Text: preview words that appear most frequently or that students will not be able to figure out given their current skill level.
- Lesson: preview vocabulary central to the content being taught.
- Two or three words in the primary grades; 3–5 words in the intermediate grades.

Examples	Nonexamples
• Preview in Context:	• Read unfamiliar words and definitions from a list of 20 words.
• Select unfamiliar words.	• Preview the word *boy* instead of the word *gingerbread*.
• Present in context.	• Post unfamiliar words but do not refer to them.
• Discuss in context.	• Preview *all* the new words in a text or lesson.
• Expand meanings.	• Look up words in the dictionary and write the definitions.
• Directly instruct students to decode new words and recite their meanings.	

FIGURE 6.3 Preteach Key Vocabulary.

hard to identify using context and/or pictures, and that the student does not yet have the skills to decode. It is not necessary to preteach *all* the words in the story that students cannot yet recognize. Rather, select those that occur most frequently and that students will probably not be able to figure out given their current skills and strategies.

Readence, Bean, and Baldwin (2004) suggested the use of the preteaching strategy "Preview in Context." This strategy asks students to look at words in context, giving them a better understanding of the specific definition of the word that will be used. Discussing key words ahead of time also gives students the opportunity to develop background knowledge for the topic to be read or discussed. Preview in Context has several key characteristics:

- Select words from the text or lesson that you think will be unfamiliar to students. Make sure to choose words that are key to the understanding of the text and don't make the list too long. It is better to have an effective lesson with a few words (two or three in the primary grades and four or five in the intermediate grades) than to have a lesson of 10 words that students forget.
- As with reviewing task-relevant material, the rate of presentation for previewing key vocabulary should be quick and effective, leaving the majority of instructional time for achievement of the current objective.
- Show students the words in context (e.g., in the text sentence in which it appears).
- Help students learn the word meaning by briefly discussing it in its context. You may want to ask questions to help lead the students to the definition.
- Expand word meanings. After students learn the initial meaning of the word, provide additional contexts for the same word. That way, when students encounter the word in a different context, they will make predictions on the basis of what they know about the word's meaning.
- Keep in mind that preteaching important vocabulary is one brief component of an e.i. lesson. It is not always possible or sensible to preview in context (e.g., when introducing new math terms). However, it is important to give students the opportunity to interact with new words by providing some e.i. and a great deal of practice reading new words.
- Have fun with new words. Students learn by the example you set. If you enjoy learning the meanings of new words or enjoy the sounds of words, your students will also become excited about words.

Nonexamples of Preteaching Key Vocabulary

- Read unfamiliar words and definitions from a list of 20 words.
- Preview the word *boy* instead of the word *gingerbread*.
- Post unfamiliar words but do not refer to them.
- Preview *all* the new words in a text or lesson.
- Look up words in the dictionary and write the definitions.

Summary

This chapter discussed three elements that can be used to prepare the knowledge base for instruction: activate prior knowledge, review previously learned skills, and preteach key vocabulary. Remember that you will not include all three of these elements in a single e.i. lesson but rather choose the most appropriate option depending on the learning objective. Now let's put it all together. Here is an example of a review from a kindergarten math lesson:

> "During yesterday's math lesson we learned that inches are the major component of a standard ruler. Many everyday items are measured in inches using rulers. Look at your rulers. Remember, each long line on the ruler equals 1 inch. How many inches are found on a standard ruler? Please close your eyes and think about the answer to this question. When I come to you and tap your shoulder, please whisper your answer in my ear." Give the students a few seconds to construct their answers. "I will begin on the left side of our semicircle. Please be prepared to give me your answer when I get to you." This quick form of assessment will determine whether you need to reteach yesterday's math lesson on the ruler. "Good! Most of you told me that a ruler contains 12 inches. This information will help us today when we will learn how to properly measure different objects to the nearest inch."

Review

1. How does prior knowledge relate to learning new material?
2. What are some strategies for actively involving all students in the activation of prior knowledge?
3. How can accessing prior knowledge help students who tend to be easily frustrated?
4. Why is reviewing especially important for less capable learners?
5. What should you do if certain students cannot handle the same material and move ahead at the same pace as the rest of the class? What might you do differently with these students? How might you explain it to them in ways that would support rather than undermine their motivation to learn?
6. What does research suggest about the benefits of incidental versus direct teaching of new vocabulary?
7. What kinds of words are especially useful to preteach?

Apply

1. You are introducing the study of pollution and the environment to your class. It is important to see what your students already know about this topic. Write a detailed plan for how you would access/activate your students' background knowledge.
2. Using a copy of a familiar text, write a detailed plan for how you would use the Preview in Context strategy to preteach two or three key vocabulary words before beginning a small-group reading lesson.
3. Following these directions are two hypothetical teaching situations. Choose one and script a review of prerequisite skills that you feel would work effectively in that situation.

   a. Situation A: Your class has been working on a math unit in measurement. During the first lesson, the students learned to measure the length of classroom objects using nonstandard units (e.g., pencils, paper clips, and paper strips). The second lesson of the unit will be measuring length using a ruler.
   b. Situation B: You class has been studying the letters *b*, *s*, and *m*. You wish to introduce the letter *l* today.

CHAPTER 7

Instruction

At this point, you have introduced the lesson to your students and prepared the knowledge base for new learning. Everything that has been done prior to this moment has laid important cognitive groundwork for the presentation of new skills, strategies, or content. The explicit instruction (e.i.) elements presented in this chapter represent the culmination of an e.i. lesson. This chapter is called "Instruction" because it is the part of the lesson where the majority of new information is explicitly presented. Instruction includes three teaching skills: cognitive modeling, guided and independent practice, and closure.

The length of this portion of the lesson will vary depending on the developmental level of your students. For example, in elementary school, teachers may model and engage students in guided practice, independent practice, and closure all within a 10- to 15-minute time frame (see Figure 7.1). In secondary school, however, it may take several days to complete all the parts of the lesson.

COGNITIVE MODELING

Research on the strategic and metacognitive aspects of learning underscores the need for modeling not only the physical, observable aspects of a task, but also the invisible mental processes that underlie it (Duffy et al., 1988; Pressley, Forrest-Pressley, Elliott-Faust, & Miller, 1985). For example, people's thought process while reading is not something that can be readily observed; just observing a reader scanning a page and then turning it gives no indication of the activity going on in the reader's mind. To reveal the thinking process, teachers verbalize their own thoughts or "think aloud"—making their thought process visible to learners. Students are required to watch observable behaviors as the instructor performs a task and to

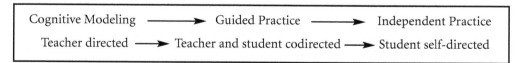

FIGURE 7.1 Relinquishing Teacher Control During Instruction.

69

listen to the instructor's self-talk. Through the detailed process of making thinking public, the teacher models both observable behaviors and the unobservable thinking processes associated with those behaviors. In this way, students are made aware of different strategies they can use. In addition, the possibility that students will misinterpret the teacher's instruction is minimized.

Being able to model unobservable thinking processes is a key component for teaching such cognitive skills as reading strategies, math problem solving, editing and revising written work, and even solving social dilemmas. This method helps students see that the answer to a problem is a logical conclusion following a sequence of reasoning rather than something the teacher "just knew" that the student must commit to memory (which, for some students, may be next to impossible). Cognitive modeling may be used in many different ways. The teacher might model self-monitoring and self-reinforcement statements (e.g., "Oh, I made a mistake. How can I go back and correct it?"), accessing prior knowledge and help (e.g., "Let me think back to what I already know about solving problems like this."), summarizing important information and planning ("Now I've finished steps 1, 2, and 3. Let me read step 4 and think about where to start."), and domain-specific modeling associated with a particular task, such as reading or math computation. ("When I come to a word I don't know, I think about the strategies I've already learned. For example, I can look at the picture for a clue.") In the course of modeling, the teacher may use one of these approaches or combine them (see Figure 7.2).

Whichever form of cognitive modeling you choose, be sure that you model the learning objective that is the focus of your lesson. This may seem like an unnecessary caveat; however,

☐ 10 minutes to ?

Essential Characteristics

- The detailed process of making thinking public or "thinking aloud."
- Students see that the answer to a problem is a logical conclusion following a sequence of reasoning.
- Two kinds of think alouds:
  a. Self-questioning—perform task while asking self-guiding questions.
  b. Self-directive—perform task while giving self-directive prompts.
- * Organize thinking before, during, and after performing a task.

Examples	**Nonexamples**
• Physically performing the task while verbally guided oneself.	• Model but do not use think-aloud.
• Describe each individual step and its importance.	• Present general background information only.
• Make predictions.	• Model only in response to student errors.
• Verbalize confusing points.	• * Model a skill/strategy unrelated to the current instructional objective.
• Demonstrate "fix-up" strategies.	

FIGURE 7.2 Cognitive Modeling.

teachers sometimes become confused about exactly what it is they are supposed to be modeling. For example, when teaching a lesson on syllabication, a beginning teacher models how to clap out the number of syllables in a word but not how syllabication can be used as a decoding strategy. This is a common mistake that typically emerges from teachers' lack of familiarity with making their thinking public. We are used to teaching students how to follow procedures; we may be less familiar with the process of teaching students how to think.

Although some concepts or procedures can be demonstrated with little or no verbalization, modeling is most effective when accompanied by verbal explanations. This procedure may seem obvious, but many teachers do not teach this way. Some teachers are uncomfortable modeling a strategy or procedure one time through without student input (again, they worry about uninterrupted segments of teacher talk). Instead, they partially model and then stop to ask, "What should I do next? Who knows the answer?" This type of modeling constitutes a well-intentioned effort to involve students in your teaching. What this type of modeling fails to acknowledge is that many students may not already know the answer. There will be certain students who need to see and hear one smooth, uninterrupted model in order to learn well. Such students will benefit from a complete and thorough cognitive model by the teacher before student input into the process is solicited. Since many students can benefit from repeated modeling, you might consider modeling one time through first using self-directive statements (e.g., "The first thing I should do is . . ."), followed by a second example using self-questioning with student input (e.g., "What should I do next?"). In this way, the teacher can promote the thinking and problem-solving processes that help all students learn how to find the answer.

Occasionally, I encounter teachers who feel uncomfortable with modeling because it closely resembles traditional teaching methods that "impart" knowledge. We are taught that democratic, student-centered teaching involves guiding students to reach their own conclusions. If we model, aren't we implicitly telling students that our way is the only correct way of doing something? In inclusive classrooms, teaching is student centered to the extent that it is effective for helping each individual student progress toward independent, self-directed learning. Once again, it is important to remember for whom e.i. is intended: students who need to acquire or accelerate progress toward mastery of skills, strategies, or content. If students can acquire and master one way of doing something, eventually they may be able to discover alternative strategies. At their current level of mastery, however, it is unlikely that they will be able to do so without e.i.

An additional consideration during cognitive modeling is the importance of examples and nonexamples. Customarily, teachers will give examples of a concept they are trying to teach, but they don't always think to provide students with nonexamples. Providing nonexamples requires anticipatory teaching because you must think ahead to how students might confuse the concept and provide useful nonexamples that will help them to filter out any potential misunderstandings. For example, let's say you were going to teach the concept of an "island." You might list the critical attributes of an island on a chart so that students can refer to it as a prompt: (a) landmass (not a continent), (b) water, and (c) land surrounded by water. In addition to the list, you might show a simple drawing in which only the critical attributes are labeled and point out each critical attribute. This could be followed by pictures of best examples, such as Hawaii, Greenland, or Cuba. As each picture is presented, you would think aloud about why each is a good example of an island, pointing out the critical attributes again. Next, you might show students both examples and nonexamples and ask questions that elicit judgments about whether each new picture is an example or a nonexample of an island. Students would have to justify their judgments by telling why or why not.

Eventually, they could even come up with their own examples and nonexamples. The number of examples and nonexamples used will depend on the extent of students' demonstrated understanding.

The cognitive modeling portion of a lesson most often involves the following characteristics:

- Both physically performing the skill or skills required for the task and verbally guiding oneself or thinking aloud while carrying out the task. The task could be overt (e.g., how to measure an object with a ruler) or covert (e.g., how to make an inference when reading a narrative text). In either case, the teacher's job is to make the internal cognitive processes explicit.
- Rate of presentation is deliberate. Any procedures or actions are performed slowly and with exaggerated motions.
- Cognitive modeling may take two forms: self-questioning (e.g., "What do I need to do next?") or self-directive statements (e.g., "The first thing I should do is . . .") (Meichenbaum & Beimiller, 1998).
- Think-alouds describe each individual step in a process and highlight the importance of each step using verbal cues (e.g., First, I. . . . Second, I. . . . Next, I should. . . . At the end, I go back and . . .).
- Modeling is structured according to what you think before, during, and after carrying out a particular task; inappropriate structuring (e.g., explaining the task as one big step) is apt to overwhelm students. Use task-directive terms that mirror this structure: first, next, then, at the end, and so on.

Examples of Teacher Statements During Cognitive Modeling

- Model what you are thinking before, during, and after carrying out the task:
  a. "My first step is. . . . Next I . . ."
  b. "Watch while I do this, and I'll tell you what I'm thinking as I work . . ."
  c. "What we might do now is go back and self-check . . ."
- Select a story to read aloud that contains unknown words. As the teacher reads the story aloud, students follow along silently, listening to how the teacher thinks through each trouble spot.
- Make predictions:
  a. "From the title, I predict that this story will tell how Arthur got the chicken pox."
  b. "In this next part, I think we'll find out why Charlie found the golden ticket."
  c. "I think this is a description of the countryside."
- Develop images. Describe the picture you're forming in your head from the information:
  a. "I have a picture of this scene in my mind. The animals are all crowded into the mitten. It's getting very tight and hot with all those furry animals in there!"
- Incorporate multiple examples and nonexamples.
- Verbalize confusing points:
  a. "This just doesn't make sense."
  b. "This is different from what I expected."
  c. "I'm getting confused. Let me see if I understand what I'm supposed to do . . ."
- Demonstrate "fix-up" strategies:
  a. "I'd better go back and do it again."
  b. "This word is new to me. I'd better check the sentence to figure it out."

    c. "That didn't work, so now I'll try . . ."
    d. "What can I do if I need help?"

Nonexamples of Cognitive Modeling

- Model but do not think aloud
- Present general background information only
- Model only in response to student errors
- Model a skill/strategy unrelated to the current instructional objective
- Model directions rather than learning (e.g., explain how to make a clock out of a paper plate rather than how to tell time to the hour)

GUIDED AND INDEPENDENT PRACTICE

We have all heard the phrase "practice makes perfect." In cognitive terms, practice serves as the rehearsal for transferring information from working memory into long-term memory. The instruction portion of an e.i. lesson can be conceptualized on a continuum that starts out as highly teacher directed during cognitive modeling, becomes teacher and student codirected during guided practice, and becomes student directed during independent practice (see Figure 7.3). From the beginning of the lesson, the teacher's ultimate goal is for students to engage in accurate, self-directed independent practice. If initial errors become engrained in working memory, they can be difficult to modify. The beginning stages of learning, therefore, are critical for determining successful future performance. As a result, students' initial attempts at practice should be carefully monitored and guided so that they are accurate and successful (Hunter, 1994). As students become more competent, the teacher gradually relinquishes control in favor of student self-direction during independent practice.

☐ 5 minutes to ?

Essential Characteristics

- Immediately follows presentation and modeling of initial concept.
- Promotes and solidifies learning achieved during earlier part of the lesson.
- Directly linked to learning objective.
- Active participation.
- Promotes student self-direction.

Examples	Nonexamples
• Practice with peers. • Group problem solving or application. • Teacher-directed individual guided practice.	• Worksheet activity at the beginning of a lesson. • *Practicing errors when working independently.

FIGURE 7.3 Guided and Independent Practice.

Practice activities are especially helpful for students with special needs because they provide extended engaged time and help promote deeper understanding of new learning. Once students are engaged in guided practice, the teacher should circulate among the class or group to make sure that instruction has "taken" before setting students free to practice independently (with limited or no help available). With teacher guidance, students need to perform all (or enough) of the task so that clarification or remediation can occur promptly if needed. In this way, the teacher can be sure that students will perform the task correctly during independent practice rather than practicing errors when working by themselves.

Guided practice is most appropriate immediately following cognitive modeling of the skill, strategy, or concept. There are several ways that teacher-organized guided practice can be accomplished, such as practice with peer partners, group problem solving or application, or teacher-monitored individual guided practice (see Table 7.1). Guided practice should be conducted in as nonevaluative an atmosphere as possible. Students should be free to risk giving incorrect responses out of which you can begin to coconstruct an accurate understanding. Any response, however inexpert or clumsy, can be the basis for learning if it is supported by appropriate corrective feedback.

In order to be successful, practice activities must be directly aligned with the learning objective. Guided practice that does not allow students to practice the learning objective or that is indirectly related to the objective will not improve student learning. For example, Darcy, a beginning first-grade teacher, taught a science lesson in which students learned the stages in the life cycle of a butterfly. She sent students back to their seats with the direction that they should rewrite and illustrate the stages in order. At each table, she provided a prompt for the students; however, the prompt listed the stages out of order, and the practice task was for students to write them in order. Darcy had omitted this from her explanation, thinking that requiring students to "figure it out" would show who really understood her lesson. On finally "figuring it out," one student remarked, "I think it was a trick!" It is only a trick if you don't explain it clearly. Students should practice precisely what you teach and model.

In addition to alignment with the learning objective, a successful guided practice activity includes several other characteristics:

- Guided practice activities must be used to promote learning that occurred during the earlier part of the lesson; in other words, avoid throwing students a curveball by introducing new information or skills during guided practice.

TABLE 7.1 Examples of Guided Practice Activities

Objective	Guided Practice Activity
Writing consonant–vowel–consonant words in cursive for handwriting practice	Dictation by teacher, work checked after every sentence
Solving math word problems with the word "more"	Students solve problems one at a time while the teacher monitors their execution of each step
Measuring with yardsticks to make a scale model of the classroom	Teacher-led group problem solving
Figuring out unknown words by reading to the end of the sentence and going back	Practice with peers

- Students with disabilities or complex learning needs are less likely to learn new information from worksheet-type activities. Although worksheets are a convenience at times, guided practice activities should be varied to enhance and extend meaningful participation by all students.
- Rate of presentation for guided practice should be deliberate while promoting the active participation of all students. Keep the pace and enthusiasm as high as possible during guided practice (e.g., "Everyone who thinks they know the answer, put your thumbs up!").

Nonexamples of Guided Practice Activities

- Worksheet activity at the beginning of a lesson
- Omitting guided practice so that students practice errors when working independently
- Guided practice for how to correctly put glue on paper (or some other activity that is not central to the learning objective)

Once the teacher and students have completed enough guided practice to facilitate independent performance, it is time to check students' understanding (see Chapter 4) and then reinforce individual proficiency with the new skill, strategy, or concept. At times, your check of student understanding may indicate that many students are still unclear. Always be prepared to provide additional guided practice when needed.

In contrast to guided practice, which is done with scaffolded teacher support, independent practice is self-directed: students work independently with little or no teacher interaction. For younger students, independent practice may be group or individual work done in class. In middle and secondary school, independent practice often takes the form of homework.

In inclusive classrooms in particular, independent practice still requires some teacher monitoring. You do not want the outcome of your carefully crafted e.i. lesson to be that some students practice errors that then become entrenched and difficult to reverse. This makes your instructional job even harder. During independent practice, teacher monitoring may consist of a quick sweep around the classroom as students begin to work independently. The teacher can immediately identify those who are having difficulty getting started and provide a small group with additional guided practice if needed.

If independent practice takes the form of written homework, obviously the teacher cannot provide additional monitoring. In that case, however, you might consider providing a procedural prompt along with one or two completed examples at the top of the homework page. This not only helps parents who may be assisting their children at home but also serves as a review for students who may have difficulty remembering back to what happened in class. Teachers are sometimes reluctant to provide such prompts, reasoning that students should have class notes to which they can refer for help. However, this conclusion includes several assumptions: (a) that students took adequate and legible notes to be able to understand when looking back, (b) that students brought their notebooks home with them, and (c) that even if the students did bring their notebooks home, they make the link between looking at their notes and completing the homework successfully. If independent practice routinely consists of homework and some students consistently fail to complete it out of frustration or confusion, you might consider creative ways to promote successful, self-directed independent performance.

Independent practice is not always written. Particularly in inclusive classrooms, teachers should work to provide students with multiple means for expressing their learning.

Independent practice should be provided in enough different contexts that skills, strategies, and concepts can be generalized to subsequent contexts—not only those in which they were originally learned. Failure to help students generalize skills and strategies is part of the reason why so many students are unable to apply their learning meaningfully in new settings.

At different times, independent practice activities may be skill based (e.g., worksheet, flash cards, game, or drill) or application based (e.g., journal entry, essay, diorama, PowerPoint presentation, dramatization, or oral presentation). Skill-based practice activities promote mastery—quick, accurate, fluent performance of skills or procedures. Application-based practice activities promote generalization to meaningful, real-life settings. Rather than consistently relying on one form of practice (e.g., worksheets), teachers can combine skill-based and application-based activities to provide students with a variety of engaging and constructive independent practice opportunities.

CLOSURE

Closure is an action, a statement, or an activity that is designed to bring an e.i. lesson to an appropriate and satisfying conclusion. Closure has several purposes. It is used to help organize student learning and facilitate storage and retrieval of the skill, strategy, or concept that has just been taught. It helps students become reflective learners by requiring them to actively consider what happened in class. Closure is also the last opportunity the teacher has during the lesson to gauge student understanding and clear up any lingering misunderstandings. Teachers will sometimes sacrifice closure in deference to classroom time constraints, particularly in secondary settings where class periods are fairly short and there is a lot of content to cover. However, the end or closure of a lesson is just as important as the beginning. Lessons that omit or include weak closure deny students the opportunity to think about and discuss what they have learned and deny the teacher important formative assessment data about the extent of student understanding (see Figure 7.4).

Weak forms of closure include asking students if there are any questions and moving on (e.g., "Are there any questions? Then let's move on to Science.") or a brief lecture, summary, or "wrap-up" statement made by the teacher (e.g., "Today you learned how to use a protractor. Here are the three take-home points . . ."). These types of statements provide closure for the teacher; however, passive students may or may not be listening and are left without a meaningful conclusion to the lesson. Like other components of e.i., effective closure is active and allows students to demonstrate their grasp of the learning objective. It should leave students with a meaningful sense of what has just been learned. In other words, you want students to go away from your lesson with whatever skill, strategy, or concept they just learned in the forefront of their minds. As a result, they will be much more likely to be able to recall the information the next time they need to use it.

For older students, closure consists of more synthesis than review. In other words, older students might be required to apply or elaborate their learning by summarizing or considering how the learning fits with what they already know about the topic. One strategy for this type of synthesis is the "three whats":

1. What did we learn today? (review and summarize)
2. So what? (how is it important, relevant, or useful?)
3. Now what? (how does it relate to our unit outcomes?)

☐ 1 to 5 minutes

Essential Characteristics

- Check that students have information they need to work on their own and achieve the instructional objective.
- Facilitates storage and retrieval of new information.
- * Provides quick teacher data: Is more practice needed? Do I need to reteach? Can I go on?

Examples	Nonexamples
• Signaled response.	• "Let's move on to social studies."
• Sampling.	• "Today you learned to read a thermometer."
• Individual private response (e.g., think–pair–share).	• "Are there any questions?"
• Individual verbal response (e.g., classroom whip-around).	• "Please put your math books away."
• Quick pencil-and-paper activity (e.g., "door pass," problem of the day, response card, learning journal, or Lesson Closure Summary Sheet; see Table 7.2).	• * Passive review in which students look and listen as teacher rereads key points.
• * Statement from students of what they learned in the lesson (e.g., the three whats or "3–2–1": three things they found interesting, two things they learned, and one thing they still have a question about).	

FIGURE 7.4 Closure.

Examples of Effective Closure Activities

- Signaled response
- Sampling
- Individual private response (e.g., think–pair–share)
- Individual verbal response (e.g., classroom whip-around)
- Quick pencil-and-paper and activity (e.g., "door pass," problem of the day, response card, learning journal, or Lesson Closure Summary Sheet; see Table 7.2)
- Statement from students of what they learned in the lesson (e.g., the three whats or "3–2–1": three things they found interesting, two things they learned, and one thing they still have a question about)

TABLE 7.2 Lesson Closure Summary Sheet

Today's lesson was about _____. One

important point was _____. This

is important because _____.

_____In sum, today I learned _____.

Nonexamples of Closure

- "Let's move on to social studies."
- "Today you learned how to turn a liquid into a gas."
- "Are there any questions?"
- "Please put your math books away."
- Passive review in which students listen as the teacher rereads key points.

Summary

This chapter discussed the three elements of instruction, the critical final portion of an e.i. lesson: cognitive modeling, guided and independent practice, and closure. Remember that you should check students' understanding throughout e.i. but especially before releasing students to engage in independent practice. Let's look at an example of instruction from an elementary math lesson in which students are taught three different ways to state time to the half hour:

Cognitive model: [Holding the large Judy clock in front of the class showing the time 1:30.] "Whenever we use the term 'half hour,' the minute hand will always be pointing to the 6 on the clock. I have to think to myself that when counting by 5s, I know that the 6 stands for 30." I'll model this by taking the minute hand, putting it on the 12, and counting by 5s until I reach the 6. "Notice on my clock that the hour hand is pointing in between the 1 and 2 and that the minute hand is pointing to the 6. This means 1:30. Now there are three different ways to say times to the half hour. Look at this chart. One way to say 1:30 would be half past 1. Another way of saying 1:30 is 30 minutes after 1. The final and tricky way to say 1:30 is 30 minutes before 2 because in thirty minutes it will be 2:00. These are the three ways of showing a time to the half hour. I am going to leave this chart on the board to help you during guided practice and independent practice."

Guided practice: "I am going to say a time. With your partner, you are going to show me that time on each of your clocks. Remember to discuss your answer with your partner before setting your clocks." Model how to do this with a student in the class. "Thumbs up if you are ready to begin. Excellent! I want you to show me 30 minutes past 7." Students will discuss time with partner and set time on miniclocks. "Five seconds. Okay, raise your clocks." Continue this method with various ways of saying a half hour.

Check student understanding: Check student understanding by walking around while the partners are discussing the correct way to show the time on the clock. While doing this, I will be able to help the students if they are confused. In addition, by raising the clocks after each time, I am using active participation to determine whether all students have grasped the concept.

Independent practice: "Boys and girls, you did a great job telling time to the half hour. Now you are going to practice this skill on your own. I am going to pass out these cards, and once everyone has their deck, we will go over the directions together." Pass out one deck of cards to each student. "You have a deck of cards. Some of the cards in the deck show clock faces to the half hour [show example]. Other cards show times in standard notation or in words [show examples]. You are going to match the clock faces to the cards that show the time either in standard notation or in words. Watch me." Model how to do one example. "When you're done, you should have 10 matched pairs. Once you have

matched all of your pairs and checked your work, raise your hand, and I will come to your desk to check your work." As students begin working, the teacher makes a sweep around the classroom to identify those who may need additional support.

Closure: "Everyone, please turn over your worksheets. I am going to give you an index card. Your card may have a time written on it, like 10:30. Or it may have one of the ways we can say time to the half hour on it, like '30 minutes before 11.' When I say go, you are going to look at your card and then try to find the other people in the group whose cards goes with yours. In the end, there will be four people in your group with four different cards: one with a digital time and three others with the three ways of saying the time. When you've found your group members, sit together on the carpet. You will have 5 minutes. Go!" Students find their group members and share with the whole group.

Review

1. Why does cognitive modeling have a powerful influence on student learning?
2. Describe in your own words the steps that are included in an effective cognitive model or think-aloud.
3. In cognitive terms, why are guided and independent practice important for student learning?
4. What are some ways that guided practice can be accomplished?
5. What are the characteristics of an appropriate closure activity?

Apply

1. You are preparing to read a familiar text to your students, and you wish to model or "think aloud" the reading strategy of prediction. Write a detailed plan for how you would use a think-aloud to model this strategy.
2. You are teaching a math lesson on recognizing sets. You have explained that a set is a group of like objects and have shown some examples (e.g., pencils, chalk, and other classroom items) and nonexamples. Now you are ready for guided practice. Each student has a pile of multicolored

lifesaver candies and a few lengths of yarn. Write a detailed plan for how you would engage your students in guided practice.

3. You are at the conclusion of a secondary history lesson on factors that led to the Great Depression. Students have just completed independent practice in which they completed a time line listing each factor and when it occurred. There are 5 minutes left for you to conduct a closure activity. Write a detailed plan for how you would engage your students in active closure for this lesson.

Creating Collaborative Relationships and Fostering Communication

From Chapter 4 of *Creating Inclusive Classrooms: Effective and Reflective Practices*, 7/e. Spencer J. Salend. Copyright © 2010 Maryann Mraz. Copyright © 2010 by Pearson Education. All rights reserved.

Jupiter Unlimited

MS. CARR AND MS. STEVENS

Ms. Cathy Carr, a general education teacher, and Ms. Sarah Stevens, a special education teacher, had worked as a co-teaching team in an inclusion program for several years. Things had gone well over the years, and the teachers tried to make improvements to their program each year. This year they decided to focus on family involvement. Because many families in the past did not know much about inclusion and their program, the teachers decided to have a meeting to explain their inclusion program to families.

There was a good turnout of family members. Ms. Carr and Ms. Stevens asked all in attendance to introduce themselves and then started talking about their program. They explained inclusion and discussed the philosophy and goals of the program, the day's schedule, communications with families, and various other aspects of the program. They also asked the paraeducators to explain their responsibilities, noting how fortunate the class was to

have their assistance for all the students in the class. They briefly explained the research on inclusion in language that families could understand and cited examples of how their students had grown academically and socially. They invited family members of a former student to speak about the program and its impact on their child.

Next the teachers solicited questions from family members. Family members asked questions like "Does the class have computers?" and "How does the teaming work?" One family member asked, "If there are two teachers in a class, which one is my child's 'real' teacher?" Ms. Carr and Ms. Stevens explained, "We both teach all the students. Sometimes one of us leads a lesson while the other helps students to participate, and sometimes we both work with groups at the same time." They concluded the meeting by thanking families for attending and participating, and inviting them to visit and volunteer in the class.

Creating Collaborative Relationships and Fostering Communication

To provide families with additional information about inclusion, they gave family members a handout that gave them resources about inclusion, and a handout of relevant Web sites that offered information and activities that families could use to support their children's learning.

At the end of the meeting, Ms. Carr and Ms. Stevens asked the family members to complete a survey that asked them to rate their satisfaction with the content, activities, organization, and scheduling of the meeting, and to identify the things they would like future meetings to address. Several family members indicated that they would like to learn more about how they could support the inclusion program. Others suggested that the teachers provide them with updates on the inclusion program, which they decided to do via a monthly newsletter and a weblog of the class's activities maintained with the assistance of the students.

Following the meeting, the professionals met to discuss it. They talked about how it went, what was successful, and what they would do differently. They also reviewed the feedback from family members and started to plan the next meeting.

What factors made this meeting successful? What strategies could professionals and families employ to collaborate and communicate to help students learn better and develop the support of their students' families for inclusion? After reading this chapter, you should have the knowledge, skills, and dispositions to answer these as well as the following questions:

- Who are the members of the comprehensive planning team?

- How can members of the comprehensive planning team work collaboratively?

- How can I foster communication and collaboration with families?

As teachers like Ms. Carr and Ms. Stevens recognize, an essential principle of effective inclusion programs is good collaboration and communication among teachers, other professionals, families, and community members and resources (Dettmer, Thurston, Knackendoffel, & Dyck, 2009). Good collaboration and communication can strengthen the connection between school and home, create a shared commitment to learning, support student learning, and build support for your inclusive classroom (Swedeen, 2009). Stivers, Francis-Cropper, and Straus (2008) provide guidelines for implementing activities throughout the school year to communicate with your students' families about your inclusive classroom. This chapter offers strategies for creating collaborative relationships and fostering communication with other professionals, families, and community members to support the development and implementation of inclusive classrooms that promote the learning of *all students*.

MEMBERS OF THE COMPREHENSIVE PLANNING TEAM

WHO ARE THE MEMBERS OF THE COMPREHENSIVE PLANNING TEAM? The comprehensive planning team (which has different names in different states and school districts), including students and their families, makes collaborative decisions about the strengths and challenges of students, and provides appropriate services to students and their families. Effective teams engage in a **wraparound process**, a multidisciplinary, interagency, strength-based, and student- and family-focused process for collaboratively designing and delivering individualized, culturally sensitive, school- and community-based educational, counseling, medical, and vocational services to address the unique strengths, challenges and behaviors of students and their families (Eber et al., 2008; Lechtenberger et al., 2008). The wraparound process guides the team in solving problems; coordinating a full range of services available to students, families, educators, and schools; and sharing the responsibility for implementing inclusion.

In addition to students, the team consists of general and special educators, administrators, support personnel, family members, peers, local community resources, and professional and family-based organizations, as shown in Figure 4.1. The members of the team and their roles vary, depending on the strengths and challenges of students, families, and educators. The roles and responsibilities of the different team members are described in the following sections.

Family Members

Relatives are key members of the planning team, and communication and collaboration with them are essential. They can provide various types of information on the student's adaptive behavior and medical, social, and psychological history. Family members also can help the team design and implement educational programs and determine appropriate related services.

School Administrators

A school administrator who supervises the districtwide services usually serves as the chairperson of the team. The chairperson is responsible for coordinating meetings and delivering services to students and their families. He or she also ensures that all legal guidelines for due process, family involvement, assessment, and confidentiality have been followed. Through their leadership and support, school administrators also can foster acceptance of and commitment to the concept of inclusion and encourage educators and families to collaborate.

General Educators

The team should include a general education teacher who has worked with the student and who can offer information on the student's strengths and challenges, as well as data on the effectiveness of specific teaching methods. General educators can provide a perspective on the academic and social rigors of the general education curriculum and classroom.

PEARSON
myeducationlab

Go to the Assignments and Activities section of the Topic *Collaboration, Consultation, and Co-Teaching* in the MyEducationLab for your course and complete the activity entitled *Understanding Collaboration*. As you watch the video and complete the accompanying questions, note the importance of true collaboration to the creation of an effective inclusive classroom.

FIGURE 4.1 Members of the comprehensive planning team

Special Educators

The special educator provides information on the student's academic, behavioral, and social skills and the student's responses to different teaching techniques and materials. When a student is to be placed in an inclusive setting, the special educator can collaborate with general education classroom teachers on curricular and teaching accommodations, learning strategies, classroom management strategies, testing accommodations, grading alternatives, assistive devices, and peer acceptance. At the secondary level, special educators also play important roles in teaching study, independence, functional, and vocational skills, and working with community agencies.

Paraeducators

Because paraeducators can perform many important roles to help you promote the educational, social, and behavioral performance of *all students* in inclusive settings, it is important for them to be part of the planning team and have a shared vision for the inclusion of students (Carnahan, Williamson, Clarke, & Sorensen, 2009; Causton-Theoharis, 2009; Suter & Giangreco, 2009). Including paraeducators on the planning team also can help them understand students' strengths and challenges, effective instructional strategies, and the goals of students' educational programs. Their participation also can clarify their roles and responsibilities in supporting you—and not replacing you—in implementing and assessing students' educational programs effectively (Giangreco & Broer, 2007; Liston, Nevin, & Malian, 2009) and in fostering the social, behavioral, and academic development of students. See Figure 4.2 for a delineation of the roles of paraeducators so that they are not asked to assume responsibilities that teachers should perform. It is important to note that the activities of paraeducators should be identified by IEP teams and must be supervised by and performed under the direction of licensed professionals (Devlin, 2008; Etscheidt, 2005; Maggin, Wehby, Moore-Partin, Robertson, & Oliver, 2009).

FIGURE 4.2 Delineating the roles and responsibilities of paraeducators in inclusive settings

Roles and Responsibilities of Paraeducators

Paraeducators can support teachers and students by
- assisting students with daily living skills and health and physical needs (e.g., toileting and feeding).
- performing clerical duties and custodial tasks (e.g., insuring proper positioning).
- supervising students during activities outside the classroom.
- recording behavior and helping manage students' behavior.
- reading to students and playing educational games with them.
- serving as a translator.
- preparing, individualizing, and adapting materials.
- providing individualized and small-group instruction and reinforcing concepts/skills taught previously.
- helping students with motor and mobility difficulties, and providing emotional support.
- observing students.
- facilitating social interactions with peers.
- modeling appropriate skills.
- ensuring student safety.
- prompting students.
- assisting with follow-up instructional activities (e.g., homework, studying for tests).

Roles and Responsibilities Outside the Scope of Paraeducators

Paraeducators should not be asked to replace teachers by
- being solely responsible for planning, delivering, and monitoring instruction to specific students.
- administering and interpreting formal and informal assessment instruments unless trained to do so or monitored by a trained professional.
- signing formal documents such as IEPs.
- assigning grades.
- disclosing confidential information.
- serving as a substitute teacher or substitute for teachers at meetings.

Sources: Carnahan et al. (2009); Causton-Theoharis (2009); Etscheidt (2005); Giangreco, Yuan, Mckenzie, Cameron, & Fialka (2005); Liston et al., (2009)

Because paraeducators often reside in the community, they may also provide valuable information regarding links to community-based services (Villa, Thousand, & Nevin, 2008). In particular, paraeducators who are educated in or have experience with students' languages and cultures can play an important role in educating students who are English language learners. Therefore, it is important that you and other members of the team treat them with respect, and appreciate and acknowledge them for the meaningful contributions they make (Causton-Theoharis, 2009; Liston et al., 2009). It is also important to communicate regularly and share information with them; solicit their perspectives; address their concerns and suggestions; and offer them support, professional development, and feedback to improve their performance (Carnahan et al., 2009; Devlin, 2008).

School Psychologists

The school psychologist is trained in the administration and interpretation of standardized tests. In addition to testing, school psychologists collect data on students by observing them in their classrooms and by interviewing other professionals who work with the students. School psychologists also sometimes counsel students and family members and assist classroom teachers in designing teaching and classroom management strategies.

Speech and Language Clinicians

Information on students' communication abilities can be provided by the speech and language clinician. To rule out or confirm a language disability, these clinicians are often the first persons to whom students learning English are referred. They can also help you improve the communication skills and academic success of students in the classroom (Kuder, 2008; Owens, 2010).

Social Workers

The social worker serves as a liaison between the home and the school and community agencies. The social worker counsels students and families, assesses the effect of the student's home life on school performance, and assists families during emergencies. In addition, the social worker can help families obtain services from community agencies, contact agencies concerning the needs of students and their families, and evaluate the impact of services on the family. Social workers also may offer counseling and support groups for students and their families.

Laura Bolesta/Merrill

School Counselors

The school counselor can provide information on the student's social and emotional development, including self-concept, attitude toward school, and social interactions with others. In schools that don't have a social worker, the counselor may assume that role. Frequently, counselors coordinate, assess, and monitor the student's program, as well as counsel students and their families. For example, during the transition period, the student may need counseling to adjust socially and emotionally to the general education classroom.

Paraeducators serve important roles in inclusive classrooms. What roles do paraeducators perform to promote the success of students in inclusive classrooms?

Vocational Educators

Vocational educators offer valuable information on the student's work experiences and career goals. They can help the team develop the transitional services component of students' IEPs. Vocational educators also provide students with vocational and career education experiences. This involves collaboration with families and employers in the community.

Anthony Magnacca/Merrill

School Physicians and Nurses

School physicians and nurses can aid the team by performing diagnostic tests to assess the student's physical development, sensory abilities, medical problems, and central nervous system functioning (Heller, 2009a). They can provide information on nutrition, allergies, chronic illnesses, and somatic symptoms. In addition, they can plan and monitor medical interventions and discuss the potential side effects of any drugs used. Since physicians' services are costly, many medically related services may be provided by school nurses.

Speech and language clinicians develop students' communication skills. How can you collaborate with them?

Physical and Occupational Therapists and Adapted Physical Educators

Students with fine and gross motor challenges may need the services of **physical** and **occupational therapists** and adapted physical educators (Heller, Forney, et al., 2009; Menear & Smith, 2008). These therapists can recommend various types of adaptive

PEARSON
myeducationlab

To enhance your understanding of the roles and responsibilities of school counselors and how you can collaborate with them, go to the IRIS Center Resources section of Topic: Collaboration, Consultation, and Co-Teaching in the MyEducationLab for your course, and complete the module entitled *Guiding the School Counselor: An Overview of Roles and Responsibilities.*

PEARSON
myeducationlab

To enhance your understanding of the roles and responsibilities of school nurses and how you can collaborate with them, go to the IRIS Center Resources section of Topic: Collaboration, Consultation, and Co-Teaching in the MyEducationLab for your course, and complete the module entitled *School Nurses: Roles and Responsibilities in the School Setting.*

equipment and suggest how to adapt teaching materials and classroom environments. The physical therapist usually focuses on the assessment and training of the lower extremities and large muscles; the occupational therapist deals with the upper extremities and fine motor abilities. The physical therapist helps students strengthen muscles, improve posture, and increase motor function and range. The occupational therapist works with students to prevent, restore, or adapt to impaired or lost motor functions. This therapist also helps students develop the necessary fine motor skills to perform everyday actions independently. Adapted physical educators offer a range of services and strategies to foster students' gross and fine motor skills and participation in physical activities.

Staff from Community Agencies

For many students, the team will need to work collaboratively with staff from community agencies. For example, if a student with a visual impairment must have an assistive device, a community agency can be contacted to help purchase it. In working with community organizations, the team should consider the unique medical, behavioral, and social needs of each student, as well as the financial resources of the student's family. Because many students may require similar services from agencies, teams can maintain a file of community agencies and the services they provide.

Professionals for Students Who Are English Language Learners

In addition to the professionals just described, teams for students who are learning English and who are referred for special education services should include personnel who are fluent in the student's native language and bicultural in the student's home culture. Therefore, planning teams working with these students should include such professionals as ESL teachers, bilingual educators, and migrant educators.

ESL Teachers ESL teachers instruct students in English. They build on students' existing language skills and experiences to enhance their learning of English. In addition, they can help the team address students' language and learning strengths and challenges, as well as offer many effective strategies for teaching English language learners.

Bilingual Educators Many students come from backgrounds where English is not spoken and need the help of a bilingual educator. This educator performs a variety of roles. These include assessing and teaching students in their native language and in English, involving families and community members in the educational program, helping students maintain their native culture and language and adjust to their new culture, and working with general educators.

Migrant Educators To help educate **migrant students**, the federal government funds migrant education programs through the states. Typically, when a migrant family moves to a new area, it is certified as being eligible for migrant status and services by a recruiter from a local migrant education agency. Then a migrant educator helps the family enroll the children in school. The migrant educator also contacts local agencies, organizations, businesses, and other community resources that can assist migrant families. Once the migrant students are in school, the migrant educator often gives them supplementary individualized instruction in small groups.

COLLABORATIVE TEAMING

HOW CAN MEMBERS OF THE COMPREHENSIVE PLANNING TEAM WORK COLLABORATIVELY? Successful comprehensive planning teams are collaborative and interactive. All members work together to achieve a common goal, are accountable to the team, share their diverse expertise and perceptions with others, and respect the code of ethics for educators (Arthaud, Aram, Breck, Doelling, & Bushrow, 2007; Bucholz, Keller, & Brady, 2007; Skinner, Garganis, & Watson, 2009). They are interdependent and empathetic, understanding their roles and roles of others. A key member of the team is the case manager, service coordinator, or support facilitator. This person promotes the team process, coordinates the services for students and their families, and provides follow-up to ensure that goals are being met (Dettmer et al., 2009).

Successful collaborative teams also develop good interpersonal and communication skills. Fleming and Monda-Amaya (2001) and Garmston and Wellman (1998) summarize the roles that team members can perform to help the team function efficiently and establish a caring, positive, trusting working environment:

- *Initiating:* All members identify problems and issues to be considered by the team.
- *Information gathering and sharing:* All members collect and share relevant information.
- *Clarifying and elaborating:* All members seek clarification, probe for specific facts and details, and provide elaboration.
- *Summarizing:* All members review and paraphrase key points discussed by the team.
- *Consensus building:* All members participate in decision making.
- *Encouraging:* All members encourage others to participate in the process and pay attention to the contributions of others.
- *Harmonizing and compromising:* All members assume that others have good intentions and seek to resolve conflict and compromise.
- *Reflecting:* All members reflect on their own feelings, comments, and behaviors, as well as those of others.
- *Balancing:* All members try to balance advocacy and inquiry.

To help the team develop these skills, the team can establish ground rules to guide their interactions and the decision-making process. Individual team members can also be assigned roles such as facilitator, recorder, timekeeper, observer, and summarizer. You can use effective communication skills to support the success of the team by (a) listening carefully and empathetically to others; (b) being tolerant of differing points of view; (c) presenting your positions, feelings, and perspectives using "I" statements, examples to support your statements, and graphics when appropriate; (d) using paraphrasing to check to make sure that you understand the comments of others; (e) understanding culturally based differences in verbal and nonverbal communication; (f) respecting the confidentiality of others; (g) disagreeing respectfully; and (h) being willing to compromise (Cancio & Conderman, 2008).

Use Person-/Student-Centered Planning

Effective teams use *person-/student-centered planning* to guide the delivery of services to students and their families (Bambara, Browder, & Koger, 2006; Dettmer et al., 2009). Person-/student-centered planning recognizes the importance of the roles that students and their families play as advocates in identifying meaningful goals and appropriate strategies and services for meeting them. It employs a variety of assessment procedures to identify the strengths, preferences, personal characteristics, cultural, linguistic, and experiential backgrounds and challenges of students and their families. These variables are then examined to develop a comprehensive and holistic plan to coordinate the students' inclusion programs.

Map Action Planning System   One person-centered planning strategy that many teams use is the **Map Action Planning System (MAPS)** (Sheehey et al., 2009). MAPS also can be used to help the team develop IEPs. In MAPS, team members, including students with disabilities, their families, and peers, meet to develop an inclusion plan by first answering the following questions:

- *What is a map?* This question allows participants to think about the characteristics of a map.
- *What is [the student's name] history?* This question helps the team understand the events that have shaped the student's life and family.

Go to the Assignments and Activities section of the Topic *Collaboration, Consultation, and Co-Teaching* in the MyEducationLab for your course and complete the activity entitled *Related Service Providers*. As you watch the video and answer the accompanying questions, consider the full team approach to inclusive teaching.

REFLECTIVE

How would you describe your communication style? What communication skills do you use that support the success of teams? What communication skills would you like to improve?

- *What is your (our) dream for [the student's name]?* This question allows team members to share their visions and goals for the student's future.

- *What is your (our) nightmare?* This question helps the team understand the student's and family's fears.

- *Who is [the student's name]?* This question gives all team members the opportunity to describe their perceptions of the student.

- *What are [the student's name] strengths, gifts, and talents?* This question helps the team focus on and identify the student's positive attributes.

- *What are [the student's name] challenges? What can we do to meet these challenges?* These questions help the team define the student's challenges in a variety of areas.

- *What would be an ideal day for [the student's name]? What do we need to do to make this ideal real?* These questions help the team plan the student's program by listing the goals and activities for the student, services and accommodations needed to achieve the goals and foster participation in these activities, and individuals responsible for delivering the services and accommodations.

Work in Co-Teaching Arrangements

Many school districts are using **co-teaching**, also called *cooperative* or *collaborative teaching*, whereby teachers like Ms. Carr and Stevens work together to educate *all students* in inclusive classrooms (Friend & Cook, 2010; Stang & Lyons, 2008). Teachers involved in co-teaching share responsibility and accountability for planning and delivering instruction, evaluating, grading, and disciplining students (Villa et al., 2008). Students are not removed from the classroom for supportive services. Instead, academic instruction and supportive services are provided where the need exists: in the general education classroom (Hines, 2008).

Co-teaching teams can use many different instructional arrangements based on the purpose of the lesson, the nature of the material covered, and the needs of students (Stivers, 2008; Villa et al., 2008). Examples of these instructional arrangements are described here and in Figure 4.3.

- **One teaching/one helping**: One teacher instructs the whole class while the other teacher circulates to collect information on students' performance or to offer help to students (see Figure 4.3a). This arrangement is also used to take advantage of the expertise of one teacher in a specific subject area, and allow the other teacher to monitor and assist students.

- **Parallel teaching**: When it is necessary to lower the student–teacher ratio to teach new material, to review and practice material previously taught, or to encourage student discussions and participation, both teachers can teach the same material at the same time to two equal groups of students (see Figure 4.3b).

- **Station teaching**: When teaching material that is difficult but not sequential, when several different topics are important or when reviewing material is an important objective of the lesson, both teachers can teach different or review content at the same time to two equal groups of students, and then switch groups and repeat the lesson (see Figure 4.3c).

- **Alternative teaching**: When teachers need to individualize instruction, remediate skills, promote mastery, or offer enrichment based on students' needs, one teacher can work with a smaller group or individual students while the other teacher works with a larger group (see Figure 4.3d).

- **Team teaching**: When it is important to blend the talents and expertise of teachers or to foster interactions with students, both teachers can plan and teach a lesson together (see Figure 4.3e).

Co-teaching is designed to minimize some of the problems of pull-out programs, such as students missing academic instruction, insufficient communication

PEARSON
myeducationlab

Go to the Assignments and Activities section of the Topic *Collaboration, Consultation, and Co-Teaching* in the MyEducationLab for your course and complete the activity entitled *Teacher Collaboration*. As you watch the video and complete the accompanying questions, consider the different types of co-teaching arrangements and their affect on inclusive classroom teaching.

FIGURE 4.3 Cooperative teaching arrangements

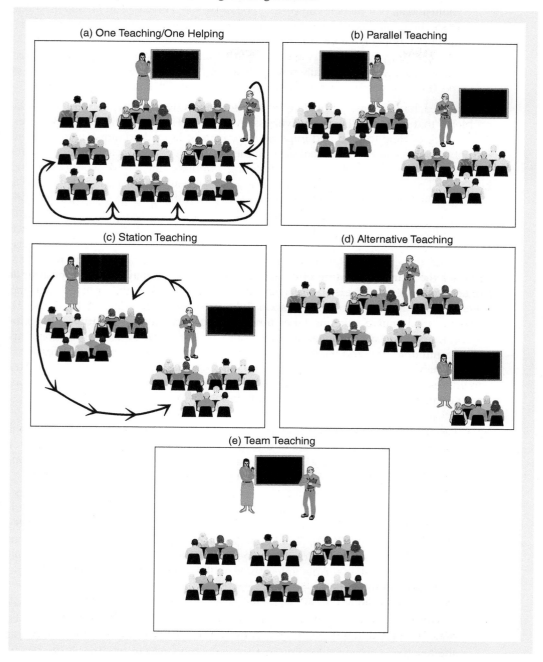

and coordination between professionals, scheduling problems, and fragmentation of the curriculum. It also allows supportive services and modified teaching for students with academic and behavioral difficulties without labeling them. In addition to helping students with disabilities, co-teaching gives *all students* the assistance and expertise of at least two professionals rather than just one (Hang & Rabren, 2009; Tannock, 2009). Teachers working in cooperative teams also note that these programs help make teaching more enjoyable and stimulating, give them new insights and experiences regarding teaching strategies, and prevent the isolation that sometimes occurs when teachers work alone (Kamens, 2007; Nevin et al., 2008).

At first, I was nervous, because you're not used to having another teacher in the classroom and all of a sudden you've got another person. I'm like, "Am I doing this right? Does she think this is okay?" Even though I knew her and I really liked her personally, I still thought, "What if she doesn't like my style of teaching? What if she thinks I'm lazy? What if she doesn't like this or that?" That sounds terrible, but the most difficult adjustment wasn't really pointed towards the kids, it was what she thought of me. (From a member of a co-teaching team) (Phillips et al., 1995, pp. 266–267)

Co-teaching teams, particularly at the secondary level, may encounter several problems that can limit their effectiveness (Alvarez McHatton & Daniel, 2008; Hines, 2008). Lack of time to plan and implement programs, limited administrative support, lack of resources and professional development, unclear roles of teaching team members, resistance from colleagues, scheduling conflicts, increased workloads, and heightened responsibilities are major obstacles to successful co-teaching (Murawski & Dieker, 2008; Scruggs et al., 2007). Teachers also report that they need to learn to work and teach together so that both members of the team assume responsibility for *all students* and perform relevant and meaningful tasks that promote student learning (Rice et al., 2007; Tannock, 2009). For instance, if one teacher is always the instructional leader and the other teacher is relegated to the role of assistant or aide for a few students, the team may not be effective. This lack of parity may particularly occur at the secondary level, where the general educator is trained in the content area and therefore may assume the major responsibilities for teaching (Harbort et al., 2007). Effective collaborative teaching takes time and requires teachers to deal with philosophical, pedagogical, historical, logistical, and territorial issues, as well as concerns about communicating and working with and being observed by another professional (Conderman, Johnston-Rodriguez, & Hartman, 2009; Murawski & Dieker, 2008). You can address these issues and work toward establishing compatibility, communication, and an equal status relationship by considering the following:

- Discuss why you want to work together, and agree on the goals you have for your classroom. It is also important to establish a common vision and ground rules for your collaboration and discuss what you expect of each other, as well as your concerns and fears about working cooperatively (Tannock, 2009; Villa et al., 2008).

- Learn about each other's abilities, beliefs, routines, teaching and communication styles, classroom management, family involvement approaches, and grading and assessment strategies (Howard & Potts, 2009; Murawski & Dieker, 2008). Conderman et al. (2009), Villa et al. (2008), and Keefe et al. (2004) present forms, surveys, and questions that co-teaching teams can use to become familiar with each other's skills, interests, teaching and communication styles, and educational philosophies.

- Understand and coordinate each other's responsibilities and areas of expertise, as well as the roles of others (Conderman et al., 2009; Linz, Heater, & Howard, 2009; Murawski & Dieker, 2008). Lodato Wilson (2008) outlines the roles that the teacher who is not leading instruction can engage in to support the teaching and learning processes.

- Consider using a variety of scheduling arrangements to coordinate the scheduling needs of teachers and students (Friend & Cook, 2010).

- Be sensitive to cross-cultural perspectives and interactions. Understand and accept multiple perspectives, and work toward accepting and responding appropriately to each other's cultural beliefs and communication styles (Taylor & Whittaker, 2009; Villa et al., 2008).

- Arrange the classroom to support collaboration. Agree on the placement of your work areas, students, and materials, and the scheduling of routines and activities (Stivers, 2008). Make sure both teacher's desks are adult-size and in prominent locations in the room, and that both of you share materials and classroom spaces and have easy access to them. Also, use a flexible layout so that your classroom can be easily adapted to the different types of collaborative teaching arrangements used.

- Establish and agree on a common set of expectations for judging and grading students' academic, behavioral, and social performance (Howard & Potts, 2009; Stivers, 2008).

- Develop communication, problem-solving, and team-building skills (Linz et al., 2009; Murawski & Dieker, 2008). Work toward honestly, respectfully, and reflectively talking to and listening to others, expressing opinions without taking a value position, and understanding each other's verbal and nonverbal communication styles (Conderman et al., 2009; Council for Exceptional Children, 2008; Tannock, 2009). Hoerr (2009) suggests that co-teaching relationships can be enhanced by striving to use *the rule of six*, which means trying to give the other person a minimum of six positive comments for each negative comment. It is also important to use self-disclosure and perspective taking, to think and communicate in terms of "we" and "our" rather than "I" and "my," and to make decisions by consensus. Consider establishing nonverbal cues to communicate such as hand signals to indicate that a break or communication is needed (Conderman et al., 2009).

- Understand that co-teaching is a developmental process, and be prepared to encounter problems at first (Cramer & Stivers, 2007; Villa et al., 2008). Successful co-teaching goes through stages and therefore involves taking time to adjust to working with another person to resolve logistical and territorial issues, to determine roles and responsibilities, and to blend skills (Dettmer et al., 2009; Murawski & Dieker, 2008).

- Share the workload and instructional materials, vary responsibilities, and don't relegate one person to a lesser role (Linz et al., 2009; Murawski & Dieker, 2008). Make sure that the contributions of all team members are recognized and valued by students, students' families, and other professionals (Stivers, 2008). For instance, place both teachers' names in prominent locations in the classroom, on communications with others, and on all teaching materials and official documents (e.g., report cards, class rosters, IEPs, etc.). At the secondary level, special education co-teachers can become members of the content area departments (Simmons & Magiera, 2007).

- Vary the arrangements used to teach students based on the purpose of the lesson, the nature of the content covered, and the strengths and challenges of students (Linz, Heater, & Howard, 2009; Sayeski, 2009). Use a range of activities that allows both team members to take a leadership role and to feel comfortable. A template to guide the planning and evaluation of co-teaching lessons is presented in Figure 4.4.

- As we saw in the chapter-opening vignette, meet periodically with families to explain the program and to share information on students' progress. It is important that both teachers attend all meetings with families and present information about their program (Howard & Potts, 2009).

- Communicate regularly to reevaluate short- and long-term goals, solve problems, plan instruction, divide responsibilities, share instructional roles and administrative tasks, brainstorm new ideas and approaches, and talk about students' progress (Conderman et al., 2009; Linz et al., 2009; Murawski & Dieker, 2008; Rice et al., 2007). In addition to addressing problems, remember to also discuss the things that are working. Howard and Potts (2009) provide a sample agenda of a co-planning meeting.

- Seek support and feedback from families and other professionals. Observe other co-teaching teams, and meet with them to discuss effective strategies and ways to improve your co-teaching (Simmons & Magiera, 2007). Solicit the support of your administrators, who can be instrumental in providing the time, professional development opportunities, and resources to facilitate the success of your

FIGURE 4.4 Cooperative teaching lesson planning template

What are our objectives, and how are they linked to our learning standards?	What individualized objectives do we have for our students with special needs?	What instructional and assessment accommodations will we use?	What co-teaching arrangements will we use?	What roles will we perform?	How can we establish an equal-status relationship?	What materials and technology will we use?	How will we arrange the classroom to support our collaboration and student learning?	How will we assess student learning and our success at working collaboratively?
Objectives Learning Standards 1. 2. 3.	Individualized Academic Objectives 1. 2. Individualized Behavior Objectives 1. 2. Individualized Social Objectives 1. 2. Other Individualized Objectives 1. 2.	Instructional Accommodations 1. 2. 3. Assessment Accommodations 1. 2. 3. Other Accommodations 1. 2. 3.	☐ One teaching/one helping ☐ Parallel teaching ☐ Station teaching ☐ Alternative teaching ☐ Team teaching	Teacher A 1. 2. Teacher B 1. 2. Paraeducator 1. 2. Other Professionals 1. 2.	1. 2. 3. 4. 5.	Materials 1. 2. 3. Technology 1. 2. 3.	1. 2. 3. 4. 5.	Assessment of student learning during the lesson 1. Assessment of student learning at the end of the lesson 1. Ways we collaborated successfully 1. Ways we can improve our collaboration 1.

Sources: Magiera & Simmons (2007); Vaughn, Schumm, & Arguelles (1997); Villa et al. (2008).

collaborative efforts (Friend & Cook, 2010; Simmons & Magiera, 2007). Linz et al. (2009), Villa et al. (2008), and Hines (2008) provide ways administrators can foster collaborative teaching arrangements and how you can encourage your administrators to support and become engaged in your co-teaching inclusive classroom.

- Address philosophical, pedagogical, logistical, and interpersonal conflicts directly and immediately (Conderman et al., 2009; Hines, 2008). Be aware of the signs of these conflicts, such as team members (a) speaking and contributing less during conversations, (b) avoiding certain topics, (c) discussing problems with others outside the collaborative classroom, and (d) failing to complete agreed-on activities (Council for Exceptional Children, 2008). Don't let conflicts escalate; resolve them by listening to each other without blame, trying to understand the other person's perspective, discussing the situation and possible solutions from your perspective, identifying the sources of the problem, examining existing roles and responsibilities, negotiating, compromising, problem solving and taking actions to address the difficulties, and scheduling future meetings to evaluate success and plan additional activities (Bradley & Monda-Amaya, 2005; Conderman et al., 2009).

A challenge for many co-teaching teams is to establish an equal status relationship. How can co-teaching teams make sure both teachers perform meaningful roles that facilitate student learning?

- Use a range of strategies to assess the impact of the program on *all students and teachers*, and revise the program based on these data (Conderman et al., 2009; Linz et al., 2009; Murawski & Dieker, 2008; Rice et al., 2007).

- Engage in self-evaluation and reflection to examine the team's success and the ways the team can improve (Linz et al., 2009; Tannock, 2009). Continually examine shared values and goals, as well as concerns, problems, misunderstandings, expectations, and plans for the future (Conderman et al., 2009; Murawski & Dieker, 2008; Villa et al., 2008). Interviews (see Figure 4.5) and surveys (see Figure 4.6) can be used to help you reflect on aspects of your co-teaching team. Other formats for examining a team's collaboration are available (Simmons & Magiera, 2007; Villa et al., 2008; Wiggins & Damore, 2006; Wilson, 2005).

- Acknowledge, celebrate, and share your success. Enjoy, share, attribute, and reflect on your accomplishments as a team, and share them with others (Magiera, Simmons, & Crandall, 2005; Murawski & Dieker, 2008).

Employ Collaborative Consultation/Problem Solving

Teachers may also use **collaborative consultation**, sometimes referred to as *collaborative problem solving*, to facilitate the success of their inclusion programs (Dettmer et al., 2009; Santangelo, 2009). This involves working together to problem solve and implement mutually agreed-on solutions to prevent and address learning and behavioral difficulties and to coordinate instructional programs for *all students*. Collaborative consultation is designed to address students' strengths and challenges and to give general education teachers improved knowledge and skills to deal with similar situations in the future (Bahr & Kovaleski, 2006).

The "consultant," usually a special, bilingual, or multicultural educator or an ancillary staff member (a school psychologist, speech/language therapist, or physical therapist), works collaboratively with the general education teacher, who has primary responsibility (Paulsen, 2008). Figure 4.7, a diary of the experiences of a collaborative consultation teacher, presents some of the services provided.

REFLECTIVE

Think about a situation in which you worked collaboratively with a team. How was the outcome affected by the collaboration? What problems and successes did the team have in working collaboratively? How did the team resolve the problems?

REFLECTING ON PROFESSIONAL PRACTICES

Working as a Co-teaching Team

Ms. Cathy Carr and Ms. Sarah Stevens remembered their first year working together as a co-teaching team. Although they had worked together before to reintegrate students with disabilities into Cathy's general education classroom for specific subject areas and activities, they were both anxious and excited about working as a co-teaching team. Initially, they had experienced some difficulties. Sarah felt out of place in Cathy's classroom. She was frustrated because she didn't know where the supplies and materials were located and frequently had to ask Cathy. She also worried that Cathy would have all the responsibilities and be the "real" teacher and that she would function as a teacher's aide.

Cathy sensed Sarah's concern and was also worried about their differences in terms of roles, teaching style, and philosophy. Sometimes she wondered whether Sarah thought she was too controlling and disapproved of her concern about getting students ready for the statewide tests. Both Cathy and Sarah were also concerned that the students and their families viewed one of them as the teacher and the other one as a teacher's assistant.

At first, Sarah and Cathy had some difficulty determining their responsibilities and blending their skills. They struggled as they attempted to teach lessons together and coordinate their instructional activities. Sometimes, while Cathy led a lesson, Sarah seemed lost and felt like a helper rather than a teacher. They also had different opinions about the abilities of the students with disabilities. Sarah worried that "her" students would not be able to keep up with Cathy's plans for all the students, and that they were not receiving the services they needed. At the first family meeting, their roles were clearly delineated, with Sarah speaking to the classified students' families separately. They quickly realized that this was a mistake and were determined to work on blending their skills.

As they worked together, they began to notice and respect each other's skills, perspectives, experiences, and areas of expertise. Cathy was impressed with Sarah's effectiveness in dealing with behavior problems, and Sarah was excited about the way Cathy made instructional activities come alive. They both wanted to learn from each other. They also started to improve in planning and teaching lessons together and performing administrative tasks. In teaching together, they began to anticipate each other's styles. Their principal observed them teaching a lesson and noticed that they were starting to teach together in a natural way even though their perspectives were different. When they completed the students' report cards together, they were amazed at how close they were in assessing students' needs and progress.

As they got to know each other, Cathy and Sarah began to experiment with new teaching methods, and both seemed to have a renewed enjoyment of teaching. They used role plays, puppets, and sometimes spontaneously acted out stories and lessons. Both teachers were surprised by how much more fun they and their students were having in class.

Although things were going well, Cathy and Sarah's concerns about teaming and their philosophical differences surfaced periodically. Sarah, who was trained in a skills-based approach, was concerned that Cathy's approach was not effective with some of the students. Sarah discussed this with Cathy, who was very understanding, and they decided to do skills work, too.

Their commitment to teaming was sustained by the positive changes they saw in their students. Sarah and Cathy were pleased that all the students had progressed developmentally, academically, and socially. They were particularly surprised and motivated by the influence of their collaboration on the sense of community in the classroom, which was seen in the students' unusual sensitivity to their peers.

Cathy and Sarah also were pleased with the support they received from their principal. The principal met periodically with them to discuss problems and solutions; to acknowledge their efforts and growth; and to offer assistance, support, and resources. The principal also rearranged their schedules to give them planning time together and encouraged them to visit schools with model programs.

Looking back on their experiences as a co-teaching team, Sarah and Cathy agreed that it was a successful year. Sarah noted, "What an incredible year! After so many years as a special education teacher, it was refreshing to interact with a greater variety of students. It was a great learning year for me. I don't think teachers know how enjoyable teaching can be when you share it." Cathy said, "This is the end of a wonderful year. The students and we as teachers became a close-knit community of learners. We all did learn and grow this year. It was like dancing with someone; sometimes you lead and sometimes you follow. We began with a lot of apprehension and ended with much enthusiasm."

- Why do you think Cathy and Sarah were initially both anxious and excited about working together as a co-teaching team?
- What problems and concerns did they have? How can these problems and concerns be addressed?
- How did working together benefit Cathy and Sarah and their students?
- What factors helped make this a successful school year?
- How would you feel if you were asked to be part of a co-teaching team?
- What resources, knowledge, skills, and dispositions do you need to teach effectively in a co-teaching team?

FIGURE 4.5 **Sample cooperative teaching interview**

- How is cooperative teaching working in your class?
- What components and practices of your cooperative teaching team appear to be effective?
- What difficulties have you encountered working as a cooperative teaching team?
- What do you enjoy the most about working in a cooperative teaching team?
- What are your biggest concerns about working in a cooperative teaching team?
- What support from others, resources, and training have you received to work successfully as a cooperative teaching team? What support from others, resources, and professional development have been most helpful? Least helpful? What additional support from others, resources, and training would be helpful?
- How has your cooperative teaching team affected the academic, social, and behavioral development of your students, and your interactions with their families? Describe the positive and negative outcomes you have observed in your students and their families.
- How do your students' families and other professionals feel about your cooperative teaching team?
- How has working in a cooperative teaching team affected you as a professional and a person? Describe the positive and negative effects for you.
- In what ways have your roles changed as a result of working in a cooperative teaching team? How do you feel about your new roles?
- How did the collaboration process change throughout the school year?
- What did you learn from working as a cooperative teaching team?
- How do you work through conflicts?
- What suggestions would you have for others interested in working in cooperative teaching teams?
- What schoolwide and districtwide practices have supported your efforts to work as a cooperative teaching team? Hindered your efforts? In what ways should these practices be revised?

Steps in Collaborative Consultation   The steps in effective collaborative consultation are (a) goal and problem clarification and identification, (b) goal and problem analysis, (c) plan implementation, and (d) plan evaluation (Dettmer et al., 2009; Santangelo, 2009).

Goal and Problem Clarification and Identification.   The first step in the consultation process is to identify goals and problems, using who, what, and where questions that help teachers clarify and agree on their goals and concerns. For example, consultation teams can address questions like these: What are the student's strengths and interests? What challenges does the student have in class? What goals do we have for the student? What can we do to address these challenges and help the student achieve our goals? Goals and problems also can be identified by examining students' IEPs and observing students in their classrooms.

Often it is best for the consultation to focus on one situation at a time. If several goals and problem areas must be handled simultaneously, it is advisable to set priorities and deal with the most important ones first. A consultation assistance request form that can be used to identify goals and problems is presented in Figure 4.8.

Goal and Problem Analysis.   In the second phase of the consultation process, educators analyze the features that appear to be related to the identified goals and problems. These may include the curriculum, the physical environment of the room, teaching strategies, grouping arrangements, teaching and learning styles, peer relationships, student ability levels, family, and the school's policies and procedures. This analysis helps educators plan appropriate intervention strategies.

FIGURE 4.6 Sample cooperative teaching survey

Directions: Please indicate your feeling about the following statements using this scale:

Strongly Disagree (1)	Disagree (2)	Neutral (3)	Agree (4)	Strongly Agree (5)

1. I like working in a cooperative teaching team.   1 2 3 4 5
2. Students benefit from being taught by a cooperative teaching team.   1 2 3 4 5
3. I feel like this is our classroom.   1 2 3 4 5
4. Students with disabilities receive fewer specialized services as a result of cooperative teaching.   1 2 3 4 5
5. My students' families are satisfied with our cooperative teaching arrangement.   1 2 3 4 5
6. Other professionals are supportive of our cooperative teaching arrangement.   1 2 3 4 5
7. Our cooperative teaching team has sufficient time to communicate effectively.   1 2 3 4 5
8. Our cooperative teaching team shares responsibility for all instructional and noninstructional activities.   1 2 3 4 5
9. Our cooperative teaching team blends the teaching styles, philosophies, talents, and expertise of both teachers.   1 2 3 4 5
10. Working in a cooperative teaching team has encouraged me to try new instructional strategies.   1 2 3 4 5
11. Our school district provides the necessary support from others, resources, and professional development to implement cooperative teaching effectively.   1 2 3 4 5
12. I enjoy teaching more because I work in a cooperative teaching team.   1 2 3 4 5
13. I like having another adult in the classroom.   1 2 3 4 5
14. It is easy to communicate with my cooperative teaching partner.   1 2 3 4 5
15. I perform a subordinate role in our cooperative teaching team.   1 2 3 4 5
16. I have benefited professionally and personally from working as a cooperative teaching team.   1 2 3 4 5
17. My workload has increased as a result of working in a cooperative teaching team.   1 2 3 4 5
18. I am satisfied with the schoolwide and districtwide policies regarding cooperative teaching teams.   1 2 3 4 5
19. I would like to continue to work in a cooperative teaching team.   1 2 3 4 5

Plan Implementation. During this phase, educators plan which interventions to use to address the identified goals and difficulties. They brainstorm and share their expertise, considering factors such as practicality, effectiveness, resources needed, and effects on others. Once the preferred interventions have been selected, they can be outlined in detail, and responsibilities and time lines can be determined.

Plan Evaluation. Once the intervention has been implemented, its effectiveness should be checked periodically. This can be done by direct observation, curriculum-based assessments, analysis of student work samples, and other techniques that assess student progress.

Follow-up evaluation can also examine how the intervention has been implemented, whether it needs to be revised, and what additional problem areas need to be solved. Feedback should be an ongoing, interactive process focused on the intervention plan rather than on the individuals involved.

Even though consultation is effective, professionals may resist its use. This attitude is often associated with frustration, professional pride, and different views of the process. Other major barriers include insufficient time for team members to

FIGURE 4.7 Diary of a collaborative consultation teacher

September 7: *I can only be in one place at a time! Juggling teacher schedules and getting to students for assistance in their academic areas of need will be a feat worthy of a gold medal. And on top of that, time has to be set aside to conference with classroom teachers. I'm frustrated!!*

September 8: *I've worried about how junior high students would accept my presence in the classroom. . . . I discussed this with Mr. T, the building principal. During the grade level orientations, Mr. T introduced me as a teacher who would be in several different classes to assist students.*

September 13: *I did it! Schedules typed, all academic areas covered. I even managed to schedule time to conference with teachers (and it's not during lunch!). Mrs. C is not too keen on meeting with me on a regular basis and voiced a great concern about how much work this would add to her already overloaded schedule. Copies of all schedules have been sent to teachers, administrators, and parents. I have contacted every parent by phone and explained the service.*

September 14: *Mrs. M came to see me. She blurted out to me that she didn't know if she could go through with having me work in her room. She indicated to me that she felt extremely intimidated and was worried about what I would think. My first reaction was, "Don't be silly." Thank goodness I didn't say that. It really wasn't silly, because, I, too, was very nervous. I told Mrs. M that I understood what she meant, and explained my own nervousness.*

September 18: *A pleasant surprise. Mr. K introduced me as a co-teacher. He told his students that if they had any questions they could ask either himself or me. . . . I was wondering exactly how this would work out, when several different students raised their hands for assistance. In the end, I put together a small group of children to work with at the back table. How nice to see that the students I expected to work with, along with other students, accepted my presence and wanted my help.*

September 20: *I met with Mrs. E today. Together we worked on J's IEP, reviewed her entire curriculum, and decided on goals which should be included. It was wonderful having her input.*

October 12: *Mrs. C asked me if I would be willing to take a group of students for the social studies lesson and work on latitude and longitude. . . . We discussed the format and objectives of the lesson. During the class, we divided the room into groups and each taught a group. After the lesson, we were able to meet and discuss the results.*

November 16: *Ms. D, a first grade teacher, approached me and asked if I could speak with her about one of her students. I do not have a student in her room. We met after school and discussed the difficulties this child was having. Ms. D then asked if I would sit in on a parent conference. I guess there is a lot more to this job than just working with my assigned students.*

November 20: *Today's consultation with Mrs. K centered on getting her feedback on a study guide I created. We went over all the points, and at the end of the conversation she asked me if I would mind if she duplicated the guide and gave it to all her students.*

December 5: *Mrs. M indicated that the whole class was having difficulty getting the concept of contractions. We discussed some strategies, and she asked if I would like to teach the lesson the following morning. At the end of the consultation session, she turned to me and said, "You know, I am still a little nervous, but I really do like this collaborative consultation."*

Source: From "Diary of a Consulting Teacher," by K. Giek, 1990, *The Forum, 16*(1), pp 5–6. Copyright 1990 by New York State Federation of Chapters of the Council for Exceptional Children. Reprinted by permission.

meet and overwhelming caseloads. Successful consultation programs have administrative support and adequate resources so the classroom teachers and support staff have time to consult with one another, and offer educators reasonable caseloads and schedules (Santangelo, 2009; Villa et al., 2008).

FIGURE 4.8 Consultation assistance request form

ASSISTANCE NEEDED

Teacher _____   Today's Date

Student _____   _____

Other _____

☐ There's a problem. Let's put our heads together.
☐ I need your help in the classroom.
☐ Develop alternative assignment or activity.
☐ Arrange cooperative learning groups & activities.
☐ Implement peer tutoring or peer partners.
☐ Produce alternative materials or locate resources.
☐ Develop a modified grading system.
☐ Create a study guide.   ☐ Plan a lesson.
☐ Modify materials.   ☐ Team teaching.
☐ Modify a test.   ☐ Classroom management.
☐ Develop guided notes.   ☐ Instructional strategies.

When? _____

Additional information:

_____
_____
_____
_____

Source: From "Collaborative Teaching in the Secondary School," by E. A. Knackendoffel, 1996, in D. D. Deshler, E. S. Ellis, & B. K. Lenz (Eds.), *Teaching Adolescents with Learning Disabilities* (2nd ed.), p. 585. Copyright 1996 by Love. Reprinted with permission.

Promote Congruence

Successful collaboration and communication requires **congruence**, a logical relationship among the curriculum, learning goals, teaching materials, strategies used in the general education classroom, and supportive services programs. A congruent program is one based on common assessment results, goals and objectives, teaching strategies, and materials.

Ideally, supplemental and remedial teaching should parallel the general education curriculum. Unfortunately, many of these programs are fragmented, based on different—and conflicting—curricula and teaching approaches. These incompatible and conflicting programs can confuse students rather than help them learn. For instance, confusion can occur when you and your school's literacy educator use different approaches to teach reading.

You can use two models for coordinating teaching so that the ancillary program supplements learning in the general education classroom: an a priori model and a post hoc model. In the **a priori model**, supportive services educators teach new content that supports the content to be learned in the general education classroom. This instruction lays the foundation for instruction in the general education classroom. For example, the ESL educator might introduce on Monday the spelling words that will be introduced on Friday in the general education classroom.

In the **post hoc model**, supportive instruction reinforces skills previously introduced in the general education classroom. Thus, rather than introducing new content, the supportive services educator reviews and reteaches content previously covered in the general education classroom. For example, while a student is learning how to add fractions in the general education classroom, the resource teacher helps the student understand the process and develop automatic methods of responding to similar items.

Meetings   Meetings such as IEP conferences also can be used to establish congruence by involving general and supportive services educators in planning and implementing teaching programs. They can agree on common objectives, teaching methods and materials, lesson plans, and evaluation procedures to assess student learning. As students master the objectives, additional meetings can be held to revise the instructional program and evaluate congruence. Meetings also can promote congruence by having teachers share lesson plans.

Student-Led Conferences and Interviews   You also can use student-led conferences and interviews to ensure and evaluate congruence (Cullotta, 2008). Specifically, students can lead conferences or complete interviews addressing, "What things are you learning in (class)?" "What type of activities do you do in (class)?" "What materials do you use in (class)?" "Does (class) help you in other classes?" and "What strategies help you learn?"

Note Card Systems   Congruence and communication between professionals can be fostered by the use of a note card system. Each professional working with the student completes a note card or technology-based file that serves as an ongoing record of the student's performance in that class for a specified period of time. The information on the card could include a rating of the student's progress, a list of the skills mastered and not mastered, upcoming assignments and tests, successful strategies, teaching materials being used, and skills other teachers can attempt to foster. One educator can be asked to categorize the information and share it with others to ensure the continuity of instruction.

Engage in Professional Development

Your ability to collaborate and communicate with others and create inclusive classrooms also can be enhanced by engaging in professional development activities to improve your teaching (Leko & Brownell, 2009). These professional development activities include attending workshops, faculty meetings, and professional conferences, reading journal articles and books, viewing Web sites and videos, joining professional organizations and learning groups, and taking classes. For example, many teachers work in collaborative learning and teaching groups to experiment and reflect on teaching strategies and programs designed to enhance student learning and inclusion (Darling-Hammond & Richardson, 2009; Herner-Patnode, 2009).

One form of professional development that is particularly helpful for beginning teachers is **teacher mentoring** (Bay & Parker-Katz, 2009; McCabe, 2008). Mentoring programs involve frequent collaborative interactions between experienced, effective teachers and new teachers to address the challenges that new teachers encounter. Mentoring dyads observe each other's classrooms, discuss their teaching, assessment, and classroom management practices, curricula, and instructional materials, and develop plans to facilitate the teaching, learning, and collaboration process. Mentors also provide information related to the field and the school district, as well as emotional support. In addition to helping mentees adjust to the profession and their jobs, mentoring programs also benefit mentors.

IDEAs to Implement Inclusion

Facing the Challenges of Being a Beginning Teacher

Ms. Salinas had always wanted to be a teacher and was looking forward to her first teaching position in an inclusion program. Before the school year began, she went into her classroom to get it ready and worked on reviewing student records, preparing lessons, and creating a newsletter for families. When school began, she was confident that she could apply what she had learned in her teacher education program. Although things got off to a good start, Ms. Salinas started feeling stressed out. Even though she arrived early and stayed late, she found herself overwhelmed by the paperwork and her unfamiliarity with the district policies. When some lessons didn't go as planned, and when she had conflicts with one of the paraeducators and a family member, Ms. Salinas started questioning her decision to be a teacher. Sensing Ms. Salinas's frustration, her principal spoke to her about being mentored by Mr. O'Connor, an experienced teacher with an excellent reputation in the school district. Ms. Salinas was reluctant, but her principal explained that what she was experiencing was typical and that mentoring is provided to all beginning teachers.

A week later Ms. Salinas and Mr. O'Connor met after school. They talked about the challenges facing a beginning teacher, and Mr. O'Connor shared some of his first-year teaching experiences, which were very similar to what Ms. Salinas was experiencing. He also told her that he wished he had the help of someone when he started teaching and that she should try not to be too hard on herself.

They made a plan to observe each other's classrooms so that they could both learn from one another. After Mr. O'Connor's first observation, he told her that she was doing fine and made some suggestions about teaching strategies she might want to try, which he modeled for her when she came to see his classroom. They also spent time talking about the district's policies, inclusion programs, the curriculum and discipline, and how to handle conflicts with other professionals and family members. Mr. O'Connor liked being helpful to Ms. Salinas, and he also learned some things from her. Ms. Salinas appreciated the support and felt better about her decision to be a teacher.

Here are some other strategies you can use to implement the IDEA in your inclusive classroom and face the challenges of being a beginning teacher:

- Recognize that teaching is a difficult and challenging job, and give yourself permission to experiment and learn from your experiences.
- Take care of your emotional and physical health. Remember your personal and family needs. Find time to socialize with friends, family, and colleagues, to do things you like to do, and to keep your life as balanced as possible.
- Learn organizational and time management strategies that help make you more effective and efficient.
- Get to know the other professionals (e.g., other teachers and service providers, paraeducators, school secretaries, janitors, cafeteria workers, and administrators) in your school and school district, and establish a good working relationship with them. Ask them about schoolwide policies and procedures, and about ways to help you and your students and their families.
- Reflect on your teaching practices. For example, maintain a journal where you reflect on your experiences as a teacher and the outcomes of your actions in specific situations.
- Take advantage of whatever professional development activities you can fit into your schedule.
- Use materials and resources (e.g., lesson plans, assessment activities, classroom management plans) that you developed or acquired as part of your participation in your teacher education program.
- Work in teacher learning cohort groups with other teachers and university professionals to establish a collaborative resource network.
- Keep in touch with your former classmates and even your professors. Use them as a resource and as a sounding board.

Sources: Bay & Parker-Katz, 2009; Cancio & Conderman, 2008; Cramer & Stivers, 2007; Nieto, 2009.

COMMUNICATION AND COLLABORATION WITH FAMILIES

HOW CAN I FOSTER COMMUNICATION AND COLLABORATION WITH FAMILIES?
As Ms. Carr and Ms. Stevens recognized in the chapter-opening vignette, a key component of effective inclusion programs is communication and collaboration with the student's family. As well as being educationally sound and in accord with the IDEA, involving family members in the education of their children can help you build support for your inclusion program (Yssel et al., 2007). You can view them as a valuable resource and partner in the educational process by (a) using a variety of ways to share information with them about your inclusion program; (b) engaging families in curriculum planning; (c) holding meetings with them to develop students' IEPs; (d) inviting them to volunteer and attend school and classroom events; (e) providing them with information and resources so that they can help their children learn and complete their

REFLECTIVE

Research indicates that family involvement in school declines significantly as students age. Why do you think this is the case? What could you and schools do to counter this pattern?

homework; and (f) soliciting information from them about their children's strengths, challenges, and progress (Floyd & Vernon-Dotson, 2008; Van Haren & Fieldler, 2008).

Gain the Trust of Families

Family involvement and empowerment are based largely on the trust established between families and educators (Angell, Stoner, & Shelden, 2009; Sebald & Luckner, 2007). If families and school personnel distrust or feel uncomfortable with each other, the family's involvement and therefore the student's performance may be harmed. You can involve and empower families by working with them using methods that are based on collaboration, empathy, understanding, honesty, and respect and that recognize the strengths of each family (Angell et al., 2009; Van Haren & Fieldler, 2008). Trust can be established when schools serve as a resource for families and collaborate with them to offer and coordinate a broad range of flexible, usable, and understandable services that support the many changing needs of families (Angell et al., 2009). You also can gain the trust of your students' families by interacting with them in many settings and by attending after-school activities and community events.

Robin L. Sachs/PhotoEdit Inc.

Family involvement and empowerment can be fostered by establishing trust between families and educators. How do you promote mutual trust with and gain the respect of your students' families?

When the experiences and expertise of family and community members are incorporated into school programs, the result is mutual respect and trust among schools, families, and the community (Checkley, 2008). Students see their families and community actively engaged in schools and classrooms. In the process, families and the community become empowered, positive partners in the educational process. Families and community members can be part of an ongoing program that allows them to share their experiences and knowledge in schools (Matuszny, Banda, & Coleman, 2007).

Learn about the strengths, experiences, cultures, communities, and attitudes of families and students, and then interact with them in ways that acknowledge their strengths and respect their values (Ramirez & Soto-Hinman, 2009; Rothstein-Fisch & Trumbull, 2008). For example, some families may have cultural beliefs that view the teacher as a highly respected person and that it is not their role to disagree with you, interfere in their children's education, or ask questions. Therefore, rather than viewing them as disinterested in their children's education, it is important for you to understand their positive beliefs about education and adjust your interactions with them accordingly (San Antonio, 2008).

In addition to understanding the cultural perspectives of your students' families, you can examine your own viewpoints, attitudes, and behaviors related to your cultural background and diversity (Nieto, 2009; Rothstein-Fisch & Trumbull, 2008). It is important to recognize how your cultural beliefs may be different from those of your students and their families and to interact with students and families in culturally sensitive ways (Dettmer et al., 2009; Harry et al., 2008). Ramirez and Soto-Hinman (2009), Rothstein-Fisch and Trumbull (2008), Richards, Brown, and Forde (2007), and Ginsberg (2007) present activities you can use to learn more about your students and their families and to increase your cultural awareness.

Advocate for Students and Their Families

You can gain the trust of families by advocating for them, their children, and your inclusive classroom, which is part of your professional responsibility (Mihalis et al., 2009; Stivers et al., 2008). In school, you can engage in advocacy informally via conversations with others and formally via your participation in comprehensive planning team meetings and other committees that influence decision making (Smith et al., 2006). You also can post articles or relevant materials in prominent locations in your school or community, and lead discussions about the issues discussed. Outside school, you can advocate by

- joining professional organizations, and other groups that offer support for advocacy efforts;
- contacting legislators and policymakers and writing letters to the editor regarding issues that affect your students and families and your profession;
- challenging myths and inaccurate and stereotypical statements made by others;
- making presentations to community groups and school boards;
- inviting community members and influential decision makers to visit your classroom and other effective programs in your school and community (Stivers et al., 2008).

You can enhance the success of your advocacy efforts by being aware of the law and related issues; developing your communication, collaboration, and conflict resolution skills; and helping students and their families learn to be effective advocates for themselves and all students (Checkley, 2008).

When advocating for students and families, you also need to be aware of the personal and professional risks. At times, your views on issues affecting your students and their families may put you in the difficult position of opposing your school district or others with whom you work. Thus, you need to comply with ethical standards for educators and be able to deal with indirect and direct pressure to conform with school district requests, and possible reprisals (Bucholz et al., 2007; Skinner et al., 2009).

Ensure Confidentiality

Ensuring students and families their right to *confidentiality*, which is specified in the Family Educational Rights and Privacy Act (FERPA) and the IDEA, is essential to establishing a trusting and collaborative relationship with families and students (Devlin, 2008; Smith et al., 2006). Educators directly involved in teaching a student may have access to his or her records, but before a school district can allow other persons to review these records, it must obtain consent from the family.

Confidentiality also guarantees the family the opportunity to obtain, review, and challenge their child's educational records. The family can obtain their child's records by requesting a copy, which the school district must provide. However, the family may have to pay the expenses incurred in duplicating the records. If the family disagrees with these records, the family can challenge them by asking school officials to correct or delete the information or by writing a response to be included in the records.

In addition to addressing protecting records, confidentiality means that professionals should refrain from

- revealing personally identifying information about students (e.g., their disability or immigration status, medical conditions and needs, test scores, etc.) and families to others; and
- speaking about students in public ways and places (e.g., teacher's room, meetings with other families, college classes and in-service sessions, etc.) that allow specific students to be identified.

Meet Regularly with Families

We knew it would be another rough year. After only 2 months, Paul's new teacher, Mr. Rodl, called and said, "Paul is falling behind, and we need to do something." Mr. Rodl asked us to come to a meeting with a team of professionals to discuss Paul's progress. He said we could schedule the meeting at a time that was convenient for us.

REFLECTIVE

What are some issues for which you would advocate for students and families? How could you advocate for your students and their families? What factors would affect your ability to advocate for them?

REFLECTIVE

Given families' and students' right to confidentiality, what would you do in the following situations? Teachers are discussing students and their families during lunch in the teachers' lounge. You notice that the students' records in your school are kept in an unsupervised area.

Going into the meeting was scary. There sat Paul's teacher, the principal, the school psychologist, and several other people we didn't know. Mr. Rodl started the meeting by introducing us to the others in the room. Then he said, "Since I work closely with Paul, I'll lead the meeting and coordinate the decisions we'll make about Paul's program. We call that being the service coordinator."

He asked each person in the room to talk about Paul. As different people spoke, others asked questions. When several people used words we didn't understand, Mr. Rodl asked them to explain the words to us. When our turn came, Mr. Rodl asked us to talk about what was happening with Paul at home, what we thought was happening with him at school, and what we would like to see happen at school.

At first, we felt very nervous. As people in the room listened to and discussed our comments, we became more relaxed. The group discussed several ways to help Paul. In the end, we all came up with a plan to help Paul learn better. Mr. Rodl summarized the plan and the roles each person would play to make it successful. We also discussed how we would continue to communicate and collaborate to help Paul, and agreed to set up a home–school contract to share information about and support Paul's progress. We left the meeting feeling really good about being part of a team that was trying to help our son.

As this vignette of Paul's family suggests, you can foster collaboration and communication with families and increase their involvement in and commitment to your inclusive classroom by improving the quality of family–educators meetings (Dettmer et al., 2009; Mueller, 2009; Sheehey & Sheehey, 2007; Whitbread, Bruder, Fleming & Park, 2007). Many educators are encouraging students to attend and take an active role in these conferences (Cullotta, 2008; Konrad, 2008).

Plan the Meeting   Plan carefully for the meeting by identifying the reasons for the meeting and developing an appropriate agenda. The agenda should allow enough time to discuss and resolve issues and address concerns of families and other educators. These issues and concerns can be determined by contacting others *before* the meeting so that they understand what will be discussed at the meeting. Share the agenda with families and other participants, encourage them to bring useful records and materials to the meeting, and give them the necessary background information to take part in the meeting. Important documents and materials such as copies of legal rights, IEPs, work samples, test results, and other teachers' comments related to agenda items and student performance can be organized and sent to participants beforehand. Some families may appreciate it if you give them a list of questions or suggestions to help them participate in the meeting, and tell them which school personnel will also be there. For example, before the meeting, you can ask family members to be prepared to discuss their goals for their child's educational programs, their perceptions of their child's feelings about school, interests, hobbies, strengths and challenges, their suggestions for effective strategies, and any questions and concerns they have. You also may want to invite family members to observe in the classroom as a way to prepare for the meeting.

Good planning also ensures that the meeting time is convenient for families and professionals (Stoner et al., 2005). Families can be contacted early in their preferred method of communication (i.e., written communication, telephone, face-to-face meetings, e-mail) to determine what times and dates are best for them, to encourage them to invite persons who are important to them, and to determine whether they need help with transportation, child care, or other special needs or circumstances. Once the meeting has been scheduled, you can contact families and professionals in advance to give them the time, place, purpose, and duration of the meeting and to confirm that they will be there. Follow-up reminders to families via mail, e-mail, or telephone will make them more likely to attend.

Structure the Environment to Promote Communication   The setting for the conference can be organized for collaborating and sharing information (Mueller, 2009). Comfortable, same-size furniture can be arranged to promote communication among all participants. Barriers such as desks and chairs should not be placed between families and teachers. Chairs and tables can be positioned so that all persons can see each other.

Welcome family members and other participants, engage in pleasant, informal conversation before the meeting starts; and offer refreshments. This will help participants feel comfortable and establish rapport. To improve participation and follow-up, you can ask the participants if they would like pads and pencils to take notes, and give them name tags.

To make sure that the meeting is not interrupted, post a note on the door indicating that a conference is in session. Distractions caused by phones and cell phones should be minimized.

Conduct the Conference   As Mr. Rodl did in the vignette with Paul's family at the beginning of this section, you should conduct the conference in a positive way that encourages understanding, participation, and collaboration (Mueller, 2009; Sheehey & Sheehey, 2007). Welcome and introduce participants or ask them to introduce themselves, review the agenda and the purpose of the meeting, and establish ground rules (Whitbread et al., 2007). One ground rule that many groups find helpful is the use of a "parking lot" for comments and questions that are important but not related to the meeting's agenda. You can establish a parking lot by having a flip chart in the room and using it to list comments and questions that can be discussed later in the meeting or during a future meeting.

The meeting can start on a positive note, with participants discussing the strong points of the student's performance. Next, participants can review any concerns they have about the student. They should present information in a way that is understandable to all and share materials such as work samples, test results, and anecdotal records to support and illustrate their comments. Some professionals find it helpful to supplement their presentations by using video, PowerPoint, and the Internet to access and share information and easels or chalkboards to record ideas and highlight important points.

You can ask families to discuss the issues or situations from their perspective or to respond to open-ended questions. Family sharing at meetings can be increased by listening attentively; by being empathetic; by acknowledging and reinforcing participation ("That's a good point"; "I'll try to incorporate that"); by avoiding asking questions that have yes/no or implied answers; by asking questions that encourage family members to respond rather than waiting for them to ask questions or spontaneously speak their minds; by informing them that there may be several solutions to a problem; by not criticizing family members; by using language that is understandable but not condescending; by explaining unfamiliar terminology; by checking periodically for understanding; by paraphrasing and summarizing the comments of family members; by using humor; and by showing respect for cultural differences and families and their feelings (Montgomery, 2005). Interpreters and translators can be used to promote the understanding of families who have difficulties with spoken or written English.

You can adjust the structure of the meeting, depending on how the family prefers to communicate. For families that value personal relationships, you can sit close by, and use self-disclosure, humor, and casual conversation. Other families may be goal oriented and respond to professionals they perceive as competent and organized. These families may expect you to structure the meeting, set goals, define roles, and ask questions of family members.

End the meeting on a positive note by summarizing the issues discussed, points of agreement and disagreement, strategies to be used to resolve problems, and roles to be played by family members and educators. At the end of the meeting, participants can agree on a plan of action, establish ongoing communications systems, and set a date for the next meeting. It is also important to share with

FIGURE 4.9 Sample schedule for a family–educators conference

❑ Greet, welcome, and thank all participants.

❑ Ask participants to introduce themselves and briefly describe their roles and the services they provide.

❑ Review the meeting's agenda, purpose(s), and ground rules.

❑ Discuss relevant information from prior meetings.

❑ Start with positive aspects of the student's performance. Ask family members and then professionals to discuss their view of the student's strengths and challenges and the issues on the agenda. Educators should be encouraged to support their statements with examples, work samples, anecdotal records, and assessment results.

❑ Discuss the comments of family members and professionals attempting to achieve a consensus.

❑ Determine a plan of action.

❑ Summarize discussions and the results of the meeting and review the future plans.

❑ Determine an appropriate date for the next meeting.

❑ Adjourn the meeting.

❑ Evaluate the meeting.

families the best ways and times to contact you and the other professionals. Feedback from families and professionals concerning various aspects of the meeting also can be solicited to identify successful factors as well as to pinpoint aspects in need of revision. A sample schedule of activities for a family–educators conference is presented in Figure 4.9.

Resolve Conflicts Constructively

Your ability to establish a trusting and collaborative relationship with families also will be affected by how you and your students' families resolve the conflicts that may occur during meetings and the school year (Mueller, 2009). These disputes often are the result of miscommunication and different views concerning academic performance and grades, student behavior and disciplinary actions, educational placement, and the availability and delivery of educational and related services. It is important that you also recognize that these conflicts may be related to families' past experiences with schools.

In addition to regularly communicating and collaborating with families using the strategies presented in this chapter, you can do several things to limit the potential negative consequences of conflicts with families and develop constructive solutions that address the concerns and issues that are at the center of conflicts (Smith et al., 2006). Recognize that families are knowledgeable about their children, and show that you care about and respect them and their children. Rather than viewing family members negatively as "overprotective," "troublemakers," "uncaring," or "uncooperative," try to identify the factors that might explain their perspectives and behavior. It also is important to understand the family's emotional reactions to their child's difficulties, which may include a combination of disappointment, fear, anger and avoidance (Smith et al., 2006).

When interacting with the family, maintain an attitude of communication, collaboration, and conciliation, and a commitment to what is best for the student (Mueller, 2009). Establish ground rules and an agenda, and serve as a neutral facilitator. Listen carefully and reflectively as family members share their concerns and perspectives without interrupting them, seeking clarification only when necessary. Avoid

A GUIDE TO ACTION
Enhancing Meetings with Families

Although a variety of techniques are possible to collaborate and communicate with families, one important strategy is meeting with families. To enhance your meetings with families, consider the following points:

- Be prepared for the meeting, and help others prepare for the meeting.
- Schedule the meeting at a time and place that is convenient for the family members and other participants.
- Address the special circumstances of families that might prevent their attendance or participation in the meeting.
- Ask for suggestions from family members and other participants about the agenda.
- Make the purpose of the meeting clear to all.
- Allow enough time for the meeting.
- Create a welcoming, positive, respectful, and comfortable environment that encourages participants to share their perspectives and work collaboratively.
- Ensure that the meeting occurs without interruptions.
- Address the issues, questions, and concerns participants want to discuss.

- Provide all participants with enough opportunities and time to present their opinions, to ask questions, and to receive feedback from others.
- Make sure that the participants discuss the strong points of the student's performance.
- Use student work samples to support your comments.
- Use technology to enhance the meeting's effectiveness.
- Listen attentively, and acknowledge and encourage participation from others.
- Communicate in a clear, nonthreatening manner using language that others can understand.
- Adjust the content, structure, tone, and interaction patterns of the meeting to be consistent with the family's cultural, linguistic, and experiential background.
- End the meeting effectively.
- Protect the family's confidentiality.
- Evaluate and reflect on the meeting.
- Take follow-up actions based on the decisions made at the meeting.

How would you rate your meetings with families? ( ) Excellent ( ) Good ( ) Needs Improvement ( ) Needs Much Improvement

Create a plan of action for enhancing your meetings with families that includes your goals, the actions you will take and the resources you will need to achieve them, and the ways you will evaluate your success.

acting emotionally, taking things personally, making assumptions or promises that you cannot keep, and rebutting each point brought up by the family (Montgomery, 2005). While you don't have to agree with families, it is important that you refrain from dismissing or diminishing their comments, recognize their role in making decisions about their children, and avoid using language that might escalate the situation. Be constructive by calmly, directly, and honestly discussing your viewpoint and the reasons for it, and citing and displaying documentation to support your statements (Smith et al., 2006). Convey your message with a respectful tone of voice and appropriate body language. Emphasize points of agreement, propose choices and options, and seek solutions that are acceptable to all parties. If conflicts cannot be resolved constructively by you and the family, seek the assistance of others who can help mediate disputes. Ultimately, it is important for you to mend fences with families.

Address the Diverse Strengths, Challenges, Beliefs, Backgrounds, Resources, and Experiences of Families

Families, like students, have diverse strengths, challenges, backgrounds, beliefs, resources, and experiences, and they are structured in different ways. In communicating and collaborating with families, be aware of these factors and how they affect families, and adjust your style and services accordingly to promote family involvement (Dettmer et al., 2009; Harry et al., 2008; Lo, 2005; Ramirez & Soto-Hinman, 2009). You can learn about your students and their families' preferences by meeting with them to discuss their daily rituals at home; their important values and customs; their feelings about their child's strengths and challenges; and their expectations of their child's behavior, their roles, the school, and you (West, Leon-Guerrero, & Stevens, 2007).

Cultural Factors   Families are interested in their children's education, but different cultural perspectives can make it hard to establish traditional school–family interactions (Araujo, 2009; Brandon & Brown, 2009; Lee et al., 2009). In designing culturally sensitive programs to involve and empower families, you should adjust to the family's level of acculturation, feelings about and knowledge of schooling, prior experience with discrimination, structure, beliefs, child-rearing practices, developmental expectations, perceptions of disability, emotional responses, and communication patterns (Harry et al., 2008).

Level of Acculturation.   The level of **acculturation**, the extent to which members of one culture adapt to a new culture, will affect a family's cultural perspective and school involvement (Olivos, 2009). Because children tend to acculturate faster than adults, children may perform some roles in the new culture that adults assumed in their native country, such as interacting with social institutions like schools. These roles involve time and stress and the dependence of adult family members on children. This can have a significant impact on adult–child relationships and the student's academic performance.

Feelings about and Knowledge of Educational System.   Family members' feelings about and knowledge of the educational system and their prior experiences with schools also can affect their involvement in school (Angell et al., 2009; Kozleski et al., 2008). Family members with limited knowledge of the educational system or negative experiences as students may not feel comfortable participating in family–school activities (Olivos, 2009). These understandings, feelings, and experiences also can influence what they expect of you and the schools their children attend. Family members who are immigrants may also have different perceptions of schooling.

Prior Experience with Discrimination.   Many families may have suffered discrimination, which can influence their behavior and attitudes (Alvarez McHatton, 2007). These families may not want to attend meetings at the school if they or others have been discriminated against or treated with disrespect there. You can increase the family's comfort in attending school-related events and establish trust and a welcoming environment by doing the following:

- Invite important extended family members to school events.
- Address elders first.
- Refer to family members by their titles, such as Mr., Mrs., Ms., Dr., or Reverend (or ask them how they like to be addressed).
- Make school facilities available for community activities.
- Speak to families in a respectful and sincere manner.
- Respond in a warm and caring way.
- Decorate the school and classrooms with icons from various cultures (Angell et al., 2009; Brandon & Brown, 2009).

Family Structure.   Most school-based strategies for involving families focus on the needs of the nuclear family. However, many cultures emphasize the value of the extended family (Pewewardy & Fitzpatrick, 2009). For example, many families live in a framework of collective interdependence and kinship interactions. They share resources and services, and offer emotional and social support. Rather than asking for help from schools in dealing with educational issues, these families may feel more comfortable relying on community members or agencies. Therefore, you need to identify and involve the informal systems that support families.

In many families, roles are hierarchical, and elders may play an important role in decision making and child care (Roopnarine et al., 2005). When working with families that value and rely on extended family members, you can involve all family members in the school program. For example, in writing to families, you could say that all family members are welcome at educational meetings.

REFLECTIVE
REFLECTIVE

What are the values and perspectives that make up your family's belief system? How do these belief affect your family's views, priorities and decisions?

Belief Systems and Child-Rearing Practices, Developmental Expectations, and Perceptions of Disability. It is essential that you understand the beliefs of your students' families and use this information to address their strengths, concerns, challenges, and goals, and adjust your interactions with them. **Belief systems** refer to the values and perspectives that inform the family's world view, way of life, priorities, and decision making (King et al., 2009).

The family's belief system impacts their views on child rearing, appropriate behavior, disability, and developmental milestones (Harry, 2008; Kozleski et al., 2008; Sheehey et al., 2009). These different perspectives also can affect how they view their children's educational program. For example, some families may stress the importance of children reaching developmental milestones at appropriate ages, but other families may not. Similarly, for some families, independence is a goal for their child, but others may view it as interfering with their preference that their child remain a part of the family. Because the behavioral and developmental expectations of schools and families may conflict, you must work cooperatively with families to develop a culturally sensitive and relevant teaching program. The program should include agreed-on bicultural behaviors, appropriate cultural settings for these behaviors, and cross-cultural criteria for measuring progress.

Families also may have different views of *disability* and its impact on the family (Harry, 2008; Kozleski et al., 2008). For example, some use a broader idea of disability that is often related to the child's ability to function at home and the family's beliefs about the child's future. As a result, they may also resist, resent, or misunderstand the labeling of their child as having a disability, which can cause them to not trust the school.

You also need to recognize that the family's belief system also has a cultural, spiritual, and religious basis (Ault & Collins, 2009; Blanks & Smith, 2009). Religious and spiritual beliefs may provide guidance, support, and strength to some families of children with disabilities (Elhoweris, Whittaker, & Salend, 2007). Some families may believe that disabilities are positive signs for the family or that a child's difficulties are caused by reprisals for rule violations by family members, spirits, failure to avoid taboos, fate, choice, and lifestyle imbalances (Masood, Turner, & Baxter, 2007). Families also may have perspectives that cause them to prefer home remedies and alternative practices, and to reject Western views of medicine and technology. Therefore, you may have to address these issues before families accept and respond to traditional educational strategies.

Bold Stock Images by Unlisted Images

Many families report experiencing positive effects as a result of having a child with a disability in the family. What might be some ways in which having a child with a disability affects the whole family?

Emotional Adjustments The family's beliefs also shape their emotional adjustment to having a child with a disability (Dettmer et al., 2009; Smith et al., 2006). Families may go through several transformative stages as they learn to adjust to and accept their child's disability (Singer, 2002). These stages, which vary from family to family based on beliefs, experience, culture, socioeconomic level, spirituality, religious beliefs, the nature of the child's disability, and the support they receive from others, may include the following:

Stage 1: Families may be shocked and dejected, and experience grief and fear.

Stage 2: Families may be confused, deny their child's disability, reject their child, or avoid dealing with the issue/situation by looking for other explanations.

Stage 3: Families may experience anger, self-pity, disappointment, guilt, and a sense of powerlessness that may be expressed as rage or withdrawal.

Stage 4: Families may start to understand and accept their child's disability and its impact on the family.

Stage 5: Families may accept, love, and appreciate their child unconditionally.

Stage 6: Families may begin to focus on living, on the benefits accrued, on the future, and on working with others to teach and provide support services to their child.

In addition to helping families as they go through these stages, be aware of the varied belief systems and culturally appropriate coping strategies that families have, and consider these values strategies when designing and delivering services (Harry, 2008; King et al., 2009). You also can aid families by being honest with them, showing genuine care and compassion, being empathetic rather than sympathetic, and encouraging them to obtain supportive services. You can also encourage them to communicate with other family members and other important persons in their lives, join family support groups, ask questions, and express their emotions.

It also is important for you to understand and help others recognize that many families report experiencing positive effects as a result of raising a child with a disability (Ferguson, 2002; Taunt & Hastings, 2002). These benefits for parents and siblings include developing coping skills and family cohesiveness; facilitating shared values and parenting; increasing one's perspective on life, sense of purpose/responsibility, and sensitivity to others and assertiveness; improving communication within the family; and expanding the family's social network.

Socioeconomic Factors Many socioeconomic factors also can affect the family's participation in their child's education (Brandon & Brown, 2009; San Antonio, 2008). Although many families face increased financial pressures related to raising and providing for their children with disabilities, these economic hardships can particularly affect families living in poverty. Long work schedules, time conflicts, transportation problems, and child care needs can be serious barriers that you and your colleagues need to address. These barriers can be reduced by the use of home visits (see Ginsberg [2007] for guidelines for conducting home visits). However, many families may consider a home visit intrusive, so you should ask for the family's permission before visiting their home.

Use Written Communication

You can use written communication such as letters and notes and other documents such as handbooks, orientation manuals, and homework guidelines to establish on-going communication with families (Brandon & Brown, 2009; Smith et al., 2006). Written communication is often used to share information on students, schedule meetings, and build support for your inclusion program. For example, you can periodically ask your students' families to complete short questionnaires to obtain feedback about your inclusion program and their children (Muscott, Szczesiul, Berk, Staub, Hoover, & Perry-Chisholm, 2008).

It is important that you evaluate written documents sent to families in terms of readability, legibility, tone, and the use of clear, respectful, welcoming, and jargon-free language (Fitzgerald & Watkins, 2006). Look at Figure 4.10, and note how the letters to family members are different. Which letter is more likely to result in family members attending the meeting? Letter A is impersonal, uses technical terms, places the school's needs above the needs of family members, can intimidate the family, and does little to encourage family participation. Letter B is welcoming and less formal, tries to establish rapport, and respects the family, their scheduling needs, and their contributions to the education of their child. It also avoids professional jargon, encourages participation and collaboration, and gives the family positive suggestions for preparing for the meeting.

You also can increase the effectiveness of your written communication with families by sharing affective and factual information; using familiar language and avoiding using acronymns; examining its readability; emphasizing positive aspects of students and their families; using examples, visuals, icons, and cultural referents; and monitoring the response rate from family members (Fitzgerald &

UDL and YOU
Understanding and Accommodating
Cross-Cultural Communication Patterns and Linguistic Factors

Rather than assuming that all of your students' families communicate in the same ways, you can apply the principles of UDL to your interactions with families by understanding and accommodating the communication patterns and linguistic factors that differ from one culture to another (Harry, 2008; Lee et al., 2009). This means that you are sensitive to linguistic and communication style differences, and interpret verbal and nonverbal behaviors within a social and cultural context (Gollnick & Chinn, 2009). For example, eye contact, wait time, word meanings, body language, facial gestures, voice quality and tone, personal space, and physical contact have different meanings and purposes in various cultures (Matuszny et al., 2007). You also need to understand that communications between cultures are affected by turn taking, by physical closeness or distance, and by spoken and unspoken rules of conversation. For example, in some cultures *yes* connotes "I heard you" or "I am listening to you" rather than agreement. Similarly, individuals from some cultures may interpret laughter as a sign of embarrassment rather than enjoyment.

Cross-cultural communication patterns also may affect communication, the discussion of certain issues, and the ways in which families view, seek, and receive assistance (Harry, 2008; Kozleski et al., 2008; Lo, 2005). Some families may not feel comfortable discussing personal problems and concerns, viewing that behavior as being self-centered or disgracing the family, while others may be reluctant to disagree in order to maintain harmony (Banks, 2004). Some families may not want to interact with the school staff because they believe that teachers know what is best for their children and that it is not appropriate for them to question the authority of teachers (Ramirez & Soto-Hinman, 2009). Community members who understand the family's needs, emotional responses, and culture can help break down these communication barriers by helping you understand and interpret the family's communication behaviors; serving as liaisons among schools, families, and communities; and orienting new families to the school.

Language factors also may block communication between schools and families (Harry, 2008; Lo, 2005). Communication difficulties may be compounded by problems in understanding educational jargon and practices that may not exist in the families' language and culture (Ramirez & Soto-Hinman, 2009). For example, some families from different cultural and language backgrounds believe that special education implies a program that is better than general education. You can correct this misconception by giving these families forms, lists of key educational terms, and information about their rights in their native languages. Learning greetings and words in the family's native language also can create a positive environment that promotes communication and respect.

Interpreters and translators can be used to promote communication between English-speaking educators and families who speak other languages (Olivos, 2009). Whereas interpreters foster oral communications during face-to-face meetings, translators focus on rewriting correspondence and documents in the family's primary language. (We will discuss the roles of translators later in this chapter.) Interpreters should speak the same dialect as the family; maintain confidentiality; avoid giving personal opinions; seek clarification from families and professionals when they have problems communicating certain information; use reverse translation when exact translations are not possible; and show respect for families and professionals. The interpreter will be more effective if you discuss the topics and terminology with the interpreter before the meeting, use nonverbal communication as well as speech, are aware of the nonverbal behaviors of family members, and ask for the interpreter's feedback about the meeting. It is also important that family members and professionals speak to each other rather than directing their comments to interpreters.

Although many families may rely on their child to interpret for them in general, the child or other students should not interpret during meetings. A child serving as an interpreter for the family can have a negative impact on the family, as this situation reverses the traditional adult–child relationship. For children, interpreting places them in the adult role in the family, which can make them anxious and frightened. For adults, being dependent on their child as their interpreter can be considered demeaning. It also may be awkward for family members to share information about their child when the child is interpreting.

Watkins, 2006). Since some family members may have difficulty accessing written information, it is always a good idea to ask families how and what they wish to communicate, and to find alternatives to written communication, and offer some form of oral communication to clarify written communications and documents (Davern, 2004).

FIGURE 4.10 Samples of written correspondence to families

LETTER A

To Whom It May Concern:

The school district has scheduled a meeting to review your child's educational program. The meeting will be held on March 15, 2008, in the conference room at the administrative offices.

The following members of the school district will be in attendance:

Mrs. Lorraine Hamilton	School Social Worker
Mrs. Constance Franks	Special Education Teacher
Mr. Patrick Hardees	General Education Teacher
Mr. Donald Fein	School Psychologist
Mrs. Joanne Frederick	Principal

If you would like the school physician to be at the meeting, please contact my office at least three days prior to the meeting.

Please contact my office if you plan to attend the meeting. My office will be able to tell you approximately what time your child will be discussed. If you are unable to attend the meeting in person, you may participate by telephone.

The meeting will take place as scheduled unless you request otherwise. I will send the results in writing after the meeting is over. Feel free to contact me with any questions or concerns related to your child's education.

Yours truly,

Donald Smith,

Director of Pupil Personnel Services

LETTER B

Dear Truman Family:

Hello. My name is Donald Smith, and I am the Director of Pupil Personnel Services for the Bellville School District. It is my job to assist you in understanding the educational system and to work with you in creating an educational program that meets the needs of your child.

Your child's teachers would like to schedule a meeting with you to discuss your child's educational program. It is important that you attend this meeting. You know your child better than anyone and can provide important information concerning your child's school performance. You may also wish to bring others with you to attend the meeting. It is also possible for you to request that the school physician attend this meeting.

If you have time, you can do several things to prepare for the meeting. You can talk to your child and his/her teachers about his/her performance in school and the ways to improve his/her learning. You also can visit your child's classroom. It also will be helpful if you bring materials to the meeting such as your child's schoolwork, school records, and reports, as well as medical information. At the meeting, we will talk about the goals for your child's education, the way your child learns best, and his/her favorite activities and interests.

I will be calling you to schedule the meeting at a time that is most convenient for your family to discuss who you would like to attend the meeting, and to answer any questions you may have. We also can assist you in attending the meeting by providing you with transportation, child care, and the services of an interpreter. I look forward to speaking with you and working with you to meet the educational needs of your child.

Yours truly,

Donald Smith,

Director of Pupil Personnel Services

Translators who help prepare written communications and community members can help you develop culturally relevant and sensitively written documents that are rewritten into the native languages of your families (Araujo, 2009). You can collaborate with translators to produce quality translated materials by using examples and activities that are culturally appropriate, including visuals and photographs that appeal to and depict the intended audience, and avoiding technical terms and jargon or including an explanation when you must use them. Software and Web-based translation programs are available to provide quick translation of material, but you should exercise caution in using them because they often fail to capture the cultural, syntactical, and linguistic meanings of the communication and address dialectical and word differences, which can result in confusing or offensive communications.

Informative Notice You can share information with families by using an *informative notice*. This is a brief written communication that alerts families to various school and classroom activities, student progress, and the materials students will need to complete their assignments. At the beginning of the school year, the informative notice can take two forms: (a) personalized postcards to students welcoming them to your class and (b) letters to families to introduce yourself and various aspects of your inclusive classroom, to explain your expectations, invite them to various school and class-related events, and to ask for their support and collaboration (Brandon, 2007; Ramirez & Soto-Hinman, 2009).

Newsletters A form of written communication that teachers like Ms. Carr and Ms. Stevens used with families is a *newsletter*, which can tell them about school and classroom events, useful resources and community services, extracurricular activities, meetings, school policies, and menus, and offer family education (Brandon, 2007; Ramirez & Soto-Hinman, 2009). Consider the following when creating newsletters:

- Create a title for the newsletter.
- Make them brief (no more than three pages).
- Present information in a clear, focused, and interesting manner.
- Consider using bulleted or numbered lists.
- Make them attractive by using graphics, columns, and colors.
- Involve students in creating them.
- Post them on the Internet.
- Focus them on information, resources, and topics that are useful to students and their families.
- Solicit feedback on their value and suggestions for future issues (Dardig, 2008).

Daily/Weekly Note The **daily/weekly note** is a brief note that alerts families to the accomplishments and improvements in their children and other issues of interest or concern (e.g., behavior, socialization, health, participation, work completion). The value of daily/weekly notes can be increased by providing a space for family members to write their messages to you. These notes can be made more effective by pairing them with praise from family members. Therefore, when family members receive these positive notes from you, they should be encouraged to read the notes promptly, praise their child in the presence of others, put the note in a prominent location (e.g., on the refrigerator door) where their child and others are likely to see it, and share their desire to receive additional notes of praise.

Two-Way Notebooks You also can communicate with families by using **two-way notebooks** and assignment folders (Sebald & Luckner, 2007). Two-way notebooks, carried to and from school by students, allow you and family members to exchange comments and information, ask questions, and brainstorm solutions. The notebook can have the student's name on it, as well as a place for family members' signatures, the date, and the number of assignments included.

Daily/Weekly Progress Reports A **daily/weekly progress report**, a written record of the student's performance in school, is effective in communicating with families. Its content and format will vary, and could include information on academic performance, preparedness for class, effort, behavior, peer relationships, and homework completion. The format should be easy for you to complete and easy for families to interpret. As students demonstrate success over a period of time, the progress report can be shared with families weekly, biweekly, and then monthly. A sample weekly progress report is presented in Figure 4.11.

FIGURE 4.11 **Sample weekly progress report**

Student:

Teachers:

Classes: **Rating**

__English/Language Arts (ELA)   1 = Unsatisfactory
__Mathematics (M)   2 = Needs Improvement
__Social Studies (SS)   3 = Good
__Science (S)   4 = Excellent
__Other (please list)

	Monday	**Tuesday**	**Wednesday**	**Thursday**	**Friday**
Academic performance	1 2 3 4	1 2 3 4	1 2 3 4	1 2 3 4	1 2 3 4
Class work completion	1 2 3 4	1 2 3 4	1 2 3 4	1 2 3 4	1 2 3 4
Direction following	1 2 3 4	1 2 3 4	1 2 3 4	1 2 3 4	1 2 3 4
Class participation	1 2 3 4	1 2 3 4	1 2 3 4	1 2 3 4	1 2 3 4
Motivation and effort	1 2 3 4	1 2 3 4	1 2 3 4	1 2 3 4	1 2 3 4
Homework completion	1 2 3 4	1 2 3 4	1 2 3 4	1 2 3 4	1 2 3 4
Classroom behavior	1 2 3 4	1 2 3 4	1 2 3 4	1 2 3 4	1 2 3 4
Socialization with peers	1 2 3 4	1 2 3 4	1 2 3 4	1 2 3 4	1 2 3 4
Cooperation with adults	1 2 3 4	1 2 3 4	1 2 3 4	1 2 3 4	1 2 3 4

Teacher Comments:

Signature: Date:

Family Comments:

Signature: Date:

Student Comments:

Signature: Date:

Sources: Battle, Dickens-Wright, & Murphy (1998); Dardig (2008).

Home–School Contracts   The daily/weekly progress report system also has been used as part of a home–school contract. *Home–school contracts* allow families to learn about their children's progress in school and reinforce their children's improved academic performance or behavior in school. You observe students in school and report your observations to families, who then deliver reinforcers to their children. These reinforcers take many forms.

Before using a home–school contract, you can discuss the specifics of the program with the family. This discussion gives both parties an understanding of the behavior to be changed, details of the communication system between home and school, potential reinforcers, and when and how to deliver the reinforcers. Once the system is in place, follow-up communication is critical to talk about the implementation and impact of the system.

Encourage and Facilitate Family Observations

Communication between the home and the school and support for your inclusion program can be fostered by encouraging family members to observe in the classroom. This experience allows family members to see and understand different aspects of the school environment and student behavior. It gives families the background information needed to discuss school-related issues with you.

Family members can be prepared for the observation if you review ways to enter the room unobtrusively, locations in the room to sit, suitable times to observe, appropriate reactions to their child and other students, and the need to maintain confidentiality. Before the observation, you can discuss with family members the purpose of the observation and the unique aspects of the educational setting. After the observation, you can meet with family members again to discuss what they saw.

Using Technology to Promote Inclusion
FOSTERING COMMUNICATION AND COLLABORATION

Technological innovations are changing the ways in which teachers, schools, students, and families interact and communicate (Ramirez & Soto-Hinman, 2009; White Englund, 2009). Many schools and families use Web sites, e-mail, multilingual hotlines, Twitter, interactive videoconferencing, automated notification systems, and telephone answering machines to communicate (Meadan et al., 2009). For example, families can use these technologies to view their children's work and grades online, see what the school is serving for lunch, check on their child's attendance record, or find out what homework has been assigned. Like Ms. Carr and Ms. Stevens did in the chapter-opening vignette, you and your students can communicate with families by maintaining a **weblog**, a journal of the class's activities and related Web links that is posted on the Internet. You can also use technology to provide families with suggestions for teaching specific skills to their children, report on student performance in school, give families information on their rights and specific programs, offer information on educational opportunities and local events of interest to students and their families, and recommend resources and other learning materials to families. Online communication also can be used by families to support, communicate, and share information with you and each other (Margalit & Raskind, 2009; Meadan et al., 2009).

If family members cannot arrange to come to school, you can use video to introduce them to various aspects of your inclusive classroom, to provide them with another opportunity to view important school and classroom activities, and to increase their awareness of their children's progress. In using video observations, you need to determine what will be recorded, as well as when, how often, and by whom will it be recorded. You also must obtain permission from your students' families to record them and share the recordings with others. It is also helpful to provide families with a format to guide them in viewing the videos such as an introduction to the activities recorded, a summary of the video, and questions they can answer as they view the video.

You also can conduct meetings via telephones and interactive videoconferencing that allow families to participate without leaving work or their homes (Patterson, Petit, & Williams, 2007). When using these technologies, you should ensure that all participants have immediate access to all the information presented and can interact directly and actively throughout the meeting. Before the meeting, all participants should receive copies of the materials that will be discussed and referred to at the meeting. As with any meeting, you also need to be sensitive to cultural and linguistic factors, and protect the confidentiality of students and their families. A telephone relay service and a TeleTYpewriter/Telecommunications Device for the Deaf (TTY/TDD) can be employed to facilitate the involvement of deaf or hard-of-hearing family members.

In addition to communicating with families, technology can be used to help you obtain information and collaborate and communicate with others and to facilitate your professional development (Frey, 2009; Walker, 2009). E-mail, blogs, Twitter, podcasts, wikis, Really Simple Syndication (RSS) feed readers, discussion groups, streaming video, and listservs allow you to obtain information, and to "talk to" and distribute communications to others (Ferriter, 2009; Kingsley, 2007; Robinson & Kelley, 2007). They can be used to share ideas and concerns, learn about model strategies and programs, develop lessons, and brainstorm solutions to problems. Online services give professionals, families, and students access to a wide range of professional development activities, resources from around the world, and opportunities to receive and exchange information and ideas with colleagues. Most professional organizations and clearinghouses offer professional development and maintain a list of online networks and resources, including discussion and support groups.

When communicating with families and colleagues via technology, remember that many individuals may not feel comfortable interacting with you in that way or may not have access to technology. Therefore, rather than assuming access, it is best for you to ask families and colleagues to identify the best ways to contact and communicate with them at the beginning of the school year.

Offer Educational Programs to Families

Because family members may need education to understand model programs like inclusion and to perform various roles in the educational process, many schools and teachers like Ms. Carr and Ms. Stevens offer family education as part of their delivery of services to students and their families (Dettmer et al., 2009; Stivers et al., 2008; Van Haren & Fieldler, 2008). Some schools have family education committees that offer schoolwide programs and activities. Other schools collaborate with national and local family-based organizations such as the Parent Teacher Association (PTA) to conduct a range of family education sessions and programs. When setting up and evaluating family education programs, you, your colleagues, and your students' families can consider the following issues.

Offer Educational Programs to All Family Members Although most programs educate mothers, education should be available to all family members, including fathers, grandparents, and siblings. For example, education and support can address the special issues of siblings and help them understand inclusion and the nature of their brother's or sister's disability and deal with the impact of having a brother or sister with special needs (Cook, 2006; Diament, 2009). Education for siblings can focus on helping them understand the causes of various disabilities, fostering the learning of their siblings, dispelling myths and misconceptions about disabilities, discussing ways of interacting with and assisting their sibling, dealing with unequal treatment and excessive demands, responding to the reactions and questions of their friends and other persons, and understanding human differences.

Focus the Content of the Educational Program on Families' Needs Generally, education should give family members the skills to understand and support your inclusion program, the skills to teach their child at home, the ability to communicate and collaborate with professionals, the ability to serve as advocates for their child, the information they need to obtain services for their child and their family, and ways to plan for their child's future (Checkley, 2008). Family members who speak languages other than English may benefit from family-based ESL and literacy programs.

Conduct the Educational Program in a Range of Settings Education can occur in the home or in the school at times that are most convenient for families. In some cases, it may be important to conduct the educational programs in nonintimidating, community-based locations (Matuszny et al., 2007).

Use a Variety of Strategies to Educate Families As Ms. Carr and Ms. Stevens did in the chapter-opening vignette, you can use a variety of strategies to educate families, including multimedia, the Internet, group discussion, role playing, simulations, presentations by professionals and other family members, and demonstrations. Print materials and education programs for families are also available from state education departments, as well as from local groups serving families and professional organizations. Experienced, skilled, and highly respected family members can be a valuable resource for educating other families (Stivers et al., 2008).

REFLECTIVE

What have been your experiences using technology to communicate with others and to engage in professional learning? What were the advantages and disadvantages? How do these systems affect the communications and the information shared? What skills do teachers, students, and family members need to use these systems effectively and efficiently?

REFLECTIVE

Do you have a family member with a disability? How has this individual affected other family members? What types of educational programs would benefit your family?

To reflect on and enhance your understanding of families of children with disabilities and ways to build positive relationships with them, go to the IRIS Center Resources section under the Topic: *Parents and Families* in the MyEducationLab for your course, and complete the module entitled *Collaborating with Families*.

What Would You Do in Today's Diverse Classroom?

★ When you volunteered to work in a co-teaching team, you and your partner were excited about the possibility of using a variety of teaching arrangements. However, you find that your team continually has the same teacher taking the lead while the other teacher monitors individual students.

★ One of your students has been acting as the class clown and fails to complete his schoolwork. His family is concerned and believes that he should receive special education services. Although you are also concerned about the student, you do not believe he needs special education services.

★ You work with a paraeducator who has developed a close and positive working relationship with Josh, one of your students. You notice that that her presence and assistance sometimes interferes with Josh's interactions with you and other classmates.

1. What challenges(s) might you encounter in each situation?
2. What factors do you need to consider in addressing them?
3. How would you address these situations?
4. What knowledge, skills, dispositions, resources, and support do you need to address these situations?

Watch Josh work with his paraeducator in his inclusive classroom by visiting the MyEducationLab for this course. Go to the *Assignments and Activities* section under the Topic *Autism Spectrum Disorders* and complete the activity entitled *Classroom Aides* to answer questions about their relationship in an inclusive classroom.

SUMMARY

This chapter provided guidelines for establishing an inclusive environment that supports the learning of *all students* by creating collaborative relationships and fostering communication among students, professionals, families, and community members. As you review the questions posed in this chapter, remember the following points:

Who Are the Members of the Comprehensive Planning Team?
CEC 1, 7, 9, 10; PRAXIS 2, 3; INTASC 10

The comprehensive planning team may consist of students, general and special educators, administrators, support personnel such as speech/language therapists, bilingual educators, paraeducators, family members, peers, local community resources, and professional and family-based organizations. The members of the team vary, depending on the strengths and challenges of students, families, and educators.

How Can Members of the Comprehensive Planning Team Work Collaboratively?
CEC 1, 7, 9, 10; PRAXIS 2, 3; INTASC 1, 3, 9, 10

Members of the comprehensive planning team can work collaboratively by using collaborative teaming, person-/student-centered planning, co-teaching, and collaborative consultation, as well as by promoting congruence and engaging in professional development.

How Can I Foster Communication and Collaboration with Families?

CEC 1, 2, 3, 7, 9, 10; PRAXIS 2, 3; INTASC 3, 10

You can foster communication and collaboration with families by gaining their trust, advocating for them and their children, ensuring confidentiality, meeting regularly with families, resolving conflicts constructively, using written and technology-based communication, encouraging and facilitating observations at the school or via technology, and offering educational programs to families. Families, like students, have diverse strengths, challenges, backgrounds, belief systems, resources, and experiences, and they are structured in different ways. In communicating and collaborating with families, be aware of these factors, adjusting your style and services accordingly to promote family involvement.

Collaboration and Teaming

From Chapter 10 of *Inclusion: Effective Practices for All Students*. Second Edition. James McLeskey, David L. Westling.

Collaboration and Teaming

A VIEW FROM TEACHERS

Why Is Collaboration an Absolute Necessity to Support Inclusion?

We interviewed teachers from Gilpin Manor Elementary and West Hernando Middle School about collaboration. All of the teachers we interviewed said that collaboration was an "absolute necessity" to support effective inclusive programs. Perhaps the main reason for this was that collaboration is used in so many ways to support teachers and inclusive programs. For example, Megan Law, first-grade teacher at Gilpin Manor, emphasized the importance of working with a team of teachers when planning lessons, as teachers provide input regarding how to differentiate instruction. "We work together so we can see which way we need to differentiate the lessons for certain students. It's such a big help because we often just keep doing the same activities . . . so we can get feedback from each other" and learn about new options for differentiation. Similar comments were made by Melissa Pratt, a preschool special education teacher at Gilpin Manor, who "goes back and forth" with teachers she works with as they "constantly modify and differentiate things together. Everybody is on the team, including the paraeducators, and we all have a voice."

Susan Davis and Lisa Hallal, who both work as co-teachers at West Hernando Middle School, elaborated further on how much teachers learn from collaboration when working as co-teachers. "Teachers bring different skills into the classroom, and collaboration provides the opportunity to share that expertise to benefit all students. Subject-matter teachers bring a deep knowledge of the content and strategies for teaching the content in interesting ways. We [special education teachers] often know much less about the content, but bring expertise in making instructional accommodations to make sure that all students learn."

Susan and Lisa continued, "Teachers learn a lot from collaboration. Special education teachers learn a lot about the content, and how to teach it from the content area expert in the general education classroom. We can't know about content in every area in a middle school: English, science, math, social studies. There's no way we can figure out how to make accommodations in instruction or on tests unless we learn about the content of the class. We learn the content by watching the general education teacher, and then we can teach some of the lessons, do re-teaching for students who don't get the information after going over it in class, and work with the classroom teacher to make accommodations in lessons and on tests.

"Content-area teachers also learn from us. One of the most important things they learn is to make accommodations for students. They see us making accommodations to help students learn

content, or we make suggestions about making accommodations during class lessons—they learn from us and then can do it themselves. We see this because they are comfortable when we have to leave their classroom. They've learned so much about how to make accommodations work. At first they are nervous to have kids with disabilities in their class when they're alone (or the only teacher). After a while they're very comfortable with that, because they've learned so much about accommodations for all of their students."

MyEducationLab

Visit the MyEducation-Lab for *Inclusion* to enhance your understanding of chapter concepts with a personalized Study Plan. You'll also have the opportunity to hone your teaching skills through video and case-based Assignments and Activities, Building Teaching Skills and Disposition lessons, and IRIS Case Studies.

Introduction

If you've ever tried to work with peers on a project in a college classroom, you know that collaboration is not a simple task. Some people readily contribute to projects, yet others don't contribute as easily. Some want to complete the project quickly and before the due date, but others want to wait until the last minute. Some attend closely to detail, yet others want to focus on the big picture. Given how difficult and time-consuming collaboration can be, why should teachers or other professionals bother collaborating?

The short answer to that question is "Two (or more) heads are better than one." That is, two or more persons collaborating on a project or activity can often come up with a better project or answer to a problem than a single person can working alone (Bahrami, Olsen, Lathan, Roepstorff, Rees, & Frith, 2010).

Collaboration obviously takes time and effort on the part of all participants. As you reflected on the successful group projects you've worked on in a college classroom, you probably noted that the group members were flexible, cooperative, worked to accommodate the preferences of others, and built on the different areas of expertise that existed in the group. When teachers and other professionals collaborate to solve problems and address student needs, these personal qualities improve the quality of collaboration.

Pause & Reflect

Consider a group project you completed in a college classroom that was very successful. What qualities of the group made the project successful? Was the content of the project better than any individual could have completed? Does this experience suggest that two heads can often be better than one? Why or why not?

As the teachers from Gilpin Manor Elementary and West Hernando Middle School illustrated in the chapter-opening vignette, "A View from Teachers," collaboration is an "absolute necessity" for effective inclusive programs. They noted that collaboration is essential primarily because general and special education teachers bring different areas of expertise to the general education classroom, and all of these areas of expertise are needed for inclusion to succeed. For example, general education teachers are most often prepared with in-depth knowledge of the content they are teaching and with methods to teach that content to large groups of students. In contrast, special education teachers are typically prepared to differentiate content and adapt instruction to meet the needs of students who struggle to learn the content. Collaboration is all about combining these areas of expertise to meet the needs of *all* students in the general education classroom.

Teachers collaborate to share knowledge and expertise and improve outcomes for students.

Collaboration: What to Expect

For most of the last century, teachers taught in relative isolation, with their classroom doors closed. They more or less depended on their own knowledge and expertise to address their students' needs. Today, this approach is gradually changing. Two major factors that have contributed to this change are increasing demands for higher levels of student achievement and the increasing diversity of the student population in schools.

Regarding *increased demands for student achievement*, success in the Information Age clearly requires all students to achieve higher levels of knowledge and skills, especially related to literacy and numeracy (Waldron & McLeskey, 2010). States have responded to this need by expecting students to master curriculum at increasingly younger ages. In addition, all states now have accountability measures in place to make certain that students meet expected standards. Thus, teachers are required to ensure that all students achieve at increasingly higher levels.

Part of the accountability system for student achievement is designed to make sure that students who live in poverty, those from different cultural and language backgrounds, and students with disabilities will meet achievement standards. The proportion of school-aged students from *culturally and linguistically diverse backgrounds* has grown substantially over the last decade (NCES, 2010). These data reveal that currently about 45% of students in public schools are from Hispanic, African American, Asian/Pacific Islander, or Native American backgrounds. Perhaps more importantly, students from culturally and linguistically diverse backgrounds make up the majority of students in ten states (Arizona, California, Florida, Georgia, Hawaii, Louisiana, Maryland, Nevada, New Mexico, and Texas). Furthermore, the number of students who live in poverty, and those who speak languages other than English is rapidly growing (Chau, Thampi, & Wight, 2010; NCES, 2010). This increasing diversity, coupled with rising demands for student achievement, makes it important that all teachers collaborate and share expertise with others to make certain that all students succeed in school.

What Is Collaboration?

Given the higher demands for achievement and related accountability measures, as well as the increasing diversity of schools across the United States, it is incumbent on teachers that they open their classroom doors and begin to collaborate with other professionals to meet students' needs. Teachers have always collaborated with others to some degree. For example, in the past when a teacher had a problem teaching a student, he often asked a fellow teacher for advice during a break between classes, during lunch, or after school. Now collaboration is more structured, it takes more forms (e.g., co-teaching, working in teams), and teachers are expected to collaborate more frequently regarding all aspects of their jobs.

Given the increasing demands for collaboration in schools, many have sought to clearly define collaboration. When we use the term *collaboration* in this book, we refer to "a style of direct interaction between at least two co-equal parties voluntarily engaged in shared decision making as they work toward a common goal" (Friend & Cook, 2010, p. 7). Several defining characteristics of effective collaboration are important to consider and are summarized in Figure 1.

When teachers initially begin to collaborate, the success of this activity will vary. However, as collaborators gain trust and respect for one another and learn to work together, collaboration will be more successful. Furthermore, this success will ensure that all participants value collaboration and are motivated to participate, especially as they recognize how much they and their students benefit from these activities.

In any inclusive school, several types of collaboration are needed. As administrators and teachers develop an inclusive school program, they must work together to change their practices, the roles they play, and the very structure of their schools. To achieve these goals, schools develop collaborative teams, which are charged with planning, implementing, monitoring, and supporting the necessary comprehensive changes (McLeskey & Waldron, 2006).

| Figure 1 | Defining Characteristics of Collaboration |

Collaboration is based on parity. Parity suggests that the contributions of everyone involved in collaboration are equally valued. A critical factor that often influences parity is the power collaborators have, or are perceived to have, in decision making. For example, collaborators may go along with suggestions from a principal because of the principal's powerful position and her responsibility for evaluating the performance of teachers. In an effective collaborative relationship, all involved must agree to equally respect the input of others and ensure that all are free to express perspectives on all issues or decisions. Otherwise, collaboration cannot succeed.

Collaborators share mutual goals. All participants in collaboration should share specific, common goals, and these goals should be important to everyone. This ensures that the purpose of collaboration is clear to all participants, and that all are motivated to work together to achieve the goals.

Collaborators share participation, decision making, and accountability. All collaborators should actively participate in decision making, reach a collective decision that all agree to support, and share accountability for the outcomes of the decision. This does not suggest that all participants should contribute to implementing the decision, which may be an intervention that one participant implements in his classroom. Rather, this suggests a perspective that "we're all in this together" and share responsibility for all aspects of collaborative decision making.

Collaborators share their resources and expertise. All participants bring valuable knowledge and skills to a collaborative activity. They also bring resources that others may not have (e.g., time, access to computers or curricular materials). It is important that all participants share their expertise, and that all participants value the expertise of others. This does not imply that an "expert" will come up with a solution to the problem, but rather that all will share suggestions to assure that the best possible information and resources are available to make a good decision. It is also important that all participants share their resources, which are often very limited in a school, to assure that resources are used efficiently and effectively to meet the needs of all students.

Collaboration is emergent. If collaboration is to succeed, some positive personal characteristics of participants must be present at the beginning of a collaborative activity, and must grow and flourish over time. These characteristics include:

1. Value collaboration and believe that "two heads are better than one."
2. Participate in collaboration in ways that ensure participants gain trust and respect for one another.
3. Work together to develop a sense of community, where all share expertise, and work together to maximize the strengths and minimize the weaknesses of all participants.

Sources: Adapted from P. Dettmer, L. Thurston, A. Knackendoffel, & N. Dyck (2009). *Collaboration, consultation, and teamwork* (6th ed.). Upper Saddle River, NJ: Merrill/Pearson Education; and M. Friend & L. Cook (2010). *Interactions: Collaboration skills for school professionals* (6th ed.). Boston: Allyn & Bacon.

In addition to this role, teachers in inclusive schools often work collaboratively with other teachers, either in a co-teaching role or as a consultant (i.e., when problems arise, one teacher assists another by problem-solving possible solutions). Still other types of collaborative roles teachers assume include the following:

- Work with other teachers and professionals in building-based support teams to solve classroom or school problems.
- Consult with other professionals regarding highly specialized student needs (e.g., consult with school psychologists, behavior specialists, physical therapists, nurses, physicians).
- Collaborate with parents to address student needs.

As you can see, all teachers in an inclusive school work in a range of collaborative roles to ensure that all students are successful. It is safe to say that no single teacher has all the knowledge and skills to address the needs of every student who might enter her classroom. Thus, working collaboratively provides the opportunity for teachers and other professionals to share expertise, learn from one another, and develop strategies that will result in more successful educational experiences for all students.

Although collaboration may seem to be a simple or even a natural skill for a teacher or other professional to engage in, that is often not the case. Understanding the basic components of effective collaboration is an important beginning point for learning to be a successful collaborator. We discuss these key components and provide more background information regarding collaboration in Strategy 1 later in this chapter.

Dispositions and Skills Needed for Successful Collaboration

Dispositions Needed for Successful Collaboration

Collaboration is not something that comes naturally for most of us. To succeed as collaborators, we need to ensure that we develop and exemplify certain dispositions and learn specific skills that lead to success in these roles. See Figure 2 for a definition of *dispositions*.

A disposition may be characterized as a habitual inclination, an attitude of mind, or a characteristic tendency. As we attempt to collaborate with others, several dispositions may interfere with collaboration; other dispositions, however, will tend to facilitate the process. Consider the following comments from teachers at Gilpin Manor Elementary and West Hernando Middle School regarding a key disposition for successful collaboration.

Collaboration works better as teachers gain trust and respect for one another.

Flexibility

When we discussed collaboration with teachers from Gilpin Manor Elementary and West Hernando Middle School, a word that was often used was flexibility. For example, when we asked Jeanne Huskins, a second-grade special education teacher at Gilpin Manor, what it took to be an effective teacher in an inclusive classroom, she replied, "Lots of flexibility." She went on to say that a good, collaborative relationship with a classroom teacher is needed, and this requires that both teachers be flexible to ensure that students' needs are met. Perhaps this flexibility is

Pause & Reflect

Recall a successful group project you completed in a college classroom. What dispositions of the members of the group contributed to the success of this project? Are the dispositions defined in Figure 2 important when working in any collaborative role? Why or why not?

Figure 2	What Are Dispositions? A Definition from the National Council for Accreditation in Teacher Education (NCATE)

Professional dispositions: Professional attitudes, values, and beliefs demonstrated through both verbal and nonverbal behaviors as educators interact with students, families, colleagues, and communities. These positive behaviors support student learning and development.

The National Council for Accreditation in Teacher Education previously provided a more complete definition of *dispositions*: The values, commitments, and professional ethics that influence behaviors toward students, families, colleagues, and communities and affect student learning, motivation, and development as well as the educator's own professional growth. Dispositions are guided by beliefs and attitudes related to values such as caring, fairness, honesty, responsibility, and social justice. For example, they might include a belief that all students can learn, a vision of high and challenging standards, or a commitment to a safe and supportive learning environment.

Source: Reprinted from National Council for Accreditation in Teacher Education. (2011). NCATE Unit Standards: Glossary. Retrieved April 22, 2011, from http://www.ncate.org/

most important when it comes to scheduling. Kim Miller, a third- and fourth-grade special education teacher at Gilpin Manor, elaborated on this idea when she said that all teachers have a schedule that should be respected by all. However, many times teachers need to be flexible regarding their schedule because the needs of students should take priority.

Susan Davis and Lisa Hallal elaborated on the need for flexibility when working in their roles as co-teachers at West Hernando Middle School. They noted that teachers take on many roles when co-teaching in an inclusive classroom—sometimes as an instructor for the entire group and at other times providing additional instruction for a small group. In addition, a co-teacher may work as a floater in class, monitoring student work, providing feedback to students, answering questions, making certain students are on task, managing behavior, and so forth. As Lisa Hallal said, "There's no end to what you do in that room." And so, we see that a key disposition that makes co-teaching successful is flexibility.

"You have to be flexible," continued Lisa Hallal, "that's the number-one thing. Some teachers prefer to do all or most of the instruction, so you have to deal with that teaching style. We've worked with teachers who like total control of dispensing information, and other teachers who are okay with us doing many of the lessons. You have to be flexible enough to say what works in this classroom, what's good for both of us, and what's going to help these kids learn the best, then that's what we'll do. You just have to do whatever it takes to make sure students are a success."

These teacher comments make a compelling case for flexibility as a key disposition for collaboration and co-teaching. Indeed, perhaps one of the most difficult issues that teachers face when collaborating is that both professionals have much knowledge and skill regarding the issue being addressed and have perspectives on how the problem might be addressed. For successful collaboration, professionals must be flexible and willing to:

- Recognize that their solution to a problem may not be the best solution.
- Look at the problem from another person's perspective.
- Compromise regarding an ultimate solution to the problem.

As you reflect on the information we've provided regarding this disposition, you will readily recognize that flexibility is certainly not always easy. All teachers in a collaborative relationship must retain a satisfying professional role and must be treated with respect. At the same time, teachers must be flexible when working with other professionals. Although this is not always easy, teachers are often motivated to be flexible because they know that flexibility leads to more successful collaboration and, most importantly, better outcomes for students.

Trust

Collaboration requires trust and respect. For example, two teachers who are co-teaching depend on each other for support when behavior management issues arise or to share responsibility for students who do not learn as much as expected. Similarly, when teacher assistance teams make recommendations to teachers who seek support for addressing a concern regarding a student, the teacher must trust that the team has her best interests and those of the student in mind as they work to develop an intervention to address the student's need.

Trust develops over time, as teachers realize that their collaborators (e.g., other teachers) are credible; demonstrate empathy for fellow collaborators (i.e., understand issues from another person's perspective); and accept other team members for who they are (Kampwirth & Powers, 2011; Snell & Janney, 2005). Furthermore, trust develops as collaborators depend on one another, become interdependent, and work to achieve mutual goals by (1) sharing resources, (2) giving help to others, (3) receiving help from others, and (4) dividing the work of the team and taking on a reasonable share of this work (Snell & Janney, 2005). As you consider how collaborators gain trust, you will readily recognize that trust is something that takes time to develop, but it can be lost in a moment (Kampwirth & Powers, 2011) if a collaborator senses that a person is not trustworthy, empathetic, or isn't working in good faith to solve a problem.

Respectful Interactions

Closely related to the development of trust is the need for collaborators to interact respectfully with one another. This suggests that collaborators will work with each other as equal partners, respecting and attempting to understand the perspectives of others. Factors that potentially interfere with parity, or working as equal partners, may include differences between collaborators related to university degrees; salary; access to resources (e.g., computers, paraeducators); gender; stature; ethnic background; facility with language; positions that differ in status in a school (e.g., principal and teacher); and a range of other factors (Walther-Thomas, Korinek, McLaughlin, & Williams, 2000).

Another aspect of respectful interactions that often influences collaboration is territoriality. That is, a general educator may view co-teaching as an intrusion on her territory because she must share the classroom with a special education teacher (Kochhar-Bryant, 2008). Similarly, a special education teacher may become territorial when others are assigned to teach "her children" in an important content area. Effective collaborators must closely examine their tendency toward protecting territory and share responsibility with other professionals, especially when this collaboration can result in better outcomes for students.

Pause & Reflect

When you interact with others, what are personal qualities that influence how much you respect and listen to the person? Are there certain qualities that cause you to shut down when listening to another? How can you address these biases to make sure that collaboration is effective?

Frame of Reference

Every collaborator brings a predisposition to respond to professional situations in a certain way, based on his frame of reference. Many factors influence a person's frame of reference, including disciplinary background and preparation (i.e., general education, special education, school psychology, etc.); previous work experience; professional socialization; and a range of other factors (Friend & Cook, 2010). For example, general and special education teachers sometimes differ with respect to how reading should be taught. Teachers and other professionals may have different frames of reference regarding the use of certain instructional strategies (e.g., cooperative learning), how classroom behavior should be managed, or who is responsible and accountable for students with disabilities.

Differing frames of reference can result in difficulty collaborating and can contribute to distortions in communication as collaborative interactions occur (Walther-Thomas et al., 2000). Frame of reference may also be influenced by the cultural identity of collaborators. For example, some cultures place great value on individual goals and achievement; others emphasize interdependence and the well-being of the group as a whole (Friend & Cook, 2010). Reflecting on one's frame of reference, understanding the frames of reference of others, and openly discussing these issues with collaborators are important in ensuring successful collaboration.

Belief in Collaboration to Meet the Needs of All Students

Beliefs about collaboration and inclusion are important dispositions as you address difficult problems faced by students and attempt to solve these problems. First is the belief that students should be included in general education classes to the maximum extent appropriate. Examining and discussing beliefs regarding what inclusion is, why it is important, and how students benefit from inclusion is an important activity for all teachers and administrators (McLeskey & Waldron, 2002), to ensure that all participants generally agree regarding these issues and support inclusive practices.

Participants in collaboration should also believe in the power of the collaborative process (Kochhar-Bryant, 2008). Confidence that collaboration can improve outcomes for all students is important to convey when working with others, and it can ensure that collaborators take the perspective that even very difficult situations can improve (Kampwirth & Powers, 2011).

Skills Needed for Successful Collaboration

Effective communication is critical for working with other professionals in a collaborative role. Many factors may interfere with effective communication and result in misunderstandings and poor collaboration. Several of these potential barriers relate to the previously described dispositions. For example, collaborators with different frames of reference will have difficulty communicating and effectively collaborating until they examine and understand the frames of reference that are creating the communication problem. Communication problems can be overcome through the development of effective skills related to listening, verbal communication, nonverbal communication, and addressing conflict. For more information regarding communications skills needed for effective collaboration, see Strategy 2 later in this chapter.

Skills for Managing Difficult Interactions

When collaboration occurs, pairs or teams of professionals can often reach consensus regarding a problem. However, at times, collaborators have very different perspectives on issues, and conflicts arise. When a conflict arises, it is important that collaborators recognize that the problem exists and then actively seek to engage and overcome the problem. Ignoring or avoiding conflict is a sure approach to undermining effective collaboration.

When conflict occurs, it is important to reaffirm the purpose of collaboration—that is, to improve outcomes for students. How collaborators address challenges depends, to a large degree, on the importance they attach to either achieving a professional goal or maintaining a good relationship with collaborators (Walther-Thomas et al., 2000). For example, when neither of these goals is important, the collaborator may simply avoid the conflict by withdrawing, and letting other collaborators make a final decision. This strategy is fine, if the goal is not important to the person who is withdrawing, or if she is not responsible for decision making. If the goal is very important, the collaborator may attempt to force others to accept a solution, which has the potential to produce conflict.

> ### Pause & Reflect
>
> Discuss with a peer how you react to conflict. Do you avoid conflict and withdraw? Confront and compete with others? Accommodate others to escape conflict? Or use a collaborative style to address issues directly and professionally? What style will you use when collaborating with other professionals?

A positive approach to addressing a challenging issue has been described as integrating (Walther-Thomas et al., 2000). When using this strategy, collaborators view the conflict as a problem to solve, and they search for a solution that both addresses the goal of the collaboration and maintains the relationship with collaborators. "This method involves collaboration between people, openness, exchange of information, reduction of tension between parties, and examination of differences to reach a solution acceptable to both parties" (Walther-Thomas et al., 2000, p. 109).

Strategies for addressing conflict include (Correa, Jones, Thomas, & Morsink, 2005):

- Clarify the goal of collaboration.
- Focus on the problem, not the people involved.
- Focus on goals that all collaborators share.
- Insist on using objective criteria to address the problem.
- Examine your feelings, and determine why they differ from others.
- Generate possible solutions collaboratively that benefit everyone.

Collaborative Roles in Inclusive Schools

As we noted previously, inclusive schools increase the necessity for collaboration by all professionals in a variety of roles and types of collaborative relationships. Three key types of collaborative relationships are working in teams, working as a co-teacher, and consulting with others for assistance.

Collaborative Teams

Teams of professionals often work together in schools to address a range of different types of issues and concerns. Most inclusive schools use inclusion-support teams to plan, implement, monitor, and evaluate inclusive school programs (McLeskey & Waldron, 2006). These teams consist of a range of professionals in different roles (e.g., teachers, principal, counselor, school psychologist) and other stakeholders (e.g., parents), who all work collaboratively to develop and support an inclusive program.

Inclusion-support teams address school-wide issues as they seek to develop a plan for school change that uses school resources effectively and efficiently to better meet the academic and social needs of all students. These teams often spend several months planning for inclusion,

Teachers often work in collaborative teams to address the needs of students who are struggling academically or socially.

as they visit inclusive schools, examine their own school, plan professional development for teachers and other school staff, and a range of other activities. (For more information regarding how these teams function, see McLeskey & Waldron, 2000, 2006.)

Another type of collaborative team addresses individual student needs. Approximately three of every four states require the use of a building-based collaborative support team to provide teachers with direct support in developing interventions to address student needs (Buck et al., 2003). These teams are often referred to as teacher assistance teams (TATs), but also are called *intervention assistance teams, student assistance teams, instructional support teams, school-wide assistance teams*, and *teacher support teams* in some states. Teacher assistance teams are relatively simple to implement, as they are designed to provide teachers with a structure to develop new ideas for their classrooms by brainstorming possible interventions for addressing student academic and social difficulties.

Teachers tend to view TATs very favorably. For example, research has revealed that from 50 to 60% of teachers view interventions developed by teacher assistance teams as using acceptable procedures and feel that the interventions were implemented with a high degree of fidelity (Lane, Pierson, Robertson, & Little, 2004). Furthermore, research on state-wide implementation of teacher support teams in Pennsylvania revealed that these teams were effective in reducing referrals to special education, and resulted in improved measures of student academic learning time (Kovaleski & Glew, 2006). For more information regarding how TATs work, see Strategy 3 later in this chapter.

Co-Teaching

A second type of collaborative role that is common for teachers in inclusive schools is co-teaching. As Susan Davis and Lisa Hallal, teachers from West Hernando Middle School, indicated in the interview in the opening vignette, co-teaching is critical to the success of inclusion in their school. As Susan Davis noted, special education teachers "can't know about content in every area in a middle school: English, science, math, social studies." Similarly, content-area teachers don't know all of the strategies that are needed to adapt for the needs of students with disabilities. Thus, having two teachers with different skills working collaboratively results in a combination of skills that benefits all students.

Co-teaching is the most frequently used model for delivering instruction in inclusive classrooms (Cook, McDuffie-Landrum, Oshita, & Cook, 2011). *Co-teaching* in inclusive classrooms is defined as a general and special education teacher working collaboratively to share responsibility for instructing a diverse group of students in a single classroom. Co-teaching uses the expertise of both general and special education teachers, and when done well provides all students with an improved educational experience.

Several issues are critical to the success of co-teaching (Cook et al., 2011; Friend, Cook, Hurley-Chamberlain, & Shamberger, 2010; Scruggs, Mastropieri, & McDuffie, 2007). For example, co-teachers emphasize the importance of administrative support to make certain that co-teaching is valued and given the resources and support needed to succeed. Co-teachers also emphasize the need for planning time before the school year begins to prepare for co-teaching; professional development to acquire necessary skills; and common planning time during the school year to continue to support co-teaching.

Perhaps most importantly, teachers emphasize the need for compatibility between co-teaching partners (Cook et al., 2011; Mastropieri, Scruggs, Graetz, et al., 2005). When co-teaching relationships work well, they are built on trust and mutual respect for the skills of the co-teaching partner and result in more effective instruction for all students (Mastropieri et al., 2005). Compatibility issues often arise because teachers have different beliefs regarding how to plan for co-teaching, or different beliefs regarding classroom instruction such as classroom routines, discipline, noise levels, and so forth (Friend & Cook, 2010; Mastropieri et al., 2005). We recommend addressing these issues by having frequent "co-teach chats" with your teaching partner. For more information on co-teach chats and ensuring compatibility and avoiding conflict when co-teaching, see Figure 3.

Figure 3	Supporting Successful Co-Teaching (and Resolving Conflict) Using Co-Teach Chats

To resolve conflicts that may arise and generally make sure that co-teaching works well, co-teaching partners should regularly schedule meetings to discuss their partnership. We recommend using the following strategies.

1. **Discuss minor issues before they escalate.** Minor issues that occur in co-taught classrooms can escalate if they are not attended to immediately by co-teaching partners. We recommend the use of weekly "co-teach chats" when beginning a co-teaching relationship. These chats should be brief (10 to 20 minutes) and should be structured to address what is working well about co-teaching and what can be improved. These meetings should be less frequent (biweekly, then monthly) as the school year progresses and teachers learn to discuss strengths and challenges of co-teaching more informally.

2. **Reflect on co-taught lessons.** Co-teach chats can be more efficient and beneficial if co-teaching partners focus on a recent co-taught lesson, and reflect on what worked well and what could be improved regarding that lesson. These discussions should begin and end with positive comments regarding the lesson, and at least twice as many positive as negative comments should be made. However, each teacher should contribute at least one area that could be improved when reflecting on each lesson.

3. **Make differences or minor disagreements opportunities to learn.** The fact that co-teaching partners bring different knowledge, skills, instructional approaches, and beliefs to the partnership is a good thing in many ways. Teachers have the opportunity to learn from one another, and experience different approaches to instruction that they may not have considered. Co-teach chats offer the opportunity to build on and discuss these differences as strengths of the partnership. This can be done if both partners remember that the strengths of working as co-teachers emerge from the equal, collaborative partnership, and not from one teacher serving as an expert who advises the other teacher or who has all the right answers.

4. **Use data on student progress to examine how co-teaching may be improved.** As a school year progresses, a source of discussion during co-teach chats should be data regarding student progress. As invariably happens in every classroom, some students will not make sufficient progress over a period of time. Data on the progress of students thus provide objective information regarding an area in which the co-taught classroom needs to improve. This provides a stimulus for discussion regarding how instruction might be altered to improve student outcomes in the co-taught classroom.

5. **Examine your approach to addressing differences, and encourage your co-teaching partner to do the same.** The approaches adults use to address conflict differ with regard to the importance of the relationship, the importance of the outcome, and their willingness to compromise. This may result in avoiding the problem, or one person making all of the decisions. A balance among the use of subsequently described approaches to conflict resolution is needed for successful co-teaching teams. Which of these approaches to conflict resolution do you prefer?

a. **Competitive:** An approach that uses power (knowledge, position, and so forth) to "win" any conflict. This approach emphasizes the importance of the outcome (winning the "battle"), and less emphasis on the relationship with the other person involved, and little emphasis on compromise. Generally, this approach leads to many problems in a co-teaching relationship, and should not be used.

b. **Avoidance:** An approach where one participant avoids or ignores differences. This approach may reflect value for the relationship more than the outcome. At times, especially when very volatile issues are the source of differences, avoidance is advisable. However, some co-teaching partners avoid minor issues, or let the other person make most or all of the decisions. This often leads to problems in the co-teaching relationship and lack of parity.

c. **Accommodation:** An approach where the relationship is valued more than the outcome. This approach results in one co-teaching partner "giving in" and accommodating the other partner to make sure that her needs are met. This approach may be used occasionally in a co-teaching partnership, but the overuse of this approach can produce dissatisfaction in the co-teaching partnership.

d. **Compromise:** The most common approach to addressing conflict is to compromise—when one person gives up some ideas and expects her co-teaching partner to do the same. This approach may be used at times, especially when time is limited. The outcome is often one that all find acceptable, but it may not be the best solution.

e. **Collaboration:** This is often the most satisfying approach to resolving conflict, but it is very time consuming. This occurs when co-teaching partners respect each other's ideas, treat each other respectfully, and consider all information and data to reach the best solution to the conflict that has arisen.

6. **Consider the following tips for constructively using differences between adults:**

a. Respect the many different perspectives that exist between thoughtful, intelligent adults.

b. Listen to your teaching partner and try to understand what she thinks, and why she thinks the way she does.

c. Try not to insist on your favorite method, approach, or preference. Instead, encourage shared or collaborative problem solving to address differences.

d. Seek input from others who are well respected when differences arise that are difficult to resolve.

e. Genuinely care about and respect your co-teaching partner's ideas and perspectives, and show this through your interactions.

Sources: P. Dettmer, L. Thurston, A. Knackendoffel, & N. Dyck (2009). *Collaboration, consultation, and teamwork for students with special needs.* Upper Saddle River, NJ: Merrill/Pearson Education; M. Friend & L. Cook (2010). *Interactions: Collaboration skills for school professionals* (6th ed.). Boston: Allyn & Bacon; D. Ploessl, M. Rock, N. Schoenfeld, & B. Blanks (2010). On the same page: Practical techniques to enhance co-teaching interactions. *Intervention in School and Clinic, 45,* 158–168.

When co-teaching is done well, many benefits accrue for students with and without disabilities (Friend et al., 2010; Hang & Rabren, 2008; Scruggs et al., 2007). These benefits include increased student achievement, fewer problems with disruptive behavior, improved student attitudes and self-concepts, and more positive peer relationships.

Co-teaching is effective for students with and without disabilities for three primary reasons. First, co-teaching provides the opportunity to capitalize on the unique knowledge and skills that both teachers bring to the classroom (Ploessl, Rock, Schoenfeld, & Blanks, 2010). Second, two teachers bring an extra pair of hands to the classroom, which provides the opportunity to structure the class and group students in ways that result in more support for students. For example, teachers can more often:

- Use effective, evidence-based instructional practices.
- Differentiate instruction.
- Employ intensive small-group or individual instruction.
- Provide immediate attention to student needs.
- Monitor student on-task behavior and intervene as needed.

Co-teaching is frequently used in inclusive classrooms to meet a diverse range of student needs.

Finally, co-teachers can combine their expertise to determine novel approaches to meet student needs (McLeskey & Waldron, 2000). This is necessary in inclusive classrooms when traditional solutions from general and special education do not readily meet the needs of all students. For example, this may occur as co-teachers determine how to use a specialized method for instruction to meet the needs of a small group of students in the general education classroom, or begin to use student resources to address needs using methods such as class-wide peer tutoring (McMaster, Kung, Han, & Cao, 2008).

Some consider co-teaching as synonymous with inclusion, but this is not the case. Many successful inclusive programs use co-teaching as a core strategy for ensuring student success, and yet others rarely use co-teaching and use other collaborative strategies to support students (e.g., consultative support from a special education teacher or paraeducators). We recommend that teachers in inclusive schools take advantage of co-teaching whenever possible. Co-teaching provides teachers with a powerful opportunity to increase their expertise. For example, special education teachers can learn in-depth information regarding the general education curriculum, methods and grouping strategies that are used in the general education classroom, and which instructional approaches fit into this setting. Similarly, general education teachers can learn methods for making accommodations for diverse student needs, grouping strategies for providing more intensive instruction to students, and so forth. In short, co-teaching provides an excellent opportunity for professional development, and after experiencing co-teaching, teachers often have significantly improved expertise for addressing diverse student needs.

Schools can implement co-teaching in any general education classroom and can use it with any subject matter. Co-teaching takes careful planning because teacher roles and responsibilities change significantly when using this approach. For more information regarding how planning for co-teaching works, see Strategy 4 later in this chapter.

Pause & Reflect

Examine the dispositions we addressed previously in this chapter. Why are these dispositions especially important for co-teachers? Do you have the necessary dispositions to be a successful co-teacher?

Collaborative Consultation

Collaborative consultation involves two persons working together to seek solutions to a mutually agreed on problem or issue. When collaboration involves two professionals, the participants will typically have different areas of expertise and different roles. For example, a special education teacher may consult with a general education teacher regarding methods for making accommodations on tests (e.g., allowing more time, breaking the test into several sessions, providing a calculator) to meet the needs of a student with a disability.

When you teach in an inclusive classroom, you will have students with highly specialized needs that you do not fully understand, regardless of whether you are the general or special education teacher. When this occurs, you will need a specialist to provide information and suggest approaches to meet student needs. For example, a special education teacher may need assistance in addressing the physical needs of a student with a severe physical disability and may seek the consultative assistance of a physical therapist. Others that may provide assistance include school psychologists, behavior specialists, curriculum specialists, speech–language pathologists, social workers, nurses, and so forth.

The steps that are typically included in collaborative consultation include the following:

- Refer a problem or issue to a consultant.
- Identify and clarify the problem to be addressed.
- Brainstorm possible solutions to the problem.
- Select an intervention by the referring teacher.
- Clarify implementation of the intervention.
- Follow up to determine the effectiveness of the intervention.

If the intervention is not effective, or if the collaborators need to address other problems or issues, they repeat the collaborative consultation cycle. Teacher assistance teams (described earlier) use a collaborative consultation approach. For a description of the steps involved in collaborative consultation when using a TAT, see Strategy 3 later in this chapter.

As a teacher in an inclusive classroom, you will not only receive assistance from consultants but also serve as a consultant to others. For example, after you have worked in a successful inclusive program for a period of time, you may be asked to consult with other teachers who are developing inclusive programs. In addition, two of the most critical consultative roles for teachers in inclusive classrooms that you will need to address relate to the work you will do with paraeducators and families.

Paraeducators (also called *paraprofessionals, instructional assistants,* or *teacher's aides*) are an important resource for many inclusive classrooms. Paraeducators are individuals who provide instruction and other services to students and who are supervised by teachers responsible for student outcomes (Fisher & Pleasants, 2011). Paraeducators can serve in a variety of roles to support classroom instruction and related activities in an inclusive setting, including the following (Correa et al., 2005):

- Tutor after a teacher provides primary instruction.
- Float in the classroom to check on student progress and respond to questions.
- Provide skill-and-drill activities to individuals or small groups of students.
- Prepare instructional materials, activities, and games.
- Read stories or content-area material.
- Conduct small-group instructional activities.
- Grade, correct homework, and handle other paperwork.
- Work on learning centers, bulletin boards, and so forth.
- Provide support for students with highly specialized needs (e.g., medical or physical needs for students with severe disabilities).

Although paraeducators can be a valuable resource in an inclusive classroom, concerns will arise at times regarding paraeducators' roles and responsibilities. For example, in some classrooms, paraeducators are assigned to one student with a disability. This type of assignment raises the possibility that the paraeducator will take on responsibility for the student (i.e., planning student lessons, assessing student progress) that should reside with the classroom teacher, and the classroom teacher will not be familiar with the student and his needs (French, 2003). In addition, if the paraeducator is "velcroed" to the student and does not work with others in the classroom, difficulty developing social relationships may result for the student.

As a teacher in an inclusive classroom, you will at times supervise paraeducators and ensure that their time is used effectively and efficiently. Some local school districts provide training in working effectively with paraeducators. We provide more information in Strategy 5 later in this chapter regarding how teachers may work effectively with paraeducators to improve outcomes for students.

Families

Two major factors have contributed to the increased involvement of families in the education of students with disabilities. First, the Individuals with Disabilities Education Improvement Act (IDEA, 2004) mandates that parents work with professionals as partners in ensuring an effective education for students with disabilities. This includes parent participation in every decision related to their child with a disability, including identification, assessment, and placement (Rosenberg, Westling, & McLeskey, 2011). Parents also have extensive rights related to the development and approval of the IEP for school-aged students or the individual family service plan (IFSP) for younger children. Parent participation in these activities is designed to ensure that parents and educators work as partners in addressing the needs of students with disabilities and that adversarial relationships are avoided.

A second reason for family involvement is research indicating this involvement can serve to enhance a student's academic achievement and improve behavior and social adjustment.

> More than 30 years of research demonstrate that when families are directly engaged with their children's education, students show increased test scores, higher academic achievement, improved attitudes toward learning, have better social behavior, higher self esteem, fewer placements in special education, higher school attendance rates, and lower dropout rates. (Kochhar-Bryant, 2008, p. 208)

These positive effects have been demonstrated across students from different economic, ethnic, and cultural backgrounds (Kochhar-Bryant, 2008).

Parents and caregivers can be involved in schools in many ways (Correa et al., 2005). For example, families can:

- Share information regarding their children with teachers and other school personnel (e.g., counselor, school psychologist).
- Reinforce and support school programs at home through activities such as a daily report card to address student discipline, or programs to ensure homework completion (Fabiano et al., 2009; Patall, Cooper, & Robinson, 2008).
- Advocate for quality services for their child.
- Volunteer to work in schools for part of the school day or in before- or after-school activities.
- Participate in school decision-making groups, such as a school advisory committee.
- Work in the community with businesses and local government to obtain support for the school.

For teachers in an inclusive classroom, parent support has the potential to significantly enhance student outcomes and increase the resources available to meet student needs. Interventions can be highly effective when teachers and caregivers work collaboratively to develop and implement interventions to address a range of student needs (Fabiano et al., 2009; Patall, Cooper, Robinson, 2008; Whitbread, Bruder, Fleming, & Park, 2007). We provide more information in Strategy 6 regarding the development of effective approaches for home–school collaboration.

Students as Collaborators: Peer Assistance in Inclusive Classrooms and Schools

In many schools, these are days of limited resources, increasing standards for student achievement, and increasing diversity in classrooms. These circumstances require that educators seek cost-effective methods for addressing student needs. Teachers who are effective use all available resources to meet student needs, and one readily available resource is the students themselves (Kauchak & Eggen, 2012). Engaging students in collaborative roles to assist or support peers in addressing the needs of those who are struggling academically or socially is an integral part of many successful inclusive classrooms. Indeed, as we have discussed throughout this text, acceptance and support of students with disabilities is a critical component of any effective, inclusive classroom.

Many peer-assisted strategies have been developed to address basic academic skills, higher-level cognitive skills, and social interactions or skill development (McDonnell, 2011). In the following section, we describe a strategy that teachers may use to support students who are struggling academically or socially in inclusive classrooms: the peer buddy program.

The Peer Buddy Program

Several researchers have found a close relationship between academic achievement and the development of friendship skills, behavior control, and self-esteem (Ginsburg-Block, Rohrbeck, & Fantuzzo, 2006). Peer-assisted learning strategies are an intervention that has the potential not only to improve academic achievement but also to improve social skills. For example, in a review of studies related to peer-assisted learning (Ginsburg-Block et al., 2006), these interventions were found to improve student social and self-concept outcomes. This is an important outcome for inclusive classrooms, because the improvement of social skills and the development of friendships are often goals for students with disabilities, especially those with more severe disabilities in these settings.

The need to improve the social skills and acceptance level of students with disabilities in general education classrooms has led to the development of a peer-assisted learning

A View from Students

How All Students Benefit from a Peer Support Program

As students with a range of disabilities were being included in general education classrooms at West Hernando Middle School, teachers and administrators recognized that teachers often do not have the time to give every student all the support that they need. To begin to address this issue, the staff developed a Peer Support program, where students volunteer to provide peer support for a student with a disability with elective course credit for this activity. Students are then provided training, and work in a general education classroom with their peer with a disability for one class period each day. Students with a range of disabilities are included in this program, including those with autism, intellectual disabilities, learning disabilities, and physical disabilities.

We discussed the impact of the Peer Support program at West Hernando with two students who have been peer buddies. One of the peer buddies, Emma (pseudonyms are used for all students in this feature), works with a student with an intellectual disability, Melissa, in a U.S. history class. Emma describes that it is "harder for Melissa to learn sometimes, and I have to go over things a few more times with her. It's easier for her if I put tidbits in there, rather than having her always learn from the dryness of the book." Another peer buddy, Susan, works with Lily, a student with autism who was formerly in a self-contained special education class before the Peer Support program started. Susan commented that in her sixth-grade geography class, Lily "likes to do things hands on, and work with other people in class. She doesn't like to be in a self-contained (special education) class because she likes being out and learning different things, not just being in one class and learning the same things over and over again."

Emma commented on the benefits of including students with disabilities in general education classrooms, noting that it is "better for them in regular classrooms because they need the interaction [with typical peers]. They need to talk with kids their age." She went on to comment that at first, "they [students with disabilities] are dependent on you, but as the program gets further along, the peers back off and let [the students with disabilities] do more themselves, helping them become more independent." Emma also commented that students with disabilities benefit from the demands of the general education classroom, because they're going to have these demands in life. "You're going to have deadlines in life. They're going to have to sit there and learn how to do things, how to write, and read. It's going to help them be independent."

Both Emma and Susan commented on how the Peer Support program had changed them and their beliefs and understandings about students with disabilities. Emma explained how she had gotten close to each of the students she had worked with as a peer buddy. "When I go home, if Melissa has had a bad day, then I have a bad day. Because we have that connection, if she's having a good day, it makes my day a lot better."

Susan further explained that working as a peer buddy helped her understand more about students with disabilities, and become more accepting of their differences. She further noted that this made accepting students with disabilities as part of the school community more natural. "I feel different about socializing with students with disabilities. Now I know what to say, if someone in the hallway is upset, I'll go up to him, talk with him, and see what's wrong. You know what to say and won't be nervous."

Susan and Emma both commented that students with disabilities are now a more accepted part of the school community as a result of the Peer Support program. Both also strongly believe that all students at West Hernando Middle School should be part of the Peer Support program. This may happen one day, as the Peer Support program has grown rapidly from 4 students when it began to 114 students who are participating this year. Obviously, many students see how this program benefits the entire school community at WHMS, and want to be part of it.

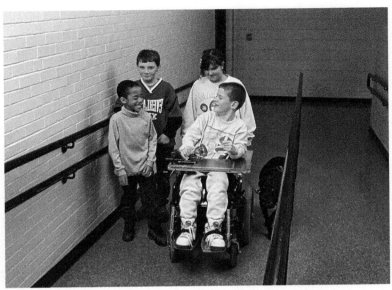

Peer buddy programs can significantly enhance academic and social outcomes for students with disabilities and their peer buddies.

strategy called the peer buddy program (Hughes & Carter, 2008). Although teachers can use the peer buddy program with any student in a classroom who needs academic support and improved social skills, it was initially developed to address the academic and social needs of students with more severe disabilities in middle and high schools (Hughes & Carter, 2008). See the "A View from Students" feature in this chapter for a description of how students provided support and benefited from a peer buddy program at West Hernando Middle School. (Note that this program is called a Peer Support program at WHMS).

As the comments from Emma and Susan regarding the Peer Support program at West Hernando Middle School reveal, these programs can be very successful in improving the acceptance levels of students with disabilities, and providing more opportunities for social interaction with typical peers. This is not always easy to achieve, as students with severe disabilities in secondary schools who are included in general education classes are often isolated and seldom interact with their peers who do not have disabilities. This occurs for many reasons, including the limited social and communication skills of many students with severe disabilities; the structure of the school day in secondary schools (e.g., emphasis on lecture and focus on academic material); and concerns among students without disabilities that they lack the skills and knowledge to interact with peers with severe disabilities. Fostering the interactions of students with severe disabilities and their peers in secondary schools requires intentional efforts by educators, and a peer buddy program provides one approach for addressing this need (Hughes & Carter, 2008). For detailed information regarding the peer buddy program, and how such a program is implemented, see Strategy 7 later in this chapter.

Summary

This chapter addressed the following topics:

Collaboration: What to expect

- Collaboration refers to "a style for direct interaction between at least two co-equal parties voluntarily engaged in shared decision making as they work toward a common goal" (Friend & Cook, 2010, p. 7).
- Teachers work in a variety of collaborative roles to meet the needs of students in inclusive schools. This collaboration is necessary because no single teacher has all the knowledge and skills necessary to meet the needs of all students. Collaboration thus provides teachers and other professionals with the opportunity to learn from one another as they share knowledge and expertise.

Dispositions and skills needed for successful collaboration

- Dispositions are characteristic tendencies or habitual inclinations.
- Dispositions necessary for effective collaboration include:
  - Flexibility in adapting to work with others in collaborative roles
  - Trust in collaborative partners to share responsibility for addressing student needs
  - Respectful interactions with collaborators
  - A frame of reference that facilitates collaboration
  - A belief in collaboration to meet the needs of all students

- Communication skills for working effectively with other professionals include:
  - Listening skills
  - Verbal communication skills
  - Nonverbal communication skills
- Skills for managing difficult interactions with other professionals are also needed for effective collaboration.

Collaborative roles in inclusive schools

- Teachers often work with teams of other professionals (e.g., teacher assistance teams) to collaboratively address student needs.
- Another frequent collaborative role of teachers in inclusive schools is working as a co-teacher.
- Teachers and other professionals may take on a collaborative consultation role. In this role, a professional provides support to another professional to address a specific problem or issue.
- Teachers often work in a collaborative role with paraeducators to provide support for students with disabilities and others who struggle in inclusive classrooms.
- Teachers and other professionals often work collaboratively with families to address the needs of students with disabilities.

Students as collaborators: Peer assistance in inclusive classrooms and schools

- Engaging students to work collaboratively to address the needs of those who struggle academically or socially can be an integral part of successful inclusive classrooms.
- Two types of peer-assisted learning strategies that are often used in inclusive classrooms are cooperative learning and peer tutoring.
- Another effective strategy for engaging students in providing academic and social support for students with disabilities is a peer buddy program.

Addressing Professional Standards

Standards addressed in this chapter include:

CEC Standards: (4) instructional strategies; (5) learning environments and social interactions; (7) instructional planning; (10) collaboration.

MyEducationLab

Go to the topic Collaboration, Consultation, and Co-Teaching in the **MyEducationLab** (www.myeducationlab.com) for *Inclusion*, where you can:

- Find learning outcomes for Collaboration, Consultation, and Co-Teaching, along with the national standards that connect to these outcomes.
- Complete Assignments and Activities that can help you more deeply understand the chapter content.
- Apply and practice your understanding of the core teaching skills identified in the chapter with the Building Teaching Skills and Dispositions learning units.
- Examine challenging situations and cases presented in the IRIS Center Resources.
- Check your comprehension on the content covered in the chapter with the Study Plan. Here you will be able to take a chapter quiz, receive feedback on your answers, and then access Review, Practice, and Enrichment activities to enhance your understanding of chapter content.

Glossary

Building-based support teams: Groups of professionals who work with teachers to address student academic or behavior difficulties.

Collaboration: Teachers' and other professionals' working together to achieve common goals.

Collaborative consultation: A formal process that includes (1) specific problem identification and goal setting; (2) analysis of factors contributing to the problem and brainstorming possible problem-solving interventions; (3) planning an intervention; and (4) evaluating the outcomes.

Consultant: A teacher (or other professional) who provides assistance to another teacher by problem solving possible solutions to a classroom problem.

Co-teaching: When used in inclusive classrooms, co-teaching is defined as a general and special-education teacher working collaboratively to share responsibility for instructing a diverse group of students in a single classroom.

Dispositions: One's temperament or tendency, generally learned over time, to act or respond in a certain way, given a certain situation.

Teacher assistance team (TAT): A widely used form of building-based support that uses a systematic approach to identify student difficulties and generate possible solutions for referring teachers.

EFFECTIVE STRATEGIES FOR COLLABORATION AND TEAMING

Putting It All Together

Today teachers are opening their classroom doors to others as they collaborate to reach increasingly higher expectations for student outcomes. With this in mind, we hope you will embrace collaboration, but keep the following ideas in mind.

1. **Start slowly.** If you're just beginning to work as a co-teacher in a school, we recommend working with only one or two co-teachers initially. It is important to start slowly with collaborative activities so that you'll have time to develop the skills and reinforce the dispositions you need to make collaboration succeed. Working with a team of teachers to plan instruction or carefully selecting initial co-teachers is often a good way to get started.

2. **Reflect on your strengths and weaknesses as a collaborator.** Every teacher has strengths and weaknesses when working in a collaborative relationship. Some teachers are quick to reach a conclusion regarding a problem, for example, and become impatient when others need more time. There are also some professionals whose perspectives you will not respect as much as the perspectives of others. It is important that you be honest in appraising how others view you as a collaborator, and use that information to improve your skills and dispositions for collaborating with other professionals.

3. **Learn and develop the skills needed for collaboration.** As you reflect on your skills and dispositions as a collaborator, you will certainly recognize some areas that need improvement. Some of these skills or dispositions will improve as you engage in collaborative activities with peers, observe their behavior (and yours) during these interactions, and try out different options to improve communication and decision making. Another critical way of gaining these skills is to take advantage of professional development related to collaboration. This includes working with and observing peers in your school to better understand how they address difficulties when collaborating, and seeking guidance from peers when difficulties arise.

4. **Enjoy the collaborative partnerships you develop.** A major benefit of collaboration for teachers is that it reduces the isolation many feel in their profession. Collaboration allows a group of experienced professionals to share and test ideas in a setting where individual and team efforts are recognized and valued, and all professionals have opportunities for growth and leadership (Waldron & McLeskey, 2010). When collaboration works well, it is very beneficial and enjoyable for all involved and creates a community of support within a school.

5. **Celebrate the successes of collaboration.** When done well, collaboration leads to the synthesis of available expertise and the discovery of new knowledge and teaching approaches that benefit all students (Kochhar-Bryant, 2008). We are sure that you will have many successes as a collaborator—be sure to take the time to recognize and enjoy your successes by celebrating them!

Strategy Fact Sheet

In the remainder of this chapter, we describe seven effective strategies, which we referred to previously in the chapter, to help you plan effectively to meet the needs of all students.

STRATEGY	DESCRIPTION	SPECIAL CONSIDERATIONS
Strategy 1: Key Components of Effective Collaboration	Collaboration allows teachers to work with other professionals to improve knowledge, teaching skills, and dispositions. The components of effective collaboration provide teachers with the knowledge and skills needed to confirm that they are well prepared for collaborative roles.	When collaborating regarding inclusion, teachers must work to ensure a respectful, equal partnership with their collaborator.
Strategy 2: Communication Skills and Successful Collaboration	The most important skills for collaborating successfully with others relate to communication. Communication problems can be overcome through the development of skills related to listening, verbal communication, and nonverbal communication.	Communication is very complex, as it consists of sending and receiving messages simultaneously, sending both verbal and nonverbal messages, and using different types of communication with different people.
Strategy 3: Teacher Assistance Teams (TATs)	This strategy provides teachers who face problems in their classrooms with a quick, efficient method to seek assistance from well-respected peers. A group of teachers meet with a referring teacher about a specific student problem, brainstorm regarding possible ways to address the problem, and support the teacher in selecting, implementing, and evaluating an intervention.	Most student problems referred to the TAT relate to work habits, classroom behavior, interpersonal behavior, attention problems, and reading difficulties. Recommended interventions are reported to be successful for almost 90% of students.
Strategy 4: Planning for Co-Teaching	Co-teaching is an approach to collaboration that allows general and special education teachers to share knowledge, dispositions, and skills as they share responsibility for student outcomes in an inclusive classroom. It is important to carefully plan before beginning a co-teaching partnership, and continue planning during the school year as co-teaching roles evolve.	Co-teaching is a dynamic process that requires teachers to change roles often, depending on the content being taught and student needs. Varying teaching roles allows teachers to learn and develop expertise from their teaching partner.
Strategy 5: Working with Paraeducators	Paraeducators, who work under the supervision of a certified teacher, provide important support for many students in inclusive classrooms. Effectively supervising a paraeducator requires that the teacher collaborate effectively with the paraeducator to be sure that responsibilities are well defined and the paraeducator is well prepared to address these responsibilities.	Paraeducators may provide support such as one-to-one or small-group instruction, support for students with highly specialized needs, grading and other paperwork, and preparation of materials for class lessons.
Strategy 6: Working with Families: Home–School Collaboration	Effective collaboration between teachers and families can result in significant improvement in student achievement and behavior. Teachers in inclusive classrooms should encourage home–school collaboration and parent involvement in a range of activities. The teacher should get to know parents well and work with parents to determine the types of involvement that will work well for them.	When collaborating with parents, teachers should be knowledgeable regarding the parents' cultural backgrounds. This allows the teacher to understand, respect, and take into account cultural experiences when working with parents.
Strategy 7: Peer Buddy Programs	Adolescents with moderate-to-severe disabilities benefit from peer interactions, just as other students do. Peer buddy programs are designed to provide academic support, as well as an opportunity for peer interactions to occur in natural school settings.	Peer buddy programs have many benefits for students with and without disabilities, but require careful planning and consistent support to succeed.

KEY COMPONENTS OF EFFECTIVE COLLABORATION

Rationale

Many professionals take the perspective that collaboration comes naturally, and is a skill that all teachers have (Friend & Cook, 2010). Research evidence indicates that this is often not the case (Correa et al., 2005; Dettmer, Thurston, Knackendoffel, & Dyck, 2009; Friend et al., 2010). Although some teachers may be natural collaborators, many teachers need to learn the skills for working effectively with others. Consideration of key components of collaboration can improve the likelihood that teachers and other professionals will succeed when engaged in these activities. For example, roles should be carefully defined and structured, teachers must understand their roles and be well prepared for them, and outcomes should be evaluated to ensure that collaboration has succeeded (Dettmer et al., 2009; Friend & Cook, 2010).

Step-by-Step

As you engage in collaboration with other professionals, you should address several key components of these activities to enhance the collaborative activities and improve student outcomes.

1. *Prepare for collaboration.* Most of us must learn collaboration skills, including those related to effective communication and addressing conflict. Participants in a collaborative relationship should participate in professional development activities together to ensure that they have the knowledge, skills, and dispositions needed for effective collaboration. Possible topics for professional development (addressed later in this chapter) include co-teaching, teaming, working with parents, and working with para-educators. Other areas of professional development that may be useful include methods for problem solving and working collaboratively to develop inclusive classrooms.

2. *Define roles.* A key to the success of any collaborative endeavor is ensuring that all participants are clear regarding their roles. For example, co-teachers can take on a range of roles (see Strategy 4 for more information on co-teaching roles), and these roles can change over time. Similarly, when professionals work on collaborative teams that address curriculum in a content area or across disciplines, or address individual needs of students and teachers, they must clearly define their roles to ensure that they provide well-coordinated, seamless support for students (Dettmer et al., 2009).

3. *Achieve role parity.* For collaboration to succeed, all participants must feel that they are important contributors, that they are equal partners in decision making, and that their contributions are valued (Friend & Cook, 2010). This becomes difficult at times when a collaborator is a principal or other professional who is in a supervisory role or is viewed as more knowledgeable than others regarding a particular topic (e.g., inclusion, classroom management). In inclusive settings, professionals often bring different expertise to collaborative deliberations (e.g., a general education teacher may have deep knowledge of a content area, or a special education teacher has skills in adapting and differentiating content). While collaborating, participants must agree to have parity and work as equal partners, even if this is not the case outside of the collaborative relationship (e.g., with a principal) or if knowledge levels regarding the content being addressed differ.

4. *Address key considerations when collaborating.* As you collaborate with other professionals, keep the following in mind (Kampwirth & Powers, 2011):

   - Reach out to your collaborators to make them feel comfortable and accepted as equal partners.
   - Make it clear to your collaborators that you strongly prefer to work collaboratively.
   - Use time efficiently, so that no one feels that time is being wasted.
   - When a problem arises, clearly define the problem and focus on finding solutions.
   - Try to understand the collaborative relationship from the perspective of other participants.
   - Continue to work on any problems until they are resolved.

5. *Evaluate the collaborative relationship frequently.* Collaborative relationships change over time, making it important for participants to frequently evaluate whether the relationship is working and how it might be changed to work better. This is true with co-teaching, which may change as student needs evolve over time or as demands on the teacher for content knowledge or differentiation of instruction change. Collaborative colleagues can use discussions to address the evolving nature of collaboration and to ensure that all participants continue to be committed to the collaborative relationship. We previously described co-teach chats (see Figure 3), which are an approach that may be used to evaluate and improve co-teaching relationships.

Applications and Examples

Teachers who are good collaborators continue to gain skills and dispositions that facilitate their work. For example, collaborators must be open to new ideas and demonstrate willingness to others to explore new perspectives, even when they contrast with their point of view. This shows respect for other collaborators and can prevent potential problems with collaborative interactions. Several essential behaviors to consider when working toward a respectful, equal partnership with a collaborator include (Dettmer et al., 2009):

- Really listen, and talk, together with collaborators.
- Describe your perspectives, but give objective examples whenever possible.
- Work toward resolutions or compromises together.
- Provide a collective summary of discussion points and tentative agreements.
- If the process is stalled, seek input from others.
- Talk after completing a collaborative activity, to reflect on outcomes and how to improve collaboration next time.

Keep in Mind

As you collaborate regarding inclusion, keep in mind that professionals often do not share common definitions of inclusion or inclusive practices. Given this variability, it is important to discuss individual perspectives on inclusion with other collaborators and to ensure that all understand your perspective and that you understand those of others. Successful collaborators determine common ground on which they can focus (e.g., improving outcomes for all students, making all students part of the academic and social community of the school), emphasize similar perspectives, and downplay differences.

Key References

Correa, V., Jones, H., Thomas, C., & Morsink, C. (2005). *Interactive teaming: Enhancing programs for students with special needs.* Upper Saddle River, NJ: Merrill/Pearson Education.

Dettmer, P., Thurston, L., Knackendoffel, A., & Dyck, N. (2009). *Collaboration, consultation, and teamwork for students with special needs.* Upper Saddle River, NJ: Merrill/Pearson Education.

Friend, M., & Cook, L. (2010). *Interactions: Collaboration skills for school professionals* (6th ed.). Boston: Allyn & Bacon.

Kampwirth, T., & Powers, K. (2011). *Collaborative consultation in the schools* (4th ed.). Upper Saddle River, NJ: Merrill/Pearson Education.

Kochhar-Bryant, C. (2008). *Collaboration and system coordination for students with special needs.* Upper Saddle River, NJ: Merrill/Pearson Education.

COMMUNICATION SKILLS AND SUCCESSFUL COLLABORATION

Rationale

The most important skills for effectively working with others relate to communication (Correa et al., 2005; Friend & Cook, 2010). Collaboration can be effective only if those involved understand each other, convey both verbal and nonverbal (e.g., body language) information intentionally, and avoid misunderstandings. Many factors may interfere with effective communication and result in misunderstandings and poor collaboration. Several of these potential barriers relate to the dispositions we discussed previously in this chapter. For example, collaborators with different frames of reference will have difficulty communicating effectively until they examine and understand the frames of reference that are creating the communication problem. It is therefore important for collaborators to learn effective communication skills to facilitate the best possible collaboration and to improve student outcomes.

Step-by-Step

Collaborators can substantially reduce communication problems by developing effective communication skills. These skills can be used to make sure that information communicated is the intended information and is understood by collaborators. The most important communication skills for collaborators relate to listening, verbal communication, and nonverbal communication.

1 *Listen.* Many factors may interfere with effective listening when collaborating (Friend & Cook, 2010). These factors include:

- Filtering certain messages that you do not want to hear. The listener hears the topic of the message and then tunes out.
- Being distracted by details that are tangential to the main point.
- Rehearsing a response while a collaborator is talking.
- Reacting to "hot" words that cause you to react strongly, such as whole language, direct instruction, inclusion, accountability, behaviorism.

Monitoring your reactions to words or topics as communication occurs and recognizing that you are engaging in these behaviors are important steps in moving beyond these barriers to effective communication. Other listening skills that will improve communication include actively listening for the real content of the message you're hearing; attending to the feelings that may be in the message; paraphrasing what you've heard, including the content of the message and the feelings behind the message; and providing the speaker with the opportunity to clarify your perspectives (Vaughn, Bos, & Schumm, 2011; Walther-Thomas, Korinek, McLaughlin, & Williams, 2000).

2 *Develop verbal communication skills.* Your verbal communication skills are important to consider as you work in a collaborative relationship. You may use several strategies to be clearly understood as you interact with others (Vaughn et al., 2011; Walther-Thomas et al., 2000), including:

- Repeat messages through multiple modes, including restating a message in a different manner (e.g., summarizing the key points of a previous message) and providing a written summary of a message.
- Practice empathy, or place yourself in the other person's shoes, in an attempt to understand your collaborator's frame of reference or perspective on a topic being discussed.
- Ensure understanding by using clear and concise language that is understandable by collaborators (e.g., avoiding the use of professional jargon and acronyms such as IEP, LRE, ASD, IDEA).
- Use questions to clarify, better understand, seek further information, and convey acceptance to the speaker.
- Summarize the content to make certain that all agree regarding what has been discussed.

Michelle Duclos, a seventh-grade science teacher at West Hernando Middle School, notes that at times, she and her co-teacher will have only a few minutes to plan before beginning a team lesson. Frequent, clear, effective communication is needed to ensure that she and her co-teacher share ideas and "play off each other, emphasizing our strengths" during the class. She also emphasizes the importance of teachers reading one another as they move through the class period, by either talking briefly or picking up on nonverbal cues as "an amazing idea comes to one of us during the lesson."

3 *Address nonverbal communication.* Many teachers who are initially involved in collaboration with other professionals and parents overlook the importance of *nonverbal communication*, which may be a more accurate representation of the intent of what is being communicated than the verbal message (Correa et al., 2005). Certain negative, nonverbal messages are sent to others by appearing to be bored, using a tone of voice that does not match comments, and exhibiting negative behaviors such as inattentiveness to comments made by certain collaborators, facial expressions or eye rolling, sighing, lack of eye contact, and so forth.

Effective collaboration requires that participants use nonverbal communication to convey attention, respect, and understanding when others are speaking. Strategies for conveying positive messages through nonverbal communication include leaning toward the speaker and maintaining eye contact, appearing relaxed and interested in the speaker, maintaining appropriate proximity to the speaker, using an appropriate tone of voice, and monitoring negative nonverbal messages (e.g., sighing, facial expressions) (Correa et al., 2005; Friend & Cook, 2010).

Applications and Examples

Several issues may result in barriers to effective communication as you work with other professionals. These potential blocks include (Kochhar-Bryant, 2008):

- Verbal or nonverbal messages that convey unequal status or lack of parity. These messages convey the perspective that "I don't view you as an equal partner or respect your point of view."
- A communication mismatch, when one collaborator needs to vent while another wants to discuss how to address a particular child's needs.
- Communications that send mixed messages. For example, a teacher says, "I'm not frustrated," but body language suggests otherwise.
- Distractions or interruptions that convey to a collaborator that his perspective is not respected.
- Focusing on the past with statements such as, "We tried that before, and it didn't work."
- Moralizing, preaching, advising, or conveying that "I know how to solve your problems."

Collaborators need to be vigilant in monitoring their own behavior as well as others' behavior to make sure that these barriers do not arise and have a negative influence or result in a total breakdown of collaboration.

Keep in Mind

Think for a moment about how difficult it is to communicate effectively. We all have experienced times when we thought we communicated clearly, but the person to whom we were sending the message did not receive the intended message. The complexity of communication is illustrated by several factors, including (Friend & Cook, 2010) the following:

- Communication consists of sending and receiving messages simultaneously.
- Messages are sent using both verbal and nonverbal information.
- The environment in which the message is sent influences communication (e.g., noise or distractions in the setting, others who are present).
- Different types of communication are used by different people.
- Different modes of communication are used to convey information (e.g., verbal, electronic, written messages).

Given the complexity of communication, it is critically important that collaborators frequently check with each other to ensure that they are sending and receiving messages clearly. This requires collaborators to send information in different formats, check understanding by using different words, and ask collaborators to rephrase information to ensure all understand the information.

Key References

Correa, V., Jones, H., Thomas, C., & Morsink, C. (2005). *Interactive teaming: Enhancing programs for students with special needs.* Upper Saddle River, NJ: Merrill/Pearson Education.

Friend, M., & Cook, L. (2010). *Interactions: Collaboration skills for school professionals* (6th ed.). Boston: Allyn & Bacon.

Kochhar-Bryant, C. (2008). *Collaboration and system coordination for students with special needs.* Upper Saddle River, NJ: Merrill/Pearson Education.

Vaughn, S., Bos, C., & Schumm, J. (2011). *Teaching students who are exceptional, diverse, and at risk in the general education classroom* (5th ed.). Boston: Pearson.

Walther-Thomas, C., Korinek, L., McLaughlin, V., & Williams, B. (2000). *Collaboration for inclusive education.* Boston: Allyn & Bacon.

Strategy 3 | TEACHER ASSISTANCE TEAMS (TATS)

Rationale

When teachers need assistance, they have typically sought help from respected colleagues by walking down the hall during a break, or catching the colleague during lunch or after school. Teacher assistance teams (TATs) formalize and simplify this source of assistance. These teams are also a source of professional development, as teachers who participate on the team learn from others about strategies to address a range of student needs.

Teacher assistance teams consist of a group of well-respected professionals who meet two to four times a month to provide assistance using collaborative consultation to other teachers who are having difficulty with a student or group of students. These teams have also been called *intervention assistance teams, student assistance teams,* and *building-based teams.* Research has shown that, when TATs are well designed and supported by teachers and the building principal, referring teachers often receive assistance that they can use in their classroom to address the identified student need (Kovaleski & Glew, 2006; Lane, Pierson, Robertson, & Little, 2004).

Step-by-Step

Teacher assistance teams typically begin their work when a teacher refers a student with a particular need to the team. Once the referral occurs, the team goes through the following steps (Chalfant & Pysh, 1989):

1 *Team members read the referral, which includes specific information regarding the child's challenges.* For example, the referral form (see Figure 4 for a sample referral form) should include a request for information regarding what the referring teacher wants the student to be able to do that she is not currently doing, what the teacher has already tried to address this problem, and the student's assets and deficits. If team members determine it is needed, one team member observes the child in the referring teacher's class to provide more in-depth information regarding the problem.

Figure 4	Teacher Assistance Team Sample Referral Form

REQUEST FOR ASSISTANCE—SOUTHSIDE ELEMENTARY SCHOOL

Name of Student   .   Age Grade

Name of Parent

Referred by:

What would you like the student to be able to do that s/he cannot currently do?

Describe what the student does well (assets).

Describe what the student does not do well (deficits).

Additional information that is relevant for the TAT to consider

2 *The team meets with the teacher for about 30 minutes.* The first step in this meeting is to explicitly identify the problem the team will address. Keep in mind that several problems might be included on the referral form, or the problem might not be clearly defined. The referring teacher is asked to work with the team to determine the most important problem to address. Once this is done, the team discusses the problem until all members agree that the problem is explicitly defined.

3 *The team, including the referring teacher, brainstorms possible solutions to the problem.* During this time, no comments are made regarding the recommendations or possible solutions to the problem. A recorder lists a recommendation, and then the team moves on to additional recommendations. Teams generate anywhere from 10 to 50 recommendations for addressing most problems.

4 *The referring teacher selects several of the recommendations.* The recommendations should fit into her classroom and approach to teaching. She may ask for further clarification regarding the recommendations, as necessary.

5 *The referring teacher selects a recommendation she will use in the classroom to address the student's problem.* The team works with the teacher to clarify any aspects of the recommendation that are unclear and logistics regarding how the intervention may be used in the teacher's classroom.

6 *The team and the teacher discuss goals for determining the success of the intervention.* This might include a specific reduction in out-of-seat behavior, handing in homework 90% of the time, and so on. The team arranges a time for a follow-up meeting.

7 *During the follow-up meeting, the teacher provides the TAT with feedback regarding how the recommended intervention worked.* If the intervention did not work, the team has three options regarding how to proceed. First, the teacher might seek additional clarification regarding the intervention that was used. This occurs if the teacher feels that she did not fully understand the intervention, and that additional clarification and support could improve the effectiveness of the intervention. Second, the teacher might select a recommendation from the list generated in the previous meeting, then the team moves though steps 5 and 6 above. Third, the team could begin at step 1 and generate additional recommendations.

Applications and Examples

Members of TATs may be appointed by the principal, be elected by teachers, or volunteer. No matter how they are selected, all teachers on the TAT should be well-respected members of the faculty who are trusted by other faculty. In most instances principals do not serve on teacher assistance teams because they are in a position to evaluate teachers and this may create parity issues. Another concern related to having a principal on a TAT relates to some teachers' perspectives that a principal may view a referral to a TAT as a sign of weakness on the part of the teacher, and this may result in a reduction in the number of referrals to the team. To make sure teachers were comfortable referring to a TAT, one principal (who was not on the team) was vocal in support of teacher assistance teams and told teachers that referrals to the TAT would be viewed in a positive way for their yearly evaluations, indicating that they were trying to improve their teaching. This resulted in an increase in referrals to the TAT.

Teacher assistance teams are designed to use the time of participants efficiently. For example, the referral form should be one page long and should include only information that is absolutely necessary for team decision making (see Figure 4 for a sample referral form). Furthermore, procedures for running the TAT meeting are designed to focus the group quickly on the problem and efficiently brainstorm and select possible interventions to address the problem. For more information regarding this process, see Walther-Thomas and colleagues (2000).

Keep in Mind

Most student problems that are referred to a TAT relate to work habits, classroom behavior, interpersonal behavior, attentional problems, and reading difficulties. The recommended interventions are reported to succeed for almost 90% of all referrals. Some students for whom recommendations are not successful may be referred to special education (if they are not already identified with a disability) to determine if they need more intensive interventions. It is noteworthy that the TAT process often significantly reduces the number of referrals to special education. Furthermore, when students are referred to special education after being referred to a TAT, they are most often identified with a disability.

Key References

Chalfant, J., & Pysh, M. (1989). Teacher assistance teams: Five descriptive studies on 96 teams. *Remedial and Special Education, 10*(6), 49–58.

Kovaleski, J., & Glew, M. (2006). Bringing instructional support teams to scale: Implications of the Pennsylvania experience. *Remedial and Special Education, 27*, 16–25.

Lane, K., Pierson, M., Robertson, E., & Little, A. (2004). Teachers' views of prereferral interventions: Perceptions of and recommendations for implementation support. *Education and Treatment of Children, 27*(4), 420–439.

Snell, M., & Janney, R. (2005). *Collaborative teaming* (2nd ed.). Baltimore: Brookes.

Walther-Thomas, C., Korinek, L., McLaughlin, V., & Williams, B. (2000). *Collaboration for inclusive education*. Boston: Allyn & Bacon.

PLANNING FOR CO-TEACHING

Rationale

When used to support inclusion, the primary purpose of co-teaching is to make sure that instruction for students with disabilities (and other students who struggle academically and/or socially) is adapted to meet individual student needs. Co-teaching thus provides students with more intense, differentiated instruction, which is built on the general education curriculum.

Co-teaching has several strengths. When teachers share responsibility for teaching a diverse group of students in one classroom, they can combine their expertise to meet the needs of all students. For students with disabilities, in particular, co-teaching provides access to the general education curriculum, reduces the fragmentation of the curriculum that results when students are pulled out of general education classrooms for instruction, and often results in improved student outcomes. Teachers also report that co-teaching provides a professional support system and leads to less feeling of professional isolation, especially for special education teachers.

Step-by-Step

During the first year of co-teaching, it is advisable to only develop one or two partnerships. Sufficient time to plan for the co-teaching partnerships should be available during the spring and summer before beginning to co-teach. Planning for co-teaching should address the following:

1 *Determine common goals for co-teaching that both teachers understand, agree to, and value.* These goals facilitate buy-in from the co-teachers and ensure interdependence in addressing and meeting the goals. Given the emphasis in schools on accountability, a critical factor in determining goals should be data on student needs. This information can be used to make decisions about instructional time, grouping patterns, and instructional methods used in class. Furthermore, data should be used to monitor student progress and make decisions about change that occur in instructional delivery. For example, if co-teachers are engaged in station teaching, it may be necessary to change the size of groups or focus on different goals if some students are not making sufficient progress. This allows co-teachers to provide students who struggle learning academic material with more intensive, direct instruction that will often accelerate learning.

2 *Discuss the strengths both teachers bring to the classroom, and how these strengths will be used to make co-teaching succeed.* All teachers are better at some things than others, or prefer to engage in certain activities (e.g., large-group instruction, small-group instruction, discussion). It is important to be candid about strengths and preferences in the classroom. Recent research has shown that collaborators are much more successful when they are knowledgeable about their strengths and weaknesses, and are candid with their collaborator about these issues (Bahrami et al., 2010).

Communicating this information during planning for co-teaching allows teachers to share expertise and determine how this expertise can be best used to meet student needs and improve outcomes.

3 *Define roles and responsibilities for both co-teachers.* Teachers' roles in co-taught classrooms should vary, depending on student needs, the content being taught, and teacher strengths/preferences. Furthermore, it is important that teachers share all roles at times, to make sure that one teacher doesn't always teach the students who are experiencing difficulty. It is also important that both teachers in a co-teaching partnership have professionally fulfilling roles and fully use their expertise. Many types of co-teaching may be used to address student needs.

Figure 5 describes several approaches to co-teaching. When planning for co-teaching, teachers should determine which approach to co-teaching will be used for a particular lesson, and the roles of both teachers should be clearly defined. This can become complex because it is typical that more than one type of co-teaching will be used during the school day. For example, with the current emphasis on tiered instructional approaches, many co-teachers use station teaching to provide small-group instruction for students who are struggling to learn academic material (Murawski & Hughes, 2009). This approach is used for part of the school day, and teachers alternate groups to make sure that they share responsibility for teaching students who are struggling. At other times during the school day, teachers may use approaches such as parallel teaching, team teaching, or one teach and one assist, depending on the content being taught, student needs, and teacher preferences.

Figure 5	Co-Teaching Options

Team teaching: Both teachers share equal responsibility for instructing the whole group, and teach the group as equal partners.

One teach, one support: One teacher teaches the content of the class, while the other teacher floats, responds to student questions, keeps students on task, addresses management issues, and so forth.

Complementary teaching: The class is divided based on student needs, and both teachers teach a group. This may include different content for the groups, review of material that a group of students has not mastered, intensive instruction for a small group of students, and so forth.

Parallel teaching: This approach consists of splitting the class into two heterogeneous groups, and one teacher instructs each group using a collaboratively planned lesson. This is designed to reduce the class size or teacher–student ratio, and thus allows the teachers to provide more attention to each student and attend to individual student needs.

One teach, one observe: Teachers rarely have the opportunity to observe a student closely during a lesson. Similarly, teachers seldom have the opportunity to observe another teacher during a lesson to learn from another professional. This approach allows these opportunities. It is important to note that this is an approach that should be used infrequently, and should strategically focus on particular opportunities that arise when intensive observation is beneficial.

Station teaching: When this approach is used, stations or centers are set up in class that address different content, and students rotate through the stations. Teachers then have the responsibility for a station, and teach all students as they rotate through the station. In many classrooms, students are expected to work independently or cooperatively in one or more stations, or a paraeducator may have responsibility for a station. This approach is used increasingly in elementary and secondary classrooms, given the emphasis on tiered instructional approaches.

④ *Participate in professional development.* Both co-teaching partners should participate in this professional development, which should address topics such as co-teaching, collaboration, communication skills, problem solving, and instructional strategies. This allows partner teachers the opportunity to develop the common skills they need to enhance the success of co-teaching. These types of activities are beneficial before co-teaching begins, as information is provided regarding the basics of co-teaching, and co-teaching partners are provided the opportunity to discuss this information with others and plan their approach (e.g., definition of roles) to co-teaching. Participating in professional development is also beneficial after beginning co-teaching, as issues invariably arise during implementation of this practice. This professional development should be tailored to the particular needs you face as a co-teacher, and may include visits to other co-taught classrooms for observation, or having a teacher with expertise in co-teaching visit your classroom to provide feedback and coaching regarding areas of concern (McLeskey, 2011).

⑤ *Develop a master plan for instruction and a general format for daily lessons that is predictable but flexible.* This can be achieved through initially collaborating to plan a unit of instruction, developing lesson plans that include accommodations for student needs, and determining the type of co-teaching used for different parts of the unit. The approach used by many teachers includes planning curriculum and instruction based on the needs and expected outcomes for all students, most students, and a few students. Using this approach, co-teachers get to know their students well, and they also get to know the preferences of their co-teaching partner. This information is useful in determining the type of co-teaching that will be used for a particular lesson. As the school year progresses, it is important to be flexible in adapting the master plan and format for daily lessons, as the needs of students and preferences of teachers will continue to evolve.

⑥ *Develop a plan for classroom management.* The plan should include how to address behavior issues proactively, rules for student behavior, consequences (both positive and negative), and who will handle delivery of consequences. This activity will allow co-teaching partners to begin to learn the preferences of their partner regarding student behavior, and preferences regarding how behavioral issues will be addressed. The plan for classroom management will also continue to evolve through the school year, as student behavior issues change over time. A co-teaching partner in the classroom offers many opportunities to address behavior issues as they arise, as well as opportunities to observe student behavior and better understand why behavior problems may arise and how they may be prevented.

⑦ *Create a common planning time for co-teachers during the school year.* During these "co-teach chats," co-teachers address student progress, instructional content, teachers' roles, accountability, and so forth. Teachers should also use this time to reflect on how co-teaching is working and make changes as needed. Teachers should agree on how to efficiently use this planning time. For example, planning routines may be developed to include activities such as the following:

- Celebrate the successes of co-teaching from the previous week's instruction.

- Discuss student needs based on the previous week's instruction and available data.
- Plan instructional content and related student accommodations for the coming week.
- Plan teacher responsibilities for the coming week, to make sure that students receive support as needed.
- Discuss how co-teaching is working, and problem solve regarding areas that need to be improved.

Applications and Examples

Co-teaching is a dynamic process. You will need to continue to make decisions with your teaching partner regarding a variety of logistical issues over the first year of co-teaching and beyond. As you enter into a co-teaching relationship, continue to acquire skills to support co-teaching and learn about your partner teacher. This makes it important that you and your co-teacher agree that it is fine to ask questions about any issues or misunderstandings that arise. You will likely need to continue to work on sharing responsibility with another professional and communicating effectively regarding student issues, as well as the logistics of co-teaching.

Another issue that you will continue to address is the roles that you and your teaching partner play as co-teachers. Student learning and related needs change over time, and you will find that student-grouping patterns and teacher responsibilities must also change. It is likely that as the year progresses, you will use the one-teach, one-assist model of co-teaching less often, and the station teaching, complementary teaching and team-teaching models more often to ensure that students receive the individual support that they need.

Keep in Mind

It is easy to fall into a pattern of often grouping low-achieving students together and assuming certain teaching roles that are traditional for general and special education teachers. For example, the general education teacher may always assume the role of content teacher for the large group, and the special education teacher always assumes the role of attending to the needs of low-achieving students. As we've noted previously, a critical aspect of effective inclusion programs is that differences become an ordinary part of the school day. Furthermore, varying the teaching roles allows teachers to learn and develop expertise from their partner teacher and to use their expertise with all students. If co-teaching is to work well, partner teachers must not revert to traditional teaching roles and grouping patterns. Rather, teachers should seamlessly share roles in the classroom, and students who are struggling should be grouped into small, homogeneous groups for only brief periods of intensive instruction. Otherwise, the grouping patterns for these students should be similar to that of their peers.

Key References

Bahrami, B., Olsen, K., Lathan, P., Roepstorff, A., Rees, G., & Frith, C. (2010). Optimally interacting minds. *Science, 329,* 1080–1085.

Correa, V., Jones, H., Thomas, C., & Morsink, C. (2005). *Interactive teaming: Enhancing programs for students with special needs* (4th ed.). Upper Saddle River, NJ: Merrill/Pearson Education.

Friend, M. (2008). *Co-Teach!* Greensboro, NC: Marilyn Friend.

Friend, M., & Cook, L. (2010). *Interactions: Collaboration skills for school professionals* (6th ed.). Boston: Allyn & Bacon.

McLeskey, J. (2011). Supporting improved practice for special education teachers: The importance of learner-centered professional development. *Journal of Special Education Leadership, 24,* 26–35.

Murawski, W., & Hughes, C. (2009). Response to intervention, collaboration, and co-teaching: A logical contribution for successful systemic change. *Intervention in School and Clinic, 53,* 267–277.

Villa, R., Thousand, J., & Nevin, A. (2008). *A guide for co-teaching* (2nd ed.). Thousand Oaks, CA: Sage.

Walther-Thomas, C., Korinek, L., McLaughlin, V., & Williams, B. (2000). *Collaboration for inclusive education.* Boston: Allyn & Bacon.

Strategy 5 — WORKING WITH PARAEDUCATORS

Rationale

The number of paraeducators working in schools has increased dramatically as inclusion has become more prevalent (Fisher & Pleasants, 2011). Many of these paraeducators have been hired to provide support for students with disabilities who require more attention and support than the general education teacher can provide. Paraeducators work under the supervision of a certified teacher and provide support such as one-to-one or small-group instruction (e.g., tutoring or drill and practice) on material already taught by the teacher, support for students with highly specialized needs, grading and other paperwork, preparation of material for class lessons, and so forth. In short, paraeducators provide support for certified teachers in much the same way paralegals provide support to lawyers or paramedics provide medical support.

Step-by-Step

Paraeducators can provide invaluable assistance in an inclusive classroom if their responsibilities are well defined and they are well prepared for the responsibilities. The supervising teacher is responsible for ensuring that this occurs. When a paraeducator is assigned, the teacher should follow several steps to ensure that she is well prepared. These steps include:

1 *Welcome and acknowledge the paraeducator.* This includes activities such as introducing the paraeducator to other professionals as part of the teaching team (and not as a helper for a specific student); providing a space for personal belongings; putting the paraeducator's name on the classroom door; and sharing routine responsibilities that communicate authority (e.g., taking roll, writing on the board) (Causton-Theoharis et al., 2007). These types of activities serve to welcome the paraeducator and communicate that she is a valued part of the professional team.

2 *Orient the paraeducator to the school.* This includes activities such as a thorough tour of the school; introductions to important staff (e.g., office staff, librarian); a review of classroom procedures, policies, and rules; provision of information regarding location of supplies and technology; and access to IEPs and support in reading and interpreting these documents (Causton-Theoharis et al., 2007).

3 *Provide training related to assigned instructional activities.* Although the school district may provide general professional development for paraeducators, the supervising teacher is in the best position to provide professional development on specific curricular materials and methods, and general procedures used in the inclusive classroom. This may include professional development related to the use of methods for tutoring, packaged programs for reading or math instruction, and so forth. As the year progresses, the supervising teacher monitors the skills of the paraeducator, provides individual professional development and support as needed, and discusses possible training opportunities offered by the district that meet specific needs related to the paraeducator's responsibilities.

4 *Plan a schedule with the paraeducator.* A critical task of the supervising teacher is to ensure appropriate use of a paraeducator's particular skills in assigned duties. The supervising teacher and paraeducator should discuss these issues and develop a weekly schedule that includes who the paraeducator will support and what the paraeducator's role will be. Addressing what the paraeducator's role should *not* be may also be important. For example, paraeducators should not be fully responsible for any student and should not be responsible for planning programs or lessons, but rather should carry out plans developed by the supervising teacher. The teacher may develop these plans collaboratively with the paraeducator, but ultimately, plans are the responsibility of the supervising teacher. After developing a schedule, the supervising teacher and paraeducator should meet frequently to evaluate how the schedule is working, and make adjustments as necessary.

5 *Communicate effectively with the paraeducator.* Teachers need regularly scheduled meetings to facilitate effective communication with paraeducators. These meetings may occur during common planning time or at other times during the school day, but they should allow adequate, uninterrupted time to address important issues and concerns. For example, it is important to use the time of the paraeducator effectively, to develop appropriate roles and responsibilities, to address any training needs, and to adjust the paraeducator's schedule as necessary. In addition to regular meetings, communication may be enhanced by the use of daily notebooks, e-mail, and checking in at the beginning and end of each day. Finally, it is important to be open to the ideas and perspectives that the paraeducator provides and to engage in active listening to ensure that these perspectives are clearly understood (Causton-Theoharis et al., 2007).

6 *Supervise the paraeducator appropriately.* The supervising teacher is responsible for supervising the work of the paraeducator. Roles related to supervision include the following (Friend & Cook, 2010):

- Monitor how well paraeducators are performing assigned tasks.
- Provide feedback, and point out strategies to improve performance.

- Model effective instructional strategies and ways to interact with students.
- Problem solve as disagreements arise with the paraeducator and other teachers.
- Make certain that the paraeducator understands school policies and ethical practices and adheres to these policies and practices.
- Support paraeducators by responding to any questions they may have and providing support and professional development.
- Publicly acknowledge the work of paraeducators.

Applications and Examples

A key to working effectively with paraeducators is to build a relationship that includes open communication and reflects respect and trust. Collaborating with paraeducators in determining their role, needed training, weekly assignments, and so forth is an important step in ensuring that this occurs. Furthermore, the effective skills for collaboration that we discussed earlier in this chapter are important when working with paraeducators.

Paraeducators were surveyed and asked what is essential for teachers to be good partners with paraeducators (Riggs, 2005). The results of this survey are summarized in Figure 6, and provide much insight into how you can work effectively with paraeducators. As we noted previously, key issues seem to be working collaboratively with paraeducators in an atmosphere of trust and respect, clearly defining the paraeducator's role, and ensuring that she receives appropriate professional development to perform assigned tasks and meet students' needs.

Keep in Mind

Paraeducators can serve in a variety of roles in an inclusive classroom. For example, they can be especially effective in providing tutoring for students using well-structured materials, or engaging students in teacher-developed skill-and-drill activities. Nonetheless, some teachers are hesitant to delegate responsibilities to paraeducators. Some of the reasons this occurs relate to concerns regarding the quality of the paraeducator's work, the need for training if the paraeducator is to engage in certain tasks, the feeling that the teacher doesn't want to be bossy, or the perspective that the teacher can do it faster herself (Friend & Cook, 2010). Teachers should work through these concerns and learn to delegate increasing levels of responsibility to paraeducators. This ensures the efficient use of resources to meet student needs, empowers paraeducators, allows them to learn new skills, and helps to create a team committed to student success (Friend & Cook, 2010).

Key References

Causton-Theoharis, J., Giangreco, M., Doyle, M., & Vadasy, P. (2007). Paraprofessionals: The "Sous-Chefs" of literacy instruction. *Teaching Exceptional Children, 40*(1), 56–62.

Fisher, M., & Pleasants, S. (2011). Roles, responsibilities, and concerns of paraeducators: Findings from a statewide survey. *Remedial and Special Education*, published online 7 February 2011, DOI: 10:1177/0741932510397762.

French, N. (2003). Paraeducators in special education programs. *Focus on Exceptional Children, 36*(2), 1–16.

Friend, M., & Cook, L. (2010). *Interactions: Collaboration skills for school professionals* (6th ed.). Boston: Allyn & Bacon.

Riggs, C. (2005). To teachers: What paraeducators want you to know. *Teaching Exceptional Children, 36*(5), 8–12.

Figure 6	What Paraeducators Want Teachers to Know

1. **Know and use the paraeducator's name.** Paraeducators are not "Kasey's helper" or invisible! They are a valuable member of the professional staff, and should be recognized and treated as such. This is an important first step in building trust, respect, and good communication.

2. **Be familiar with rules and policies in your district regarding paraeducators.** It is important that the supervising teachers and others understand the ground rules regarding paraeducators. A special education supervisor or school administrator should have this information readily available.

3. **Work with the paraeducator as a valued team member.** The working relationship that develops between a paraeducator and teacher should reflect professionalism, cooperation, and camaraderie. It logically follows that paraeducators should be recognized as a valued member of the professional team.

4. **Explicitly share your expectations.** Paraeducators want to know what to do, as well as what not to do in the classroom. Teachers should explicitly share information regarding expectations regarding classroom management, student behavior, expectations for certain students, and so forth.

5. **Define roles and responsibilities for paraeducators and teachers.** Avoid disagreements and conflicts by explicitly defining the role of paraeducators in a job description and ensuring that their role is clearly differentiated from the role of the teacher.

6. **The teacher should supervise and direct paraeducators.** Paraeducators are often confused regarding who should provide them with direction in a co-taught, inclusive classroom. Teachers should be explicit regarding who provides direction and supervision, and should be clear about what is expected and how to do it.

7. **Ensure effective communication.** Determining effective methods to provide formal and informal feedback to paraeducators regarding their work is a critical role for the supervising teacher. A time should be set aside for discussing how things are working, and improvements that may be needed.

8. **Recognize that paraeducators have knowledge and expertise to share in the classroom.** Paraeducators often gain extensive information regarding students as they perform tasks across a range of settings. Furthermore, paraeducators gain valuable skills as they work with teachers and students over a number of years. Respecting and valuing the knowledge and skills paraeducators bring to their jobs helps to create a good working relationship, and can have a positive effect on student learning.

9. **Take ownership of all students.** Teachers should be classroom leaders for all students, and not put paraeducators in the position of taking responsibility for some students (e.g., a student with a disability). When a paraeducator works individually with a student for a long period of time, the teacher may not be familiar with the student and his needs. It is important to make sure that this does not occur, and the teacher knows and works with *all* students in the classroom.

10. **Respect paraeducators.** If teachers model respect for paraeducators, students will likely model this same behavior. In addition, the job satisfaction and retention of paraeducators are influenced by the extent to which they are valued and respected for the work that they perform.

Source: Information adapted from C. Riggs (2005). To teachers: What paraeducators want you to know. *Teaching Exceptional Children, 36*(5), 8–12.

WORKING WITH FAMILIES: HOME–SCHOOL COLLABORATION

Rationale

Home–school collaboration is defined as a teacher and parent or significant caregiver working collaboratively to develop interventions to address student needs. Interventions that have proven effective related to home–school collaboration include simple activities such as parent monitoring of homework or dispensing consequences based on a daily report card, to more extensive interventions that require parent training, such as parent tutoring in reading and math or improving a student's self-determination skills (Cox, 2005; Fabiano et al., 2009; Kochhar-Bryant, 2008; Patall, Cooper, & Robinson, 2008). Research has shown that home–school interventions are more successful when school personnel collaborate with caregivers and treat them as equals (Cox, 2005).

Family involvement and support are especially important for inclusive programs. More-over, caregivers for students with disabilities are in a unique position to become involved in their child's education and to work as a partner with educators, given the high level of parent involvement that is required as part of IDEA (Correa et al., 2005; Whitbread et al., 2007). Unfortunately, many parents are not engaged in their child's education. Some of this lack of engagement can be explained by a parent's choice not to become involved, while other parents want to be involved but may have family responsibilities and stressors that make it very difficult to be involved (Kochhar-Bryant, 2008). Still other parents may not be involved because of cultural issues that impede clear, effective communication between school and home (Matuszny, Banda, & Coleman, 2007).

Step-by-Step

An important responsibility you will have as a teacher in an inclusive classroom is to encourage home–school collaboration and other forms of parent involvement in their children's education. The following steps will help ensure that parents have an opportunity to participate and serve as a resource to improve their children's education.

1 *Get to know parents as individuals, build trust, and open lines of communication.* Some parents may immediately want to become involved in their child's education, but for others, you will need to get to know the parent before you can develop home–school collaborative interventions. It is important to engage parents in informal settings early in the school year to begin this process. For example, the school might sponsor a kick-off-the-year event that allows teachers and parents to meet in an atmosphere that is informal, comfortable, and stress free (Matuszny et al., 2007). Talking with parents before and after school about topics unrelated to their child is also helpful.

After initially getting to know the parents, you should engage in activities such as inviting parents into the classroom and providing information the parents will find useful to further build a positive relationship. Finally, you could give parents choices regarding alternatives for participating in school-related activities and ask them for input in decision making (Matuszny et al., 2007).

2 *Try to understand, respect, and take into account the parents' perspective.* Most families have some difficulty adjusting to the needs of a child with a disability. For example, after determining that a child has a disability, some parents may deny that a disability exists and need time before they can accept the disability. Other parents may have stressors in their lives that are exacerbated by having to address the child's disability in home and in school. Understanding the parents' perspectives by talking with them and/or visiting in the home will lead to the conclusion that some parents do not have the time to participate in home–school collaboration, and others choose not to participate, often for very understandable reasons.

3 *Determine the types of involvement that will work for particular parents.* A group of parents likely will be willing and prepared to engage in home–school collaboration on an intervention that will improve student achievement and/or behavior. We advise beginning with a small group of parents who are interested in using a single intervention. This allows teachers the opportunity to "work out the bugs" with the intervention while working with a group of parents who will provide feedback and aren't likely to be discouraged if some aspects of the intervention need to be adjusted.

④ *Design, implement, and evaluate the intervention collaboratively with parents.* The intervention should be well structured and easily understood by participating parents, and resources should be available to support the intervention, as needed. Information on possible interventions related to homework, student behavior, tutoring, self-determination, and so forth is widely available. Other teachers in your school and special education consultants are likely to be good sources of information on these types of interventions that have proven to be effective.

Applications and Examples

When engaging parents in home–school collaboration, or otherwise encouraging parent involvement in school activities, an important consideration is the parents' cultural background(s). To ensure that teachers understand, respect, and take into account parents' cultural background(s), we recommend the following activities (Correa et al., 2005; Harry, Kalyanpur, & Day, 1999):

- Identify cultural values that are embedded in the teacher's interpretation of a student's difficulties or in recommendations for services.
- Explore whether the family understands and values how teachers interpret the student's difficulties, and, if not, have the family share how their values differ from those of the teacher.
- Respect any differences that exist regarding the student that are embedded in the cultural background of the family.
- Determine ways to adapt the teacher's recommendations or interpretations to the value system of the family.

For guidelines regarding how teachers can encourage involvement of parents from culturally diverse backgrounds, see Figure 7.

Figure 7	**Guidelines for Encouraging Involvement of Parents from Diverse Cultural and Language Backgrounds in Their Child's Education**

1. **Empower families with knowledge and skills to:**
   - Adapt and cope with the school system, which will likely be very different than their previous experience.
   - Work with their children and reinforce educational programs at home in ways that are natural and functional.
2. **Provide the family with assistance in moving from their native culture to the mainstream culture**, recognizing that cultures vary significantly within such groups. This requires that the teacher learn about the family's cultural experiences, including their expectations regarding schools, interaction patterns with teachers, and desire for involvement in school.
3. **Work as a culture broker** and support the family in contacts with the school. This may involve serving as an advocate or mediator for students from certain ethnic backgrounds, and/or linking with community leaders to enhance home–school collaboration.
4. **When communicating with families, determine the preferred means of communication** that will remove barriers related to cultural, language, and communication differences, and enhance communication between school and home.
5. **Collect information regarding the family related to:**
   - Experiences in their native country
   - The roles of extended family members and siblings
   - The amount of available community support
   - Religious, spiritual, and cultural beliefs
   - Parenting practices related to discipline, independence, and so forth
6. **Provide the family with information** in written and/or oral forms that enables family members to understand exactly what is being conveyed. Ensure that linguistic and cultural barriers do not impede this communication.

Source: Adapted from V. Correa, H. Jones, C. Thomas, & C. Morsink (2005). *Interactive teaming: Enhancing programs for students with special needs* (4th ed.). Upper Saddle River, NJ: Merrill/Pearson Education.

Keep in Mind

Home–school collaboration is especially important for teachers in inclusive settings, but it is only one type of interaction teachers have with parents. Teachers often will be involved in providing information to parents regarding their child's academic and social development, legal issues that influence the child's special education program, and so forth. Teachers may also be involved in reporting and interpreting evaluation and test results for parents; encouraging and preparing parents to work as volunteers in school activities (e.g., working in an after-school tutoring program or participating in a school decision-making group); and/or providing training to build parenting skills (e.g., communicating with children, discipline). Of course, all of these activities are important and should be done while keeping in mind the step-by-step guidelines for effectively working with parents, and information related to working with parents from different cultural backgrounds.

Key References

Correa, V., Jones, H., Thomas, C., & Morsink, C. (2005). *Interactive teaming: Enhancing programs for students with special needs* (4th ed.). Upper Saddle River, NJ: Merrill/Pearson Education.

Cox, D. (2005). Evidence-based interventions using home–school collaboration. *School Psychology Quarterly, 20*(4), 473–497.

Fabiano, G., Pelham, W., Coles, E., Gnagy, E., Chronis, A., & O'Connor, B. (2009). A meta-analysis of behavioral treatments for attention-deficit/hyperactivity disorder. *Clinical Psychology Review, 29*, 129–140.

Harry, B., Kalyanpur, M., & Day, M. (1999). *Building cultural reciprocity with families: Case studies in special education*. Baltimore: Brookes.

Kochhar-Bryant, C. (2008). *Collaboration and system coordination for students with special needs*. Upper Saddle River, NJ: Merrill/Pearson Education.

Matuszny, R., Banda, D., & Coleman, T. (2007). A progressive plan for building collaborative relationships with parents from diverse backgrounds. *Teaching Exceptional Children, 39*(4), 24–31.

Patall, E., Cooper, H., Robinson, J. (2008). Parent involvement in homework: A research synthesis. *Review of Educational Research, 78*, 1039–1101.

Whitbread, K., Bruder, M., Fleming, G., & Park, H. (2007). Collaboration in special education: Parent–professional training. *Teaching Exceptional Children, 39*(4), 6–14.

| Strategy 7 | # PEER BUDDY PROGRAMS |

Rationale

As students enter adolescence, they spend more time with peers, increasing the influence of these interactions on their development (Carter & Hughes, 2005). Adolescents with moderate-to-severe disabilities benefit from peer interactions, just as other students do, while they make friends, learn social skills, and experience an enhanced quality of life. Unfortunately, even when students with moderate-to-severe disabilities are included in general education classes and participate in daily activities in a school (e.g., lunch), they often remain substantially isolated socially from their peers without disabilities. Thus, students with moderate-to-severe disabilities need teachers to intervene and facilitate social interactions with peers (Carter & Hughes, 2005).

Many middle and high schools across the United States have implemented peer buddy programs, which have proven effective in increasing social interactions between students with disabilities and their peers. These programs offer students the opportunity to earn course credit and participate in service learning, as they interact with students with disabilities in school, leisure, and/or work settings.

Step-by-Step

Peer buddy programs are a strategy for promoting inclusion and "ensuring a positive experience both for the students with severe disabilities and their general education peer buddies" (Hughes, Guth, Hall, Presley, Dye, & Byers, 1999, p. 32). These programs may also be effective for students with mild-to-moderate disabilities. Hughes and colleagues (Hughes & Carter, 2006; Hughes et al., 1999) suggest the following steps in developing a peer buddy program in a middle or high school.

1 *Develop a course that offers students course credit and an opportunity to fulfill service-learning requirements for participating in the peer buddy program.* This course provides time for peer buddies to spend at least one class period per day with their partners. The content of the course offers participants the opportunity to learn about persons with disabilities and gain knowledge and skills necessary for successfully interacting with and supporting their peer buddies.

2 *Recruit peer buddies to participate in the program.* This involves promoting the program to teachers, administrators, school staff, and students. Students may be recruited in inclusive classrooms that include a student who would benefit from a peer buddy, or in classes where disability-related issues are being discussed (e.g., health, civics, literature). After the program is in place, peer buddies can provide support in recruitment.

3 *Screen students who apply to be peer buddies.* Screening criteria may include good attendance (always a key criterion), an adequate grade-point average, recommendations of teachers, written applications, and interviews. Peer buddies should be willing to take the initiative and require minimal supervision, should be open-minded and tolerant regarding individual differences, and they should demonstrate personal qualities such as caring, flexibility, responsibility, and so forth. Keep in mind that peer buddies may not be the highest-achieving students, and students with disabilities may be peer buddies.

4 *Match students with peer buddies.* Students should be tentatively matched by a teacher or counselor based on common interests, student preferences, and so forth. Students should then have the opportunity to interact, observe in classes, and clarify the role of the peer buddy to determine if the match is a good one. Students, teachers, and/or counselors should participate in making the final matches for peer buddies.

5 *Develop expectations, and communicate those expectations to peer buddies.* Teachers should communicate expectations to peer buddies through an orientation session. Peer buddies from previous years may assist with this session. Expectations should address attendance, role and responsibilities of the peer buddy, and other program procedures and expectations.

6 *Prepare peer buddies to ensure success.* Training sessions should address topics such as student information (regarding each student's peer buddy) and confidentiality, disability awareness, instructional strategies, interaction and communication strategies, suggestions for activities, addressing challenging behaviors, and handling emergencies.

Applications and Examples

On the entrance to West Hernando Middle School is a quote from Booker T. Washington: "If you want to lift yourself up, lift up someone else." The school lives this quote in many ways, including its peer buddy (or Peer Support) program. This was illustrated earlier in this chapter as two students from West Hernando, Emma and Susan, described the benefits of their Peer Support program. West Hernando has 114 peer buddies, making its peer buddy course the second-most popular elective in the school. Students who serve as peer buddies include those with and without disabilities. Maureen Finelli, a teacher who directs the Peer Support program at West Hernando reports that these students supply teachers in inclusive classrooms with invaluable assistance, as they provide support during academic activities and build natural social relationships with students with disabilities.

Benefits of peer buddy programs are included in Figure 8. It is noteworthy that these benefits accrue not only for the student with a disability but also for the peer buddy, teachers, and administrators. However, the most important benefits of peer buddy programs are for students with disabilities. As Lisa Hallal, a teacher at West Hernando, noted, "We have

Figure 8	Benefits Associated with Peer Buddy Programs

For students who do not have disabilities
- Friendships develop with students with disabilities.
- Knowledge regarding disabilities increases.
- Advocacy skills are improved.
- Interpersonal skills are enhanced.
- Expectations for peers with disabilities are increased.
- Learn from students with disabilities in areas where they are positive role models.
- Explore careers in human services.
- Experience a sense of accomplishment and personal growth.

For students with disabilities
- Develop friendships.
- Engage in more social interactions with peers.
- Acquire new academic, social, and life skills.
- Learn from age-appropriate peers in areas where they are positive role models.
- Receive natural, effective peer support in inclusive settings.
- Increase their independence and self-confidence.

For teachers
- Gain assistance to support students with disabilities in learning academic and social skills.
- Provide all students with more opportunities to socialize.
- Increase diversity in the classroom.
- Experience professional growth and personal satisfaction.

For administrators
- School climate and sense of school community are improved.
- Gain assistance in supporting students with disabilities in all school settings.
- Support efforts to improve inclusion and align school practices with school reform efforts and legislation related to inclusion

For parents
- Their children are more enthusiastic about school.
- Their children have opportunities for new friendships and increased social activities.
- Their children experience academic and social growth.

Source: Adapted from C. Hughes & E. Carter (2008). *Peer buddy programs for successful secondary level inclusion.* Baltimore: Brookes.

seen so many benefits. Like Albert, who now goes to the lunchroom. He never went to the lunchroom before. Now he goes with his peers, not his peer buddy. He gets to do what everybody else is doing. That's the beauty of it."

Keep in Mind

Peer buddy programs have many benefits, but to realize these benefits, the program must be carefully planned and consistently supported. Students who have participated in these programs recommend the following to ensure success (Copeland et al., 2004):

- Offer activities for all students that increase awareness of students with disabilities.
- Ensure that peer buddies receive information about their partner, as well as training regarding how to provide effective support.
- Encourage friendships between students with disabilities and their peers, to increase participation in academic and social activities.
- Provide structures that support the peer buddy program. Sources of structure that are beneficial include a daily schedule of suggested activities, a peer buddy manual that includes information about disabilities, regular conversations with a supervising teacher regarding the peer buddy experience, and writing in a reflective journal.

Key References

Carter, E., & Hughes, E. (2005). Increasing social interaction among adolescents with intellectual disabilities and their general education peers: Effective interventions. *Research & Practice for Persons with Severe Disabilities, 30*(4), 179–193.

Copeland, S., Hughes, C., Carter, E., Guth, C., Presley, J., Williams, C., & Fowler, S. (2004). Increasing access to general education: Perspectives of participants in a high school peer support program. *Remedial and Special Education, 25*(3), 342–352.

Hughes, C., & Carter, E. (2008). *Peer buddy programs for successful secondary level inclusion.* Baltimore: Brookes.

Hughes, C., Guth, C., Hall, S., Presley, J., Dye, N. & Byers, C. (1999). "They are my best friends": Peer buddies promote inclusion in high school. *Teaching Exceptional Children, 31*(5), 32–37.

Westling, D., & Fox, L. (2009). *Teaching students with severe disabilities* (4th ed.). Upper Saddle River, NJ: Merrill/Pearson.

References

Bahrami, B., Olsen, K., Latham, P., Roepstorff, A., Rees, G., & Firth, C. (2010). Optimally interacting minds. *Science, 329* 1080–1085.

Buck, G., Polloway, E., Smith-Thomas, A., & Cook, K. (2003). Prereferral intervention processes: A survey of state practices. *Exceptional Children, 69*(3), 349–360.

Causton-Theoharis, J., Giangreco, M., Doyle, M., & Vadasy, P. (2007). Paraprofessionals: The "Sous-Chefs" of literacy instruction. *Teaching Exceptional Children, 40*(1), 56–62.

Chalfant, J., & Pysh, M. (1989). Teacher assistance teams: Five descriptive studies on 96 teams. *Remedial and Special Education, 10*(6), 49–58.

Chau, M., Thampi, K., & Wright, V. (2010). *Basic facts about low-income children, 2009. Children under age 18. Fact sheet.* New York: National Center for Children in Poverty, Columbia University.

Cook, B., McDuffie-Landrum, K., Oshita, L., & Cook, S. (2011). Co-teaching for students with disabilities. A critical analysis of the empirical literature. In J. Kauffman & D. Hallahan (Eds.), *Handbook of Special Education* (pp. 147–159). New York: Routledge.

Copeland, S., Hughes, C., Carter, E., Guth, C., Presley, J., Williams, C., & Fowler, S. (2004). Increasing access to general education: Perspectives of participants in a high school peer support program. *Remedial and Special Education, 25*(3), 342–352.

Correa, V., Jones, H., Thomas, C., & Morsink, C. (2005). *Interactive teaming: Enhancing programs for students with special needs.* Upper Saddle River, NJ: Merrill/Pearson Education.

Cox, D. (2005). Evidence-based interventions using home–school collaboration. *School Psychology Quarterly, 20*(4), 473–497.

Dettmer, P., Thurston, L., Knackendoffel, A. & Dyck, N. (2009). *Collaboration, consultation, and teamwork for students with special needs.* Upper Saddle River, NJ: Merrill/Pearson Education.

Fabiano, G., Pelham, W., Coles, E., Gnagy, E., Chronis, A., & O'Connor, B. (2009). A meta-analysis of behavioral treatments for attention-deficit/hyperactivity disorder. *Clinical Psychology Review, 29*, 129–140.

Fisher, M., & Pleasants, S. (2011). Roles, responsibilities, and concerns of paraeducators: Findings from a statewide survey. *Remedial and Special Education*, published online 7 February 2011, DOI: 10:1177/0741932510397762.

French, N. (2003). Paraeducators in special education programs. *Focus on Exceptional Children, 36*(2), 1–16.

Friend, M., & Cook, L. (2010). *Interactions: Collaboration skills for school professionals* (6th ed.). Upper Saddle River, NJ: Pearson.

Friend, M., Cook, L., Hurley-Chamberlain, D., & Shamberger, C. (2010). Co-teaching: An illustration of the complexity of collaboration in special education. *Journal of Educational and Psychological Consultation, 20*, 9–27.

Ginsburg-Block, M., Rohrbeck, C., & Fantuzzo, J. (2006). A meta-analytic review of social, self-concept, and behavioral outcomes of peer-assisted learning. *Journal of Educational Psychology, 98*(4), 732–749.

Hang, Q., & Rabran, K. (2008). An examination of co-teaching: Perspectives and efficacy indicators. *Remedial and Special Education, 30*, 259–268.

Harry, B., Kalyanpur, M., & Day, M. (1999). *Building cultural reciprocity with families: Case studies in special education*. Baltimore: Brookes.

Hughes, C., & Carter, E. (2006). *Success for all students: Promoting inclusion in secondary programs through peer buddy programs*. Upper Saddle River, NJ: Prentice Hall.

Hughes, C., & Carter, E. (2008). *Peer buddy programs for successful secondary school inclusion*. Baltimore: Brookes.

Hughes, C., Guth, C., Hall, S., Presley, J., Dye, M., & Byers, C. (1999). "They are my best friends": Peer buddies promote inclusion in high school. *Teaching Exceptional Children, 31*(5), 32–37.

Individuals with Disabilities Education Improvement Act (IDEA) of 2004, Public Law 108-446 (2004). Retrieved November 24, 2008, from http://frwebgate.access.gpo.gov/cgi-bin/getdoc.cgi?dbname108_cong_public_laws&docidf:publ446.108

Kampwirth, T., & Powers, K. (2011). *Collaborative consultation in the schools: Effective practices for students with learning and behavior problems* (4th ed.). Boston: Pearson Education.

Kauchak, D., & Eggen, P. (2012). *Learning and teaching: Research-based methods* (6th ed.). Upper Saddle River, NJ: Pearson Education.

Kochhar-Bryant, C. (2008). *Collaboration and system coordination for students with special needs*. Upper Saddle River, NJ: Merrill/Pearson Education.

Kovaleski, J., & Glew, M. (2006). Bringing instructional support teams to scale: Implications of the Pennsylvania experience. *Remedial and Special Education, 27*, 16–25.

Lane, K., Pierson, M., Robertson, E., & Little, A. (2004). Teachers' views of prereferral interventions: Perceptions of and recommendations for implementation support. *Education and Treatment of Children, 27*(4), 420–439.

Mastropieri, M. A., Scruggs, T. E., Graetz, J., et al. (2005). Case studies in co-teaching in the content areas: Successes, failures, and challenges. *Intervention in School and Clinic, 40*(5), 260–270.

Matuszny, R., Banda, D., & Coleman, T. (2007). A progressive plan for building collaborative relationships with parents from diverse backgrounds. *Teaching Exceptional Children, 39*(4), 24–31.

McDonnell, J. (2011). Instructional contexts. In J. Kauffman & D. Hallahan (Eds.), *Handbook of special education* (pp. 532–543). New York: Routledge.

McLeskey, J. (2011). Supporting improved practice for special education teachers: The importance of learner-centered professional development. *Journal of Special Education Leadership, 24*, 26–35.

McLeskey, J., & Waldron, N. (2000). *Inclusive schools in action: Making differences ordinary*. Alexandria, VA: Association for Supervision and Curriculum Development.

McLeskey, J., & Waldron, N. (2002, September). School change and inclusive schools: Lessons learned from practice. *Phi Delta Kappan, 84*(1), 65–72.

McLeskey, J., & Waldron, N. (2006). Comprehensive school reform and inclusive schools: Improving schools for all students. *Theory into Practice, 45*(3), 269–278.

McMaster, K., Kung, S., Han, I., & Cao, M. (2008). Peer-assisted learning strategies: a "Tier 1" approach to promoting English learners' response to intervention. *Exceptional Children, 74*, 194–214.

Murawski, W., & Hughes, C. (2009). Response to intervention, collaboration, and co-teaching: A logical combination for successful systemic change. *Intervention in School and Clinic, 53*, 267–277.

National Center for Education Statistics. (2010). *Condition of education 2010*. Washington, DC: U.S. Department of Education, Institution of Education Sciences. Retrieved January 25, 2011, from http://nces.ed.gov/programs/coe/

Patall, E., Cooper, H., & Robinson, J. (2008). Parent involvement in homework: A research synthesis. *Review of Educational Research, 78*, 1039–1101.

Ploessl, D., Rock, M., Schoenfeld, N., & Blanks, B. (2010). On the same page: Practical techniques to enhance co-teaching interactions. *Intervention in School and Clinic, 45*, 158–168.

Riggs, C. (2005). To teachers: What paraeducators want you to know. *Teaching Exceptional Children, 36*(5), 8–12.

Rosenberg, M. S., Westling, D. L., & McLeskey, J. (2011). *Special education for today's teachers* (2nd ed.). Upper Saddle River, NJ: Merrill/Pearson Education.

Scruggs, T., Mastropieri, M., & McDuffie, K. (2007). Co-teaching in inclusive classrooms: A metasynthesis of qualitative research. *Exceptional Children, 73*(4), 392–416.

Snell, M., & Janney, R. (2005). *Collaborative teaming.* Baltimore: Brookes.

Vaughn, S., Bos, C., & Schumm, J. (2011). *Teaching students who are exceptional, diverse, and at risk in the general education classroom* (5th ed.). Boston: Pearson.

Waldron, N., & McLeskey, J. (2010). Establishing a collaborative school culture through comprehensive school reform. *Journal of Educational and Psychological Consultation, 20*(1), 58–74.

Walther-Thomas, C., Korinek, L., McLaughlin, V., & Williams, B. (2000). *Collaboration for inclusive education.* Boston: Allyn & Bacon.

Whitbread, K., Bruder, M., Fleming, G., & Park, H. (2007). Collaboration in special education: Parent–professional training. *Teaching Exceptional Children, 39*(4), 6–14.

Photo Credits

Differentiating Instruction
for Diverse Learners

Emi DiScuillo

JULIA AND TOM

In addition to several students with learning disabilities, Ms. Taravella's inclusion class included Julia, a student with a visual disability, and Tom, a student with significant cognitive disabilities. To assist Ms. Taravella in teaching her students, her teaching team included Ms. Stoudamire, a special education teacher, and Mr. Howry, a paraeducator. Ms. Steckler, a vision specialist, also was available periodically to help the team teach Julia, and Ms. Camac, the school's technology specialist, also helped Ms. Taravella use technology to teach her students.

As part of the districtwide curriculum related to the study of the solar system, the class was working on a unit about the sun, the moon, and the planets. Before implementing the unit, Ms. Taravella and her teaching team collaborated to plan it. They began by discussing the essential information they wanted their students to learn and agreeing on their curricular goals. They consulted assessment information and IEPs, and determined individualized goals for

their students. Whereas all of their students' curricular goals were aligned to the districtwide curriculum, Tom's goals also reflected several of the functional goals in his IEP. Because of their prior knowledge and level of mastery, the goals for Julia and several other students were enhanced to include learning about the derivation and meaning of the planets' names.

The team then used these curricular goals to create a menu of student products that varied in both difficulty and learning style to assess student mastery. The activities included creating a new planet; making visual displays and dioramas; giving oral or PowerPoint/Keynote presentations; writing a paper, a blog, or a wiki highlighting the unique characteristics of the sun, the moon, or a planet; and creating a podcast or a digital video about life on the sun, the moon, or a planet. The team then outlined their learning activities and the teaching strategies, student groupings, and resources they needed to use to support the participation and learning of their students.

Differentiating Instruction for Diverse Learners

Ms. Taravella, Ms. Camac, and Ms. Stoudamire led the students in performing a variety of individualized large- and small-group learning activities. The teachers presented a series of digital videos on the solar system to show colorful and animated video segments of the sun, the moon, and the different planets. Occasionally, they repeated segments or paused the presentation to highlight different features. Ms. Camac helped Ms. Steckler obtain a wireless headphone system so that Julia could hear a running description of the visual material being presented. To help students identify, organize, and remember the important points of the presentation, the teachers used an interactive white-smartboard to lead the class in creating a graphic organizer and playing a game (Name That Planet) comparing the planets. The students were particularly excited about using the white-smartboard to view Web sites that offered webcams of different planets.

The team also implemented instructional accommodations and arrangements for the students, including Julia and Tom, which were consistent with their IEPs. To support the learning of Julia and several of her classmates, the teachers and their colleagues paired visually presented information with tactile/kinesthetic- and auditory-based learning activities. They gave these students opportunities to learn by using hands-on replicas of the sun, the moon, and the different planets. Ms. Steckler used a software program to prepare enlarged handouts for Julia and collaborated with Mr. Howry to create charts of the sun, the moon, and the planets with string so that Julia and her classmates could access visual information through tactile experiences.

Ms. Taravella and Ms. Stoudamire used many of the same materials in different ways to support Tom's learning. While Ms. Taravella worked with students classifying and comparing the planets, Tom worked with Ms. Stoudamire sorting replicas of the planets by size and color. Tom also used the tactile planet chart to compare the sizes of the planets and to count the number of planets. Under the guidance of Ms. Taravella, Tom, Julia, and their classmates who have difficulty accessing text used digital teaching materials to have text highlighted, defined, enlarged, or read aloud by the computer. These materials also allowed the students to record their responses by typing text, drawing, speaking, or entering words from a list. Marta, an English language learner, used these materials in both English and Spanish.

The educators also created a webquest designed to guide the students in learning about the early study of and beliefs about the solar system by cultures around the world. Students worked in collaborative groups to access Web-based information related to early explorations of the sun, the moon, and the planets and the different cultural meanings regarding them. They learned about the different early observatories that had been set up throughout the world, and the various tools that the early astronomers used to observe and calculate the movements in the solar system. They also learned how different calendars and rituals were established based on these movement patterns. The groups then shared their findings with their classmates and others by postings on the class's website.

After completing the unit of instruction, the students chose a strategy for sharing their learning from the list of activities that the teachers had created. To make sure that students selected appropriate activities, Ms. Taravella and Ms. Stoudamire focused their choices. They also kept a record of students' choices and encouraged them to try new activities. Julia and Tom chose to work with several other students to create a web page about Saturn. Julia volunteered to design and create the Web page, and Tom worked with Mr. Howry to draw pictures and reproduce pictures of Saturn, which were then added to the group's Web page via use of a digital camera. The group's Web page and the other products students completed were then posted on the class's Web site, which also included a weblog of the class's learning activities and digital pictures of the students' assignments with accompanying narration.

What other strategies could Ms. Taravella and Ms. Stoudamire and their colleagues use to differentiate instruction for Julia, Tom, and the other students? After reading this chapter, you will have the knowledge, skills, and dispositions to answer this as well as the following questions:

- How can I differentiate instruction for students?
- How can I differentiate instruction for students who have difficulty reading and gaining information from print materials?
- How can I differentiate instruction for students from diverse cultural and language backgrounds?
- How can I use instructional technology and assistive devices to differentiate instruction for students?

Julia, Tom, and the other students were successful learners because Ms. Taravella and her colleagues used a variety of curricular and teaching accommodations to differentiate instruction for their students. To accommodate the diverse learners in their classrooms, educators differentiate

- *content* (what they teach),
- *process* (how they teach),
- *product* (how students demonstrate content mastery),
- *affect* (how students connect their thinking and feelings), and
- *learning environment* (how the classroom is designed and what instructional groupings they use) (Price & Nelson, 2007; Tomlinson et al., 2008).

They use varied curricula and instructional arrangements, strategies, resources, materials, and technology to address their students' individual learning strengths and challenges, preferences, and styles, as well as their developmental levels, interests, and experiential, cultural, and language backgrounds (van Garderen & Whittaker, 2006). This chapter describes proven strategies for differentiating instruction to address the many unique learning strengths and challenges of students. While these strategies can be used to help various types of students learn, they also can be used to differentiate instruction for *all students*. For example, Ms. Taravella and her colleagues used instructional accommodations not only to differentiate instruction for Julia and Tom but also to ensure the learning of *all* of their students.

DIFFERENTIATING INSTRUCTION

HOW CAN I DIFFERENTIATE INSTRUCTION FOR STUDENTS? Like Ms. Taravella and Ms. Stoudamire, you can engage in a variety of professional practices to differentiate instruction for your students so that they can succeed in the general education curriculum (see Figure 8.1). These effective practices are discussed in the following sections. In reflecting on their use, consider their potential impact; prior effectiveness; and the skills, resources, support, and time requirements you need to implement them.

Tailor Curricular Goals and Teaching Strategies to Your Students and Your Learning Environment

As we saw in the chapter-opening vignette, the types of curricular goals and teaching strategies used to differentiate your instruction should be tailored to your students and your local and statewide learning standards, and your learning environment (Childre, Sands, & Tanner Pope, 2009; Parish & Stodden, 2009). Therefore, you need to consider your students' strengths and challenges and the variables you control in your classroom (Lee et al., 2009).

PEARSON
myeducationlab

Go to the Assignments and Activities section of the Topic *Instructional Practices and Learning Strategies* in the MyEducationLab for your course and complete the activity entitled *Differentiating Instruction.* As you watch the video and answer the accompanying questions, consider how differentiating instruction benefits *all students* in your classroom.

FIGURE 8.1 **Differentiated instruction practices**

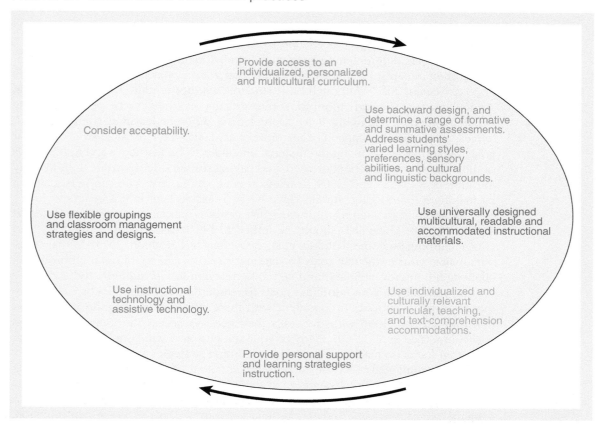

Provide access to an individualized, personalized and multicultural curriculum.

Consider acceptability.

Use backward design, and determine a range of formative and summative assessments. Address students' varied learning styles, preferences, sensory abilities, and cultural and linguistic backgrounds.

Use flexible groupings and classroom management strategies and designs.

Use universally designed multicultural, readable and accommodated instructional materials.

Use instructional technology and assistive technology.

Use individualized and culturally relevant curricular, teaching, and text-comprehension accommodations.

Provide personal support and learning strategies instruction.

In planning lessons and units of instruction that are tailored to your students and your classroom, you and your colleagues can consider the following issues:

- What are the themes, goals, and objectives of the lesson/activity?
- What teaching materials and arrangements will be used in the lesson/activity?
- When, where, and how long will this lesson/activity occur?
- Will all students be able to participate in this lesson/activity in the same ways as their classmates?
- What supports, personal assistance, learning strategies, instructional accommodations, and/or instructional technology/assistive devices are needed to help students participate fully?
- How can the curriculum and student assessment be supplemented or changed to address the different learning styles and challenges of students?
- How can the lesson/activity be differentiated to reflect students' learning styles, language, culture, experiences, behavioral needs, motivation, interests, talents, strengths, challenges, and IEPs?
- How can the lesson/activity be differentiated in terms of the complexity of the content, type and amount of work, teaching materials used, grouping patterns, support needed, location, pace and time, and the products produced?
- Can students participate in the activity but work on other skills or work with others on an activity that has different goals?
- How can the lesson/activity be differentiated to motivate and engage students and provide them with choices?
- What materials will be needed to engage students in the lesson/activity?
- How can the classroom environment be differentiated to engage students in the lesson/activity?
- How can student mastery of the content of the lesson/activity be assessed throughout and at the end of the lesson/activity?

Individualize and Personalize Your Curriculum

An initial step in differentiating instruction is individualizing your curriculum by identifying the concepts, principles, and skills you want to teach (Fisher & Frey, 2008; Price & Nelson, 2007). Although most students will not require accommodations in curricular goals, the curriculum for some students may need to be personalized by supplementing or changing it to address their different learning strengths, challenges, and styles (Thompson, 2008; Voltz et al., 2005). Individualize your curricular goals by adding or reducing the material and skills to be learned, varying the levels of difficulty of the content addressed, and having students demonstrate their mastery in different ways (Salend, 2009; Tomlinson et al., 2008). You also can personalize it by making it more multicultural, which we will discuss later in this chapter.

In addition to aligning your curricular goals to national, statewide, and district standards, your goals also should be linked to big ideas, essential questions, and critical learning outcomes (Childre et al., 2009; Parish & Stodden, 2009). You also can personalize your curricular goals by making sure they are meaningful, appropriate, challenging, interdisciplinary, and culturally relevant for *all students* and their lives (Thompson, 2008). Your curricular goals for students who have IEPs or 504 accommodation plans should be consistent with these documents and individualized so that they are provided with the skills they need to access the general education curriculum (Lee et al., 2009). Many of your students also will benefit from curricular goals that focus on teaching them to use learning strategies.

Curriculum goals for your students also should relate to your assessment of their existing levels of mastery. Therefore, at the beginning of a lesson or unit of instruction you can use a variety of classroom-based assessment techniques to assess your students' prior knowledge and various levels of mastery. This assessment information, combined with your examination of your curriculum, can help you individualize your curricular goals for your students by determining the following:

- What levels of content mastery and skills do my students have?
- What content and skills do I expect *all* my students to learn?
- What content and skills do I expect *most* of my students to learn?
- What content and skills do I expect *some* students to learn? (Lenz, Bulgren, Kissam, & Taymans, 2004)

Use Backward Design, and Determine a Range of Formative and Summative Assessments

Prior to planning your instructional activities, use **backward design**, a process for planning units of instruction and individual lessons by which you first determine the assessments you will use to evaluate your students' learning (Childre et al., 2009). Once you determine these assessments, you use them to guide you in designing and sequencing the instructional activities that your students will engage in to achieve your learning outcomes (Parrish & Stodden, 2009).

In planning and implementing your assessments, consider using both *formative* and *summative* assessment to evaluate your students' learning and your teaching (Salend, 2009). **Formative assessment** relates to your use of assessment strategies during instruction to monitor your students' learning progress and to use this information to make ongoing decisions about the effectiveness of your teaching and ways you can improve it (Brookhart, Moss, & Long, 2008; Tomlinson, 2008b). **Summative assessment** focuses on your use of assessments at the end of instruction to assess student mastery of specific content, topics, concepts and skills taught, and to communicate this information to others (Chappuis & Chappuis, 2008).

Tiered assignments during and at the end of instructional units allow you to differentiate your assessments to meet the strengths and challenges of individual students (Painter, 2009). In this method, you identify concepts that need to be learned, delineate multiple ways in which students can show mastery that differ in complexity and learning style, and allow students to select how they want to demonstrate their learning (Salend, 2009). For example, at the end of the unit, Ms. Taravella and Ms. Stoudamire identified and gave their students a menu of choices about how they could demonstrate their learning. They also made sure that students selected appropriate activities, and tried new activities.

Use Curricular Accommodations

Once the curricular goals and assessment strategies are delineated, you can use curricular accommodations to help a diverse group of students access and master them (Lee et al., 2009; McKinley & Stormont, 2008). Some individualized curricular accommodations that you may consider include

- giving students choices about what they learn and how they learn it;
- collaborating with students to create learning contracts that specify learning goals, activities, and products;
- altering the instructional content, tasks, and pace;
- enhancing the multicultural aspects of the content;
- designing alternative projects to allow students to demonstrate mastery;
- focusing on fewer or different objectives; and
- modifying students' requirements and assessments.

Your lessons and curricular areas can be differentiated for academically diverse students by using multilevel teaching and curriculum overlapping (Downing, 2008; Giangreco, 2007; Lee et al., 2009). In **multilevel teaching**, students are given lessons in the same curricular areas as their peers but at varying levels of difficulty. Some students may work on a reduced or increased number of items or more or less complex

UDL and YOU
Using Universally Designed Curriculum and Teaching Materials

An essential aspect of differentiating instruction for your students is the use of universally designed curriculum and teaching materials (Metcalf & Evans, 2009). This use of universally designed curriculum and teaching materials provide you with ways to differentiate your instruction based on your students' learning styles and cognitive, physical, sensory, motivational, cultural, and language characteristics (Dukes & Lamar-Dukes, 2009). They also allow you to offer a wide range of flexible options that so that your students can select to access and respond to information of varying levels of difficulty in a variety of formats (Kurtts, Matthews, & Smallwood, 2009). Thus, directions, content, and learning activities are clearly presented in multiple formats, and learners choose the appropriate formats that fit their learning styles and preferences (Sopko, 2008). In addition, assessment, motivation, prompting, and feedback are available throughout the learning experience.

One example of UDL curriculum and teaching materials that Ms. Taravella and her colleagues used involved providing their students with digitally presented, interactive teaching activities. Digitally presented learning activities such as electronic books foster reading fluency and text comprehension for a broad range of students through help menus that connect them to

- *text-to-speech capabilities and translation resources* that offer help through the use of digitized reading in multiple languages and definitions of words or video clips of sign language translations;

- *teaching resources and/or strategy prompts* that are embedded in the selection to allow students to review

material, understand context cues, look ahead to preview material, respond to questions, ask questions about the material, engage in games and simulations, pay attention to underlined or highlighted information, receive corrective feedback, and construct mental pictures;

- *reader-friendly resources* that allow readers to select the text size, the language read, and the page display, add color highlights, and note where the reader last read;

- *illustrative resources* that offer students access to examples; comparisons; and visuals of concepts through the use of graphics, animation, and sound;

- *informational or supplementary resources* that provide additional information and enrichment via access to multimedia presentations, electronic encyclopedias, dictionaries, and databases;

- *summarizing resources* that offer students graphics, outlines, and overviews of the structure, content, and major features of the text;

- *collaborative resources* that allow students to work together;

- *notational resources* that allow students to take notes, construct sticky notes, summarize main points, add color, and highlight text electronically as they read; and

- *assessment resources* that record ongoing data on student performance and make it readily available to students and teachers. (Anderson-Inman, 2009; Douglas, Ayres, Langone, Bell, & Meade, 2009)

REFLECTIVE

Think about a lesson you recently taught or are planning to teach. How did/could you use multilevel teaching to adapt the lesson to the needs of a student with a significant disability? A student with a mild disability? A student who is gifted and talented? An English language learner?

learning objectives. For example, while other students were classifying and comparing the planets, Tom was sorting replicas of the planets by size and color. Similarly, because of her advanced level of mastery, Julia's instructional program was supplemented so that she was learning about the derivation and meaning of the planets' names.

Curriculum overlapping involves teaching a diverse group of students individualized skills from different curricular areas. In this method, teaching of a practical, functional, specific skill related to the student's academic program is embedded in learning activities across the curriculum. For example, when the class was working on science, Tom also worked on counting the planets.

Use Individualized Teaching/Instructional Accommodations

The use of *individualized teaching/instructional accommodations*—changes in the ways information is presented or the ways students respond—are essential aspects of differentiated instruction (Byrnes, 2008; McKinley & Stormont, 2008). Rather than being disability specific, teaching accommodations for students should be individually determined based on students' individual characteristics, including their cultural, linguistic and experiential backgrounds. They also should be consistent with research and districtwide policies, appropriate for the content to be learned, and acceptable to students, educators, and families. They should be selected and implemented to help students access their learning strengths, overcome their learning challenges, and demonstrate their mastery of content being taught (Bianco et al., 2009). Finally, it is essential that the effectiveness of teaching accommodations in fostering student learning be evaluated (Salend, 2009).

Stough (2002) offers a continuum for delineating differentiation techniques based on their impact on the individual profiles of students and the level of curriculum mastery expected of students. The first level of the continuum refers to *access differentiation techniques*. These techniques provide students with access to the curriculum and do not affect the level of mastery expected of students. They help students like Julia participate at the same level as others and do not require adjustments in the structure or content of the curriculum. Examples of *access differentiation techniques* include Braille, sign language, bilingual dictionaries, and instructional and assistive technology.

The second level of the continuum relates to *low-impact differentiation techniques*. Although these techniques involve adjustments in teaching methods, they have minimal to no impact on the level of curricular mastery expected of students. These instructional techniques alter the ways students are taught, but do not require significant adjustments in the structure or content of the curriculum. Examples of these types of techniques include content enhancements, word processing and spell checkers, learning strategies instruction, and peer-mediated instruction.

The third level of the continuum addresses *high-impact differentiation techniques* that affect curricular expectations. These instructional techniques, sometimes referred to as *modifications*, alter the content of the curriculum, as well as the ways students are taught, and require adjustments in the structure and content of the educational program that affect the level of curricular mastery expected of students. Examples of this level of the continuum include some of the accommodations used to teach Tom, such as the use of multilevel teaching and curriculum overlapping.

Decisions about individualized teaching accommodations for students are made based on data to determine whether and how students' disabilities affect their educational performance, and whether and to what extent individual students will need teaching accommodations to access the general education curriculum (Byrnes, 2008). You and your colleagues can use a variety of methods and sources to collect data concerning students' skills, strengths, challenges, learning and testing styles and preferences, self-concept, attitudes, and health (Salend, 2009). Sample questions that can guide you and your colleagues in analyzing student information to determine appropriate teaching accommodations for individual students include the following:

- Does the student exhibit academic and social behaviors that interfere with his or her learning or the learning of others? If so, what are these behaviors and what strategies and resources are needed to address them?
- What instructional methods, approaches, strategies, specialized equipment, technology, materials, and/or classroom designs have been successful in supporting the student's learning?
- What strategies and resources are needed to help the student understand directions and respond to classroom activities?
- What are the student's learning and testing style preferences?
- Does the student have sensory, medical, and/or attention conditions that affect his or her classroom performance?
- Does the student require more time and or additional motivation to complete assignments?

Use Instructional Materials Accommodations

Varying the instructional materials to accommodate your students and their varied academic abilities, interests, experiential and cultural backgrounds, and learning preferences is another way you can differentiate instruction (McKinley & Stormont, 2008). In addition to many of the strategies presented in this text, you can use the following instructional materials accommodations:

- Vary the amount of the material that students are exposed to and asked to complete (e.g., students read half the assignment and complete only the first three questions).
- Vary the format of the materials (e.g., have Julia, Tom, and other students access the materials digitally and via other forms of technology).
- Supplement the materials (e.g., provide Julia, Tom, and other students with manipulatives, replicas, visuals, graphic organizers, cues, and prompts).
- Use materials that present similar content at lower readability levels.
- Use alternative materials (e.g., create a chart with string so that Julia, Tom, and their classmates can tactilely access visual information).

Provide Personal Supports

As was evident in the chapter-opening vignette, you can differentiate your instruction for students by providing them with personal supports from other professionals, paraeducators, and peers. In addition to using a variety of cooperative-teaching instructional formats and consultation with specialists like Ms. Steckler, personal supports can be provided by using paraeducators like Mr. Howry and grouping arrangements where students learn in cooperative learning groups. Paraeducators also may be asked to provide physical supports so students with physical, sensory, or cognitive disabilities can access all aspects of the learning environment (Suter & Giangreco, 2009).

Paraeducators can be invaluable in helping you and your students, but if used improperly, they can hinder the school performance and independence of students (Giangreco & Broer, 2007). When paraeducators work too closely with specific students (sometimes called the Velcro effect), it is important for you to make sure that they don't impede effective inclusion programs by

- allowing general educators to avoid assuming responsibility for educating students with disabilities (e.g., saying, "She is so good with Mitchell that I just let her handle it");
- fostering the separation of students with disabilities from the rest of the class (e.g., working with a student with disabilities in a separate location);
- creating dependence on adults (e.g., prompting and assisting students when it is not necessary);
- limiting interactions with peers (e.g., being near the student can intimidate peers and reduce socialization);
- teaching ineffectively (e.g., not adjusting an unsuccessful activity);
- causing the loss of personal control (e.g., making decisions for students with significant communication, physical, and/or sensory difficulties);
- causing the loss of gender identity (e.g., taking students to the bathroom based on the gender of the paraeducator, not the student);
- interfering with the teaching of other students (e.g., using behaviors that distract other students) (Causton-Theoharris, 2009; Giangreco & Broer, 2007; Liston et al., 2009).

To prevent these situations from occurring, clarify their roles and make sure they are performing duties that are commensurate with their job descriptions (Carnahan et al., 2009; Causton-Theoharis, 2009). It also is essential for you to collaborate and communicate with paraeducators to differentiate instruction and deliver appropriate services to support the learning of *all students*. Also, take actions to help them perform the job and address their concerns (Devlin, 2008; Liston et al., 2009). For example, orient them by sharing your teaching philosophy, providing a tour of the school, introducing them to key school personnel, describing relevant programs and daily routines, and reviewing the dress code and other standards of decorum. In the orientation program, you can also explain the need for and rules on confidentiality, and discuss scheduling, handling emergencies, and other school procedures.

In addition, you can offer paraeducators an education program so that they understand and have the skills to perform their roles (Carnahan et al., 2009; Causton-Theoharis, 2009; Devlin, 2008). Such a program includes many types of information. It explains the roles of paraeducators inside and outside the classroom, as well as their legal and ethical responsibilities. It identifies the special medical, social, and academic strengths and challenges of students and the technology they use. It provides an overview of the curriculum, teaching, and behavior management techniques and reviews the communication system you will be using.

Because it is your job to make curriculum decisions and to supervise paraeducators when they provide instruction, it is important to monitor their actions and communicate regularly with them (Causton-Theoharis, 2009; Liston et al., 2009; Maggin et al., 2009). Collaborate with them to jointly plan and coordinate activities, monitor student performance, and deal with problems and conflicts. It is also important to treat them respectfully, give them feedback on their performance, solicit their point of view about their roles, strengths, and challenges and acknowledge their contributions (Carnahan et al., 2009; Devlin, 2008).

Address Students' Learning Styles and Preferences

When choosing methods to differentiate instruction, you should address students' learning styles and preferences (Tomlinson, 2008). Use learning style assessments, and note the situations and conditions that appear to influence individual students, and then adjust learning and assessment activities to accommodate students' learning styles and preferences (Beam, 2009; Servilio, 2009). You can use different types of reinforcement and feedback to increase students' motivation and acknowledge their performance. You also can structure the classroom so that noise levels, students' nearness to others, distractions, movement, and desk arrangements are acceptable to students and consistent with their preferences. For example, you can let students choose whether to work at their desks or in some other place. Finally, when planning the length and nature of learning activities and daily and weekly schedules, you can think about the various learning style and preferences of students such as attention span, ability to move while learning, time of day, and grouping considerations such as learning alone or in groups and with or without adults present.

Learning and teaching styles also are classified as either *field independent* or *field dependent* (Levine & McCloskey, 2009). Field-independent students appear to work best on individual tasks such as independent projects and relate formally to teachers; field-dependent students prefer to work in groups and establish personal relationships with others, including teachers. Field-independent teachers foster learning through competition and independent assignments; field-dependent teachers use personal and conversational teaching techniques.

Learning styles can be affected in other ways by cultural factors. For example, some cultures emphasize learning through verbal rather than visual descriptions; other cultures emphasize physical modeling over pictorials. Students' socioeconomic status can also influence their learning and cognitive styles.

Address Students' Sensory Abilities

Students with sensory disabilities have unique challenges, which you need to address when differentiating your instruction for them. For students like Julia, who have visual disabilities, you must present information orally; for students who are deaf and hard of hearing, you should use visual forms. At all times, you should encourage independence. Because the sensory functioning of students with sensory

REFLECTIVE

How do you prefer to learn and teach? How do you adapt when the teaching strategy and environment are different from the way you prefer to learn? Should teachers match students' learning styles all the time? Should students be taught to adapt their learning styles to the various teaching styles they will encounter in schools?

disabilities varies tremendously, you need to consider their unique needs and abilities when modifying your teaching methods, and the learning environment.

Differentiating Instruction for Students with Visual Disabilities   As the teachers did in the chapter-opening vignette, you can collaborate with vision and mobility specialists to design and implement many strategies to differentiate instruction for students with visual disabilities (Li, 2009; Taylor et al., 2009). Many of these strategies also can be used for students who are visual learners. Help them; follow along in class by giving important directions verbally or recording them; phrasing questions and comments so that they include students' names; and using peers to read directions and materials, describe events in the classroom, and take notes.

You also can help these students learn by giving them opportunities to learn by doing, and by providing with physical prompts and pairing verbal and tactile cues (Bruce, Randall, & Birge, 2008; Lewis, 2010; Swift et al., 2008). It also is suggested that you use real objects and manipulatives that are familiar, meaningful, and motivating to students and provide them with large-print books, photo-enlarged handouts and tests, tactile books, Braille reference books and dictionaries, adaptive computer software, and audio-based materials (Howell, 2008; Spungin & Ferrell, 2007). However, understand that as students grow older, they may be reluctant to use special materials in the presence of their peers. When providing students with tactile learning experiences or asking them to respond orally, it is important to give students sufficient time to interact with all aspects of the learning materials or answer, and provide the supports students need to benefit from the tactile representations. You also might find it helpful to experiment with the materials yourself by using them with your eyes closed.

You also can use technology to produce large, clear typewritten materials with high contrasts (i.e., black type on a white background) (Swift et al., 2008). Tracing over the letters, numerals, and pictorials with a black felt-tip marker or black ballpoint pen makes it easier to see them, and placing a piece of yellow acetate over a page of print enhances the contrast and darkens the print. Students with visual impairments may experience visual fatigue during activities that require continuous use of visual skills. In these situations, it may be helpful to present one visual item at a time, to give students additional time to complete assignments and tests or to reduce the number and length of activities that call for visual concentration.

Student learning can also be promoted by using several strategies to help students locate learning materials and move around the classroom and the school (Heward, 2009). You can use *o'clock* directions to describe the location of an object on a flat surface (e.g., "Your book is at three o'clock, and your pencil is at nine o'clock"). If an object is nearby and in danger of being knocked over, guide the student's hand to the object or hand the student the object by gently touching his or her hand with the object. When giving directions to specific places in the classroom or school, use nonvisual statements and remember that directions for going left and right should be in relation to the student's body rather than yours.

Differentiating Instruction for Deaf and Hard-of-Hearing Students   Many strategies are available for differentiating instruction for deaf and hard-of-hearing students, which also can be used for students who are auditory learners (Howell, 2008; Taylor et al., 2009). These strategies include using good communication techniques, which are (a) standing still and facing the person when speaking; (b) speaking clearly, at a moderate pace, and using short sentences; (c) speaking in a normal voice; (d) maintaining a proper speaking distance; (e) keeping the mouth area clear; (f) using facial and body gestures; (g) speaking in an area where the light is on your lips and face; and (h) providing transitions to indicate a change in the subject. Try to limit movement and unnecessary gestures, and present all spelling and vocabulary words in sentences (context), as many words presented in isolation look alike to lip readers. In addition, you can use visual signals to gain the student's attention, and use instructional technology such as interactive white-smartboards to present material so that the student can view the material and your lips simultaneously. If necessary,

PEARSON
myeducationlab

To enhance your understanding of instructional accommodations that can support the performance of students with visual disabilities in your inclusive classroom, go to the IRIS Center Resources section of the Topic *Visual Impairment* in the MyEducationLab for your course, and complete the modules entitled *Instructional Accommodations: Making the Learning Environment Accessible to Students with Visual Disabilities* and *Accommodations to the Physical Environment: Setting up a Classroom for Students with Visual Disabilities*.

rephrase, repeat, summarize, or simplify your comments and questions, as well as those of other students, to make them more understandable, and ask questions to check understanding of orally presented directions and content. When using multimedia, shine a light on the speaker's face when the room is darkened for films or slides, and give the student the script of a video, or a recording to help the student follow along.

You also can use visually oriented techniques such as experiential and hands-on learning to help students learn (Roberts, 2010; Wurst et al., 2005). Offer demonstrations and provide examples. Create a visually rich learning environment and use written materials, visual aids such as graphic organizers to present content and summarize the main points of lessons, and cues to support instruction. Supplement information presented orally with real objects, manipulatives, and concrete visual aids (e.g., maps, globes). Write daily assignments, the schedule, important directions and information, technical terms, and new vocabulary on the board, and give students test directions, assignments, vocabulary lists, models, feedback, and lecture outlines in writing. Teach students to look up difficult-to-pronounce words in the dictionary.

Deaf and hard-of-hearing students may need the service of an educational interpreter. What have been your experiences working with educational interpreters?

Using Educational Interpreters Effectively. An *educational interpreter*, a professional who helps transfer information between individuals who do not communicate in the same way, can assist you in differentiating instruction for deaf and hard-of-hearing students. Depending on the student's preference, many educational interpreting methods exist. Early in the school year, you and the interpreter can meet to agree on the responsibilities of both persons. The teacher has primary responsibility and the interpreter aids communication. To help teachers and interpreters communicate, planning meetings can be scheduled on a regular basis.

Because interpreters may not know the content and teaching strategies used in the classroom, it is helpful to orient them to the curriculum and to give them copies of textbooks and other relevant materials. A knowledge of class routines, projects, and long-term assignments can assist interpreters in helping students understand assignments. With a difficult unit, including technical vocabulary and other content that may be hard to explain by alternative means, you and the interpreter can meet to discuss key terms. For example, when teaching about the geological history of the earth, you could give the interpreter a list of key terms and copies of lesson plans so that the interpreter can plan in advance how to translate and explain terms such as *Paleozoic era, Oligocene epoch*, and *Jurassic period*.

To maximize the effectiveness of the interpreter in your classroom, try these tips:

- Be sensitive to the time delays caused by interpreting.
- Talk to the students, not to the interpreter.
- Avoid directing comments to the interpreter during class time. Signals can be used to indicate the need for discussion after class.
- Encourage the interpreter to seek help when communication problems arise during class that affect the translation process.
- Avoid involving the interpreter in disciplining the student for misbehavior unless this misbehavior is directed at the interpreter. When the interpreter is involved in disciplinary actions, help students understand the roles and perspectives of the persons involved.
- Place the interpreter in a position that makes interpretation easy.

Consider Acceptability

When selecting strategies to differentiate instruction, another important factor to consider is **acceptability**, the extent to which you and your colleagues view a specific assessment, curricular and teaching practice as easy to use, effective, appropriate for the setting, fair, and reasonable (Carter, 2008). Reasonableness can be assessed by examining your practices in terms of

- which individuals will be responsible for implementing it;
- how much extra time and what materials, resources and technology are needed to implement it;
- whether it will require important changes in your teaching style;
- whether it is consistent with your philosophy;
- whether it requires preparation and practice for students and educators to implement;
- whether it is intrusive;
- how it will affect others; and
- how much it will cost.

An important aspect of treatment acceptability is the impact of your practices and accommodations on specific students and their peers (Salend, 2009). You are more likely to use strategies you perceive as fair and benefiting *all students*. Other factors related to students include age appropriateness, risks such as student embarrassment or isolation, intrusiveness into the student's personal space, and student cooperation. For example, giving a student a math assignment while the other students are working on social studies can isolate the student. Make sure that the accommodation does not adversely affect either the students or their classmates.

When adapting your curricular and teaching practices, you also need to consider students' reactions to and perceptions of these changes. In general, students prefer teachers who adapt their methods and believe that *all students* benefit from these accommodations. Some students, however, particularly those with disabilities, are concerned that accommodations in tests, textbooks, and homework may isolate them from their general education peers.

DIFFERENTIATING INSTRUCTION FOR STUDENTS WHO HAVE DIFFICULTY READING AND GAINING INFORMATION FROM PRINT MATERIALS

HOW CAN I DIFFERENTIATE INSTRUCTION FOR STUDENTS WHO HAVE DIFFICULTY READING AND GAINING INFORMATION FROM PRINT MATERIALS? You probably present a lot of content to your students using print materials. However, because many students have difficulty reading and gaining information from print materials, you may need to use the teacher- and student-directed strategies presented here. When selecting and using these methods, it is important for you to teach your students about the different types of text structures and how to use learning strategies to support their text comprehension (Englert, 2009; Faggella-Luby & Deshler, 2008). It also is important for you to collaborate with your school's literacy specialist and provide *all students* with numerous opportunities to develop their decoding skills and vocabulary and to read selections across the curriculum that they find motivating and that relate to their prior knowledge and experiential backgrounds (Ebbers & Denton, 2008).

Use Teacher-Directed Text Comprehension Strategies

Previewing   Before assigning a reading selection, you can use prereading activities to preview new vocabulary and word pronunciation, text structures, motivate students, and activate their prior knowledge (Roberts, Torgesen, Boardman, &

Scammacca, 2008; Williams, 2005). Scanning the selection and discussing the meaning of boldfaced or italicized terms is helpful. New vocabulary words can be placed in a word file of index cards by chapter. English language learners also may find it helpful for you to write critical vocabulary in their native language and link new vocabulary to visuals and cognates in their native languages (Denton, Wexler, Vaughn, & Bryan, 2008; Dong, 2009).

Previews, structured overviews, self-monitoring checklists, and prereading organizers can help students understand the purpose of the reading selection, identify the text structures employed, and direct their attention to the relevant information in the selection (Faggella-Luby & Deshler, 2008; Roberts et al., 2008; Whalon & Hanline, 2008). For example, you can give students an outline of the selection's main points and discuss them before reading or have students complete an outline as they read the selection. As students read the assignment, emphasize key points by underlining and highlighting them; repeating, discussing, and summarizing them; and questioning students about graphs, pictures, and diagrams.

You also can use cues to help students identify and understand essential information presented in print. Prompt students to focus on important content by highlighting it or labeling it as important in the margins. Margin notes, like the ones in this text, can be written on textbook pages that include definitions, statements, questions, notes, and activities that help students understand and interact with the material. You also can teach your students to understand and use text features such as headings, visuals, and highlighted words to support their ability to focus on and understand important text (Fisher & Frey, 2008).

Activating or priming students' prior knowledge before reading the selection also can help them understand the new material and vocabulary (Englert, 2009; Gately, 2008; Vacca & Vacca, 2008). This can be done by using brainstorming, and discussing and predicting text structures and components of the story. You and your students also can learn to use different types of graphic organizers based on the nature of information being presented (Whalon, Al Otaiba, & Delano, 2009) (see Figure 8.2b). You can introduce your students to important background information by displaying and reviewing some of the key and motivating illustrations in the reading selection. You also can use a *K-W-L* strategy: *K* (students identify what they **K**now about the reading selection and the topic), *W* (students create questions or statements related to what they **W**ant to learn from reading about the topic), and *L* (students discuss what they have **L**earned from reading about the topic).

You can improve students' comprehension skills by asking them to do a writing activity related to the assignment before they read the selection (Roberts et al., 2008). Learning logs, study guides, written summaries, and questions related to readings can be used to help students understand the material by allowing them to organize their thoughts.

Questioning   A popular strategy for guiding text comprehension—having students individually or in groups respond to or generate questions about the text before, during, and after reading—can focus attention on the purpose of the assignment (Falk-Ross et al., 2009; Fink Chorzempa & Lapidus, 2009; Whalon et al., 2009). You can use

- *literal questions*, which ask about the facts presented in the selection (who, what, where, when, why, and how);
- *literacy-based questions*, which are related to the written and oral language components of the selection;
- *inferential questions*, which cause students to make interpretations about and reflect on the material;
- *ponderable questions*, which present dilemmas or situations that have no right or wrong answer;
- *elaborative questions*, which ask students to incorporate their prior knowledge into information presented in the selection.

You can help students answer questions by teaching them about the different kinds of questions and by modifying the language, type, and timing of the questions (Fink Chorzempa & Lapidus, 2009; Sanacore, 2005). At first, present literal questions that deal with factual information in the reading selection. Then move to those that require inference and evaluation on the part of students and more complex skills. You also should try to phrase your questions so that *all* students feel comfortable responding. Open-ended questions can be used so that different students can provide different responses and insights to questions. When students have difficulty responding to open-ended questions, you can rephrase them, using simpler language or a multiple-choice format. You can help students gain information from books by using *prequestions* posed before the selection is read and *postquestions* posed afterward. Postquestions are particularly effective in promoting recall by establishing the need for review. Be careful in using prequestions; they can cause students to focus too much on information related to the answers while ignoring other content. You can help students develop text comprehension skills by asking them to generate their own questions and summarize a selection's content in their own words.

One questioning strategy that teachers and students can learn is Question the Author (QtA) (Salinger & Fleischman, 2005). When using this strategy with your students, you ask them questions to guide and assess their text comprehension and reading strategies. For example, as students read text, you can ask them to identify important information ("What is the important information in that paragraph? Why is it important?"), understand key terminology ("Why did the author choose this word? What does it mean in the context of the sentence?"), and question content ("Do you agree with the author? Why or why not?").

Another effective text comprehension strategy that involves students responding to questions about the text and story structure (e.g., who, what, where, when and how questions about the story) is Reread-Adapt and Answer-Comprehend (RAAC) (Therrien, Gormley, & Kubina, 2006). You implement RAAC by (a) prompting students to read the selection as fast as they can and to pay attention to what they have read so that they can answer questions about the story; (b) having students read who, what, where, when, and how questions about the story; (c) asking students to reread the story aloud while you correct their errors and praise their improvements; (d) having students adapt and answer questions about the story while you prompt them if they make errors; and (e) evaluating student progress and making decisions about future reading selections based on their progress.

Reciprocal Teaching Text comprehension skills also can be improved by *reciprocal teaching*, which involves a dialogue between you and your students (Ash, Kuhn, & Walpole, 2009; Gately, 2008). Here you ask students to read a selection silently, summarize it, discuss and clarify problem areas and unclear vocabulary, use questions to check understanding, and give students the opportunity to predict future content. After you model these strategies, students take the role of the teacher while you provide help through prompting ("What type of question would a teacher ask in this situation?"), instructing ("A summary is a short statement that includes only essential information"), modifying the activity ("If you can't predict what's going to happen, summarize the information again"), praising students ("That was a good prediction"), and offering corrective feedback ("What information could help you make your prediction?").

Collaborative Strategic Reading A multicomponent reading comprehension strategy that is based on reciprocal teaching is Collaborative Strategic Reading (CSR) (Brigham, Berkley, Simpkins, & Brigham, 2007; Vaughn & Edmonds, 2006). In CSR, teachers use modeling and talking aloud to teach students why, when, and how to use the following strategic reading comprehension strategies:

- *Previewing:* Students read the selection, recall what they know about it, and predict what it is about.
- *Click and clunk:* Students identify difficult parts of the selection and create fix-up sentences to make the sentences understandable.

PEARSON
myeducationlab

Go to the Building Teaching Skills and Dispositions section of the Topic *Reading Instruction* in the MyEducationLab for your course and complete the activity entitled *Teaching Comprehension Skills and Strategies.* As you watch the video and answer the accompanying questions, consider how comprehension strategies can help all students gain information from text.

- *Get the gist:* Students read and restate the important aspects of the selection.
- *Wrap-up:* Students summarize the important aspects of the selection and generate easy, harder and hardest questions that might be on a test. *Easy questions* are those whose one or two word answers are in the text. *Harder questions* are those that involve one or two sentences combining information presented in the text. The *hardest questions* are those that require students to use prior knowledge and information from the selection.

Once students learn the strategic reading strategies, three to five students work collaboratively to read the text and apply the strategic strategies. To assist each group, ask them to maintain a log of their activities, progress, and use of the strategies or assign students to perform roles (e.g., group leader, the click and clunk or gist experts, recorder, timekeeper). You also can implement technology-based collaborative strategic reading (Kim, Vaughn, Klingner, Woodruff, Reutebuch, & Kouzekanani, 2006).

Collaborative Reading Groups   Your students also can work in collaborative reading groups to foster their text comprehension (Chiang & Lin, 2007; Fisher & Frey, 2008; Guthrie et al., 2009). In collaborative reading groups, students share responsibility for reading the text and making sure that all group members comprehend it. You can foster the success of these groups by teaching your students how to work collaboratively and assigning them different roles to support the success of the group. Possible roles include the *questioner* (who prompts the group to generate questions), *page master* (who identifies special text features and important sections and prompts the group to summarize them), *vocabulary enricher* (who helps the group identify and define important and difficult vocabulary), *connector* (who assists the group in making connections between the text and their lives and learning), and *illustrator* (who guides the group in creating pictures or graphic organizers depicting the key elements and information from the selection) (O'Brien, 2007). When using collaborative reading groups, try make sure that *all students* have the opportunity to perform a range of the roles within the group.

Story/Text Mapping   Some students may benefit from *story/text mapping*, in which you help them identify the major elements of a story or passage using a visual representation (see Figure 8.2a) (Gately, 2008; Stone, Boon, Fore, Bender, & Spencer, 2008). Give students story/text maps that contain pictorial prompts paired with text and spaces for them to list the key elements of the story or passage such as the setting (characters, time, and place), the plot or problem, the goal, the action, the outcome, and the characters' reactions (e.g., graphics of individuals paired with "Who are the characters?") (Whalon & Hanline, 2008). As students read information on the components-of-the-story/text map, ask them to discuss the information and write the correct response on their map. As students learn to do this, they can complete the story/text map independently. Boyle and Weishaar (1997) have developed TRAVEL, a type of map that helps students create cognitive organizers to help them understand text.

Communicative Reading Strategies   Communicative reading strategies offer students corrective feedback designed to support their independent use of text

PEARSON
myeducationlab
To enhance your understanding of how to use collaborative strategic reading strategies to foster your students' text comprehension, go to the IRIS Center Resources section of the Topic *Instructional Practices and Learning Strategies* in the MyEducationLab for your course, and complete the module entitled *CSR: A Reading Comprehension Strategy.*

Scott Cunningham/Merrill

Story and text maps can facilitate students' text comprehension. What strategies do you use to foster your students' reading comprehension?

comprehension strategies (Fisher & Frey, 2008). This involves your monitoring students' text comprehension as they read, and intervening to assist them by engaging them in conversations about the text, offering prompts and cues to help them focus and understand the topic, simplifying sentences, defining and explaining new vocabulary, summarizing passages, highlighting and explaining pronoun references, and linking ideas and words, and text across passages and chapters.

Teach Student-Directed Text Comprehension Strategies

Students may learn to use a variety of student-directed comprehension strategies (Englert, 2009; Faggella-Luby & Deshler, 2008; Schumaker et al., 2006). You can help your students learn to employ these strategies by modeling and role-playing their use, thinking aloud as you use them, and offering opportunities for guided/collaborative and independent practice (Fink Chorzempa & Lapidus, 2009; Servilio, 2009). You can foster their use of these strategies by providing them with or posting pictorial prompts and self-monitoring checklists such as the ones presented in Figure 8.2 (Guthrie et al., 2009). You also can give them sticky notes and ask students to use them to summarize text, list main ideas, supporting details, and specific story elements, and prompt students to ask questions or make comments (Stormont, 2008).

Finding the Main Idea   Students can learn to identify the main idea of a paragraph, which is usually embedded in the topic sentence (Coyne, Zipoli, & Ruby, 2006; Guthrie et al., 2009).Therefore, you can teach your students how and where to find topic sentences. For example, you can display a paragraph on a PowerPoint slide and model and prompt students in identifying the main idea (Kroeger, Burton, & Preston, 2009). Students also can be taught how to identify main points by looking for repetition of the same word or words throughout the paragraph, examining headings and subheadings, and delineating major and supporting ideas (Anderson, 2006). They also can be taught to ask who, what, where, when, and how questions to identify the main ideas in paragraphs.

Predicting   A good reading comprehension strategy for students to use is predicting (Englert, 2009). Individually or in pairs or small groups, students can read sections of a selection and make predictions about it (Alber-Morgan, Matheson Ramp, Anderson, & Martin, 2007; Whalon & Haline, 2008). As students continue to read, they check their predictions and reflect on why their predictions were correct or incorrect. When students finish reading, they summarize the selection using no more than 10 words and discuss and receive feedback on their predictions.

Surveying   Students can be taught to survey reading assignments through use of *SQ3R*, a technique that consists of the following steps:

> *Step 1. Survey*. Surveying allows students to look for clues to the content of the chapter. In surveying, students can do the following: (a) examine the title of the chapter and try to anticipate what information will be presented; (b) read the first paragraph to try to determine the objectives of the chapter; (c) review the headings and subheadings to identify main points; (d) analyze visual aids to find relevant supporting information and related details; and (e) read the final paragraph to summarize the main points.

> *Step 2. Question*. Questioning helps students identify important content by formulating questions based on restating headings and subheadings and their own reactions to the material.

> *Step 3. Read*. Reading enables students to examine sections more closely and answer the questions raised in the questioning phase.

> *Step 4. Recite*. Reciting helps students recall the information for further use. In this step, students can be encouraged to study the information they have just covered.

> *Step 5. Review*. Reviewing also helps students remember the content. This can be done by having them prepare an oral or written summary of the main topics.

FIGURE 8.2 **Sample text comprehension prompts and self-monitoring checklists**

(a) Story/Text Mapping
(Use to identify the major elements of the story/passage.)

Setting

Where and when does
the story occur?

Characters

Who is in the story? What
are their characteristics?

Actions

What happens in the story?
What does each character do?

Conflicts/Problems

What conflicts and or problems
are presented?

Solution

What happens to the characters?
How are the problems solved?

Ending

How does the story end?

(Continued)

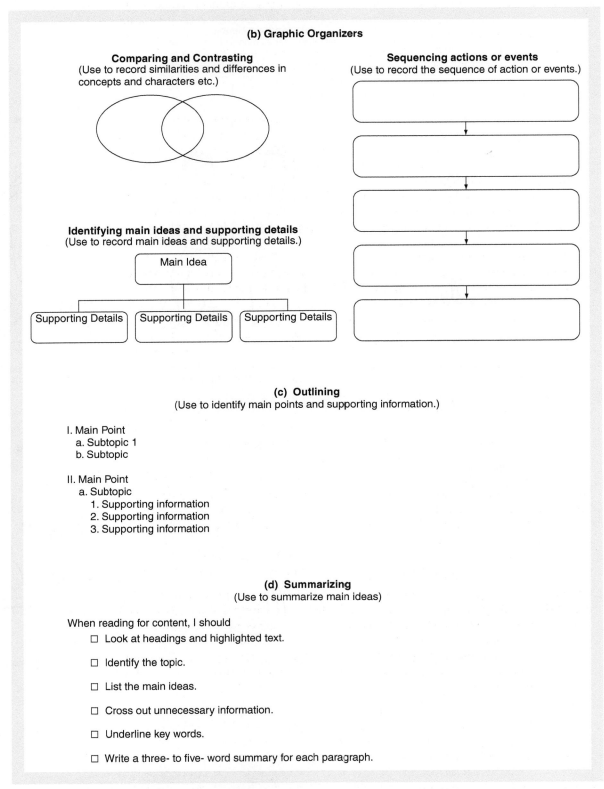

(b) Graphic Organizers

Comparing and Contrasting
(Use to record similarities and differences in concepts and characters etc.)

Sequencing actions or events
(Use to record the sequence of action or events.)

Identifying main ideas and supporting details
(Use to record main ideas and supporting details.)

Main Idea

Supporting Details   Supporting Details   Supporting Details

(c) Outlining
(Use to identify main points and supporting information.)

I. Main Point
  a. Subtopic 1
  b. Subtopic

II. Main Point
  a. Subtopic
    1. Supporting information
    2. Supporting information
    3. Supporting information

(d) Summarizing
(Use to summarize main ideas)

When reading for content, I should
  ☐ Look at headings and highlighted text.

  ☐ Identify the topic.

  ☐ List the main ideas.

  ☐ Cross out unnecessary information.

  ☐ Underline key words.

  ☐ Write a three- to five- word summary for each paragraph.

Sources: Casteel, Isom and Jordan (2000); Whalon and Hanline (2008).

A modified version of SQ3R is *multipass*, in which students review the content of a reading selection three times. In the first pass, or *survey*, students become familiar with the structure and organization of the selection. The second review, the *size-up* pass, helps students identify the main points of the chapter. In the final or *sort-out* pass, students read the selection again and answer the accompanying questions.

Other similar techniques—such as *SOS* (Schumaker, Deshler, Alley, & Warner, 1983), *OK5R* (Pauk, 1984), *PQST* (Pauk, 1984), *PARTS* (Ellis, 1996), and *SCROL* (Grant, 1993)—also can be selected based on students' ability levels.

Self-Questioning   Students can be taught to use several self-questioning procedures to improve their text comprehension skills (Englert, 2009; Faggella-Luby & Deshler, 2008; Roberts et al., 2008). In one self-questioning technique, students determine the reasons for studying the passage, identify the passage's main ideas by underlining them, generate a question associated with each main idea and write it in the margin, find the answer to the question and write it in the margin, and review all the questions and answers. Students also can use self-questioning to deconstruct sentences to determine their meaning. For example, students can ask themselves, "What is this sentence about? What is the subject? The verb?" (Anderson, 2006).

You can teach your students to use the learning strategies to generate questions. The Self-Questioning Strategy involves students composing questions addressing the selection they are reading, predicting answers to their questions, and locating and discussing the answers as they read the selection (Schumaker et al., 2006). You also can teach them to use the mnemonic RAM to: (1) **R**ead the passage and ask yourself who, what, where and why questions; (2) **A**nswer the questions while you read the text; and (3) **M**ark your answers with a meaningful symbol (Brigham et al., 2007).

Your students also can work in groups to pose and discuss text comprehension questions by using Socratic discussions (Fink Chorzempa & Lapidus, 2009) and reciprocal questioning (Whalon & Hanline, 2008). You can implement *Socratic discussions* by having your students generate questions after reading text, which are then discussed by the class to identify, examine, and reflect on the information presented in the reading selection. *Reciprocal questioning* involves your students working in collaborative pairs to generate text questions.

Paraphrasing   Paraphrasing requires students to read text, ask questions about it to determine the main idea and other relevant information, and paraphrase the answers to these questions (Dieker & Little, 2005). Paraphrased statements should consist of a complete sentence, be correct and logical, and provide new and useful information. Students can learn to use *RAP*, a learning strategy that involves **R**eading the paragraph, **A**sking yourself what was the main idea and the important supporting details, and **P**utting the main idea and details in your own words (Hagaman & Reid, 2008).

Outlining   Outlining chapters allows students to identify, sequence, and group main and secondary points so that they can better understand what they have read (Joseph & Konrad, 2009; Margolis & McCabe, 2006; Siegle & McCoach, 2005) (see Figure 8.2c). Students can learn to use a separate outline for each topic, identify essential parts of a topic using Roman numerals, present subtopics by subdividing each main heading using capital letters, and group information within a subdivision in a sequence using Arabic numerals.

Summarizing   Another approach to teaching text comprehension skills is *summarization* (Englert, 2009; Faggella-Luby & Deshler, 2008; Whalon et al., 2009) (see Figure 8.2d). The five basic summarization rules students can employ are (a) identify and group main points, (b) eliminate information that is repeated or unnecessary, (c) find the topic sentence, (d) devise topic sentences for paragraphs that have none, and (e) delete phrases and sentences that fail to present new or relevant information (Anderson, 2006). You can foster your students' summarization skills by having them read paragraphs and underline key words and phrases, and write three- to five-word summaries in the margins (Nilson, 2007).

Paragraph Restatements and Paragraph Shrinking *Paragraph restatements* help students actively process reading material by encouraging them to create original sentences that summarize the main points of the selection. The sentences should include the fewest possible words. They can be written in the textbook, recorded as notes on a separate sheet, or constructed mentally. In *paragraph shrinking*, students read a paragraph orally and then state its main idea in 10 words or less by identifying the most important information about who or what the paragraph is about (Kroeger et al., 2009).

Visual Imagery Visual imagery or visualizing requires students to read a section of a book, create an image for every sentence read or paragraph, contrast each new image with the prior one, and evaluate the images to make sure they are complete (Anderson, 2006). You can teach students to use visual imagery by asking them to create visual images for concrete objects, having them visualize familiar objects and settings, asking them to create images while listening to high-imagery stories, and having them devise images as they read (Hart & Whalon, 2008). You also can teach them to use *SCENE*, a learning strategy that involves **S**earching for picture words, **C**reating or changing the scene, **E**ntering details, **N**aming the parts, and **E**valuating your picture.

Verbal Rehearsal In verbal rehearsal, students pause after reading several sentences to themselves and verbalize to themselves the selection's content. At the beginning, you can cue students to use verbal rehearsal by placing red dots at various points in the selection.

Combinations of Student-Directed Comprehension Strategies. In addition to learning the previously discussed student-directed text comprehension strategies, students also may benefit from learning how to combine these strategies (Faggella-Luby & Deshler, 2008; Roberts et al., 2008; Whalon et al., 2009). One such strategy is *TWA*, which involves the following:

> **T** (Think Before Reading): Think about (a) the author's purpose, (b) what you know, and (c) what you want to learn.
> **W** (While Reading): Think about (a) reading speed, (b) linking knowledge, and (c) rereading parts.
> **A** (After Reading): Think about (a) the main idea, (b) summarizing information, and (c) what you learned (Mason, Meadan, Hedin, & Corso, 2006; Rogevich & Perin, 2009).

Enhance the Readability of Materials

Students with reading and learning difficulties must often use commercially produced and teacher-developed print materials whose readability levels are too high for them. You can increase students' understanding of reading matter by modifying the material, making the text less complex, and using instructional technology.

Highlight Essential Information Highlighting helps students identify main points and locate essential information. Cues linking questions with the location of the answers in the selection can help students learn how to find the answers. For example, you can color-code study questions and their answers in the text. Pairing questions with the numbers of the pages containing the answers, simplifying vocabulary by paraphrasing questions, defining important and difficult terms, breaking multiple-part questions into separate questions, or recording questions on digital recorders and including the pages where the answers occur are other helpful methods.

Use Instructional Technology The use of instructional technology also can foster text comprehension. As we saw earlier in this chapter, you can use a variety of digital materials which read text to students and offer a variety of supports including access to dictionaries and thesauri and pronunciation guides (Izzo, Yurik, & McArrell, 2009). Many of these materials also have multiple highlighters that allow for *dynamic and dual highlighting*. Whereas *dynamic highlighting* helps students focus their attention

REFLECTIVE

Try the various comprehension strategies using material in this text or in a text for the grade you would like to teach. Which were easiest? Which were most effective?

on important text by simultaneously color coding and reading it, *dual highlighting*, also called *masking*, uses two colors so that one color highlights the text and another color highlights the text that is being read (Silver-Pacuilla et al., 2004).

You also can use software and web-based programs to offer students access to self-paced, interactive activities to develop their comprehension of written text (Hasselbring & Bausch, 2006; Zorfass & Clay, 2008). Many of these programs include visual and auditory cues designed to assist students in decoding the material and using effective text comprehension strategies such as highlighting main ideas and other important information, summarization, questioning, and story grammars. For example, many digital, software, and Web-based materials include *rebus prompts*, which assist students in comprehending written text by pairing important words with their pictures. Software programs that allow teachers and students to create graphic organizers and cognitive maps also can improve students' text comprehension (Reeves & Stanford, 2009). You also can use Microsoft Word AutoSummarize to condense and summarize longer text selections into shorter versions.

Readability software programs also are available to help you prepare readable materials for your students (Salend, 2009). In addition to computing the readability of your materials, many of these programs guide you in making them more readable. For instance, these programs can identify difficult words that can then be replaced with more readable alternatives such as synonyms that are more appropriate for your students. When using these programs, keep in mind that the content-based terms that are essential to student learning cannot and should not be simplified.

Audio- and video-based materials also can be used by students. Audio recordings of text-based materials that are available in digital formats have the added advantages of allowing users to determine the playback rate, and to set bookmarks.

Teachers can use the principles of typographic design to produce highly readable and legible materials for use with students. How successful are you at using these principles?

IDEAs to Implement Inclusion

Adjusting the Complexity of Text Language

Ms. Mantel's class had several students whose reading abilities varied widely. Sometimes they were able to read the material and understand it. At other times, they struggled. Ms. Mantel noticed that her students' reading abilities appeared to be related to the linguistic complexity of the text. She decided to break up the reading selections that caused her students the most trouble into several smaller sections and began to simplify the choice and arrangements of words and sentences in the selections. First, she examined the length of sentences and shortened them. She broke long sentences into two or three shorter sentences. Second, she highlighted main ideas, concepts, and words, and introduced only one idea at a time. Third, she helped her students understand the order of the concepts presented by using signal words such as *first, second*, and *third*. Fourth, because her students had difficulty understanding the relationship between concepts, she used words that show relationships, such as *because, after*, and *since*.

Here are some other strategies you can use to implement the IDEA in your inclusive classroom and reduce the linguistic complexity of text:

- Eliminate unnecessary words and sections that may distract students.

- Use easy-to-understand language and words with which students are familiar rather than uncommon or unusual words (e.g., *use* rather than *utilize*).

- Refrain from using proper names, irregularly spelled words, ambiguous terms, and use of multiple terms for the same word or concepts as well as double negatives, abbreviations, contractions, acronyms, quotations, and parentheses.

- Use clear pronoun references and word substitution to clarify relationships.

- Rephrase paragraphs so that they begin with a topic sentence followed by supporting details.

- Present a series of events or actions in chronological order, and cluster information that is related.

- Embed definitions and examples of new words and concepts, and avoid using different words that have identical meanings.

- Insert text and examples to clarify main points.

- Present text in the present tense and avoid use of the passive voice.

- Create visual aids that present content and depict processes.

Sources: Kozen, Murray, and Windell (2006); Salend (2009).

Using Technology to Promote Inclusion
PREPARING READABLE AND LEGIBLE MATERIALS

An important factor in differentiating instruction for your students is providing them with access to high-quality instructional materials that support their learning. The visual look of text affects its readability and legibility. Technology—including the use of word processing programs, scanners, laser printers, and digital cameras—offers you access to various dimensions of typographic design that can help you produce universally designed text-based instructional materials for students that promote speed, clarity, and understanding (Ferreri, 2009; Salend, 2009). These dimensions, which are outlined here, also can be used to prepare all the materials you use to teach and assess your students and to communicate with families and colleagues. It is also important to include page numbers when preparing materials that have multiple pages, to use bullets to present essential information that does not have a numerical or hierarchical sequence, to display significant information in text blocks with an appropriate border, and to date materials when the date is an important factor.

Type Size

Type that is too small is difficult to decipher, and type that is too large requires excessive eye movements to follow the text and can cause the reader to pause more often while reading a line.

In terms of type size, 12- to 14-point type is easier to read than smaller or larger print at typical reading distances. However, larger type of at least 18-point may be more appropriate for young students who are beginning to read and for students who have visual difficulties (Ferreri, 2009). Larger type can reduce eye fatigue. Larger type also should be used when preparing materials that students will view at a distance of greater than 10 feet such as PowerPoint presentations.

Typefaces/Fonts

You can make material more readable by using typefaces, also referred to as *fonts*, with simple designs, as well as those familiar to students. Most printed materials use a serif font such as Times Roman, which promotes the reading of text via the use of small lines that are part of the serif strokes to align the text on the line. However, students who struggle with reading may benefit from materials that are prepared using sans serif fonts such as Arial, which can make letter and word identification a little easier because the text will resemble hand lettering. It also is important not to mix fonts as it can make text more difficult to read.

Case

Lowercase letters provide cues that help readers perceive, discriminate, and remember differences in letters and word shapes. For this reason, text should be printed in lowercase and capital letters where grammatically appropriate. ALL-CAPITAL PRINTING CAN SLOW DOWN THE READING PROCESS, and its use should be limited to short, noncontinuous important text that needs to be HIGHLIGHTED, such as headings and subheadings, or an essential word or phrase in a sentence or paragraph.

Style

Style refers to variants such as *italics* and **boldface.** *The use of italics or boldface variants slows reading of continuous text* and should be used only to **emphasize** and *highlight* small amounts of text embedded in sentences and paragraphs or to make headings stand out. Italics and boldface are preferable to underlining to highlight important material; underlining can distract the reader and make it harder to discriminate letters. For example, underlining can cause students to perceive *y* as *v* or *u* and *g* as *a*. Excessive boldface can make the page appear darker and more dense, which makes it more difficult and less motivating to read. Furthermore, readers also may find boldface used in the middle of sentences to be distracting as it tends to focus their attention on the highlighted words.

Proportional and Monospaced Type

Monospaced or fixed type uses the same horizontal space for all letters, whereas proportionally spaced type varies the horizontal space of letters, depending on their form. Although proportionally spaced type makes reading easier by providing additional perceptual cues for letter recognition and enhancing the flow of the text, some learners may prefer monospaced type.

Line Length

Line length refers to the number of characters and spaces in a line. Material that is printed in long lines may cause fatigue by making it difficult to find the next line to read, whereas text that is printed in short lines
demands that students' eyes
change lines frequently.

You can use several strategies to design materials that have an appropriate line length of about 4 inches. One method is to count characters and spaces and to maintain a line length and character count of between 40 and 70. Another method is to structure the material by using line lengths of 7 to 12 words. This method adjusts the line length to the linguistic complexity of the material and therefore the reading skill of students.

Another factor to consider is whether the material has word clusters, a series of words that need to be presented together in order to provide the context for understanding the material. Where possible, word clusters should be presented on the same line.

Spacing

When designing print materials, it is useful to view space as a hierarchy that proceeds from smallest to largest, as follows: (a) space between letters, (b) space between words, (c) space between lines, (d) space between paragraphs, (e) space between columns, (f) space between sections, and (g) space from the text area to the edge of the page. Failure to follow these spatial relationships can confuse and frustrate readers. For

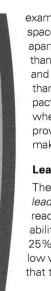

example, if the space between letters exceeds the space between words, the words appear to "fall apart," and if the space between words is greater than the space between lines, the lines break up and the eye may be tempted to move down rather than across. Therefore, you should examine the impact of all spaces on a page and make adjustments when necessary. It is also recommended that you provide space between paragraphs and columns to make them more readable.

Leading

The vertical space between lines, referred to as *leading*, can be adjusted to make materials more readable. In general, you can increase the readability of your materials by making the leading 25% to 30% of the point size. For students with low vision, it is important to increase the leading so that the space between lines of text is greater.

Justification

Justification refers to the alignment of the edges of text. Left-justified or aligned text and staggered right margins are the best choices for readability at all reading levels, as it makes it easier for the reader to see and track the text. Right-justified text results in uneven word and letter spacing of text and can cause students with and without reading difficulties to experience problems tracking the flow of text.

Centered text slows the reading process and is best used for special purposes like titles or lists.

Right-aligned text disturbs the flow of reading because the eye does not know where to go to begin reading the next line.

It is important to read through materials you develop from left to right and top to bottom to make sure that the organization and spacing are consistent and provide a logical structure for the reader to follow. When preparing materials that are to be stored in notebooks, it is important to use a wider left margin so that there is sufficient space for punch holes.

Background and Contrast

Students' ability and motivation to read, and eye strain also can be affected by the color contrast between the text and the background. Contrast also can attract or distract the reader to the critical content being presented. Therefore, the color of the text and background should differ so that it is easier for students to locate important information. When selecting colors, choose those whose lightness differs as much as possible. While using colored type can help highlight text, it should be used carefully. It is suggested that materials consist of black or blue text on an off-white, pale, or matte pastel background. It is also important to avoid gray backgrounds, especially when essential information is presented. In addition to increasing the expense of producing materials, specific colors such as yellow or light green may be difficult for students to read.

Varying the contrast also can help focus the readers' attention to important content. Important content can be made to stand out by surrounding it with white space and/or by embedding it in thick and dark borders. For example, important directions for an assignment or test items can be placed in boxes that are bordered by white space.

Visuals

Visuals can enhance the reading process and make materials more understandable and motivating. When using visuals, make sure they are necessary by determining whether they (a) support the reading process and are linked to the text, (b) help students understand and identify important information, (c) enhance the visual presentation of the material and do not distract the students' attention, and (d) are integrated and labeled appropriately, current, age-appropriate, and culturally sensitive.

Sources: Acrey, Johnstone, and Milligan (2005); Beddow, Kettler, and Elliott (2008); Rotter (2006); Salend (2009); Voss (2005).

Many of these audio recordings are becoming available electronically via Recordings for the Blind and Dyslexic (www.rfbd.org), the Internet, and electronic libraries (e-libraries). For example, Bookshare (www.bookshare.org) allows individuals with visual, learning and physical disabilities that hinder their ability to read print to download digital books and textbooks and software that reads text aloud, or displays it on a Braille device or a computer screen (Harrison, 2009). Through LibriVox (www.librivox.org), you and your students can volunteer to read and create audiofiles of text-based materials which can then be downloaded by others. Dyck and Pemberton (2002) offer guidelines for preparing audio-presented text-based materials.

Video of content that is related to or parallels the material presented in textbooks and other print materials also can orient students to content in these materials. Video also provides direct visual experience with the material that can improve students' understanding and memory of the content to be mastered.

DIFFERENTIATING INSTRUCTION FOR STUDENTS FROM DIVERSE CULTURAL AND LANGUAGE BACKGROUNDS

HOW CAN I DIFFERENTIATE INSTRUCTION FOR STUDENTS FROM DIVERSE CULTURAL AND LANGUAGE BACKGROUNDS? In addition to using cooperative learning and the other strategies presented in this text, you can consider the following guidelines when adjusting your curriculum and teaching methods for students from diverse cultural and language backgrounds. Again, these guidelines can be used to enhance instruction for *all students*.

Use a Multicultural Curriculum

As Ms. Taravella and her colleagues did in the chapter-opening vignette, one means of making learning relevant, interdisciplinary, and challenging for *all students* is by using a *multicultural curriculum*, which acknowledges the voices, histories, experiences, and contributions of all ethnic and cultural groups (Banks, 2009; Gollnick & Chinn, 2009; Taylor & Whittaker, 2009). The goal of a multicultural curriculum is to help *all students* do the following: (a) understand, view, and appreciate events from various cultural perspectives; (b) understand and function in their own and other cultures; (c) take personal actions to promote racial and ethnic harmony and to counter racism and discrimination; (d) understand various cultural and ethnic alternatives;

A GUIDE TO ACTION
Creating Readable and Legible Materials

You can foster your students' learning by providing them with readable and legible materials. To create effective readable and legible classroom materials and tests, consider the following points:

- Make sure your materials are not too wordy.
- Highlight key terms and concepts.
- Use words that students can read and understand.
- Embed definitions and examples of new and difficult words and concepts in the text.
- Make sure the lengths of sentences and paragraphs and sentence structures are appropriate.
- Make sure that sentences contain no more than one complex idea.
- Avoid using double negatives, abbreviations, contractions, acronyms, quotations, and parentheses.
- Refer directly to important points, objects, or events rather than using pronouns.
- Begin paragraphs with a topic sentence and present information and events logically and in chronological order.
- Number or letter directions, lists, and steps.
- Establish clear transitions to and connections between concepts.
- Make sure that the graphics are necessary, current, age-appropriate, culturally sensitive, placed in the right locations; and that they explain, highlight, or summarize the material.
- Avoid overuse of visuals and unnecessary stimuli or text.
- Check to see that the materials are grammatically correct and presented in a tense and voice your students can understand.

- Use type sizes and typefaces (fonts) that are appropriate for and familiar to students.
- Present text in lowercase and capital letters when grammatically appropriate.
- Use brief, highlighted headings.
- Use boldface and italics sparingly and only to highlight headings or small amounts of text within sentences or paragraphs.
- Use appropriate spaced type, line lengths, spacing, and leading.
- Use left-justified margins, staggered right margins, and wider margins at the bottom of the page.
- Make the overall spacing consistent so it provides a logical structure for students to follow.
- Make sure that the length of the materials are appropriate, and number the pages.
- Create an appropriate contrast between lettering color and background color.
- Make important content stand out by surrounding it with white space and/or by embedding it in thick and dark borders.
- Use bullets to present essential information that does not have a numerical or hierarchical sequence.
- Present important information in text blocks with an appropriate border and surrounding.
- Date materials when the date is an important factor.

How would you rate the readability and legibility of your classroom materials? ( ) Excellent ( ) Good ( ) Need Improvement ( ) Need Much Improvement

Create a plan of action for improving the readability and legibility of your classroom materials that includes your goals, the actions you will take and the resources you will need to achieve them, and the ways you will evaluate your success.

(e) develop their academic skills; and (f) improve their ability to make reflective personal and public decisions and to choose actions that contribute to enhancing and changing society (Banks, 2008).

Multicultural education is often seen as focusing on the needs of students of color and students who speak languages other than English. However, a true multicultural curriculum should teach information about *all groups* and should be directed at *all students* (Gollnick & Chinn, 2009; Nieto & Bode, 2008). A multicultural curriculum also should address content integration and the knowledge construction process, use an equity pedagogy, and foster prejudice reduction and an empowering school culture and social structure (Banks, 2008; Taylor & Whittaker, 2009). Figure 8.3 provides definitions and examples of these dimensions of multicultural education.

A multicultural curriculum should teach information about *all groups* and should be directed at *all students*. How could you make your curriculum more multicultural?

The multicultural curriculum should address all content areas. For example, a science lesson on plants can include a discussion of plants in other countries and in various regions of the United States. The Native American counting technique that uses knots in a rope can be taught as part of a math lesson.

Four hierarchical methods for incorporating multicultural information into the curriculum have been identified (Banks, 2008, 2009). In the *contributions* approach, various ethnic heroes, highlights, holidays, and cultural events are included to the curriculum. In the *additive* approach, content, concepts, themes, and issues related to various cultures are added to the curriculum. In both of these approaches, no substantive changes are made in the organization or goals of the curriculum. As a result, while students are introduced to the contributions of various cultural groups, they are often given little information about various cultural groups, and fail to understand the social and political realities behind the experiences of these groups (Taylor & Whittaker, 2009).

The *transformation* approach to multicultural curriculum reform tries to enhance the curriculum by encouraging students to examine and explore content, concepts, themes, issues, problems, and concerns from various cultural perspectives. In this approach, students learn to think critically and reflect on the viewpoints of different cultural, gender, and social class groups. For example, a lesson on the impact of the North American Free Trade Agreement (NAFTA) can compare its impact from the perspectives of groups in all countries of North America.

The *social action* approach, although similar to the transformation approach, encourages and teaches students to identify social problems and take action to solve them. Students are given opportunities to challenge and change practices that they consider unfair. For example, as part of their unit, Ms. Taravella's and Ms. Stoudamire's class might analyze data on the number of people of color and females working as scientists studying the solar system. They can then propose and evaluate actions to address the problems that discourage people of color and females from becoming scientists.

Parallel lessons, which allow students to learn about individuals and content from both the mainstream culture and other cultures, also help make a curriculum multicultural. For example, a lesson on Abraham Lincoln could be paired with lessons on a comparable historical figure in other countries.

Use Multicultural Teaching Materials

A multicultural curriculum should contain teaching materials that reflect a wide range of experiences and aspirations (Gollnick & Chinn, 2009; Taylor & Whittaker, 2009).

REFLECTIVE

How has your cultural background influenced your perspectives? How are your cultural perspectives similar to and different from those of others? How would multicultural education influence your cultural perspectives?

FIGURE 8.3 Dimensions and examples of multicultural education

Category	Definition	Examples
Content Integration	Content integration deals with the extent to which teachers use examples and content from a variety of cultures and groups to illustrate key concepts, principles, generalizations, and theories in their subject area or discipline.	• Biographies of women or persons of color who are scientists and mathematicians • Learning about demographics of diverse groups in mathematics • Using primary documents about the history of non-Anglo European peoples • Reading and creating multicultural literature • Including images of many kinds of families in the curriculum
The Knowledge Construction Process	The knowledge construction process relates to the extent to which teachers help students to understand, investigate, and determine how the implicit cultural assumptions, frames of references, perspectives, and biases within a discipline influence the ways in which knowledge is constructed within it.	• Examine the degree to which authors who are female or people of color are included in the curriculum • Including the perspectives of both the dominant and nondominant cultures in any description of historical conflict • Examining labels applied to persons with disabilities from the perspective of the person • Validating the importance of languages other than English • Discussing the difference between Western and non-Western views on science • Interviewing community elders about their immigration experiences
An Equity Pedagogy	An equity pedagogy exists when teachers modify their teaching in ways that will facilitate the academic achievement of students from diverse racial, cultural, and social-class groups. This includes using a variety of teaching styles that are consistent with the wide range of learning styles within various cultural and ethnic groups.	• Knowing the cultural background of students and incorporating them into classroom instruction and procedures • Using cooperative learning or group experiences with students who learn best collaboratively • Placing students in pairs to encourage question and answer exchanges
Prejudice Reduction	This dimension focuses on the characteristics of students' racial attitudes and how they can be modified by teaching methods and materials.	• Using heterogeneous groups by gender, race, and language in cooperative learning groups • Developing racial identity (e.g., through a family tree) • Teaching the concept of race as a social, not biological, construct • Studying various religions in the context of a winter holiday season or historical event
An Empowering School Culture and Social Structure	Grouping and labeling practices, sports participation, disproportionality in achievement, and the interaction of the staff and the students across ethnic and racial lines are among the components of the school culture that must be examined to create a school culture that empowers students from diverse racial, ethnic, and cultural groups.	• Including students in determining classroom rules or allowing them choice of assignment • Including students with disabilities or all students who try out for a performance • Actively recruiting and hiring teachers of color • Reducing the numbers of African Americans and Hispanics who are inappropriately placed in special education programs • Working with community groups to provide mentoring and tutoring programs • Involving families in school decision-making bodies

Source: From "Planning Differentiated Multicultural Instruction for Secondary Inclusive Classrooms," by D. van Garderen and C. Whittaker, 2006, *Teaching Exceptional Children*, 38(3), pp. 12–20. Copyright 2006 by The Council for Exceptional Children. Reprinted with permission.

Therefore, materials that reflect cultural, ethnic, linguistic, and gender diversity should be used frequently and should be fully integrated into the curriculum (Banks, 2008; Nieto & Bode, 2008). Guidelines for evaluating multicultural teaching materials are presented in Figure 8.4.

FIGURE 8.4 **Guidelines for evaluating multicultural teaching materials**

To what extent do the materials include the various groups in U.S. society?

How are various groups portrayed in the materials?

Are the viewpoints, attitudes, reactions, experiences, and feelings of various groups accurately presented?

Do the materials present a varied group of credible individuals to whom students can relate in terms of lifestyle, values, speech and language, and actions?

Are individuals from diverse backgrounds depicted in a wide range of social and professional activities?

Do the materials show a variety of situations, conflicts, issues, and problems as experienced by different groups?

Are a wide range of perspectives on situations and issues offered?

Does the material incorporate the history, heritage, experiences, language, and traditions of various groups?

Are the experiences of and issues important to various groups presented in a realistic manner that allows students to recognize and understand their complexities?

Are culturally diverse examples, situations, experiences, and anecdotes included throughout the materials?

Are the materials factually correct?

Are the experiences, contributions, and content of various groups fully integrated into the materials and the curriculum?

Are graphics accurate, inclusive, and ethnically sensitive?

Do the materials avoid stereotypes and generalizations about groups?

Are members of various groups presented as having a range of physical features (e.g., hair texture, skin color, facial features)?

Is the language of the materials inclusive, and does it reflect various groups?

Do the materials include learning activities that help students develop a multicultural perspective?

Use Culturally Relevant and Responsive Teaching Strategies

Teaching strategies should be relevant and responsive to your students' experiences, cultural perspectives, language backgrounds, and developmental ages (Diaz-Rico & Weed, 2010; Gollnick & Chinn, 2009). They should reflect and be aligned with your students' cultural and linguistic backgrounds and preferred learning styles, which in turn requires you to be aware of your students' cultural values (Banks, 2008). It also means that you teach in a way that helps your students find relevant connections between themselves and the subject matter, the instructional strategies used, and the tasks they are asked to perform (Cartledge & Kourea, 2008; Nieto & Bode, 2008).

Research has identified effective strategies for teaching students from diverse cultural and language backgrounds, and other groups of students:

- *Emphasizing verbal interactions:* Use activities that encourage students to respond verbally to the material in creative ways such as group discussions, role plays, storytelling, group recitations, choral and responsive reading, and rap.

- *Teaching students to use self-talk:* Encourage and teach students to learn new material by verbalizing it to themselves, such as thinking aloud.

- *Facilitating divergent thinking:* Encourage students to explore and devise unique solutions to issues and problems through activities such as brainstorming, group discussions, debates, and responding to open-ended questions.

- *Using small-group instruction and cooperative learning:* Allow students to work in small groups, and use cooperative learning arrangements including peer tutoring and cross-age tutoring.

- *Employing verve in the classroom:* Introduce *verve*, a high level of energy, exuberance, and action, into the classroom by displaying enthusiasm for teaching and learning, using choral responding, moving around the classroom, varying your voice quality, snapping your fingers, using facial expressions, and encouraging students to use their bodies to act out and demonstrate content.

- *Focusing on real-world tasks:* Introduce content, language, and learning by relating them to students' home, school, and community life, and to their cultures and experiences.

- *Promoting teacher–student interactions:* Use teaching methods based on exchanges between students and teachers. Ask frequent questions, affirm students' responses, give feedback, offer demonstrations and explanations, and rephrase, review, and summarize material (Gay, 2004; Goldenberg, 2008; Obiakor, 2007; Shealey & Callins, 2007).

Use Reciprocal Interaction Teaching Approaches

You can supplement teaching activities that emphasize the development of skills with *reciprocal interaction teaching approaches (RITA)* that foster learning through verbal and written dialogues between students and teachers and among students. In using reciprocal interaction, you use students' prior knowledge and experiences to add a context that promotes comprehension and incorporates language development and use. The curriculum and teaching focus on meaningful, authentic activities related to students' lives, and they target higher-level critical thinking skills rather than basic skills.

When implementing RITA, you also use student–centered teaching and dialogues, student–student interactions, problem-solving situations, and guided questioning to help students control their learning. Higher-level thinking is promoted through teacher modeling and thinking aloud, presenting new information as collaborative problems to be solved, posing open-ended questions, asking students to justify their responses and explain their reasoning, helping students explore alternative perspectives, encouraging students to evaluate and monitor their thinking and that of others, and viewing students' miscues as opportunities to discuss new information.

You also can employ **scaffolding**, breaking down comments and concepts students don't understand or a task students have difficulty performing into smaller components that promote understanding or mastery (Echevarria, Vogt, & Short, 2010). Scaffolding methods include relating the task to students' prior knowledge, using visual and language cues, modeling effective strategies, and highlighting the key parts of the task (Levine & McCloskey, 2009; Paxton-Buursma & Walker, 2008). As students gain skill or mastery, scaffolding supports are gradually removed so that students function independently to understand, apply, and integrate their new learning.

When using RITA, you also can promote teacher–student interactions through the use of confirmation checks ("Are you saying . . . ?"), comprehension checks ("Do you understand what I just said?" "Tell me in your own words what I'm saying"), clarification requests ("Can you explain that again?" "In a different way?"), repetitions, and expansions. Conversational interactions also can be fostered by you and your students asking questions related to who, where, why, when, and what.

Use Effective ESL and Dual-Language Approaches and Techniques

Instruction for English language learners can be differentiated by using effective ESL and dual-language approaches and techniques such as total physical response, sheltered English, natural language approaches, and new vocabulary and concept instructional techniques (Diaz-Rico & Weed, 2010; Echevarria et al., 2010; Lessow-Hurley, 2009; Levine & McCloskey, 2009; Whelan Ariza, 2010).

Total Physical Response *Total physical response (TPR)* improves students' vocabulary through modeling, repeated practice, and movement. In TPR, you model the message by emphasizing physical gestures and objects. (You state the message, model, and physically emphasize movements related to the concept of, say, sharpening a pencil.) Next, the class as a group responds to your directions. (You ask the students to sharpen their pencils and the students, as a group, make the appropriate motion.) Finally, individual students respond to verbal commands given by you and their peers. (Individual students are asked by you and their peers to sharpen a pencil.) As students develop skills, the complexity of the language skills taught increases.

Sheltered English   **Sheltered English**, or *content-based instruction*, uses cues, gestures, technology, manipulatives, drama, and visual stimuli and aids to teach new vocabulary and concepts. As part of your use of sheltered English, you need to simplify your vocabulary and grammar. When using a sheltered English approach, present lessons that cover grade-level content and teach students the terminology needed to understand the concepts in specific content areas. Create a context; present information orally and visually; use hands-on activities and media; and help students learn by restating, paraphrasing, simplifying, and expanding the material. It is also important to connect the curriculum to students' culture, experiences, and language and to promote interactions among students.

Lessons using a sheltered English approach typically are organized in the following sequence:

1. Identify, define, and teach terminology that is essential to understanding the lesson and related to the curriculum. Key terms are posted as a visual reference for students and are added to students' word banks.

2. Select and explain the main academic vocabulary and concepts to students.

3. Help students learn and understand the main concepts by presenting content using visual aids, objects, physical gestures, facial expressions, manipulatives, and technology. Where possible, allow students to experience the concepts.

4. Make instruction meaningful by giving students opportunities to relate the concepts to their prior knowledge and experiential background.

5. Check students' understanding, encourage them to seek clarification, and offer feedback.

6. Encourage students to work and interact with their peers (Freeman & Crawford, 2008; Short & Echevarria, 2005).

Natural Language Techniques   You also can help students develop language by using and prompting your students to use natural language techniques: expansion, expatiation, parallel talk, and self-talk (Paxton-Buursma & Walker, 2008). **Expansion** allows you to present a language model by expanding on students' incomplete sentences or thoughts or ask your students to expand on a classmate's statement. **Expatiation** occurs when you or one of your students adds new information to the comments of others. **Parallel talk** involves describing an event that students are seeing or doing. **Self-talk** consists of talking about one's actions, experiences, or feelings.

New Vocabulary and Concept Teaching Techniques   Effective teaching for English language learners requires you to help them learn new vocabulary and concepts. To aid these students, focus on essential vocabulary key words and concepts that students use often, and are related to their lives and the material they are learning. In addition, teach vocabulary in context rather than in isolation; teach related words and concepts together; and teach using concrete examples, visuals, pictorials, and physical movements to highlight the important features of new vocabulary words when possible (Denton et al., 2008). For example, you can teach words like *cold* or *frigid* by pretending to shiver. When introducing new vocabulary and concepts, you can consider the following sequence:

Step 1. Analyze the concept to be taught and identify its key features, including the concept's structure and characteristics. Determine whether the context is important for understanding the concept.

Step 2. Introduce and label the concept in a variety of situations. If possible, present the concept using clear, consistent language, concrete materials, manipulatives, and visuals.

Step 3. Show and discuss examples and nonexamples of the concept, moving from easy to difficult. Present and use the concept in many naturally occurring situations, and elaborate on the characteristics that define the concept and distinguish it from others.

REFLECTIVE

Watch a television show or film in a new language. What factors helped you understand the content?

IDEAs to Implement Inclusion

Differentiating Instruction for English Language Learners

Ms. Phalen's class included several English language learners. The class was learning about the cycle of the butterfly. First, Ms. Phalen read and discussed a book on this topic with her students. They talked about such terms as *caterpillar, cocoon*, and *butterfly*. Then Ms. Phalen had the students reenact the cycle of the butterfly. She told them to roll themselves into a little ball. Then she asked them to pretend they were caterpillars. They acted like caterpillars, and then became a cocoon and broke out of the cocoon as butterflies. With their arms outstretched like butterflies, the students then "flew" around the room. After this activity, Ms. Phalen had her students work in small groups to draw pictures of the cycle of the butterfly.

Here are some other strategies you can use to implement the IDEA in your inclusive classroom and differentiate instruction for English language learners:

- Establish a relaxed learning environment that encourages students to take risks and attempt to use both languages, and emphasize communication rather than language form. For example, correct students indirectly by restating their incorrect comments in correct form. (If the student says "My notebook home," you say, "I see—your notebook is at home.")

- Make it easier for students to understand and respond by articulating clearly in a normal tone of voice; pausing often; limiting the use of idiomatic expressions, slang, and pronouns; highlighting key words through increased volume and slight exaggeration; using rephrasing, simple vocabulary, and shorter complete sentences; and giving students enough wait time.

- Begin new lessons with reviews of relevant previously learned concepts, and show the relationships between previously learned concepts and new material.

- Relate material and examples to students' experiences, use cultural referents, and use real-world language and meaningful, functional activities.

- Be consistent in your use of language, and use repetition to help students acquire the rhythm, pitch, volume, and tone of their new language.

- Use gestures, facial expressions, voice changes, pantomimes, demonstrations, rephrasing, visuals, props, manipulatives, and other cues to provide a context that conveys the meaning of new terms and concepts.

- Introduce new material in context, discussing changes in the context while it is occurring. Talk about what has occurred in context so that ambiguities are reduced.

- Develop students' language competence by using modeling, questioning, art forms, drama, simulations, role plays, storytelling, music, and games.

- Supplement oral instruction and descriptions with demonstrations; hands-on activities; and visual materials such as charts, maps, graphs, pictures, graphic organizers, and chalkboard writing.

- Allow students to express their knowledge, understanding, and intended meaning nonverbally. For example, rather than asking a student to define a word or concept, ask the student to draw a picture depicting it.

- Encourage and show students how to use bilingual dictionaries, pictionaries, and glossaries.

- Offer regular summaries of important content, and check students' understanding frequently.

Sources: Diaz-Rico and Weed (2010); Dong (2009); Echevarria et al. (2010); Goldenberg (2008); Lessow-Hurley (2009); Levine and McCloskey (2009); Whelan Ariza (2010).

Step 4. Contrast the concept with other related concepts.

Step 5. Allow students to practice using the concept in functional activities related to their interests and learning levels.

Encourage Students to Respond

You may need to encourage English language learners and students with speech and language difficulties to respond verbally (Goldenberg, 2008; Zwiers & Crawford, 2009). You can promote student responding by using open-ended questions, allowing students to use gestures until they develop language competence, and praising and expanding on students' contributions and seeking more information when necessary. Give students enough time to interact with and discuss material before responding, and encourage students to share their opinions, ask questions, and expand on the comments of others. You also can stimulate the use of language by providing experiences that encourage discussion, such as introducing new objects into the classroom; changing the classroom environment; allowing students to work and play together; sending students on errands; creating situations in which students need to ask for help; asking students to recount events or talk about doing something while doing it; and using visuals that display pictorial absurdities.

USING INSTRUCTIONAL TECHNOLOGIES AND ASSISTIVE DEVICES

HOW CAN I USE INSTRUCTIONAL TECHNOLOGY AND ASSISTIVE DEVICES TO DIFFERENTIATE INSTRUCTION FOR MY STUDENTS? You can employ a range of instructional technologies and assistive devices to support your use of differentiated instruction and UDL (Wissick, Gardner, & Dempsey, 2009). In choosing which technologies to use, consider whether they match your curricular and instructional goals and educational philosophy and your students' strengths and challenges (King-Sears & Evmenova, 2007). Also, evaluate their impact on your students' learning and including whether they are age-appropriate and your students feel comfortable using them.

Instructional Technology

Recent technological developments allow you to use a wide range of instructional technologies and interactive multimedia to present content in multiple modalities and to create motivating and contextualized learning environments and ways for *all students* to show their learning (Dell et al., 2008; Rao, Dowrick, Yuen, & Boisvert, 2009). Interactive multimedia can link text, sound, animation, video, and graphics to present information to students in a nonlinear, instantaneous fashion that promotes critical thinking skills and social interactions. These technologies can be integrated across the curriculum to differentiate instruction so that you address students' diversities and varied learning strengths and challenges, and allow students to be more actively engaged in directing and showcasing their learning (Mulrine, 2008; Salend, 2009).

Computer-Based Instruction   You can supplement and individualize teaching by using *computer-based instruction* (Campbell & Mechling, 2008). Computers can help you individualize your instruction and assessment by directing students to items related to their skill levels and allowing students to work at their own pace. Through the use of computers, you can differentiate your instruction by providing your students with access to drill-and-practice, instructional games, tutorials, simulations, and problem-solving programs (Parette & Peterson-Karlan, 2007). For example, software tutorial programs can monitor students as they use the program, analyze students' errors, and offer individualized feedback prompts (e.g., "Did you look at the signs for all the numbers?"), and additional items to foster student learning. Technology also can be used by students to demonstrate their mastery of content and present their work to others (Salend, 2009).

However, the effectiveness of computer-based instruction depends on the software program used. Many programs are open to criticism; you should carefully evaluate the ones you use (Boone & Higgins, 2007). A form for evaluating software programs is presented in Figure 8.5.

Video-Based Digital Materials

Video-based digital materials have many multimedia features that can help you differentiate your instruction. As we saw in the chapter-opening vignette, you can present content via video-based digital materials containing sequential or nonlinear frames of realistic graphic displays, video segments, slides, motion pictures, audio information, text, and animation and sound effects. With remote control, you can quickly access high-quality visual and auditory information randomly or continuously, and you can halt the presentation to highlight critical information or to ask students questions. Thus, digitally based teaching allows students to hear explanations in various languages, and view colorful, animated, and expressive visual displays and demonstrations, computer graphics, and sound effects that accurately depict concepts and material in a gradual and systematic way.

Digital materials also have the added advantages of allowing content to be presented through the use of music, speech, and dynamic illustrations to motivate students and promote concept and vocabulary development across content areas, as well as reading and listening comprehension. These materials can present text and

FIGURE 8.5 Sample educational software evaluation form

Software Features	Yes	No	Comments
Content and Instructional Considerations			
Curricular and instructional goals are identified and appropriate.			
Content is up-to-date, valid, relevant, unbiased and supported by references.			
Content and visual images are developmentally and age appropriate and can be presented in multiple formats.			
Instructional activities are appropriate, varied, and motivating.			
Content can be differentiated based on levels of difficulty and complexity.			
Content can be differentiated based on students' responses.			
Many opportunities to respond to and interact with similar and differentiated content are provided.			
Ease of Use Considerations			
Program loads easily, quickly, and reliably.			
Program is welcoming and user friendly and can be used independently by students.			
Language is age-appropriate and free of biases.			
Menus and navigational features are easy to access and use, logical, and presented in multiple formats (text, icons, and audio).			
Relevant features are easily identified and clearly labeled.			
Prerequisite educational and technological skills students need to use are identified.			
Tutorials and opportunities to practice related to how to use the program and its features are available.			
Help and search features are readily available and helpful.			
Page layouts present directions and content in an organized, predictable, nondistracting, sequential, and logical manner.			
Directions are easy to understand and follow, available in multiple formats (text, audio, video), and can be presented on demand.			
Content and directions are presented in readable and legible text.			
Formats for responding are differentiated, intuitive, and easy to use.			
Limited keyboarding skills are necessary for use.			
Error minimization techniques are provided.			
Links are identified, appropriate, active, and helpful.			
Individualization Considerations			
Options to revise content are provided.			
Options to provide access to students with a range of disabilities and English language learners are available, intuitive, and easy to use.			
Alternate input devices and other technologies for students with special needs easily interface with the program.			
Options to access digital speech of text and audio descriptions of visual images are provided.			
Adjustments can be easily made in text size, font, color, style variants, spacing, and backgrounds.			
Adjustments in the speed, amount, time, and sequence of the presentation of and response to content can be easily made.			
Strategies for highlighting important content can be easily accessed (e.g., color cuing, bold, italics).			
Animation and sound features can be used, turned off, and individualized.			
Personalized visual and auditory cues, prompts, reminders and reinforcement are available and foster student performance, attention, and motivation.			
Feedback and Assessment Considerations			
Options to provide individualized and personalized informative and corrective feedback are available.			
Feedback provided to students is immediate, positive, and consistent.			

(Continued)

FIGURE 8.5 **Continued**

Software Features	Yes	No	Comments
Feedback and Assessment Considerations			
Opportunities for students and teachers to review individual and cumulative responses are provided.			
Student responses can be easily retrieved and revised.			
Student responses are recorded automatically and reliably.			
Valid student performance data are provided and accessed easily in varied understandable formats for students and teachers.			
Support and Documentation Considerations			
Hardware and software requirements are listed.			
Information about the credentials of the program developer is provided and establishes the developer's credibility.			
Documentation and research to demonstrate effectiveness are provided.			
Contact information is presented.			
Follow-up support is readily available and helpful.			
Cost is reasonable.			

Comments:

Sources: Boone & Higgins (2007); Salend (2009).

illustrations using different voices and languages for the various characters, including sign language. Individual words and text can be repeated, defined, presented in sign language, or translated into another language by highlighting the text to be pronounced or pressing a button. Digital technology also allows you and your students to adjust the pace of the oral reading, magnify the text, vary the colors of the illustrations, and compare their reading with the oral reading.

Video-based digital materials are also being used to make teaching and reference materials more accessible and understandable to students (Anderson-Inman, Terrazas-Arellanes, & Slabin, 2009). Because this technology integrates graphics, spoken text, captioning, video segments, animation, and sound effects, information presented in digital encyclopedias and dictionaries can become more meaningful and motivating to students.

Digital equipment that allows you and your students to develop materials and products also is available. For example, you and your students can use technologies such as presentation software and digital stories to foster and showcase student learning.

Presentation Software   You and your students can use presentation software such as PowerPoint and Keynote to make classroom presentations more effective, motivating and interactive (Doyle & Giangreco, 2009; Salend, 2009). PowerPoint presentations are especially helpful for your deaf and hard-of-hearing students and English language learners as they allow you to present material so that students can view the material, visuals, and your lips simultaneously. Using presentation software you can prepare a digital task analysis that demonstrates to your students how to perform specific academic, social, behavioral, transitional, and functional skills (Schleibaum, 2007). This involves taking digital images (video or pictures) of each step in a task analysis and converting the digital images into presentation software slides that include brief written and oral descriptions of each step in the task analysis.

Digital Videos/Stories   Your instruction and student learning also can be enhanced by use of digital videos and stories (Rao et al., 2009). Digital videos or stories created by you and your students presenting role plays, documentaries, narratives, news reports, essays, poems, book reports, interviews, and skill demonstrations can be integrated into your instructional program across the curriculum (Sprankle, 2008). These programs allow your students to record narrations to describe learning products, processes, and outcomes and to integrate music and artwork.

Digital, Document, and Web Cameras   Digital cameras give you and your students access to digital technology in order to create video-based teaching and learning projects and increase visual literacy skills (Sopko, 2008). Users can immediately see the recorded image, store it in memory, delete it, or download it so that it can be edited, enlarged, e-mailed, embedded in Web pages, imported to other documents, added to student products or learning materials, or printed. Digital cameras are particularly useful for visually presenting learning tasks that are completed in a series of sequential steps. Document cameras are replacing overheads in classrooms as they allow teachers to display text, images, documents, three-dimensional objects, and Web sites. Web cameras (webcams) allow you and your students to view live events. When using webcams, it is important for you to preview the sites to make sure they are appropriate for your students.

Captioning Television, Interactive White-Smartboards, and Liquid Crystal Display Computer Projection Panels   Captioning and liquid crystal display (LCD) computer projection panels are other valuable teaching methods, particularly for deaf and hard-of-hearing students and English language learners (Sopko, 2008). The dialogue that accompanies closed-caption materials can be presented on the screen in real time via a device that receives closed-caption signals connected to the screen. Real-time closed-captioning can be used with a wide variety of students, including those with reading difficulties and those who speak different languages; it provides an auditory and a visual context for learning new vocabulary and information (Anderson-Inman, et al., 2009). For example, set-top television translators can convert closed captions from one language into another. As we saw in the chapter-opening vignette, students with visual disabilities like Julia benefit from descriptive video services, a specialized sound track system that enhances television and CD/DVD viewing by providing a running description of the images, events, characters' actions and body language, and scenes.

Via an Internet connection and a special slate and stylus and/or remote control device, interactive white-smartboards can help you differentiate your instruction across the curriculum for students by accessing and displaying information and images from the Internet or software programs; presenting digital graphics, text, video clips, and stereo sound; playing educational games; and recording, storing, and sending notes, handouts, and assignments to students (Mounce, 2008). For example, you can pair text with visual cues such as icons and pictorials to help students read words and understand information. You and your students can access the boards by touching the screen and icons displayed on the screen, or from anywhere in the room by writing on them electronically using a slate and a special stylus, or wireless and remote control devices such as handheld devices (Auchincloss & McIntyre, 2008).

LCD computer projection panels promote information sharing by interfacing a computer with a digital projector so that students can view more easily the information displayed on the monitor. With LCD projection, you can display images from multimedia sources with more colors and sharper resolution. You can also teach content in ways that are interesting, multidimensional, motivating, and tailored to students' needs.

Technology-Based Simulations and Virtual Reality   Technology-based simulations and virtual reality systems allow students to engage in a range of learning experiences that present digitally generated images and accompanying text depicting real or imaginary interactive and three-dimensional learning environments (Gee & Levine, 2009; Sayeski, 2008). Via problem-solving, simulation, and virtual learning software programs and Web sites, your student can have access to a range of learning experiences and multidimensional dilemmas and situations across the curriculum that can foster their academic, critical thinking, social, and metacognitive skills (Okolo, Englert, Bouck, & Heutsche, 2007; Salend, 2009). Virtual reality systems, which are available via software programs and the Internet, range from relatively simple simulations to more sophisticated lifelike learning, social and community-based environments (Cafiero, 2008; Cote, 2007; Cummings, 2007). For example, virtual reality can provide students with a safe environment to learn and practice how to cross the street or to conduct scientific experiments.

Internet The Internet provides you and your students with access to information, as well as many exploratory and discovery-based learning and communication experiences (Richardson, 2009). It allows you to access national, state, and district learning standards, as well as digital instructional activities and materials aligned with the standards. It allows students to control their learning more effectively, and it offers them options related to what and how they learn.

Some of the ways you and your students can use the Internet to differentiate instruction to support learning are presented here. When using the Internet as an instructional tool, keep in mind that it is essential for you to address issues of accessibility and to teach students how to be good digital citizens who use technology safely, appropriately, and respectfully.

Address Accessibility Issues When using the Internet with students, you need to make sure that *all students* can use Web sites and Web-based and digital materials by examining them in terms of their success at incorporating the principles of universal design (Krach & Jelenic, 2009). To do this, you can use Web accessibility software tools that guide you in evaluating and enhancing the accessibility of Web-based content and digital materials (Skylar, 2007). For example, these resources and materials can be made more accessible for *all students* by pairing graphic images with text and audio descriptions; using appropriate typeface and fonts, style variants, colors, and contrasts; and making sure that the site is easy to navigate, allows adjustments in timed responses, and is not visually distracting (Hartley & Boone, 2005).

Software programs are available that help students with a range of disabilities access the Internet (Dell et al., 2008). These programs, which are available in several languages, allow individuals with visual, dexterity-based, cognitive, and reading disabilities to tailor their browsing and navigating the Internet by using audio descriptors and prompting, closed captioning and text labels, error minimization strategies, and mouse and keyboard accommodations, reducing and reorganizing the visuals presented on the screen, presenting text and images that are read aloud, or enlarging text, graphics, browser controls, mouse pointers, and busy indicators (the hourglass). These programs also provide users with choices related to the text, images and backgrounds in terms of colors, fonts, spacing, and layout (presenting text in a single column) and whether to eliminate backgrounds, animations, time requirements, and images.

Teach Students to Be Good Digital Citizens Who Use Technology Safely, Respectfully and Appropriately Students need to learn how to be good digital citizens who use technology in a safe, respectful, and appropriate manner (Mustacchi, 2009; November, 2008; Richardson, 2009). When using technology, it is vital that you establish and teach rules, etiquette, and common sense for using the Internet and protecting privacy. As part of this instruction, you need to teach your students to avoid inappropriate Web sites and to refrain from posting or giving out personal information and pictures. They should be taught about viruses and spam and how to avoid them. Your students should learn how to conduct searches, identify the most appropriate links, and interact with others as well as what constitutes and how to avoid plagiarism (Moore Howard & Davies, 2009) and cyberbullying (Mustacchi, 2009). It is important that you teach your students how to evaluate Web sites and Web-based information (Badke, 2009; Richardson, 2009) (see Figure 8.6). Monitor your students' use of technology during instruction to

FIGURE 8.6 Guidelines for evaluating Web sites and Web-based information

- Who produced the site? When and why did they produce it?
- Does the title of the site reflect the content presented?
- Is contact information for the site available?
- Is the site produced by a credible individual, organization, or group?
- What are the goals and purposes of the site?
- Does the site have a specific agenda and any biases?
- Is the information provided current, accurate, helpful, and detailed?
- Is the information presented free of opinions, errors, emotional appeals, and biases?
- Are useful supporting visuals provided?
- Who provided the information for the site?
- Are the credentials of the author(s) of the information provided? Appropriate?
- Are sources of the information provided, relevant, and cited correctly?
- Are relevant links to other sites provided? Are these links active, up-to-date, appropriate, and useful?
- Is the site frequently updated?
- When was the site last updated?

Source: From Salend, S. J. (2009). *Classroom testing and assessment for all students: Beyond standardization.* Thousands Oaks, CA: Corwin Press. Reprinted with permission.

make sure students are using it appropriately (e.g., not e-mailing others or playing video games).

If you share your students' work with others using online formats, take precautions. Therefore, prior to posting student work electronically, you should

- obtain permission from students, their families, and your school district;
- delete confidential and personally identifying information from students' work;
- check to see that your students used pseudonyms and numbers instead of their real names;
- make sure that visuals of students are blocked out;
- evaluate the content and visuals to make sure they are appropriate for viewing by others;
- use password protection to control who can post and view student work; and
- limit access so that only your students and their families can view their work (November, 2008).

Use the Internet to Have Students Communicate with Others The Internet allows students to learn and communicate with others. Bulletin board folders, e-mail, video- and Web conferencing, and chat groups offer students opportunities to talk to, share information and experiences with, and learn from others (Richardson, 2009). Internet bulletin boards allow students to locate and meet others with whom they may want to interact. E-mail gives them the chance to send private messages to and receive them from other individuals. Videoconferencing and chat groups offer students a forum to talk with others. Through the Internet, students and classes can have digital pals from other schools in the district, geographic region, country, and world with whom they communicate and learn. These interactions give students direct opportunities to learn about and with others, to experience different ways of life, and to learn and use a new language.

Use the Internet to Access Electronic Resources The Internet provides you and your students with access to an enormous electronic library of lesson plans, learning activities, videos, resources, pictorials, videos, wikis, podcasts, encyclopedias, webcams, and databases containing information about virtually every subject and content area and in every language (Richardson, 2009). For example, you can locate and share classroom-appropriate video clips by using video sharing and streaming video sites such as TeacherTube (*www.teachertube.com*) and SchoolTube (*www .schooltube.com*). When using these video sharing sites, preview the videos to make sure that they are appropriate for your students and align with your instructional goals. Internet connections allow you and your students to examine and browse through these electronic documents and resources. You and your students also can visit and access information from museums and webcams via the Internet.

Your students also can access information, and share their learning by using **wikis**, which are Web sites that offer content on a range of topics created and edited by users. Thus, your students can learn about or demonstrate what they know about a specific topic by creating a new wiki or editing an existing wiki (Knobel & Wilber, 2009; Schweder & Wissick, 2009). They also can receive feedback on their wiki entries by periodically viewing the wiki to see the comments and changes made by others. Because wikis are edited by users, it is important to teach students to carefully evaluate and verify the information obtained from wikis (Badke, 2009) (see Figure 8.6).

Podcasts available via the Internet allow your students to watch or hear live or prerecorded events and learning activities occurring throughout the world. They also can be made by you to present information that your students can view at their convenience and by your students to showcase their work (Langhorst, 2007; Williams, 2007). For example, video and audio-podcasts can consist of you reviewing key terminology prior to a test, or students reading, giving presentations, discussing issues, or solving problems. When creating podcasts to share with others, it is helpful to include markers, which allow others to easily locate or access specific parts of the podcast.

You and your students can access electronic resources by using **RSS Site Summary (RSS)**, which is also referred to as *Really Simple Syndication* (Richardson, 2009). RSS compiles brief summaries of the content on particular topics available at various Web sites so that users can identify relevant online content without having to access multiple sites.

Use the Internet to Create Web Sites, Weblogs, Webquests, and Tracks   You also can use the Internet to create accessible, easy-to-use classroom Web sites, weblogs, webquests, and tracks. Creating a Web site or page for your class is a good way to involve students in learning about the Internet and communicating with other students, families, and individuals throughout the world. For example, your class can work as a group to plan, design, and create a classroom Web page relating to important aspects of your class. Like Ms. Taravella and Ms. Stoudamire, you also can post students' work on your class's Web page, and students can receive and respond to inquiries from others about their Web page. You also can use your Web site to make important learning materials available to students.

You and your students also can create *weblogs* (or *blogs*), online diaries that are easily and continuously updated to present information about your class's activities (Davis & McGrail, 2009). Teachers also use blogs as a way to extend classroom discussions or question and answer sessions beyond the confines of their classrooms. Individual and groups of students also can maintain blogs to share information about things they are learning, to comment on their experiences and events around the world, and to interact with others (Knobel & Wilber, 2009). For example, your students can maintain blogs to present their assignments and to share their knowledge of a specific topic and across the curriculum (Schweder & Wissick, 2007). In addition to text, blogs can include **video blogs**, **vlogs**, as well as audio files such as music or narrations, and links to other related websites.

Another type of Internet-based instructional activity that is becoming more common in classrooms is a **webquest** (Skylar, Higgins, & Boone, 2007). This is an inquiry-oriented, cooperatively structured group activity in which some or all of the information and content that your students use comes from resources on the Internet or videoconferencing. For example, Ms. Taravella and her colleagues had students work in collaborative groups to complete webquests that asked them to use the Internet to gather and present information on the early explorations of the solar system and the corresponding cultural beliefs of different groups. Webquests can be structured in a variety of ways, including as Internet hunts, puzzles, projects, and study guides.

Tracks are online lessons that guide student learning related to a specific topic by directing them to a variety of instructional activities presented by accessing a series of teacher-specified Web sites. Students then visit these sites to engage in learning activities which include producing products that demonstrate their learning or completing an online quiz of material presented via the track.

Assistive Technology

Technology has been used to develop many assistive devices to promote the learning, independence and communication abilities of students with various disabilities like Julia and Tom. These devices are an integral part of students' IEPs. They also can be used to create assistive technology toolkits, a list of technology devices and services that teachers and students can use to support the learning and socialization of students in inclusive classrooms.

Devices for Students with Physical Disabilities   For students who have difficulty speaking intelligibly, augmentative and alternative communication systems devices are invaluable. Low-technology devices, such as communication boards with pictures/words/objects, which are nonelectric and tend to be homemade by clinicians, also are useful. Some students may benefit from use of a Picture Exchange Communication System (PECS) that allows them to communicate via use of a pictorial-based system (Beck, Stoner, Bock, & Parton, 2008; Sulzer-Azaroff, Hoffman, Horton, Bondy, & Frost, 2009).

High-technology augmentative communication systems, sometimes referred to as speech-generating devices or voice output communication aides, based on computer hardware and software and output devices transform strokes and/or word input into speech can increase communication and student learning (Thunberg, Ahlsen, & Dahlgren Sandberg, 2009; Wilkins & Ratajczak, 2009). Students can input a phrase or press a key or icon that activates the technology's speech capabilities. Specific vocabulary sets can be programmed based on students' educational and communicative needs, as well as the setting in which they need to communicate. As the technology evolves, these devices are being made smaller and more portable and with digitized speech that sounds more natural.

Some students, including those with physical disabilities, also may have problems inputting information into technology in traditional ways (e.g., pressing more than one key at a time). To meet their needs, alternative methods have been developed (see Figure 8.7). These students also may benefit from accommodations to the standard keyboard such as keyboard overlays or larger, ergonomic and alternative keyboards that can be placed at different angles and have different letter/key and spacing arrangements. Other alternatives are auditory keys that offer oral feedback when they are accessed, keyguards, stickers to signify keys, key locks, and word prediction and speech recognition programs. They also may need to use specialized keys that increase the accessibility of the keyboard (see Figure 8.8). Students with tremors and/or uncontrolled hand or finger movements may need to use an adapted more accessible mouse, joystick, trackball or touchpad that can adjust for extraneous movements (Lotempio, 2008). Some students also may benefit from other built-in accessibility features including on-screen keyboarding, screen magnification, visual and auditory warnings, text-to-speech recognition, text narration, and enhanced mouse visibility and movement. Students also may benefit from mouse and typing echo systems that orally describe cursor and keyboard movements.

Voice/speech recognition and voice-activated systems are allowing students with a range of disabilities to use technology, access and browse the Internet, and interact and share their ideas with others (Fitzgerald, 2008; MacArthur, 2009). These

REFLECTIVE

What instructional technologies and assistive devices did you use as a student? As a teacher? What were the positive and negative effects of these technologies on your learning and your students' learning?

FIGURE 8.7 Alternative methods of inputting information into computers

1. *Voice recognition:* The computer recognizes the user's speech and converts it into action

2. *Key guard:* A device that modifies the traditional keyboard to change the size and spacing of the keys. It may include a key lock that automatically toggles specialty keys

3. *Keyboard alteration programs:* Programs that modify the keyboard in terms of key accept time and key repeating

4. *Graphics tablet:* A small slate that may be covered by templates of words, pictures, numerals, and letters that are input when touched by a special stylus

5. *Adapted switches:* Switches controlled by pressure or body movements. They can be activated by foot, head, cheek, chin, tongue, or eye movements

6. *Scanning systems:* An array of letters, phrases, and numerals displayed on the screen at a rate that is adjusted to the student's need. The student selects the message from the scanner by using the keyboard or a switch

7. *Touch screens/on-screen keyboards/light pens:* Devices that allow the student to activate the computer by touching or writing on the screen

8. *Joystick:* A stick that is moved in different directions, controlling the movement of the cursor

9. *Vocal joystick:* A microphone-like device that is connected with a sound card that allows cursor movements to be controlled by auditory sounds made by users

10. *Mouthstick:* A tool that is placed in the mouth and used to press buttons and activate switches

11. *Headband:* A headband-like device that is worn by the student to control the computer through head or eye movements

12. *Sip and puff systems:* A long command tube attached to a computer or wheelchair on which the student sucks

13. *Skateboard:* A block of wood on rollers attached to the student's arm that is moved in different directions to control cursor movements

14. *Mouse:* A mouselike object that is moved in different directions to control the computer. Adaptations of the mouse can be controlled by using the numeric pad of the keyboard (keyboard mouse) or by a headsetlike device, such as a headband, that conveys directions to the computer via head movements

15. *Eye gaze:* Use of eye gazes and scanning to select stimuli that appear on the computer screen

16. *Sensors:* Sensors are attached to the user and the computer and activated by facial movements or physical gestures

FIGURE 8.8 Specialized keys for using technology

- *StickyKeys*, which results in one key press taking the actions associated with multiple keys being pressed simultaneously
- *MouseKeys*, which allows movement of the mouse pointer through use of the numeric keypad
- *ToggleKeys*, which activates an auditory sound when specific features are activated, such as the lock keys NUM LOCK, CAPS LOCK, or SCROLL LOCK
- *FilterKeys*, which contains a range of features that vary the keyboard response time and address the inadvertent pressing of keys
- *RepeatKeys*, which provides users with control over whether repeated key strokes are converted into actions and allow users to set the repeat start time and rate
- *BounceKeys*, which allow users who tend to bounce when activating or releasing a key to access only one action or keyboard character at a time

Source: Salend (2009).

systems, which are also available on many devices, can convert spoken words into text or into actions that activate technology (Parette et al., 2007). For example, students can access menus or Web site links by stating an action or a name/number or write papers by dictating their ideas and then editing them via use of word processing (Zhao, 2007). These systems continue to have improved accuracy rates and can recognize the different accents of students from different regions in the United States (e.g., Great Lakes, southern United States, etc.) and students from other parts of the world (e.g., Australia, Britain, Southeast Asian, India, Mexico, Spain, etc.) (Pogue, 2008b). However, keep in mind that these systems are still being perfected; the programs will need to be taught to recognize a student's voice and students will need training to use them effectively.

Assistive devices also help individuals with disabilities organize and take notes in class. Some students use tablet personal computers (tablet PCs) and laptop computers with word processing programs and lightweight, voice-activated digital recorders or digital dictation systems for note taking. Portable devices including PDAs and wireless tablet PCs allow students to access online material, to receive motivational prompts and organizational reminders, to take notes that include illustrations and to receive and send notes and class and homework assignments to and from teachers and classmates (Bouck et al., 2007; Smith Myles, Ferguson, & Hagiwara, 2007). They also allow teachers to monitor students' understanding of instruction and provide feedback to students on their performance via active responding systems. These devices provide access to information and resources available through other technologies such as the Internet. PDAs and paging systems also can help students engage in appropriate social skills, recall and access information, and remember to use the correct sequence of tasks and routines, as well as organize schedules, information, and events (Taber-Doughty et al., 2008). These devices can be programmed to deliver reminders to students via pictures, speech, audio, video, and text (Cihak et al., 2008; Mechling, 2008).

Scanning and form-typing software is available to help students complete forms and worksheets (Thompson, Bakken, Fulk, & Peterson-Karlan, 2005). Using this technology, hard copies of forms or assignments are scanned into a digital format and then completed by students using their computers.

Valerie Schultz/Merrill

Instructional and assistive devices are helping students succeed in inclusive settings. What technologies help your students?

Computer technology including advances in design, sensors, and robotics has also helped increase the independence of individuals with physical disabilities (Lotempio, 2008). The Independence Enhanced Wheelchair is a robotic wheelchair that uses computer and GPS technology to allow individuals to input where they want to go, which is then processed by the device to plan and execute the most effective path to get there including ways to get around barriers such as furniture and other individuals. Robotic devices and computerized systems and sensors in the home can be programmed to turn on the oven, reconnect a phone left off the hook, shut off lights, lock doors, and adjust the sound of the television so that these individuals can live on their own. Infrared remote control systems and voice activation also allow individuals to control and operate learning and independent living devices and appliances.

Devices for Students with Visual and Reading Disabilities Several assistive devices have been developed to help use print materials. Various lightweight text scanners and optical character-reading systems with speech synthesis recognize letters, group letters into words, read words, and provide the correct pronunciation of words in a sentence in several languages. Printed materials are scanned and stored in memory. Students can then view the printed page, hear the text being read aloud, look up the meaning of unfamiliar words, highlight important content, and insert bookmarks. When selecting a scanning-based reading adaptive device, you should consider the ability of the scanner to scan accurately and the availability of an automatic document/page feeder.

Technology-based screen- and text-reading programs read text aloud by word, letters or by phonetic markers; or convert words, sentences, and paragraphs into fluent speech (Auchincloss & McIntyre, 2008; Izzo et al., 2009). Using these programs, students can hear text read aloud as they read along (as the text read is digitally highlighted) (Harrison, 2009). These programs, which can read in different voices and languages, allow users to search for or highlight words, sentences, and paragraphs that can be read aloud. These programs also can be customized to create pronunciation dictionaries and to control the speed, pitch, and volume of the speech.

Screen- and text-reading technologies also are available on many devices (Parette et al, 2007). For instance, the "Save as DAISY XML" feature can convert text-based Word documents, such as your tests and other print materials, into Digital Accessible Information SYstem (DAISY) files, accessible formats that can be orally presented to your students with visual impairments and students with reading difficulties.

Also available are smaller and more portable optical character reading systems such as the Kurzweil-National Federation of the Blind Reader Mobile (KNFB Reader Mobile), the ReadingPen, and the C-pen. These devices allow users to scan printed materials, which are then read aloud to them; they are also useful for your students who are learning English. When considering using these devices, it is important to remember that they are most helpful for reading words or sentences rather than paragraphs or pages.

Low-tech devices can be used to assist students with reading (Ferreri, 2009; Higbee Mandlebaum, Hodges, & Messenheimer, 2007). Line guides or masks such as reading rulers, windows, or index cards can assist students who have difficulty tracking and maintaining their place on a line. Some students also may benefit from placing color acetate overlays on their reading materials to help them adjust the contrast in the text.

As we discussed earlier in this chapter, digitized books help students use printed materials, including textbooks. Talking calculators, globes, and other devices are available to support the learning of these students. For example, electronic dictionaries with digitized speech help students define unfamiliar words. Screen magnification programs enlarge text and graphics to an appropriate size and adjust the colors on the screen to offer users the best contrast (Swift et al., 2008). Many of these programs contain zoom features that allow users to zoom in on specific areas of the screen. Font enlargement features also allow users to adjust the size of the fonts in which text is presented (Ferreri, 2009). Students with visual difficulties can benefit from use of Braille, larger keys, flicker-free monitors that have a higher resolution and contrast, and external magnification devices that are placed over the existing monitor.

Technology also is available to help students like Julia access information media and technology presented information (Ely et al., 2006). An eDescription, like the descriptive video system used by Julia, can provide access by offering a description of visually presented images and text. Students with visual disabilities also may use a tactile graphics display (TGD), so they can tactilely access electronic images and text.

Technology also is available to assist students and professionals in converting electronic files and print materials into audio, large-print, or Braille formats (Dell & Newton, 2008), and to assist students with visual disabilities in taking

Braille-based notes (Hopkins, 2006). Technology allows you and your students and colleagues to scan print materials, and then enlarge or enhance them or translate and convert them into Braille materials for use by students. For example, Visiprint (www.visiprintsoftware.com) provides software that can help you prepare large-print documents that can be tailored to the different needs and preferences of your students. You also can label items in your classroom with a Braille labeler or via a talking bar-code scanner and reader, and provide these students with access to a handheld color identifier that verbally identifies colors of objects (Wolfe Poel, 2007). Students with visual disabilities also may benefit from using a refreshable Braille note taker, a portable assistive device that converts electronically produced text into Braille or speech.

A variety of optical aids to help students with low vision access visual images and text are available (Eisenberg, 2008). In addition to goggles, handheld pocket magnifiers, magnifiers mounted on a base, and magnifiers attached to eyeglass frames or incorporated in the lenses to magnify printed materials for individuals with visual disabilities, lightweight and portable electronic optical devices have been developed. Electronic optical devices are also available to make reading and seeing easier by allowing individuals to make choices about the size, contrast, and colors of text/images and their backgrounds. During reading activities, typoscopes can be used with these students to direct and focus their attention on specific words (Wolfe Poel, 2007).

Communication systems for individuals with visual disabilities also exist. Tele-Braille helps deaf and blind individuals communicate by converting a message typed on a Braille keyboard into print on a video monitor, which is read by a sighted person. The sighted person then types a response, which is converted into a Braille display. Devices with large-print, Braille, and voice output capabilities also allow students with visual disabilities to communicate. These students also may benefit from the use of Braille printers, refreshable Braille displays, and Braille note takers.

Electronic travel aids can increase the independent movement of students with visual disabilities. These students can use a handheld electronic device that vibrates to alert students to barriers in their path and to indicate the distance to obstacles. The Laser Cane emits three laser beams that provide a sound signaling objects, dropoffs, or low-hanging obstacles in the user's path. Students with visual impairments as well as those with other disabilities can carry a cell phone or PDA with small GPS receiver offering orally or Braille presented step-by-step directions that can guide them in moving around schools and classrooms and finding locations, objects and materials (Bouck et al., 2007).

Devices for Deaf and Hard-of-Hearing Students Technology is making a profound improvement in assistive devices for deaf and hard-of-hearing students. New types of hearing aids based on digital technology contain smaller and more powerful computer chips that recognize and selectively amplify human speech, filter out background noises, deliver more realistic sound, and tailor the sound to the individual's needs and acoustic setting. Technologies are fostering communication between individuals with and without hearing. IP-RELAY (*www.ip-relay.com*) uses Internet telephony to allow deaf and hard-of-hearing individuals to communicate with others. Using this technology, a confidential operator fosters telephone conversations by converting speech to text for deaf and hard-of-hearing individuals and text to speech for individuals who have hearing.

PDAS, cell phones and two-way pagers with amplification, text messaging and video features allow deaf and hard of hearing individuals to communicate, develop their independence, and foster learning. Speech-to-text translation systems provide these students access to oral presentations by viewing a monitor that presents the speaker's comments (Hopkins, 2006).

PEARSON
myeducationlab

To enhance your understanding of assistive technology devices that can support the performance of students with visual disbilities in your inclusive classroom, go to the IRIS Center Resources section of the Topic *Visual Impairment* in the MyEducationLab for your course, and complete the module entitled *Accommodations to the Physical Environment: Setting Up a Classroom for Students with Visual Disabilities.*

These students also can access technology-based information via systems with closed-captioning and where the text and graphics appear on the video monitor accompanied by a video of a signer who signs the text. For students who have some hearing, a digitized voice can read the text as it is presented via closed-captioning or as the signer signs it. Some students who rely on speechreading may benefit from a classroom speechreading technology system that involves a live video transmission of the speaker's lips to a desktop monitor located on students' desks.

Devices for Students from English Language Backgrounds   The academic performance and language learning of students who are English language learners can be enhanced through many of the instructional technology and assistive devices previously discussed, which they can access using their preferred language. They also may benefit from technology that provides meaningful, active, and motivating learning experiences, sensory-based support, and captioning and translating in their primary and new languages (Lowdermilk et al., 2008). Using the Internet, they can access authentic text, audio and video resources, and media sites in multiple languages (e.g., online radio and television broadcasts). They also can use the Internet to read, hear, and write in multiple languages and communicate with native speakers of many languages via Web sites, e-mail, chat rooms, and blogs.

Translation software can be used to foster language development and communication with individuals who speak other languages. English language learners can use translation software and handheld talking translators that can convert verbal statements or text from one language into another. When using these programs, it is important for you and your students to understand that they may at times provide inaccurate translations and may not cover the range of dialects associated with specific languages.

Technology also is available that promotes English language acquisition (Lowdermilk et al. 2008; Mulholland, Pete, & Popeson, 2008). Programs that build on students' prior linguistic and cultural knowledge and employ colors, 3-D visuals, videos, vignettes, audio, sounds, and animation to present the meanings and pronunciation of words and sentences and their semantic relationships can be particularly helpful for your students who are English language learners. Effective software programs for these students also should provide them with numerous opportunities to practice labeling and requesting items; repeating words, phrases, and sentences; identifying things and their related features; understanding gestures; and engaging in reading and writing.

Bilingual software programs, Web sites, translation, and word processing provide bilingual online assistance with content presentation, dictionaries, thesauruses, and spelling and grammar checkers. Interactive programs offer access to bilingual glossaries, captioning, visual presentations, and many opportunities for students to develop their vocabulary, word recognition, and reading and listening comprehension skills. PowerPoint presentations and videos of visuals paired with text of key words and questions also can be used with these students to develop their vocabulary and expressive language skills (Reagon, Higbee, & Endicott, 2007). Technology can be used to help students learn their new language by allowing them to see mouth movements associated with sounds, hear the pronunciation of words and sentences, and then record and receive feedback on their own attempts to speak.

The Language Master is a handheld device that contains electronic dictionary, thesaurus, and grammar and spell checker that pronounces words, gives definitions and synonyms, corrects the spelling of phonetic words, and offers educational games involving targeted vocabulary words (Lindsey-Glenn & Gentry, 2008). The Language Master allows you and your students to develop their vocabulary by playing, recording, and erasing oral material on stimulus cards and writing on the stimulus cards to provide visual cues.

PEARSON
myeducationlab

To reflect on and enhance your understanding of how you can differentiate your curriculum and instruction to plan and implement lessons that foster your students' access to the general education curriculum, go to the IRIS Center Resources section of the Topic *Instructional Practices and Learning Strategies* in the MyEducationLab for your course, and complete the module entitled *Content Standards: Connecting Standards-Based Curriculum to Instructional Planning.*

REFLECTING ON PROFESSIONAL PRACTICES

REFLECTING ON PROFESSIONAL PRACTICES

Using Instructional and Assistive Technology to Differentiate Instruction

Ms. Taravella and Ms. Camac, the school's technology specialist, were excited about developing and teaching a unit on the Vietnam War using instructional technology. They started to develop the unit by searching the Internet for content, online lesson plans, and teaching resources about Vietnam and the war. They also participated in a chat room related to teaching and technology, which also provided suggestions for the unit. Then they identified and reviewed interesting and relevant Web sites and resources and created their unit. They also visited the sites, which provided help in designing various Web-based activities.

Because their students' experience with the Internet varied, Ms. Taravella and Ms. Camac began by teaching students about the Internet and how to use it appropriately. They modeled and provided an overview of how to access and navigate the Internet and evaluate sites and Web-based information. They paired experienced users with novices to perform a World Wide Web scavenger hunt that required them to conduct searches for various topics. They had students go online to access activities that taught them how to use the Internet safely, responsibly, efficiently, and effectively. They brainstormed with students and framed rules for use of the Internet by having students respond to such questions as "What would you do if you were asked for personal information or your password?" "What would you do if someone wanted to meet you or sell you something?" and "What would you do if you received or encountered offensive material?" They also told students not to believe everything they read or heard via the Internet. They gave students guidelines for examining and verifying sites and information, which included identifying the individuals who created the site, the dates on which it was created and updated, the location and organizational affiliation of the site, and the content of the site.

Once they were convinced that students could use the technology appropriately, Ms. Taravella and Ms. Camac assigned students to work in groups. Each group selected a variety of learning activities from a menu that included

- gathering information about the war from Web sites and wikis;
- viewing a video that portrayed actual battles and presented interviews with soldiers;
- taking a three-dimensional panoramic tour of the Vietnam Memorial through pictures that Ms. Camac had taken the previous summer with a digital camera;
- watching videos of news reports from the 1960s and 1970s and documentaries about the Vietnam War and antiwar activities throughout the United States and the world;
- exchanging e-mail messages with military experts and leaders of the antiwar movement;

- examining primary-source documents online;
- viewing and listening to podcasts that contained discussions about the war, including eyewitness accounts of the war from the viewpoint of soldiers, protesters, and Vietnamese citizens;
- making a virtual visit to an exhibition on the Vietnam War at the Smithsonian Museum; and
- establishing a keypal online relationship with Vietnamese and U.S. students and their families.

While the groups worked, the teachers and the other professionals in the room helped them. When computers froze because students tried to download too much information, they helped students reboot them. They also aided students who had difficulty accessing information from websites (like Julia) by using an Internet screen reading program that read the text and images aloud and reformatting the text and images so that they were easier for students with reading difficulties to read.

Ms. Taravella and Ms. Camac also allowed each group to choose its own final product. Group projects included writing and making a video and podcast of a play about the Vietnam War, completing a webquest, wiki, or a track about the war, preparing a presentation about the war using presentation software and digital photos, conducting an online survey of the community's knowledge of the Vietnam War, and creating a memorial to Vietnam Veterans and the peace movement. All students helped develop their group's project. Tom, a student with a severe disability, used his assistive communication system to speak lines in his group's play, and Marta, an English language learner, helped her group translate their community survey into Spanish.

The teachers and their students used the class's Web page to create a weblog that provided an ongoing summary of the class's learning activities that also included digital photos of the groups' projects with accompanying narration. They were pleased when they received e-mail messages from other teachers and their students' families commenting on the students' products and requesting to use activities from their unit.

- What strategies did Ms. Taravella and Ms. Camac use to differentiate instruction for their students?
- What process and resources did they use to create and implement their technology-based unit?
- What do you think the students and their families thought about this unit?
- What difficulties might you encounter in using instructional technology activities in your classroom?
- How could you attempt to solve these difficulties?

What Would You Do in Today's Diverse Classroom?

Your class includes the following students:

★ Alexis is an inconsistent reader. Her reading difficulties are greatest when she is asked to read handouts and tests. She also has trouble understanding text. Alexis likes to work with others, and works hard to please her teachers and her family.

★ Raymond, a student with cerebral palsy, has difficulty walking and limited use of his hands. Although he can speak, it is very hard to understand him. Because of his communication difficulties, it is hard to assess his cognitive abilities. However, you notice he learns best using technology.

★ Carrie, a student with a moderate hearing loss, has difficulty following orally presented information and directions. She relies heavily on gestures and visual stimuli and the services of an educational interpreter. Usually she can understand face-to-face communications. Although her speech is intelligible to others, she sometimes needs to be prodded to speak in class.

1. How would you determine the appropriate strategies to differentiate instruction for these students?
2. What strategies would you use to differentiate instruction for these students?
3. How could you use instructional technology and assistive devices to differentiate instruction for these students?
4. What difficulties might you encounter in differentiating instruction for these students?
5. What knowledge, skills, dispositions, and support do you need to differentiate instruction for these students?

PEARSON myeducationlab Watch Carrie and her educational interpreter discuss Carrie's educational strengths and challenges by visiting the MyEducationLab for this course. Go to the *Assignments and Activities* section under the topic *Hearing Loss and Deafness*, and complete the activity entitled *Sign Language Interpretation* to answer questions about differentiating instruction for students like Carrie in inclusive classrooms.

SUMMARY

This chapter offered guidelines for differentiating instruction to address the diverse learning strengths and challenges of your students. As you review the questions posed in this chapter, remember the following points:

How Can I Differentiate Instruction for Students?

CEC 2, 3, 4, 5, 7, 9, 10; PRAXIS 3; INTASC 1, 2, 3, 4, 5, 6, 7, 9

You can tailor your curricular goals and teaching strategies to the individual strengths and challenges of your students and your learning environment. It is also important to use backward design to determine a range of formative and summative assessments; individualized curricular, teaching, and instructional materials and accommodations; and universally designed materials. You also can provide personal support; address students' learning styles, preferences, and sensory abilities; and consider acceptability.

How Can I Differentiate Instruction for Students Who Have Difficulty Reading and Gaining Information from Print Materials?

CEC 2, 4, 7, 9; PRAXIS 3; INTASC 2, 3, 4, 7, 9

You can use a variety of teacher- and student-directed text comprehension strategies. In addition, you can make materials more readable by modifying them, reducing their linguistic complexity, incorporating the principles of typographical design, and using instructional technology.

How Can I Differentiate Instruction for Students from Diverse Cultural and Language Backgrounds?

CEC 1, 3, 4, 5, 6, 7, 9, 10; PRAXIS 3; INTASC 1, 2, 3, 4, 5, 6, 7, 8, 9, 10

You can use a multicultural curriculum, multicultural instructional materials, culturally relevant and responsive teaching strategies, reciprocal interaction, and effective ESL and dual-language approaches and techniques. You can also encourage students to respond.

How Can I Use Instructional Technology and Assistive Devices to Differentiate Instruction for Students?

CEC 6, 7, 9; PRAXIS 3; INTASC 4, 6, 7, 9

Recent developments in instructional technology allow you to create differentiated, interactive, motivating, and contextualized learning environments for students by using computer-based instruction, video-based digital materials, presentation software, digital videos/stories, digital, document, Web cameras, captioning interactive white-smartboards, liquid crystal display projection panels, and technology-based simulations. The Internet provides you and your students with access to information, as well as many learning and communication experiences. You also can use a wide variety of assistive devices to help students learn, communicate with others, use technology, be organized, take notes, increase their range of movements and mobility, read text, hear sounds, and learn a new language. When using these technologies, make sure you address accessibility issues, and teach your students to be good digital citizens who use technology safely, appropriately, and respectfully.

Effective Practices for Students from Diverse Backgrounds

From Chapter 12 of *Inclusion: Effective Practices for All Students*. Second Edition. James McLeskey, David L. Westling.

Effective Practices for Students from Diverse Backgrounds

A VIEW FROM THE TEACHER

Navigating Cultural Responsiveness at Heritage High School

Melanie Buckley knows that cultural diversity is not just an urban issue. As an English teacher and department chair at Heritage High School in suburban (some may even say rural) Leesburg, Virginia, Melanie has observed that too many students from culturally and linguistically diverse (CLD) backgrounds have difficulty meeting academic and behavioral standards. This is a major challenge: Approximately 45% of the Heritage student population comes from CLD backgrounds, with substantial numbers of students (over 10%) from Hispanic, African American, and Asian backgrounds.

Melanie has considerable teaching experience at both the high school and community college levels. Her experience has taught her that "all teachers must be culturally aware and culturally responsive. This means that teachers must be cognizant of their students' lives outside of school, actively learning of their varied cultural backgrounds and the media-saturated popular culture contexts in which they live." She and her team have initiated a number of professional development activities to assist teachers at Heritage. These activities—known as *purposeful pedagogy*—have helped teachers connect elements of the secondary curriculum to the lives of their students from CLD backgrounds. One of the curriculum development sessions, "Beyond Dead White Men and Why You Should Diversify Your Literature Curriculum," was useful and popular with the faculty of the English department.

Melanie recognizes that professional development for teachers must be supplemented by specific actions that engage students and families from culturally and linguistically diverse backgrounds. Recognizing that school personnel need consistent family support to address the learning needs of their students, Melanie and the Heritage team developed "Success Nights," a strategy to involve families that had a history of limited contact with the school. To engage these families, the team used Success Nights to recognize the accomplishments of students and showcase how modest achievements could serve as a foundation for greater academic and social success. In addition to recognizing student accomplishments, guest speakers presented important topical information in an accessible, jargon-free fashion. Instead of being formal and authoritative, Success Nights were social occasions for community team building and letting families know that their input was welcome and needed by the school faculty and administration.

Melanie and her colleagues know that being culturally responsive requires problem solving and experimentation. For example, after reviewing the Heritage standardized test data, it was discovered that a disproportionately high number of students from the English language learner subgroup did not achieve acceptable levels of academic performance. Recognizing that merely assigning more work would not address the challenge, Melanie and the Heritage team wrote a grant

proposal to examine various ways of motivating this group of learners. A similar group process was used to devise a series of ways to increase homework completion among these same students.

Melanie recognizes that far too many students from diverse backgrounds struggle to meet academic expectations. This results in an achievement gap between these students and European American students and higher dropout rates and special education placements for students from CLD backgrounds. Through understanding, reflection, and creative experimentation, Heritage High School remains committed to navigating the intersection of ethnicity, language, and disability, and enhancing cultural responsiveness across all aspects of the school community.

MyEducationLab
Visit the MyEducationLab for *Inclusion* to enhance your understanding of chapter concepts with a personalized Study Plan. You'll also have the opportunity to hone your teaching skills through video and case-based Assignments and Activities, Building Teaching Skills and Disposition lessons, and IRIS Case Studies.

Introduction

Imagine that you are about to begin working in an inclusive school with students who are from diverse backgrounds. In most schools, you will have a significant number of students who come from homes of poverty, and many students of color. Unfortunately, as Melanie Buckley observed in the opening vignette for this chapter, many of these students likely will be behind in both reading and/or mathematics on state assessments (NCES, 2010). Some of these students will be learning English as a second language, others will have disabilities, and some will qualify for gifted and talented programs. Such a diverse classroom context challenges the skills of any teacher who is committed to ensuring that all students achieve at high levels. Success will require finding ways to engage students who may be resistant to learning. Success will also require meeting the individual needs of each student with special needs and finding ways to communicate with students and families whose backgrounds vary considerably from yours.

There is a widespread misconception that diverse schools exist only in urban settings. Heritage High School, in Leesburg, Virginia, is one of many schools that suggest otherwise. In fact, the population of the United States is changing rapidly and dramatically, and understanding the needs of **culturally and linguistically diverse (CLD)** learners is critical to the success of teachers in all settings, particularly teachers with a commitment to inclusive education. Indeed, students with disabilities are just as diverse as—and in some cases more so than—the general population of students. Many students with disabilities are thus from diverse **cultures** and **ethnic groups** (i.e., non-European American backgrounds, where **standard English** is often not spoken in the home), as well as from low-income families.

To better meet the needs of students with disabilities from diverse backgrounds within inclusive schools and classrooms, all teachers should:

- Understand their students' cultural and language backgrounds.
- Learn how they can adapt their teaching based on information about students' cultural and language backgrounds.
- Provide supports to ensure each student's success, and that each student is involved as an active participant in the academic and social community of the school (Banks et al., 2005; Gay, 2010; Ginsburg, 2005; Irvine, 2002).

Pause & Reflect

Our choice of the words we use to describe ourselves is one way we define our identity. Take a moment and list every word that you would use to describe yourself. Include words that define your physical characteristics, but be sure to go beyond that and list words that describe who you are and the various roles you play. Share your list with a peer, and discuss your commonalities and differences.

In this chapter, we begin with a description of students from diverse backgrounds, and what you can expect as you teach these students in an inclusive classroom. Understanding your own background provides a context for reading about and understanding the experiences of students from diverse backgrounds that we discuss in this chapter. Before reading the rest of the chapter, take a moment to reflect on your background in the "Pause & Reflect" exercise.

Students from Diverse Backgrounds: What to Expect

Are today's students different from the students who entered school 15 to 20 years ago? Are schools more diverse? To answer these questions we'll need to examine how individual characteristics of the student population have changed and continue to change.

What to Expect Regarding Student Diversity

Students with disabilities come from a diverse range of cultural, language, and ethnic backgrounds.

Throughout the history of the United States, a substantial majority of the population has been European American (although we use this term, the U.S. Census Bureau and the U.S. Department of Education use the term *non-Hispanic Whites*). This is rapidly changing, especially among school-aged students. Currently, just over 25% of all students are European American in California (NCES, 2010). In nine other states (Arizona, Florida, Georgia, Hawaii, Louisiana, Maryland, Nevada, New Mexico, and Texas), the majority of students are from non-European American backgrounds. Many other states have a large proportion of students from non-European American backgrounds, as about 45% of all students are from diverse backgrounds.

The number of students who speak a language other than English at home continues to increase rapidly across the United States. Today, 1 of every 5 school-aged students (almost 11 million students) speaks a language other than English when they are at home, and about 1 in 10 students is designated as an **English-language learner (ELL)** and entitled to general educational services to address his limited-English proficiency (LEP) (NCES, 2010). As the number of second-language learners increases, the need for services will also increase, and the majority of teachers entering the profession will need to be prepared to meet those students' needs. Indeed, this is already true in some states. For example, in Florida, all teachers are required to have proficiency in addressing the needs of students who are English-language learners.

The poverty rates in the United States may surprise you. About 15 million children under 18 years of age live in families with incomes below the federal poverty level (Chau, Thampi, & Wright, 2010), an increase of 33% since 2000. Even more problematic is how ethnicity is intertwined with poverty, as disproportional percentages of African American, Hispanic, and American Indian children live in poor families (Chau, Thampi, & Wright, 2010). Figure 1 gives additional information on ethnic disparities in poverty rates.

What to Expect Regarding Diversity in Special Education

Understanding the intersection of ethnicity, language, and disability is important, but this issue goes deeper than

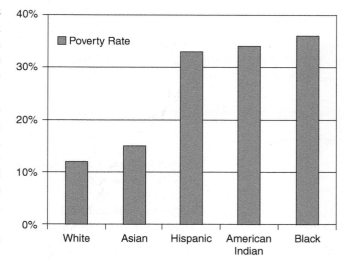

Figure 1

Statistics on Children Living in Poverty by Ethnicity in 2009

Source: Data from M. Chau, K. Thampi, & V. Wight (2010). Basic facts about low-income children, 2009. The National Center for Children in Poverty. Retrieved January 10, 2011, from http://www.nccp.org/publications/pub_975.html

Just the Facts — About Student Diversity and Disability

What percentage of school-aged students in the United States are from different ethnic groups?	European American 55% Hispanic 21.5% African American 17% Asian/Pacific Islander 5% American Indian/Alaska Native 1%
What is the prevalence of disability by diversity factors? That is, what percentage of all students from each group is identified with a disability?	• Homeless 30 to 40% • Foster care 16% • English-language learner 8% • American Indian/Alaska Native 12.5% • African American 11.3% • Hispanic 8.6% • European American 7.7% • Asian/Pacific Islander 4.5%
Are there differences in ethnicity by disability category?	• Substantially more African American and American Indian/Alaska Native students are identified with disabilities than are students from other ethnic groups. • African American and American Indian/Alaska Native students are overrepresented in the categories of intellectual disability, learning disability, and emotional and behavioral disabilities.
How do graduate and dropout rates compare for different ethnic groups?	• Overall, 52% of students with disabilities graduate with a regular diploma. This includes 61.5% of European Americans, 39.2% of African Americans, 47.1% of Hispanics, and 49.4% of American Indian/Alaska Natives. The dropout rate for students with disabilities by ethnic background is 4.8% of European American students, compared to 14.6% of American Indian/Alaska Native students, 9.9% of African American students, and 18.3% of Hispanic students.
Where are students educated?	• African American students with disabilities are the least likely of any ethnic group to be educated in a general education classroom. Of these students, 49% are educated in separate settings for much of the school day, compared to 38% of European American students. • African American students with disabilities are also more likely than other ethnic groups to be educated in a separate class or separate school setting.
Who is living in poverty?	• Students with disabilities are more likely to be poor than are students in the general population. • About 25% of elementary and secondary students with disabilities live in poverty, compared with 21% of the general population.

overall statistics. Some groups of students are overrepresented in special education. This means that for some demographic groups, the proportion of students identified for special education is higher than the proportion of that group in the general population. Specifically, African American and American Indian/Alaska Native students with disabilities are overrepresented in the learning disability, intellectual disability, and emotional and behavioral disability categories (U.S. Department of Education, 2011). Overrepresentation of these students has been a longstanding issue and concern for special educators (Skiba, Simmons, Ritter, Gibb, Rausch, Cuadrado, & Chung, 2008).

Further complicating this issue are the specific student placements and outcomes for different demographics. The ethnicity or language of a student strongly influences their classroom placement. For example, African American, Hispanic, American Indain/Alaska Native, and ELL students with disabilities are more likely to be taught in separate classrooms or schools than students who are European American or Asian and Pacific Islander (Skiba, Poloni-Staudinger, Gallini, Simmons, & Feggins-Azziz, 2006). Additionally, although all students with disabilities have low graduation rates, Hispanic, American Indian/Alaska Native, and African American students with disabilities have substantially lower gradua- tion rates than do European American students (U.S. Department of Education, 2010). See "Just the Facts" for more information regarding diversity and students with disabilities.

The population of students entering classrooms today differs substantially from students in the 1990s, and this diversity is predicted to further increase in the future. Moreover, the disproportionate number of these students with disabilities necessitates that educators adapt their inclusive classroom practices to meet the particular needs of students from diverse backgrounds. This need becomes especially obvious when examining the low academic achievement levels and the higher-than-expected dropout rates for many of these students, including both those with and without disabilities.

What You Need to Know about Student Diversity and Academic Achievement

As the opening vignette with Melanie Buckley revealed, a significant achievement gap was found at Heritage High School, as a large number of students from diverse backgrounds did not meet performance standards. Unfortunately, this finding is common across many schools. For example, the U.S. Department of Education (NCES, 2010) reports that although the achievement gap has narrowed in reading and mathematics, European American stu- dents continue to score at higher levels than students from Hispanic and African American backgrounds. This is illustrated by the results from the 2009 administration of the California Standards Test, which revealed large differences in student proficiency by subgroup for third- grade students. In English/language arts, 29% of Hispanic and 29% of African American students were rated proficient or better, compared to 63% of European American students (Kids Data, 2009). Similar achievement gaps were found for high school students in math- ematics. Perhaps even more troubling, only 20% of students designated as English-language learners were at or above proficiency.

These gaps also are reflected in the number of students who drop out of school before graduation. For example, in 2008, the percentage of 16- to 24-year-olds who were not en- rolled in school and had not earned a diploma was 4.8% for European American students, 9.9% for African Americans, 18.3% for Hispanics, and 14.6% for American Indian/Alaska Native students (NCES, 2010). Data on students with disabilities' graduation rates reveal that about 52% of these students will graduate from high school with a regular diploma (U.S. Department of Education, 2010). Graduation rates for European American students with disabilities were 61.5%, but were considerably lower for African American (39.2%), Hispanic (47.1%), and American Indian/Alaska Native (49.4%) students.

Poverty also poses a serious challenge to children's potential for success in school. Growing up in poverty can negatively impact children's mental and behavioral development as well as their overall health, which can make it more difficult for them to learn (Darling- Hammond, 2010). As such, the achievement gap is often pronounced for students living in poverty. To illustrate, data from the National Assessment of Educational Progress (NCES, 2010) reveal that students in grades 4 and 8 in high-poverty schools from across the United States score substantially lower in reading and mathematics than do students from low- poverty schools.

Given the diversity that currently exists in classrooms across the United States, no mat- ter where you teach, you will have a diverse range of students in your classroom. If you teach in a state that is highly diverse (e.g., Arizona, California, Florida, Georgia, Hawaii, Louisiana, Maryland, Nevada, New Mexico, and Texas), the majority of your students may well be from diverse backgrounds, including those with disabilities. This level of diversity makes it especially important that all teachers who teach in inclusive classrooms know ef- fective principles and practices for addressing the needs of all students. Although many of the practices that we describe throughout this text will often work well with students from diverse backgrounds, in this chapter we provide descriptions of practices that are especially effective for students from culturally and linguistically diverse backgrounds.

Principles and Practices to Support Effective Instruction

As you may know, the diversity that exists in the student population does not exist in the teaching force. According to data from the National Center for Educational Statistics (2010), the teaching workforce in the United States is largely European American (83%) and female (75%). Furthermore, the percentage of non-European American teachers has increased, but only by about 2% between 1999 and 2008.

This lack of diversity in teacher backgrounds creates a *demographic divide* in many schools. Consider that although 45% of all students are of African American, Hispanic, Asian, and American Indian/Alaska Native descent, only 17% of their teachers are from similar backgrounds (NCES, 2010). This problem is even more extreme in some states, and in many of the nation's largest school systems.

In presenting these data, we do not mean to suggest that teachers from the majority culture cannot successfully teach all students. This is certainly not the case. However, it is important that the teacher workforce include at least a reasonable proportion of teachers who share the cultural and language experiences of their students. These teachers can serve as a rich resource for other teachers and ensure that the diverse backgrounds of students are used to enrich the lives of everyone in the school. Regardless of background, all teachers must bridge the demographic divide by learning about students' backgrounds and experiences, and how these cultural experiences influence student achievement and behavior in school.

How Teachers Establish Connections across the Demographic Divide

A critical issue related to our ability to accept and teach persons from different cultural groups is whether we view differences as typical and acceptable. All too often, many of us perceive difference as a way of dividing people into two groups: those who are typical (similar to me) and those who are atypical (different from me), rather than seeing human variation along a continuum (Baglieri & Knopf, 2004). We view those who are most like us as being within an acceptable range of typical behavior, while those who differ from us in ways we view as important are viewed as atypical (or even "abnormal"). For most people, these perceptions are implicit feelings. Try a little experiment to help you think about your perceptions of "typical" and how hard it is to alter perceptions.

Cross your arms across your chest in the way that you habitually cross them. Notice which arm is on top. Now cross your arms so that the *other* arm is on top. Many people find

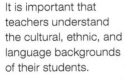

It is important that teachers understand the cultural, ethnic, and language backgrounds of their students.

this so "atypical" that it takes several tries to cross their arms in the nonhabitual way, but there is nothing inherently "typical" about having one's left (or right) arm on top. Yet even when you *know* that there is nothing atypical about the new position, it feels weird. Without deliberate intention, you will habitually return your arms to their accustomed position.

In school, teachers often define "typical" and thus acceptable students as those who come prepared to behave in particular ways and to handle a specific type of academic structure. A number of culturally specific behaviors have been identified that often challenge teachers (Lewis & Doorlag, 2011). Consider whether the following behaviors, which are "typical" behaviors within specific cultural contexts, might seem problematic for you:

- Students talk out, often talking over you or other students in a form of communal participation.
- Students are very reticent to participate, or to ask and answer questions.
- Students come to school or school functions late.

European American, middle-class teachers who have spoken English from birth may expect all students to exhibit behaviors such as taking turns speaking in class, looking teachers in the eye when reprimanded, and asking questions when they don't understand. Yet, each of these behaviors is outside the norm for one or more cultural groups. This can mean that the teacher perceives actions that fall within the norms for a certain student's culture as atypical, and perhaps unacceptable.

These implicit judgments can lead teachers to blame students or their families for lack of success in school, disrupting their connections with students and creating barriers to success. It's important to keep in mind that "what we learn through our culture becomes our reality, and to see beyond that is often difficult" (Chamberlain, 2005, p. 199). *When a teacher's cultural assumptions lead to the conclusion that a student's academic or social behavior is outside the norm of appropriate, the teacher may make well-intended decisions that undermine the student's educational success.*

What Is Culture and Why Is It So Important?

Culture is a concept that helps teachers understand the implicit evaluations they make and the reasons behind some of the student behaviors that "seem" atypical or abnormal. *Culture* has been defined as "the values, traditions, worldview, and social and political relationships created, shared, and transformed by a group of people bound together by a common history, geographic location, language, social class, religion, or other shared identity" (Nieto & Bode, 2008, p. 171). As this definition suggests, culture is dynamic, or changing, and is created or socially constructed by those who participate in it. Culture has also been referred to as an iceberg (Oetzel & Ting-Toomey, 2006). The part that we see and hear on the surface includes such variables as dress, music, food, and language. What is below the surface includes the deeper culture such as traditions, beliefs, values, norms, and worldviews. It is this invisible part of the iceberg that can confuse people as they interact with different cultural groups.

Some Examples of Cultural Norms in School

Culture can influence how students interact in schools, especially students who are new to the United States. Dimensions of culture include styles of communication and interaction, concepts of self, behavioral expectations and management styles, time, and spatial proximity (Oetzel & Ting-Toomey, 2006). It is important to note that cultural dimensions are not characteristics that students either have or don't have but are aspects that fall along a continuum (Salend & Duhaney, 2005). For example, some groups tend toward an *individualist orientation* in their culture and communication style, but others tend toward a *collectivist orientation*. **Individualist cultures** emphasize individual achievement and initiative and promote self-realization (Gudykunst & Kim, 2003). Students in individualist cultures typically are motivated by individual recognition. For such students, the teacher might create a public display of achievement by hanging stellar student work on the wall. A common manifestation of this orientation in schools is the selection of a citizen of the week.

In **collectivist cultures**, working for the common good is more highly valued than individual achievement. Students from collectivist cultures may prefer to work in groups, and each member's contribution is judged "successful" only to the degree that it enhances the whole group. Individual awards, praise, or displays of accomplishment may not motivate individuals from collectivist cultures; instead, they may be motivated by group productivity and accomplishment (Trumbull, Rothstein-Fisch, & Greenfield, 2000). Although cultural groups have tendencies toward individualism or collectivism, these cultural traits fall along a continuum, and all cultures have both individual and collective traits. In addition, individuals within cultures differ with regard to these traits.

Cultural tendencies impact the way students participate in education. Figure 2 describes several classroom situations and some cultural dimensions to consider. This figure will help you see how a teacher might misinterpret the behavior of a student from a diverse culture. Cultural differences may cause educators to inaccurately judge students as poorly behaved or disrespectful. Consider also that as effective professionals, teachers must be culturally responsive and accept responsibility for learning about cultural differences and helping build bridges between home and school cultures. Because cultural

Figure 2	Cultural Perspectives on Education
Classroom Situation	**Cultural Dimensions to Consider**
Cultural Dimension: Styles of Communication	
A student nods his head "yes" when asked in front of the whole class if he understands the solution to the math problem. Yet the student clearly did not understand the concept as he is unable to even successfully complete any problems on an individual practice assignment.	Consider that the student comes from a culture where he would be embarrassed to admit that he did not know the answer. Direct communication and "calling attention" to individuals may not be encouraged. The teacher could wait and ask the student, individually, to show him how to solve the problem or use response cards during small group.
Cultural Dimension: Concept of Self	
Students in a small group are asked to play "Jeopardy" as a way of solving social studies questions. The winner will receive an award and be allowed to choose a toy from the class store. Lucia, a student from the Ukraine, does not attempt to answer any of the questions.	Consider that the student comes from a culture that promotes collaboration and collectivism. The nature of the competition may make this student uncomfortable. The teacher could set up small teams to work together in answering the Jeopardy questions.
Cultural Dimension: Management Style	
A new student arrives from Central America. The teacher uses a lot of cooperative learning strategies in the classroom. The student seems confused and does not want to leave his desk.	Consider that the student came from a class where the teacher lectures and the students' roles are more passive. The teacher can use a buddy system to help the new student adjust to more "open" classroom activities.
Cultural Dimension: Time	
A student arrives to class late and without his notebook. He's visibly upset. His friend offers to let him borrow a notebook, but the student refuses and remains distracted throughout the class period.	Consider that the student comes from a culture that has a monochromic perspective. Time commitments are taken very seriously and so is personal property Borrowing or lending is seen to intrude on privacy.
Cultural Dimension: Proximity	
A new student who speaks very little English is having a problem getting along with the other students. He has fights on the playground every day, which he seems to provoke by constantly touching the other boys.	Consider that the student comes from a culture where it is appropriate to get close in personal space and touch each other. The other students do not feel comfortable with the close proximity and touching and respond with anger. The teacher needs to speak to the students about personal space and encourage students to express their comfort with proximity.

differences are implicit, students may have a great deal of difficulty perceiving that their actions are inconsistent with teacher expectations and may find themselves reprimanded by teachers but fail to understand what they did that caused concern.

Becoming a Culturally Responsive Teacher

Culturally responsive teachers are simultaneously curious about culture and introspective (Irvine, 2003; Stormont, 2007). They know that culture affects people's perceptions, knowledge, and interactions, and that the impact of cultural assumptions is often implicit. These teachers strive to learn more about themselves, what they believe, and how their beliefs and experiences influence their perceptions of and interactions with students and their families.

Cultural background can influence how students interact and work together in school.

Learning about Culture and Difference

No teacher will possess comprehensive knowledge about all of the possible cultures, languages, disabilities, and economic influences on learning. A teacher's underlying curiosity about individuals, culture, and difference is vitally important (Banks et al., 2005). As Melanie Buckley noted in the opening "A View from the Teacher" feature in this text, "All teachers must be culturally aware and culturally responsive. This means they must be cognizant of their students' lives outside of school, actively learning of their varied cultural backgrounds." A teacher who is culturally curious and responsive recognizes that all people are influenced by their background, culture, and experience, and that variations within cultures are as significant as variations across cultures.

While we are all inevitably influenced by our culture, the pervasiveness and dominance of one's own culture (European American, heterosexual, middle-class for a large proportion of teachers) can make certain cultural characteristics invisible to many who have grown up inside that culture. Remember your response to the "Pause & Reflect" exercise that addressed understanding your own background. If you are female, your list may include *sister, friend, sorority member, runner, good student, motivated, strong-willed.* Look back at your list to see if you also listed any descriptive words such as *White, middle class, monolingual, heterosexual, Christian, European American.* Persons from European American, middle-class backgrounds seldom include these terms when describing themselves, suggesting parts of their culture may be invisible to them.

Pause & Reflect

Are certain parts of your culture largely invisible to you or taken for granted? Discuss with a friend or classmate from a different cultural background how this might influence your interactions with friends or your interactions with students in a classroom. Why is it important for a teacher to recognize these aspects of her culture?

Reflecting on Your Beliefs

Working effectively with students from diverse backgrounds requires you to constantly question your reactions to students and their families and to check the human tendency to judge different as atypical and unacceptable. This is difficult to do. Recall how weird it felt to cross your arms in an uncharacteristic way. Even though you know (a cognitive reaction) that there is nothing abnormal about putting the opposite arm on top, it still feels weird (an affective reaction). Suspending judgment and blame means constantly questioning your reactions to determine when cultural difference might be a factor in your interactions with students.

Unfortunately, there are no road signs to tell you when you are likely to encounter a cultural incongruity with students or with parents. Suspending judgment means you constantly scan your environment through a cultural lens, looking for the possibility that culture could explain a challenge you are facing. Additionally, suspending judgment means you question yourself to identify possible stereotypes that might undermine your expectations for students.

Demonstrating Care

Most people become teachers because they care about children and youth. For culturally responsive teachers, care means developing comprehensive knowledge about students and their lives so that you are able to link new learning to prior experience and use students' strengths to build their capacity to achieve (Gay, 2010). It also means being tough when you need to be. Teachers who care treat students with respect, require them to treat others with respect, perceive them as capable, and accept them unconditionally, even as they help them change undesirable behavior (Ross, Bondy, Gallingane, & Hambacher, 2008). To do this requires that you know, understand, and value the particular students you teach each year.

Getting to Know Your Students

Culturally responsive teachers must really *know* their students to teach them effectively. This information is acquired using different strategies. To get to know students, it is important to spend time in their communities, visit homes, interact with families, and attend relevant cultural and family-oriented activities. Even teachers who live outside the community in which they teach find ways to become part of the community. Parents know the teachers and see them in the community, and the teachers know families well enough to know the cultural and experiential resources in students' homes. This has been called knowing the funds of knowledge within students' homes (Gonzalez, Moll, & Amanti, 2005).

Other strategies for learning about students include informal conversations with students and parents, observations of student behavior in different settings (i.e., in the classroom, with peers, and with family), and analysis of students' work. Moreover, it is important to become a student of children's culture. What are their favorite television shows? Movies? Music? Video games? Where do they go, and what do they do after school? What significant events have happened in the community? The more you know about the students and their communities, the greater your capacity to link schoolwork to their background knowledge and experience.

Pause & Reflect

Adopting an asset orientation matters a great deal. Consider how your interactions with a student would be different if you believed the student to be stubborn (a deficiency) versus determined (an asset), wild versus energetic, or whiny versus sensitive? How can we teach ourselves to see assets instead of deficits?

Using an Asset-Oriented Lens

Once you have gotten to know your students, it's important to maintain an "asset-based" view as you teach them (Garcia & Ortiz, 2006). All students present an array of strengths and weaknesses. At times it is challenging to see beyond what students do not know, and take an "asset-based" perspective on the strengths that might be used in teaching them. For example, one teacher encountered a fifth-grade student who had mastered few basic math facts. Previous teachers had tried numerous strategies to get him to learn—urging him to practice, requiring him to complete mad-minute practices, drilling him on flash cards, testing him, providing peer tutoring, and failing him. The teacher learned that the student loved video and computer games and enjoyed being a leader. She used these assets to engage the student as she created a series of games for the Smartboard focused on math facts. As the student worked with the teacher to develop the games and helped to guide others in playing the games, he learned the math facts.

Taking an asset-oriented approach may seem obvious, but it is often not easy. As teachers work to develop an asset orientation, they must spend time investigating students' assets. For example, teachers may learn whether students have significant home responsibilities for younger siblings, if they provide translation assistance for adults in their families, or if they have

It is important that teachers learn about the lives of their students outside of school.

outside jobs or activities. Teachers can then make a list of the skills required to succeed in each academic content area. This type of information helps identify strengths that will be useful in reaching every student.

Becoming a Warm Demander

Research suggests that teachers support the achievement motivation of culturally diverse students by adopting the stance of a *warm demander*. Teachers who are warm demanders are culturally responsive, do not lower their standards, and are viewed as willing to help students (Ware, 2006). See the following "A View from a Teacher" feature for a perspective from warm demander Jan Patterson, an eighth-grade language arts teacher at West Hernando Middle School with a reputation for working successfully with students from diverse backgrounds.

A View from a Teacher

Jan Patterson Embraces the Role of a Warm Demander

Jan Patterson is an eighth-grade language arts and reading teacher at West Hernando Middle School. She has a reputation among her fellow teachers for being demanding, and also for working well with students from diverse backgrounds. We interviewed Ms. Patterson about her approach to teaching, and discovered that her beliefs align well with the characteristics of a warm demander. She is supportive of her students and she treats them respectfully, but she demands that they meet performance expectations for their behavior and academic achievement.

Ms. Patterson began by stating that she looks at "inclusion as affecting every student. They all come in as individuals." She goes on to note that all her students come into her classroom as teachers: "They bring in their culture, and I honor that. If there's a topic going on and it's something that is relevant to a student, then they become a teacher." She describes an example of a student in her class from Haiti who returned to her homeland during the holiday break, and experienced firsthand the devastation from an earthquake. "What a good source of information [she was. Students] have background and experience that none of us will ever have. I tell their parents too, 'You're all teachers. If you have something to bring [into the classroom], please feel free to come in, keep us company, and add to the classroom.'"

There are many other ways in which Ms. Patterson shows respect and warmth for students. For example, she states, "I believe all my students are young adults, so I address them as 'Mr.' and 'Ms.' to show them respect. That applies to all students. How you handle and address that [respect for students] often takes care of the rest of the issues. I respect them all as unique individuals." She also is very supportive of students who need additional assistance to master their academic work. She tells her students, "I'm here on Tuesday, Wednesday, and Thursday after school for tutoring. What we are looking at is skill building, not the grade. You can retake anything you want as many times as you want for full credit. I don't care how many times you want to take that test. Because you're going to eventually master the skills. You take the responsibility of retaking that test, and you need my individual attention, I'm right there for you, my door is always open if you need me."

Clearly respectful and supportive of her students, Ms. Patterson is also steadfastly demanding that they master academic material and behave appropriately. She clearly articulated her "no excuses" perspective when she said, "An adolescent sentence structure is this—Truth, Conjunction, and Excuse. I stop listening at the conjunction. In a nice way, I'm saying, 'Come on, I don't need to hear an excuse.' A student's background is never an excuse for bad behavior or not mastering skills." She goes on to say that in her classroom, a student can't give up. "No! I can't help you if you tell me 'I don't get it' or 'I don't know where to start.' That tells me that you've given up. You can't give up. You need to do this one way or another!"

Ms. Patterson believes in working closely with parents to provide students with support to learn and behave appropriately. "I make a call to their house when they misbehave or don't do their homework. I really believe in having contact with the parents because we're working for the same cause. They want their children to be successful, and so do we. When they do something extremely creative, I also call the house. Why should I deny their parents the opportunity to know what's happening, [so] I call the house!"

According to Ms. Patterson, no matter what the student's background is, everyone must behave appropriately and master academic content in her classroom. Culture or disability or family background is never an excuse. "You still have to do what's required. You still have to do your work. I don't ever want to be in a position where I have to excuse somebody because of who [he or she is]!" She emphasizes with students and their families that she accepts no excuses because her job is to "teach students how to be successful in the real world. You need to understand the power of language, the power of body language, you need to understand people's immediate perceptions of you as an adult."

Ms. Patterson's success with students from a broad range of backgrounds attests to the success of her warm-demander philosophy. Students respect her and the demands that she makes on them, while at the same time they realize that she returns that respect, and will do anything she can to help them succeed.

Research on positive classroom environments (Patrick, Turner, Meyer, & Midgley, 2003), the development of resilience (Benard, 2004), culturally relevant pedagogy (Gay, 2010), and culturally relevant classroom management (Weinstein, Tomlinson-Clarke, & Curran, 2004) reflects many of the perspectives that Jan Patterson shares regarding her role as a warm demander. This research and Jan's comments indicate that there are three characteristics of classroom environments that support academic achievement (Ross et al., 2008): (1) a respectful, caring relationship between students and the teacher; (2) respectful relationships among peers; and (3) clear and high expectations for behavior and achievement. These are consistent with the characteristics of warm demanders.

Care Is the Foundation for the Warm Demander. The foundation of any effective classroom is that students know the teacher cares about them. This is the "warm" part of being a warm demander. Keep in mind the previous discussion of what it means to care. *Warm* doesn't mean being nice, and it isn't about gentle nurturing, which often becomes benign neglect (Gay, 2002). As noted previously, *warm* means the teacher believes in students and cares enough about their futures to create a community where it is safe to take risks, where achievement is valued, where support is provided, and where students are never "let off the hook." Most importantly, it means caring enough to demand that students behave and achieve.

Warm Demanders Create a Respectful Community. Community is a key part of many cultural groups. Within a community, each member's individual needs are met (Gay, 2002). A key task for a culturally responsive teacher is building a community so that it is safe for every student to take the risks necessary to learn. Culturally responsive teachers bring themselves into the classroom and enable students to do the same. To do this, teachers share their families, their interests, and their lives with their students and use structures such as class meetings to enable students to share information and get to know one another. They communicate that respect for others is highly valued by respecting and listening to students and teaching students to respect and listen to one another. As Jan Patterson from West Hernando Middle School noted, all students should be shown respect as unique individuals.

These classrooms are the opposite of a "collection of strangers," a description that unfortunately fits many classrooms. When students are strangers, it is impossible to create a network of caring peers who support one another through learning challenges. In addition, classroom-management problems escalate when students do not know one another. Yet, the significance of creating community is often forgotten, particularly in secondary classrooms. For example, a high school teacher initiated a community-building class meeting with a group of ninth-grade students who were in a transition classroom because of poor performance on the eighth-grade state assessment test. Within two meetings, students began to share personal information, and after the second session, the teacher overheard a student say, "Going to this class is like being in a club." The fact that the student saw this class as so different from his other classes suggests how rare it is that some high school students feel a true sense of belonging.

Warm Demanders Explicitly Teach Classroom Rules, Routines, and Procedures. It is critically important to teach expectations, particularly social skills, in diverse, inclusive classrooms (Harriott & Martin, 2004). This means that culturally responsive teachers *never* assume that students know what is expected. Even when teaching in high school, culturally responsive teachers teach the behaviors they expect students to demonstrate. In fact, explicitly teaching specific rules and procedures is a long-established principle of effective classroom management (Evertson & Emmer, 2009). If rules and procedures are not taught, classroom management can become an escalating sequence of consequences and punishments. The result is the development of a negative, often punitive, classroom environment where many fail to thrive.

The following principle may help you: Assume that students will behave respectfully and appropriately if they know and remember what the teacher expects. Culturally responsive classroom teachers teach their academic and behavioral expectations using multiple strategies (Bondy et al., 2007). These strategies include:

- Stating their expectations
- Providing models and demonstrations
- Providing humorous negative examples
- Requiring student restatement of expectations
- Providing opportunities for practice with feedback
- Repeating instructions as necessary
- Reminding students of and reinforcing appropriate behavior

Protecting the Classroom Community through Teacher Insistence. A key difference between teachers who establish environments that support achievement motivation and those who do not is that effective teachers strategically and respectfully insist that students abide by rules and procedures and that they respect one another and the teacher (Patrick et al., 2003). Yet in their "insistence," effective teachers always preserve the respectful and caring connection to each student. As one middle school student commented, "She's mean out of the kindness of her heart" (Wilson & Corbett, 2001, p. 91). The view that Jan Patterson provided earlier in this chapter reflects this perspective well.

All teachers want their students to abide by classroom rules. Yet, some give multiple "chances" that send inconsistent messages to students. Others become punitive and threatening. These responses undermine the expectation that students must be respectful of one another—the former by allowing disrespectful behavior, and the latter by treating students disrespectfully. Charney (2002) provides guidelines to help teachers say what they mean. In addition to keeping demands simple and short, she directs teachers to clearly communicate what is negotiable and what is not and to remind only twice. An effective "reminder" strategy that she suggests is to ask students to "rewind" when inappropriate behavior surfaces. This gives the student a clear directive and a chance to correct inappropriate behavior but maintains a lighter tone likely to be effective particularly with secondary-level students.

High Expectations: What Does "No Excuses" Really Mean?

We've already noted that culturally responsive teachers convey a belief in the potential of students that enables them to transcend barriers to learning. Enacting this belief requires that teachers view student learning as a puzzle that they are constantly striving to solve (Banks et al., 2005; Corbett et al., 2002). They use a variety of activities and strategies for instruction and work to match their methods to students (Cole, 2001).

Teaching Is Guided by Assessment and a Problem-Solving Approach

Culturally responsive teachers use a continual assessment system to determine who is and who isn't learning. They also constantly search for another way to make learning comprehensible (Gay, 2002). If one way isn't working, they modify instruction and reteach (Garcia & Ortiz, 2006). These are teachers who simply refuse to believe there is any student who cannot be reached, and they actively communicate this belief to students. This belief is a guiding principle of inclusive practice and differentiated instruction.

> The basic premise of differentiated instruction is to systematically plan curriculum and instruction that meets the needs of academically diverse learners by honoring each students' learning needs and maximizing each student's learning capacity. (Van Garderen & Wittacker, 2006, p. 12)

In short, instruction should be culturally responsive for all students in inclusive classrooms. The central theme here is that teaching and learning are not culture free, and therefore student failure should initially be viewed as a mismatch between the school's culture and environment and the student's needs (Garcia & Ortiz, 2006).

Insisting on Completion and Quality

Insistence is just as important in establishing high academic expectations as it is in establishing a respectful learning community. Culturally responsive teachers do not allow students to do less than their best (Corbett et al., 2002). They insist that students complete and revise their work until it meets high standards. In a study of urban middle school students' perspectives about effective teachers, students valued teachers who made them do their work, even when they didn't want to do it (Wilson & Corbett, 2001). Others have made the same point in stressing that important learning inevitably involves struggle (Weinstein, 2002). Effective teachers not only convey that the struggle is important but insist that students persist through barriers and provide them with support until they succeed. They encourage students to try, refuse to allow them to get by with incomplete or sloppy work, give them opportunities to make up work, provide tutoring, make work relevant to students' lives, and reteach using varied strategies until everyone understands and succeeds (Wilson & Corbett, 2001).

Pause & Reflect

Mr. Newsome believes he has high standards. As evidence, he reports that his tenth-grade math students get zeros if they do not turn in homework. He says with pride that he does not just "pass students through." One third of his class got D's or F's last term, and he says, "They earned them." Do these practices suggest that Mr. Newsome has high expectations?

Using a Diverse Curriculum

Motivation to achieve is influenced by factors such as culture, values, and language (Ginsberg, 2005). It also is influenced by the nature of the curriculum. The school curriculum is not culturally neutral. The curriculum as represented in texts, national and state standards, and the experience of most teachers, is a reflection of the European American culture. The school curriculum "promotes its own (a) cultural values, practices and perceptions; (b) psychological, social, economic, and political needs; and (c) elevated status within the larger society" (Hollins, 1996, p. 82).

Teachers should view their curricular materials with a critical eye (Gay, 2002). The text may include a few multicultural historic figures, but that is often not enough. Gay cautions that when the same few figures are taught repeatedly, students learn that their ancestors really did not contribute much. Similarly, she notes that it is inappropriate to focus more attention on African Americans than on other ethnic groups. In addition, the fiction and nonfiction that students read needs to be diverse so that they see their lives and cultures reflected in the characters, setting, and plot of the stories. When students see themselves in their books, they are more likely to enjoy reading, make a connection to literature, and build vocabulary and language skills that assist them academically. To be effective, teachers need "wide ranging knowledge of subject matter content, so that they can construct a curriculum that includes multiple representations addressing the prior experiences of different groups of students" (Banks et al., 2005, p. 251).

Literature is not the only strategy to broaden the curriculum. Teachers should draw on their communities for curricular content and take a risk and teach controversial topics such as ethnicity and poverty (Gay, 2002). Additional strategies for incorporating diversity in the curriculum include

Using material from different cultural groups for instruction can motivate students to learn.

ideas such as teaching thematic units organized around countries or languages; studying and comparing fashion, religious and marriage customs, games, and hair styling from around the world; and subscribing to magazines from around the world that help teachers and students learn about students' cultures and provide possible curricular topics (Jones, 2005).

Summary

This chapter addressed the following topics:

Students from diverse backgrounds: What to expect

- The demographics of public school students are rapidly changing in terms of ethnicity, language, poverty, and disability as classrooms across the United States become more diverse.
- Although about 55% of school-aged students are European American, in 10 states the majority of students are from non-European Americans backgrounds.
- Students with disabilities include students from all ethnicities, language backgrounds, and socioeconomic levels.
- Some groups of students are overrepresented in special education. For example, students who live in poverty and those from ELL backgrounds are more likely to be in special education. African American and American Indian/Alaska Native students are also overrepresented in special education.
- A significant achievement gap exists across students from different ethnic, language, and socioeconomic backgrounds.
- The lack of connection between teachers' and students' background knowledge, experience, and culture (i.e., the demographic divide) is a key contributing factor to this achievement gap.

Principles and practices to support effective instruction

- Culturally responsive teaching is designed to foster resilience in students, improve student outcomes, and enhance the educational futures of students.
- Culturally responsive teachers are those who
  - Study culture and the ways that students differ.
  - Believe that every student has the capacity to succeed.
  - Learn to suspend judgment and blame when interacting with students and families.
  - Show students that they sincerely care about them.
  - Develop depth of knowledge about their students.
  - Develop the skills and stance of a warm demander.
  - Hold students to high expectations.
  - Make the curriculum meaningful.
  - Connect instruction to students' interests and experiences.

Addressing Professional Standards

Standards addressed in this chapter include:

CEC Standards: (1) foundations, (2) development and characteristics of learners, (3) individual learning differences, (4) instructional strategies, (5) learning environments and social interactions, (6) language, (9) professional and ethical practice.

MyEducationLab

Go to the topic Cultural and Linguistic Diversity in the **MyEducationLab** (www .myeducationlab.com) for *Inclusion,* where you can:

- Find learning outcomes for Cultural and Linguistic Diversity, along with the national standards that connect to these outcomes.
- Complete Assignments and Activities that can help you more deeply understand the chapter content.
- Apply and practice your understanding of the core teaching skills identified in the chapter with the Building Teaching Skills and Dispositions learning units.
- Examine challenging situations and cases presented in the IRIS Center Resources.
- Check your comprehension on the content covered in the chapter with the Study Plan. Here you will be able to take a chapter quiz, receive feedback on your answers, and then access Review, Practice, and Enrichment activities to enhance your understanding of chapter content.

Glossary

Collectivist cultures: Cultures in which working for the common good is more highly valued than individual achievement.

Culturally and linguistically diverse (CLD): Backgrounds that are non–European American and, in some instances, non–English speaking, including African American, Hispanic, Native American/ Alaskan Native, and Asian/Pacific Islander.

Culture: The values, beliefs, traditions, and behaviors associated with a particular group of people who share a common history.

English-language learner (ELL): Includes students who are learning English as a second language or those previously called students with limited English proficiency.

Ethnic group: A group in which individual members identify with one another, usually based on ancestry. Ethnic groups often share common practices related to factors such as culture, religion, and language.

Funds of knowledge: The cultural and experiential resources within a student's home that a culturally responsive teacher may use to provide effective, successful curriculum and instruction.

Individualist cultures: Cultures that value individual achievement and initiative and promote self-realization.

Standard English: A controversial term that is most often used to refer to the dialect of English spoken by educated people.

EFFECTIVE PRACTICES FOR STUDENTS FROM DIVERSE BACKGROUNDS

Putting It All Together

No matter where the school, almost all teachers in the United States have a diverse range of students in their classrooms. Although many of the evidenced-based practices that we discuss throughout this text are effective with these students, they often need more than this. Several considerations to keep in mind when working with students from diverse backgrounds include:

1. **Know yourself.** To work effectively with students from different cultural backgrounds, you must be intimately aware of your own cultural background, and how this background influences your expectations of students in your classroom. Most teachers take for granted that they understand their cultural backgrounds, but evidence from classrooms reveals that this is all too often not the case.

2. **Know your students.** Throughout this text, we've emphasized the need to get to know your students' academic and social-behavioral strengths and weaknesses. This is especially important when teaching students from diverse backgrounds. Get to know them personally, including information about their family background, cultural experiences, and interests.

3. **Use this knowledge.** Knowing your students' backgrounds can provide many benefits for an effective teacher in an inclusive classroom. This knowledge helps build rapport with students, and conveys to students that you value and care about them. This information can also be used as a foundation for instructional experiences in class, and improves the likelihood that students will be engaged in these activities.

4. **Keep learning about all your students.** Although in this chapter we have emphasized students from culturally diverse backgrounds, it is also important to apply these principles to *all* students in your classroom. All students benefit from teachers who are warm demanders—teachers who care about them, respect them, provide them with needed supports, and demand success from them.

In the remainder of this chapter, we describe five effective strategies to help you meet the needs of students from culturally and linguistically diverse backgrounds. The *Strategy Fact Sheet* summarizes these strategies.

Strategy Fact Sheet

STRATEGY	DESCRIPTION	SPECIAL CONSIDERATIONS
Strategy 1: Culturally Responsive Teaching	Culturally responsive teaching involves providing supports to students from culturally and linguistically diverse backgrounds to make sure they are active participants in the academic and social communities of the school, and have a successful school experience.	All too often, an achievement gap exists between students from CLD backgrounds and their European American peers. Culturally responsive teaching is needed to address this gap and improve academic outcomes for students from CLD backgrounds.
Strategy 2: Teaching Reading to Students who are English-Language Learners (ELLs)	Research has identified five components of instruction that lead to improved reading outcomes for students who are English-language learners.	Many students who are English-language learners lag behind their peers in learning to read. As part of this instruction, it is important to focus on developing academic language or the language of schools.
Strategy 3: Highly Effective Instructional Practices for Students from CLD Backgrounds	Highly effective instructional practices have been identified that ensure that students from CLD and high poverty backgrounds do not continue to fall further behind in learning the skills needed for school success.	Closing the achievement gap for students from CLD and high poverty backgrounds should have a positive impact on dropout rates, and should also reduce discipline referrals for many students.

(Continued)

STRATEGY	DESCRIPTION	SPECIAL CONSIDERATIONS
Strategy 4: Culturally Responsive Classroom Management	Expectations for appropriate behavior are often influenced by culture. A cultural divide between teachers and their students makes this problem even worse. To address this issue requires the use of culturally responsive forms of classroom management.	The achievement gap for many students from CLD backgrounds is significantly influenced by a discipline gap, as students from diverse backgrounds are more frequently subjected to school disciplinary sanctions. Culturally responsive classroom management can be effective in reducing this discipline gap as well as improving achievement.
Strategy 5: Double-Check: A Culturally Responsive Approach to Classroom Management	Double-check is a framework to support teachers in delivering culturally responsive classroom management. This approach uses evidence-based components to address culturally responsive practices in the classroom.	Professionals agree that there is a need to provide more culturally responsive approaches to classroom management, but few alternatives are available. The Double-check framework begins to address this need.

CULTURALLY RESPONSIVE TEACHING

Rationale

As you learned earlier in this chapter, an achievement gap exists in reading and math between students from culturally and linguistically diverse backgrounds (including students who are African American, Hispanic, and American Indian/Alaska Natives) and European American students (NCES, 2010). Although this gap has narrowed in recent years, it remains substantial. Providing instruction to students from CLD backgrounds that significantly improves achievement has proven to be more difficult than many expected. To effectively address the needs of students from CLD backgrounds, teachers must be responsive to students' cultural and linguistic backgrounds, and adapt their instruction based on this information. Furthermore, culturally responsive teachers must provide supports to students from CLD backgrounds to make sure that they are active participants in the academic and social communities of the school (Gay, 2010; Sheets, 2005).

Step-by-Step

Culturally responsive teaching is designed to improve the achievement of all students in a learner-centered, culturally supported context that recognizes student strengths and uses these strengths to improve achievement (Richards, Brown, & Forde, 2006). Recent research has identified critical components of effective instruction in culturally responsive classrooms (Cartledge & Kourea, 2008).

1 *Identify and address the academic needs of CLD students.* Evidence indicates that many students from CLD backgrounds begin school behind their European American counterparts (NCES, 2010). These differences are often greatest among students from low socioeconomic backgrounds. This suggests the importance of a sense of urgency in identifying areas of academic weakness as early as possible, and intervening with intensive instruction to ensure that academic deficits do not increase (Cartledge & Kourea, 2008). More specifically, when high-quality instruction is delivered to small groups of three to five students who have similar needs for short periods of time, evidence reveals that this instruction often significantly reduces the achievement gap, and may prevent the labeling of students with disabilities (Cartledge, Gardner, & Ford, 2009; Fletcher et al. 2007; Torgesen, 2009).

2 *Provide frequent academic monitoring.* Given the difficulty professionals have had in closing the achievement gap for students from CLD backgrounds, it is especially important to monitor student academic progress often (Cartledge & Kourea, 2008). For example, curriculum-based measures (Deno, 2007) should be used to determine student skill development in reading and mathematics as they begin school. For students who have areas of weakness, more intensive instruction should be provided to address these needs, and student progress should be frequently monitored using curriculum-based measures to determine whether the student's academic progress is accelerating. Providing tiers of increasingly focused, intensive instruction for students who do not make sufficient academic progress has been shown to be highly effective in improving academic outcomes for students from CLD backgrounds in reading (Torgesen, 2009) and math (Fuchs, Fuchs, Craddock, et al., 2008).

3 *Engage students in a high level of academic responding.* An academic achievement gap exists between students from CLD backgrounds and their European American peers at least in part because CLD students lack opportunities for active academic responding in most classrooms (Cartledge & Kourea, 2008). Furthermore, for many students from culturally and linguistically diverse backgrounds, learning is not just cognitive and technical; it is also active and emotional (Gay, 2010). Thus, instruction should often reflect novelty, variability, and active participation. To support active student engagement, the following strategies should be considered (Boykin & Bailey, 2000).

- Use movement that is expressive and purposeful.
- Encourage open expression of thoughts, ideas, and emotions.
- Use activities that encourage or support high levels of physical stimulation.

- Use music, dance, and rhythm when teaching academic tasks.
- Include multiple stimuli and activities when teaching.
- Use cultural practices originating in the home as part of academic tasks.
- Encourage student bonding or interconnectedness.

4 *Use an appropriate pace of instruction.* Instructional pace relates to the speed at which academic information is presented. Obviously, a faster pace influences the amount of content that is covered in a class, allowing more opportunities to learn. This is an important consideration for students from CLD backgrounds who may have had more limited opportunities to learn academic content than their European American peers. A brisk academic pace also is more likely to keep students actively engaged and reduce off-task and disruptive behavior (Cartledge & Kourea, 2008). Thus, use a brisk pace of instruction whenever possible. It is important to note that the effectiveness of a brisk pace is dependent on the provision of high-quality instruction that is carefully planned and structured. In addition, this type of instruction provides the opportunity to build on cultural themes that relate to improved instruction for students from CLD backgrounds, including active engagement and movement as part of instruction, and having students engage in more than one task simultaneously (Boykin, Tyler, & Miller, 2005).

5 *Develop a community of learners to support the learning of all students.* A key component of culturally responsive instruction is the development of a supportive learning environment that employs a community of learners to support the learning of all students. Such a learning environment has been shown to be effective in working with students from a wide range of cultural backgrounds. As Gay (2010) noted, "Underlying values of human connectedness and collaborative problem solving are high priorities in the cultures of most groups of color in the United States" (p. 187). Thus, developing a learning community and actively engaging students in working with one another is especially effective for students from cultural groups that emphasize a collectivist or communal orientation (Boykin, Tyler, & Miller, 2005).

Involving students in their own learning using strategies such as cooperative learning and peer tutoring are approaches that may be used to develop a community of learners. For example, research has shown that peer tutoring improves student motivation, creates more opportunities for teacher–student interactions, provides a framework that teaches students that they need to work collaboratively to meet instructional goals, increases student engaged time, and often results in significantly improved academic outcomes for students from CLD backgrounds (Cartledge & Kourea, 2008).

Applications and Examples

When cooperative groups are used in classrooms, teachers often control the groups by determining group membership, assigning roles to group members (leader, note-taker), and encouraging competition within and across groups (Sheets, 2005). When this occurs, the cohesiveness and engagement of cooperative groups is decreased. A collaborative approach should be used when students work cooperatively in small groups. This approach enhances group responsibility, focuses participation more on learning and sharing, and results in a process that is more natural and communal. To prepare students for collaborative group work, teachers attend to the following (Sheets, 2005):

- Keep competition to a minimum.
- Focus responsibility for the learning of all group members on the group.
- Provide for self-selection of group members by students.
- Encourage students to develop social bonds.
- Work to ensure that students equally participate in group activities.
- Support students in developing communication, negotiation, problem solving, and self-evaluation skills.
- Employ some open-ended learning activities.

Keep in Mind

As we have noted previously, a demographic (or cultural) divide often exists between teachers and their students. Given the diverse range of students that currently are in classrooms in most parts of the United States, it is important that all teachers develop their knowledge and skills to provide more culturally responsive instruction. Several activities that may be useful in this regard include (Richards, Brown, & Forde, 2006):

- *Learn about the experiences and history of persons from CLD groups.* This provides perspective on how different historical experiences have influenced attitudes and values of different groups. This type of activity also will allow teachers to begin to see how their values differ from those of other cultural groups. This learning can be facilitated by interacting with members of cultural groups, or by reading literature written by member of a cultural group.
- *Visit students' families and communities.* This activity helps teachers get to know their students as part of their cultural world outside of school. More specifically, it helps teachers develop the perspective that a student is not just another person in the classroom, but is part of a complex social and cultural network that likely has a significant influence on the student's attitudes and values.
- *Read about teachers who have been successful working in diverse settings.* Books, articles, blogs, or other writing by these teachers can provide insight into effective, culturally responsive methods (e.g., see Codell, 2009; Esquith, 2007). To learn even more, visiting the classroom of a teacher who has been highly successful working with students from CLD backgrounds can provide firsthand knowledge of how culturally responsive instruction is provided.
- *Develop an appreciation of diversity.* To be effective in a culturally diverse setting, a teacher must come to view differences as a typical part of society, and actively reject the notion that any one group is more competent than another. To do this, teachers might examine their affiliations with different groups (e.g., gender, ethnicity) and the advantages or disadvantages that come from this membership. Developing an appreciation of diversity results in a respect for differences, and provides a clear understanding regarding why it is important to teach from this perspective. The key to this understanding will likely be the realization that the teacher's views of the world are not the only views, and cannot always be the most important views.

Key References

Cartledge, G., Gardner, R., & Ford, D. (2009). *Diverse learners with exceptionalities: Culturally responsive teaching in the inclusive classroom.* Upper Saddle River, NJ: Pearson Education.

Cartledge, G., & Kourea, L. (2008). Culturally responsive classrooms for culturally diverse students with and at risk for disabilities. *Exceptional Children, 74*(3), 351–371.

Gay, G. (2010). *Culturally responsive teaching: Theory, research, and practice.* New York: Teachers College Press.

Richards, H., Brown, A., & Forde, T. (2006). *Addressing diversity in schools: Culturally responsive pedagogy.* Tempe, AZ: National Center for Culturally Responsive Educational Systems, Arizona State University.

Sheets, R. H. (2005). *Diversity pedagogy.* Upper Saddle River, NJ: Pearson Education.

| Strategy 2 | **TEACHING READING TO STUDENTS WHO ARE ENGLISH-LANGUAGE LEARNERS (ELLS)** |

Rationale

Many students who are English-language learners lag behind those who are not ELL in the development of reading skills. Although this achievement gap has narrowed in recent years (NCES, 2010), it remains substantial. Fortunately, evidence now exists to shed some light on instructional methods that are most likely to increase reading achievement levels for English-language learners at the elementary level (Gersten et al., 2007; Kamps et al., 2007). This research has identified five components of reading instruction that are particularly important for teaching reading to students from ELL backgrounds.

Step-by-Step

1 *Assess students who are English-language learners using English-language measures on the components of early reading instruction (i.e., phonological awareness, alphabetic knowledge, reading words, and reading text).* As with other students who struggle with learning to read, curriculum-based measures should be used to (a) screen for reading problems, (b) assess reading skills, and (c) monitor reading progress over time. The same measures can be used with students who are native English speakers and those who are English-language learners, and the same standards or performance benchmarks can be used for both groups.

2 *Provide explicit, direct instruction to students who are at risk for reading problems in the five core areas of beginning reading (i.e., phonological awareness, phonics, reading fluency, vocabulary, and comprehension).* Areas of focus for the instruction should be determined by assessment measures, and intensive instruction should be provided to small groups of students who have similar educational needs. Provide this small group instruction daily for at least 30 minutes in groups of three to five students. Consider intervention programs such as Read Well (Sprick, Howard, & Fidanque, 1998) or SRA Reading Mastery (Engelmann & Bruner, 2003) to deliver this instruction. These programs may be used as a central component of reading instruction for 30 to 50 minutes of intensive, small-group instruction per day, as both employ the principles of direct, explicit instruction and address core areas of beginning reading instruction.

3 *Throughout the school day, provide students high-quality vocabulary instruction.* This should include in-depth instruction related to content words that are frequently used as part of instruction. Ideally, these words should be from the student's reading program, and from texts used in other content areas (i.e., mathematics, science, social studies). Use instructional time to teach the meanings of common or everyday English words, phrases, and expressions that are known to most students who are native English speakers, but that ELL students may not have yet learned.

4 *Provide students with support to develop formal or academic English, especially related to reading and mathematics.* Daily English instruction should be part of the core curriculum at the earliest grades, preferably for a specified block of time each day. This instruction should begin before students learn to read and write, and should be focused on the development of age-appropriate English morphology, syntax, and vocabulary. Focus this instruction on the use of appropriate verb tense, plurals, and the use of adverbs and adjectives. Offer opportunities to practice these features of English in natural, meaningful contexts of oral and written communication, and in a range of situations (e.g., describing events, summarizing content, telling stories).

5 *Have students work in pairs for approximately 90 minutes a week.* Use these activities to allow students the opportunity to practice and extend material already taught. Students at different levels of academic ability should be paired, or at different levels of English proficiency. Peer-assisted strategies such as class-wide peer tutoring (CWPT) (Greenwood, Arreaga-Mayer, Utley, Gavin, & Terry, 2001) and peer-assisted learning strategies (PALS) (Saenz, Fuchs, & Fuchs, 2005) have been demonstrated as effective with students across a range of age levels and content areas.

These strategies may be used with English-language learners for instruction related to basic skills in reading and language, or for older students to provide feedback regarding vocabulary and comprehension. Students may also work in pairs to support English-language development. For example, students could work together reading text, and discussing this text using a structured format (e.g., practice summarizing the text with feedback).

Applications and Examples

Vocabulary instruction for students from ELL backgrounds should be more explicit and structured than instruction that is typically provided in general education classrooms (Gersten et al., 2007). Furthermore, the goal of this instruction is to provide students with an understanding of words so that this vocabulary can be used in natural communication and as a basis for further language learning. Vocabulary instruction for students from ELL backgrounds should be intense and rich. It should also:

- Include multiple exposures to the selected vocabulary words over time, and across opportunities to read, write, and speak.
- Place an emphasis on definitions that are student friendly.
- Engage students in the use of word meanings in natural contexts related to reading, writing, speaking, and listening.
- Include regular review across these contexts.

Keep in Mind

Many potential barriers may impede the use of effective strategies for teaching ELL students. Some particular barriers to keep in mind include:

- Some teachers believe that reading problems may resolve themselves after oral language proficiency is attained by ELL students.
- Some instruction focuses too much on what is tested, and too little on vocabulary development and comprehension.
- Teachers may not be comfortable identifying students for additional reading instruction if the student's English-language skills are low.
- Developing a grade-level or building-level schedule to deliver the instruction needed by ELL students may be difficult, and requires the involvement of all teachers and administrators.

For additional information regarding these and other barriers to providing instruction to ELL students in reading and English language instruction, see Gersten and colleagues (2007), which is available from the U.S. Department of Education, Institute for Education Sciences as part of their "Practice Guides" series at http://ies.ed.gov/ncee/wwc/publications/practiceguides/.

Key References

August, D., & Siegel, L. (2006). Literacy instruction for language-minority children in special education settings. In D. August & T. Shanahan (Eds.), *Developing literacy in second-language learners: Report of the National Literacy Panel on Language-Minority Children and Youth* (pp. 523–553). Mahwah, NJ: Erlbaum.

Gersten, R., Baker, S., Shanahan, T., Linan-Thompson, S., Collins, P., & Scarcella, R. (2007). *Effective literacy and English language instruction for English learners in the elementary grades.* NCEE-2007-4011. Washington, DC: U.S. Department of Education-Institute for Education Sciences.

Greenwood, C., Arreaga-Mayer, C., Utley, C., Gavin, K., & Terry, B. (2001). Classwide Peer Tutoring learning management system: Applications with elementary-level English language learners. *Remedial and Special Education, 22*(1), 34–47.

Kamps, D., Abbott, M., Greenwood, C., Arreaga-Mayer, C., Wills, H., Longstaff, J., Culpepper, M., & Waiton, C. (2007). Use of evidence-based, small-group reading instruction for English language learners in elementary grades: Secondary-tier intervention. *Learning Disability Quarterly, 30*(3), 153–168.

Vaughn, S., & Linan-Thompson, S. (2007). *Research-based methods of reading instruction for English language learners, grades K–4.* Alexandria, VA: ASCD.

HIGHLY EFFECTIVE INSTRUCTIONAL PRACTICES FOR STUDENTS FROM CLD BACKGROUNDS

Rationale

Highly effective instructional practices are needed to ensure that students from CLD backgrounds do not continue to fall further behind in learning basic skills that are needed for school success. Several research-based practices have been identified that are particularly effective for students from CLD and high-poverty backgrounds (Borich, 2011; Cartledge, Gardner, & Ford, 2009). Using these practices should result in many benefits for students from CLD backgrounds. For example, narrowing of the achievement gap should have a significant and positive influence on student dropout rates, and should reduce discipline referrals for many students (Gregory, Skiba, & Noguera, 2010).

Step-by-Step

1 *Ensure that the qualities of effective instruction are used to guide classroom instruction.* Although many research-based practices have been shown to work with students across cultural and language groups, some practices are particularly effective, given the diverse backgrounds and life experiences of many students from CLD backgrounds. Borich (2011) recommends the following practices as particularly effective for students from high-poverty backgrounds.

- Use progress monitoring to ensure that students are learning the material and making adequate academic progress. Charts and graphs should be used to illustrate the progress that is being made by the student.
- Begin by teaching the most concrete information, then move to applications of this information, followed by teaching patterns and abstractions.
- Provide immediate assistance to students who indicate a need for help in the classroom. The use of peer assistants or peer tutoring may be useful in providing this assistance.
- Provide time for practice with feedback immediately after material has been learned.
- Plan transitions from one activity to another in advance, to maintain the structure and flow of activities and to maintain momentum.

2 *Provide appropriate praise.* Much research evidence has documented that teachers are less likely to praise low-achieving students for their academic performance, and are more likely to praise those achieving at high levels (Rodriguez & Bellanca, 2007). Furthermore, teachers tend to give fewer reasons for praise to low achievers, with typical responses such as "OK" or "Good job." Teachers should provide praise to low-achieving students when they make significant progress, especially when the student fails to recognize this progress. This praise should be natural, sincere, private, and focused on a specific accomplishment (Rodriguez & Bellanca, 2007).

As students are receiving high levels of intensive instruction in the classroom, provide both praise for student progress, as well as corrective feedback for responses that are incorrect. High levels of academic responding are worthwhile only if students receive feedback to correct inaccurate responses, preventing continued practice of incorrect responses (Rodriguez & Bellanca, 2007). Provide feedback by using a graph of the student's progress, which can be reinforcing and instructive for the student, especially when corrective feedback is provided (Cartledge & Kourea, 2008).

3 *Treat students respectfully.* Research has shown that teachers tend to be less respectful and courteous to low-achieving students, yet demand respect from these students (Rodriguez & Bellanca, 2007). These negative teacher behaviors often consist of sarcasm, put-downs, and interruption of student responses in class. These behaviors tend to produce a group of "low-status" students in the classroom, reduce the students' interest in academic content, and may lead to behavior problems as students express frustration over their low status. Furthermore, when a teacher engages in these behaviors, higher-achieving students who receive more respectful treatment are likely to model the teacher's behavior toward these so-called low-status students.

In contrast to a classroom that produces a group of low-status students, research from a range of sources has shown the power of culturally responsive caring in the classroom (Gay, 2010). When teachers take this approach, all students are valued and treated with respect and courtesy, and teachers are characterized as warm demanders (Ross et al., 2008). These teachers develop a respectful relationship with students, ensure that students treat one another respectfully, develop a task-oriented environment in the classroom, and have clear and high expectations for all students. In short, they are caring for all students, while also demanding high levels of achievement from all students.

④ *Ensure that students are asked high-level questions and are engaged in high-level material.* Students who are perceived by teachers as low performing are often asked low-level, factual questions during classroom discussions, but students perceived as higher performing are asked questions that require the application and evaluation of ideas (Rodriguez & Bellanca, 2007). Asking high-level questions has been shown to improve students' critical thinking and formation of concepts (Borich, 2011).

Teachers who successfully use questions to facilitate discussion in diverse, inclusive classrooms provide an appropriate wait-time for a student response to a question. Rather than expecting an immediate response, effective teachers wait at least 2 to 3 seconds, or more, and don't immediately respond to questions or add additional questions (Rodriguez & Bellanca, 2007). Increase the effectiveness of questions in facilitating discussions by having students engage in discussions in settings that are similar to their sociocultural experiences. For example, some students are more comfortable responding to questions and engaging in discussions in small groups with informal structures (Borich, 2011).

Research has shown that teachers tend to call on high-achieving students more often than they call on low-achieving students (Rodriguez & Bellanca, 2007). This research has also revealed that teachers tend to call on students in the front row and in seats toward the middle of the classroom more often than they call on students in the back of the room. To address this issue, monitor your behavior to ensure that questions are equally distributed across all students in the classroom, thus ensuring that all students have the opportunity to engage in high-level classroom discussions.

⑤ *Provide opportunities for student self-regulation.* To achieve academic success, all students benefit from activities that are self-directed. These activities tend to increase the confidence of students, and improve student motivation, especially for students from diverse backgrounds (Borich, 2011; Rodriguez & Bellanca, 2007). Self-regulated strategies have been developed for teaching students mathematics (Montague, 2008) and writing (Mason, Harris, & Graham, 2011).

Strategies that may be used to promote self-regulated instruction for students from CLD backgrounds include (Borich, 2011):

- *Provide the student with a choice regarding learning activities.* When students pursue topics on their own, they will often choose topics that are culturally relevant. In addition, these activities allow students to construct their own meaning and interpretations related to classroom activities, as they participate in and direct their own learning.
- *Use challenging problems for instruction.* These problems should be focused so that the student must make decisions regarding what is important for a solution. This allows the student to have control over problem solving, and provides an opportunity to see learning as self-directed.
- *Include problems from the real world that require problem solving.* This allows learners to become investigators in their communities as they solve actual problems. As students engage in these activities, they must apply classroom knowledge to a practical problem, thus increasing their interest in the problem while reinforcing information they have learned.
- *Use group activities to support self-directed instruction.* These group activities may add to the comfort level of some students as they begin to engage in self-directed learning. Furthermore, working in groups allows students the opportunity to gain information from others, and then create new or unusual variations on this knowledge that can be applied during self-directed learning.

Applications and Examples

One approach that can be used to develop self-directed learning for students from CLD backgrounds is cooperative learning. This approach to learning has been shown to be effective for students from a range of culture and language backgrounds (Gay, 2010). However, when students work in cooperative groups, it becomes obvious that there is great variety among students with regard to independence, persistence, and flexibility (Borich, 2011). These characteristics are influenced, at least to some degree, by a student's cultural background, and may influence the quality of each student's participation in a cooperative group (Gay, 2010). To ensure that all students engage in high-quality activities in cooperative groups, teachers should attend closely to students who need more structure (i.e., shorter attention span, tend to ask fewer questions), and those who need less structure (i.e., enjoy discussion, want to solve problems). Teachers should also monitor student persistence in working on activities and flexibility in working with others to solve problems (Borich, 2011). Adjusting the cooperative group structure and process to accommodate student preferences ensures that all students are actively engaged in these groups, and learn to work well with others who may have different approaches to learning.

Keep in Mind

A key consideration for teachers when using effective instructional strategies to improve educational outcomes for students from diverse backgrounds relates to teacher expectations. Research has revealed that teachers may have low expectations for academic success for students who are from CLD backgrounds, those from high-poverty backgrounds, students with disabilities, and students who have not achieved at expected levels in the past. Teachers who have these low expectations tend to hold on to them tenaciously, and, as might be expected, these low expectations influence the quality of learning opportunities that are provided to certain students (Gay, 2010). Recent research reveals that a combination of high expectations and high-quality instruction can significantly increase academic achievement levels for many of these students (Borich, 2011; Gay, 2010; Rodriguez & Bellanca, 2007; Torgesen, 2009). Thus, it is important that all teachers closely examine their expectations for student success, and adjust low expectations so that *all* students are given an equitable opportunity to receive high-quality instruction and achieve at a high level.

Key References

Borich, G. (2011). *Effective teaching methods: Research-based practices* (7th ed.). Upper Saddle River, NJ: Pearson Education.

Cartledge, G., Gardner, R., & Ford, D. (2009). *Diverse learners with exceptionalities: Culturally responsive teaching in the inclusive classroom.* Upper Saddle River, NJ: Pearson Education.

Cartledge, G., & Kourea, L. (2008). Culturally responsive classrooms for culturally diverse students with and at risk for disabilities. *Exceptional Children, 74*(3), 351–371.

Gay, G. (2010). *Culturally responsive teaching: Theory, research, and practice.* New York: Teachers College Press.

Rodriguez, E., & Bellanca, J. (2007). *What is it about me you can't teach? An instructional guide for the urban educator.* Thousand Oaks, CA: Corwin Press.

| Strategy 4 | **CULTURALLY RESPONSIVE CLASSROOM MANAGEMENT** |

Rationale

The achievement gap that exists for many students from diverse backgrounds may be significantly influenced by a discipline gap; that is, students from diverse backgrounds are more frequently subjected to school disciplinary sanctions, including removal from the classroom or school (Gregory, Skiba, & Noguera, 2010; Wallace, Goodkind, Wallace, & Bachman, 2008). This discipline gap is likely influenced by the demographic divide that exists between teachers and many of their students, who often are from different cultural backgrounds that reflect different expectations for student behavior (Cartledge, Gardner, & Ford, 2009; Gay, 2010; Weinstein, Curran, & Tomlinson-Clarke, 2003). These differences become a problem at times because expectations for appropriate behavior are often influenced by culture, "and conflicts are likely to occur when teachers and students come from different cultural backgrounds" (Weinstein, Tomlinson-Clarke, & Curran, 2004, p. 26). Culturally responsive classroom management is needed to reduce the discipline gap and provide a more equitable classroom experience for students from CLD backgrounds.

Step-by-Step

Culturally responsive classroom management is designed to create a setting in which student behavior is appropriate—not because of fear of punishment or a desire for a reward, but because students have a sense of personal responsibility (Weinstein, Tomlinson-Clarke, & Curran, 2004). The teacher therefore places an emphasis on teaching students to make good decisions about their behavior, rather than emphasizing an overreliance on external control. Research provides support for several key components of culturally responsive classroom management (Cartledge & Kourea, 2008; Weinstein, Curran, & Tomlinson-Clarke, 2003; Weinstein, Tomlinson-Clarke, & Curran, 2004).

1. *Recognize your own biases and ethnocentrism (Weinstein, Curran, & Tomlinson-Clarke, 2003; Weinstein, Tomlinson-Clarke, & Curran, 2004).* We are all cultural beings who have assumptions, beliefs, and biases related to human behavior. It is critical that teachers recognize that cultural differences exist, and that schools often reflect some of these biases. More specifically, schools most often adopt a European American, middle-class worldview that influences how most classrooms operate (i.e., placing an emphasis on efficiency, independence, and individual achievement). By examining your own cultural, ethnic, and socioeconomic class biases, you are much less likely to misinterpret the behavior of students from different cultural backgrounds and treat them inequitably.

2. *Be aware of and knowledgeable about the cultural backgrounds and related behavior patterns of your students (Weinstein, Curran, & Tomlinson-Clarke, 2003;* *Weinstein, Tomlinson-Clarke, & Curran, 2004).* Many classrooms include students from a range of cultural backgrounds. At least some of these students are likely to have patterns of behaviors and beliefs that vary from the expectations in a typical classroom. For example, Delpit (1995) has pointed out that many African American students from working-class families are accustomed to experiencing very direct language from authority figures (e.g., "Sit in your seat and get to work"), rather than the indirect, or polite language that is often used in classrooms (e.g., "Are you ready to get in your seat and get to work?"). Teachers can learn about students' backgrounds and gain valuable information that informs culturally responsive classroom management by learning about (a) the experiences and history of persons from CLD backgrounds; (b) students' families and communities; (c) interpersonal relationship styles and discipline practices; and (d) cultural conceptions of time and space (e.g., how students think about punctuality).

3. *Establish clear expectations for behavior (Cartledge & Kourea, 2008; Weinstein, Curran, & Tomlinson-Clarke, 2003; Weinstein, Tomlinson-Clarke, & Curran, 2004).* As we noted previously, different cultures may have different views regarding appropriate behavior. For example, in some cultures, making eye contact is a sign of respect for authority figures, yet in other cultures, averting the eyes is viewed as more appropriate. In many classrooms, teachers expect students to sit and listen while others speak. This expectation may be inadvertently disregarded by some African American students who are more accustomed to being active participants by using a call-response pattern of interaction. When using

this interaction style, there are frequent interactions between the speaker and others (e.g., responses are often provided when the speaker makes statements).

It is important to note that when a mismatch occurs between a student's cultural background and classroom rules, the teacher must make a decision regarding whether or not this difference should be accommodated. This practice of mutual accommodation (Nieto & Bode, 2008) suggests that at times teachers should adjust rules based on students' cultural backgrounds, while at other times they should maintain rules that are needed to meet the requirements of school (e.g., attendance, punctuality, homework completion), and that are important to ensure academic progress and success.

Any good classroom management system is built on clear rules for behavior that students from all cultural groups understand. Typically, classrooms have three to six rules that are stated in a positive way (e.g., "follow teacher directions," "complete assignments on time") and are associated with success in the classroom. To ensure that students understand and have ownership for the rules, the teacher and students should develop these rules collaboratively. Students should also be engaged in discussions regarding the rules, and opportunities should be provided for modeling and practice to ensure understanding.

④ *Organize the classroom to support culturally responsive practices (Weinstein, Curran, & Tomlinson-Clarke, 2003).* The physical environment of the classroom can be used to convey respect for cultural diversity. This may be done in many ways, including the following:

- Display a map of the world that highlights students' countries of origin.
- Use different languages on signs and posters in the classroom that welcome students.
- Depict persons from different cultural groups in pictures that are displayed.

- Emphasize literature from different cultures, and ensure that books promoting diversity are prominently displayed.

The physical environment of the classroom can also be used to affirm connectedness among students and a sense of community that accepts and supports all students. For example, arranging desks in clusters that allow students to work together, engage in discussions, share materials, and assist one another on academic tasks can be done to facilitate the connectedness among students and the development of a sense of community.

⑤ *Create a caring setting (Cartledge & Kourea, 2008; Weinstein, Curran, & Tomlinson-Clarke, 2003).* In any classroom, management of student behavior is more successful when a climate of trust, respect, and caring is developed. This is especially important when students are from a different cultural background than the teacher. Developing a sense of community within the classroom can be an important component of a caring classroom. Teachers can begin to develop a sense of classroom community by having students explore how they are similar and different. Other activities such as morning meetings and cooperative learning activities allow students to get to know one another better and highlight students' unique backgrounds and abilities.

The teacher can play a key role in developing a sense of caring and respect for others within the classroom by engaging in activities that model these behaviors. This can be done by (a) greeting students in their native language and having other students learn words or phrases in this language; (b) modeling respect for diversity by including examples from different cultures in instructional activities; and (c) taking on the role of a warm demander (Ross et al., 2008) by not only caring for the students but also having high expectations and holding students accountable for their behavior and the quality of their work.

Applications and Examples

A critical element of culturally responsive classroom management is fairness (Cartledge & Kourea, 2008). There are many ways teachers can ensure fairness in a culturally diverse classroom. One important consideration is to ensure that behavioral consequences match any violation of rules that may occur, and are not viewed by students as an overreaction to an infraction. Another critical consideration is that disciplinary actions should not be discriminatory against any group of students or individual, or allow privileges for certain groups. For example, Weinstein and colleagues describe the dress code at a school where European American students were allowed to wear pants with holes in the thighs, while African American students were punished with 10-day suspensions for not snapping the straps on their overalls (Weinstein, Tomlinson-Clarke, & Curran, 2004).

A key concern that arises regarding fairness in the classroom is when students begin to discern unfairness, they not only become angry but they may also begin devaluing the importance of education and disengage from school (Cartledge & Kourea, 2008). These behaviors are more likely to occur if classes seem to have standards that favor the advantaged group, and thus reflect ethnic injustice.

Keep in Mind

Teachers may engage in many actions and activities that promote culturally responsive caring and respect for all students. Caring in action may be reflected in behaviors such as the following (Gay, 2010).

- Ensure that students from different ethnic groups feel valued, recognized, respected, seen, and heard in the classroom.
- Demonstrate personal and academic knowledge of culturally diverse students.
- Be confidants, resources, and advocates for culturally diverse students.
- Help students develop a sense of who they are, what they value, and what they can accomplish.
- Support students to develop competence, confidence, compassion, courage, and courtesy.
- Be academically demanding and personally supportive.
- Treat each student in the classroom with equal human worth.
- Acknowledge differences among students without making judgments.

Key References

Cartledge, G., Gardner, R., & Ford, D. (2009). *Diverse learners with exceptionalities: Culturally responsive teaching in the inclusive classroom.* Upper Saddle River, NJ: Pearson Education.

Cartledge, G., & Kourea, L. (2008). Culturally responsive classrooms for culturally diverse students with and at risk for disabilities. *Exceptional Children, 74*(3), 351–371.

Gay, G. (2010). *Culturally responsive teaching: Theory, research, and practice.* New York: Teachers College Press.

Hoover, J., Klingner, J., Baca, L., & Patton, J. (2008). *Methods for teaching culturally and linguistically diverse exceptional children.* Upper Saddle River, NJ: Pearson Education.

Weinstein, C., Curran, M., & Tomlinson-Clarke, S. (2003). Culturally responsive classroom management: Awareness in action. *Theory into Practice, 42*(4), 269–276.

Weinstein, C., Tomlinson-Clarke, S., & Curran, M. (2004). Toward a conception of culturally responsive classroom management. *Journal of Teacher Education, 55*(1), 25–38.

| Strategy 5 | DOUBLE-CHECK: A CULTURALLY RESPONSIVE APPROACH TO CLASSROOM MANAGEMENT |

Rationale

Professionals are in agreement that more culturally responsive approaches to classroom management are needed to address the needs of students from culturally and linguistically diverse backgrounds (Gay, 2010). These practices should be based on current evidence regarding effective practices, and must address the needs of teachers and students from a diverse range of cultural backgrounds. The double-check framework has been developed to support teachers in delivering culturally responsive behavior management (Hershfeldt, Sechrest, Pell, Rosenberg, Bradshaw, & Leaf, 2009; Rosenberg, 2007). This approach uses evidence-based components to address culturally responsive practices in the classroom.

Step-by-Step

Double-check is a five-step framework for supporting teachers in developing more culturally responsive classroom management strategies.

1 *Engage in reflective thinking about cultural group membership.* Double-check begins by having teachers examine their own cultural group membership, as well as those of their students. As this is done, teachers begin to understand the concept of culture, and recognize why culture is important to understand for effective classroom practice. Teachers examine their thinking regarding culture by (a) being aware of their own group membership and history; (b) being aware of their students' group memberships and histories; (c) considering how classroom behaviors of students are influenced by past and present circumstances (e.g., life experiences, cultural practices); (d) examining their own (the teacher's) biases, and how these biases might influence the interpretation of classroom behavior; and (e) making efforts to reach out to students and understand differences. These activities are best completed in collaboration with other teachers. We later describe a self-assessment instrument that can be used to facilitate this process.

2 *Develop sensitivity to students' cultural and situational messages.* As we noted previously, getting to know your students' cultural backgrounds and histories, as well as examining your own cultural history and biases are important steps in developing sensitivity to students' cultural experiences and practices. Given the many different cultural backgrounds of students, and the differences that exist within a given cultural group (Gay, 2010), it is important that teachers interpret student behavior based on the student's cultural background. For example,

Townsend (2000) has noted that some teachers respond negatively to a communication style of some African American students that is viewed as argumentative during classroom discussions. Interpreting this communication style through a cultural lens allows the teacher to realize that viewing this behavior as argumentative is a misinterpretation, as the students are expressing a passionate feeling about the topic being discussed—a behavior that is highly valued and appreciated by most teachers.

3 *Develop an authentic, caring relationship with students.* In any classroom, fewer behavior problems occur when the teacher and students have a positive relationship. This is especially important when working with students from a range of cultural backgrounds, as most students value a caring relationship with their teacher. Teachers who demonstrate caring for their students are interested not only in the students' academic achievement but also their social and emotional well-being. Moreover, when a teacher has a caring, authentic relationship with a student, the teacher is in a better position to address any behavior issues with a plan that aligns with the student's cultural background.

Indicators that teachers are initiating and maintaining authentic, caring relationships with students include:

- Examples of the teacher's involvement in the student's personal life
- Discussion of the student's behavior rather than reacting immediately to behavior
- Examples of recognition that situational factors (e.g., need to save face) influence behavior

319

- Increased levels of positive attention directed toward the student (e.g., engagement during instructional activities)
- Evidence of caring and trust directed toward the student

4 *Develop effective communication with students from CLD backgrounds.* As we noted previously, many students from CLD backgrounds have distinctive communication styles that may not be a good fit for typical expectations of teachers. Teachers who have a culturally responsive approach to addressing these communication styles should seek to understand the intended communicative function of the student's behavior. Furthermore, the teacher's behavior should reflect civility and respect, even when this may be difficult to do. Finally, culturally responsive teachers should recognize that some issues that arise may be explained by the student's lack of facility with code-switching (Gay, 2010)—that is, the student may not recognize that different contexts require different types of communication.

5 *Connect the student's experiences with the curriculum.* Using examples from a student's cultural background in classroom lessons and activities tangibly demonstrates that the teacher values the student's background. Furthermore, these experiences help the teacher develop more authentic relationships with students, and model acceptance of diversity to all members of the class. This connection to the curriculum should occur on an ongoing basis, and should be reflected in books that are read in class, coverage of historical events from different cultural perspectives, and so forth. This ensures that the value of different cultures permeates the curriculum, and that the cultural backgrounds of all students are represented in the curriculum.

Applications and Examples

Examining one's cultural background and experiences is not an easy task. This is especially true when a person is from the majority or dominant culture (i.e., European American in most U.S. schools). We would recommend that as teachers examine their cultural group membership and their biases, they should work collaboratively with other teachers. Ideally, some of these teachers should be from different cultural backgrounds. To facilitate this process, we recommend using the self-assessment from Hershfeldt and colleagues (2009) or a brief, adapted version of that self-assessment in Figure 3 as a starting point for this examination and discussion. All school personnel should complete the assessment anonymously. Each item in the assessment should be interpreted individually. This assessment can be used as a catalyst for discussion among small groups of school professionals or at faculty meetings, or the data may be aggregated to provide a building-level needs assessment and suggest possible directions for professional development.

Figure 3 Double-Check Self-Assessment

Review and provide a rating for each item below

Program Components	Evidence				
	4—See regularly in my school or classroom	3-See most of the time	2-Rarely see	1-Never see	U-Does not apply in my school
Reflection on students' group memberships					
I understand culture and why it is important.					
I reflect on how my actions contribute to student behavior.					
My views of differences are positive and constructive.					
Developing authentic relationships with students					
I encourage positive interactions among all students.					
I display to students tangible evidence of caring and trust.					
I am genuinely interested in the personal lives and activities of my students.					
Effective communication					
I have high expectations for all of my students.					
I am civil and respectful in all of my communications with students.					
I am not judgmental in my communications with students.					
I know about and recognize "code switching."					
Connections to the curriculum					
I use examples from students' cultural backgrounds in my lessons.					
I use activities in instruction that reflect the cultural backgrounds of my students.					
I highlight cultural differences in a positive way.					
Sensitivity to cultural and situational messages					
I know how situations related to health, poverty, dress, and so forth may influence behavior.					
I am aware that students need to address multiple groups.					
I am aware of students' social and political consciousness.					

Open ended questions. Review the items above that were rated below a "4". Those rated "3" may require additional practice or attention. Those rated "2" or "1" may require additional instruction and practice. Please respond to the items below by prioritizing the areas in which you would like resources and support to address cultural responsiveness to students.

Additional professional development in the following areas would be useful:

Additional practice (e.g., role play, coaching) in the following areas would be useful:

Note: This assessment is abbreviated and adapted from Rosenberg (2007) and Hershfeldt et al. (2009). For the full Self-Assessment, see Hershfeldt et al. (2009).

Keep in Mind

Current research evidence strongly supports a positive system of behavior support for all students, and suggests that negative responses to behavior and punishment can quickly become ineffective when addressing the behavior of any student. To keep classroom management as positive as possible, and to address student discipline and the occasional need for punishment, Cartledge, Gardner, and Ford (2009) recommend the following:

- Avoid disproportionate use of disciplinary actions for certain cultural or ethnic groups.
- Keep punishment to a minimum, and ensure that consequences directly relate to the infraction and are fair and brief.
- Emphasize positive relationships and show respect for all students, even when punishment is being used.
- Communicate high expectations for social behavior for all students.
- Appeal to students' backgrounds and integrity as reasons for behaving appropriately.

Key References

Cartledge, G., Gardner, R., & Ford, D. (2009). *Diverse learners with exceptionalities: Culturally responsive teaching in the inclusive classroom.* Upper Saddle River, NJ: Pearson Education.

Cartledge, G., & Kourea, L. (2008). Culturally responsive classrooms for culturally diverse students with and at risk for disabilities. *Exceptional Children, 74*(3), 351–371.

Gay, G. (2010). *Culturally responsive teaching: Theory, research, and practice.* New York: Teachers College Press.

Hershfeldt, P., Sechrest, R., Pell, K., Rosenberg, M., Bradshaw, C., & Leaf, P. (2009). Double-check: A framework of cultural responsiveness applied to classroom behavior. *Teaching Exceptional Children Plus, 6*(2), Article 5. Retrieved January 21, 2011, from http://escholarship.bc.edu/education/tecplus/vol6/iss2/art5

Rosenberg, M. (2007, September). *Double check: Application of culturally responsive behavior management principles.* Paper presented at the initial training for PBIS Plus, Baltimore, MD.

References

August, D., & Siegel, L. (2006). Literacy instruction for language-minority children in special education settings. In D. August & T. Shanahan (Eds.), *Developing literacy in second-language learners: Report of the National Literacy Panel on Language-Minority Children and Youth* (pp. 523–553). Mahwah, NJ: Erlbaum.

Baglieri, S., & Knopf, J. H. (2004). Normalizing difference in inclusive teaching. *Journal of Learning Disabilities, 37*(6), 525–529.

Banks, J., Cochran-Smith, M., Moll, L., Richert, A., Zeichner, K., LePage, P., Darling-Hammond, L., Duffy, H., with McDonald, M. (2005). Teaching diverse learners. In L. Darling-Hammond & J. Bransford (Eds.), *Preparing teachers for a changing world: What teachers should learn and be able to do* (pp. 232–273). San Francisco: Jossey-Bass.

Bondy, E., Ross, D., Gallingane, C., & Hambacher, E. (2007). Creating environments of success and resilience: Culturally responsive classroom management and more. *Urban Education, 42*(4), 326–348.

Borich, G. (2011). *Effective teaching methods: Research-based practices* (7th ed.). Upper Saddle River, NJ: Pearson Education.

Boykin, A. W., & Bailey, C. (2000). *The role of cultural factors in school relevant cognitive functioning: Description of home environmental factors, cultural orientations, and learning preferences* (Report 43). Washington, DC, and Baltimore: Howard University and Johns Hopkins University, enter on the Education of Students Placed at Risk (CRESPAR).

Boykin, A. W., Tyler, K., & Miller, O. (2005). In search of cultural themes and their expressions in the dynamics of classroom life. *Urban Education, 40*(5), 521–549.

Cartledge, G. W., Gardner, R., & Ford, D. Y. (2009). *Diverse learners with exceptionalities: Culturally responsive teaching in the inclusive classroom.* Upper Saddle River, NJ: Merrill/Pearson.

Cartledge, G. W., & Kourea, L. (2008). Culturally responsive classrooms for culturally diverse students with and at risk for disabilities. *Exceptional Children, 74*(3), 351–371.

Chamberlain, S. P. (2005). Recognizing and responding to cultural differences in the education of culturally and linguistically diverse learners. *Intervention in School and Clinic, 40*(4), 195–211.

Charney, R. (2002). *Teaching children to care.* Greenfield, MA: The Northeast Foundation for Children.

Chau, M., Thampi, K., & Wright, V. (2010). *Basic facts about low-income children, 2009. Children under age 18. Fact sheet.* New York: National Center for Children in Poverty, Columbia University.

Codell, E. (2009). *Educating Esme: Diary of a teacher's first year* (expanded edition). Chapel Hill, NC: Algonquin.

Cole, R. W. (2001). *More strategies for educating everybody's children.* Alexandria, VA: Association for Supervision and Curriculum Development.

Corbett, D., Wilson, B., & Williams, B. (2002). *Effort and excellence in urban classrooms.* New York: Teachers College Press.

Darling-Hammond, L. (2010). *The flat world of education: How America's commitment to equity will determine our future.* New York: Teachers College Press.

Delpit, L. (1995). *Other people's children: Cultural conflicts in the classroom.* New York: New Press.

Deno, S. (2007). Curriculum-based measurement. In J. McLeskey (Ed.), *Reflections on inclusion: Classic articles that shaped our thinking* (pp. 221–249). Arlington, VA: Council for Exceptional Children (CEC).

Engelmann, S., & Bruner, E. (2003). *Reading mastery classic.* Chicago: Science Research Associates.

Esquith, R. (2007). *Teach like your hair's on fire: The methods and madness inside room 56.* New York: Penguin.

Evertson C., & Emmer, E. (2009). *Classroom management for classroom teachers* (8th ed.). Upper Saddle River, NJ: Pearson Education.

Fletcher, J., Lyon, R., Fuchs, L., & Barnes, M. (2007). *Learning disabilities: From identification to intervention.* New York: Guilford.

Fuchs, L., Fuchs, D., Craddock, C., Hollenbeck, K., Hamlett, C., & Schatschneider, C. (2008). Effects of small-group tutoring with and without validated classroom instruction on at-risk student's math problem solving: Are the two tiers of prevention better than one? *Journal of Educational Psychology, 100*(3), 491–509.

García, S., & Ortiz, A. (2006). Preventing disproportionate representation: Culturally and linguistically responsive prereferral interventions. *Teaching Exceptional Children, 38*(3), 64–68.

Gay, G. (2002). Preparing for culturally responsive teaching. *Journal of Teacher Education, 53*(2), 106–116.

Gay, G. (2010). *Culturally responsive teaching: Theory, research, & practice.* New York: Teachers College Press.

Gersten, R., Baker, S., Shanahan, T., Linan-Thompson, S., Collins, P., & Scarcella, R. (2007). *Effective literacy and English language instruction for English learners in the elementary grades.* NCEE-2007-4011. Washington, DC: U.S. Department of Education, Institute for Education Sciences.

Ginsberg, M. G. (2005). Cultural diversity, motivation and differentiation. *Theory into Practice, 44*(3), 218–225.

Gonzalez, N., Moll, L. C., & Amanti, C. (2005). *Funds of knowledge: Theorizing practices in households and classrooms.* Mahwah, NJ: Erlbaum.

Greenwood, C., Arreaga-Mayer, C., Utley, C., Gavin, K., & Terry, B. (2001). Classwide Peer Tutoring learning management system: Applications with elementary-level English language learners. *Remedial and Special Education, 22*(1), 34–47.

Gregory, A., Skiba, R., & Noguera, P. (2010). The achievement gap and the discipline gap: Two sides of the same coin? *Educational Researcher, 39*(1), 59–68.

Gudykunst, W. B., & Kim, Y. Y. (2003). *Communicating with strangers: An approach to intercultural communication.* New York: McGraw-Hill.

Harriott, W., & Martin, S. (2004). Using culturally responsive activities to promote social competence and classroom community. *Teaching Exceptional Children, 37*(1), 48–54.

Hershfeldt, P., Sechrest R., Pell, K., Rosenberg, M., Bradshaw, C., & Leaf, P. (2009). Double-Check: A framework of culturally responsiveness applied to classroom behavior. *Teaching Exceptional Children Plus, 62*(2), Article 5. Retrieved January 21, 2011, from http://escholarship.bc.edu/education/tecplus/vol16/iss2/art5/

Hollins, E. R. (1996). *Culture in school learning: Revealing the deep meaning.* Mahwah, NJ: Erlbaum.

Irvine, J. J. (2002). *In search of wholeness: African American teachers and their culturally specific practices.* New York: Palgrave/St. Martins Press.

Irvine, J. J. (2003). *Educating teachers for diversity: Seeing with a cultural eye.* New York: Teachers College Press.

Jones, T. (2005). Twenty ways to incorporate diversity into your classroom. *Intervention in School and Clinic, 41*(1), 9–12.

Kamps, D., Abbott, M., Greenwood, C., Arreaga-Mayer, C., Wills, H., Longstaff, J., Culpepper, M., & Waiton, C. (2007). Use of evidence-based, small-group reading instruction for English language learners in elementary grades: Secondary-tier intervention. *Learning Disability Quarterly, 30*(3), 153–168.

Kids Data. (2009). *Kidsdata.org data groups.* Retrieved January 25, 2011, from http://www.kidsdata.org/data/demographic/

Lewis, R., & Doorlag, D. (2011). *Teaching students with special needs in general education classrooms* (8th ed.). Upper Saddle River, NJ: Pearson Education.

Mason, L., Harris, K., & Graham, S. (2011). Self-regulated strategy development for students with writing difficulties. *Theory into Practice, 50*(1), 20–27.

National Center for Education Statistics. (2010). *Condition of education 2010.* Washington, DC: U.S. Department of Education, Institution of Education Sciences. Retrieved January 25, 2011, from http://nces.ed.gov/programs/coe/

Nieto, S., & Bode, P. (2008). *Affirming diversity: The sociopolitical context of multicultural education* (5th ed.). Boston: Allyn & Bacon.

Oetzel, J. G., & Ting-Toomey, S. (Eds.). (2006). *The SAGE handbook of conflict communication: Integrating theory, research, and practice*. Thousand Oaks, CA: Sage.

Patrick, H., Turner, J., Meyer, D. K., & Midgley, C. (2003). How teachers establish psychological environments during the first days of school: Associations with avoidance in mathematics. *Teachers College Record, 105*(8), 1521–1558.

Richards, H., Brown, A., & Forde, T. (2006). *Addressing diversity in schools: Culturally responsive pedagogy*. Tempe, AZ: National Center for Culturally Responsive Educational Systems, Arizona State University.

Rodriguez, E., & Bellanca, J. (2007). *What is it about me you can't teach? An instructional guide for the urban educator*. Thousand Oaks, CA: Corwin.

Rosenberg, M. (2007, September). *Double Check: Application of culturally responsive behavior management principles*. Paper presented at the initial training for PBIS Plus, Baltimore.

Ross, D., Bondy, E., Gallingane, C., & Hambacher, E. (2008). Promoting academic engagement through insistence: Being a warm demander. *Childhood Education, 84*(3), 142–146.

Saenz, L., Fuchs, L., & Fuchs, D. (2005). Peer-assisted learning strategies for English language learners with learning disabilities. *Exceptional Children, 71*(3), 231–247.

Salend, S., & Duhaney, L. (2005). Understanding and addressing disproportionate representation of students of color in special education. *Intervention in School and Clinic, 40*(4), 213–221.

Sheets, R. H. (2005). *Diversity pedagogy*. Boston: Pearson Education.

Skiba, R., Poloni-Staudinger, L., Gallini, S., Simmons, A., & Feggins-Azziz, L. (2006). Disparate access: The disporprotionality of African American students with disabilities across educational environments. *Exceptional Children, 72*, 411–424.

Skiba, R., Simmons, A., Ritter, S., Gibb, A., Rausch, M., Cuadrado, J., & Chung, C. (2008). Achieving equity in special education: History, status, and current challenges. *Exceptional Children, 74*(3), 264–288.

Sprick, M., Howard, L., & Fidanque, A. (1998). *Read well*. Longmont, CO: Sopris West.

Stormont, M. (2007). *Fostering resilience in young children at risk for failure*. Upper Saddle River, NJ: Merrill/Pearson Education.

Torgesen, J. (2009). The response to intervention instructional model: Some outcomes from a large-scale implementation in reading first schools. *Child Development Perspectives, 3*(1), 38–40.

Townsend, B. (2000). The disproportionate discipline of African American learners: Reducing school suspensions and expulsions. *Exceptional Children, 66*, 381–391.

Trumbull, E., Rothstein-Fisch, C., & Greenfield, P. M. (2000). *Bridging cultures in our schools: New approaches that work. Knowledge brief*. San Francisco: WestEd.

U.S. Department of Education. (2010). *Twenty-ninth annual report to Congress on the implementation of the Individuals with Disabilities Education Act, 2007*. Retrieved January 25, 2011, from http://www2.ed.gov/about/reports/annual/osep/index.html

U.S. Department of Education. (2011). *Individuals with Disabilities Education Improvement Act (IDEA) data: Data Accountability Center*. Retrieved January 10, 12, and 25, 2011, from www.ideadata.org

van Garderen, D., & Whittaker, C. (2006). Planning differentiated, multicultural instruction for secondary inclusive classrooms. Teaching Exceptional Children, 38(3), 12–20.

Vaughn, S., & Linan-Thompson, S. (2007). *Research-based methods of reading instruction for English language learners, grades K–4*. Alexandria, VA: Association for Supervision and Curriculum Development.

Wallace, J., Goodkind, S., Wallace, D., & Bachman, J. (2008). Racial, ethnic, and gender differences in school discipline among U.S. High school students: 1991–2005. *Negro Educational Review, 59*, 47–62.

Ware, F. (2006). Warm demander pedagogy: Culturally responsive teaching that supports a culture of achievement for African American students. *Urban Education, 41*(4), 427–456.

Weinstein, C., Curran, M., & Tomlinson-Clarke, S. (2003). Culturally responsive classroom management: Awareness in action. *Theory into Practice, 42*(4), 269–276.

Weinstein, C., Tomlinson-Clarke, S., & Curran, M. (2004). Toward a conception of culturally responsive classroom management. *Journal of Teacher Education, 55*(1), 25–38.

Weinstein, R. (2002). *Reaching higher: The power of expectations in schooling*. Cambridge, MA: Harvard University Press.

Wilson, B. L., & Corbett, H. D. (2001). *Listening to urban kids*. Albany, NY: SUNY Press.

Photo Credits

Credits are listed in order of appearance.

Scott Cunningham/Merrill; © Comstock Images, a division of JupiterImages Corporation; © Bill Aron/PhotoEdit; © Big Cheese Photo LLC/Alamy; Ryan McVay/Photodisc/Getty Images Inc.; © Richard Hutchings/PhotoEdit

CHAPTER 14

Professional Development and Teacher Leadership
Personal Responsibilities

From Chapter 14 of *Curriculum and Instructional Methods for the Elementary and Middle School*, 7/e. Johanna Kasin Lemlech.
Copyright © 2010 by Pearson Education. Published by Allyn & Bacon. All rights reserved.

Requirements for teacher credentialing as well as the roles and responsibilities of teachers have changed dramatically during the last several years. In this chapter, performance expectations and some of the ways that teachers are performing leadership roles are discussed. The hierarchical, bureaucratic governance structure of schools has also changed. Although reform strategies in schools do not cause teachers to be leaders, participation beyond the doors of the classroom certainly is related to teachers' shared decision making in schools.

New professional roles require that teachers concern themselves with their own professional development and the development of their colleagues. This chapter explains the ways that teachers can reflect on their practice, self-assess, and grow professionally. Teacher portfolios are a means for authentic assessment, and many teachers are preparing them to exhibit their professional prowess and excellence.

Teachers' legal rights and responsibilities and students' rights conclude the chapter. Teachers are affected by tenure laws, malpractice and negligence, and copyright laws. These legal issues are discussed, along with teacher benefits and salary issues.

Advance Organizer

The following questions are intended to guide your reading and understanding of the content of this chapter.

1. What are some ways to continue your own professional education?
2. In what ways have teachers' responsibilities been expanded in some schools?
3. Why is it important to develop collegiality for professional development?
4. How can clinical supervision assist the beginning teacher?
5. What are some purposes of staff development programs?
6. How will you collect data for self-evaluation, and can you set a timeline for improvement?
7. Which professional association would you like to join?
8. How does copyright law affect teachers in the classroom?
9. In what ways do tenure and dismissal procedures affect teachers?
10. Under what circumstances are teachers liable?
11. What instructional, supervisory, and assessment responsibilities should teachers assume?

INTASC

INTASC Standards

This chapter focuses on teachers' professional responsibilities. Standards 9 and 10 speak to those issues; however, to demonstrate those two standards, teachers need to be proficient in Standards 1–8. To accomplish Standards 9 and 10, a competency checklist of teaching performance is included in the chapter to help you assess your own capabilities.

Professional Lexicon

collegiality The establishment of a professional relationship for the purpose of service and accommodation through the mutual exchange of perceptions and expertise.

comparative negligence Negligence in which the teacher is held responsible commensurate to the extent of negligence when both teacher and student are liable for an injury.

continuing contract A type of employment contract that protects nontenured teachers from "summer dismissal"; notification of dismissal must occur by a certain date, usually May 1.

contributory negligence Negligence in which the injured person fails to exercise reasonable self-care.

indefinite contract A type of employment contract for tenured teachers that is renewed automatically each year without mutual action.

in loco parentis Literally "in place of the parent"; the ability of teachers to act in a parent's place in school situations.

negligence Failure to exercise reasonable care and judgment to protect students from injury.

participation rights The rights of children to participate in decisions that affect their lives and futures.

restructuring Reorganizing schools to improve student achievement and develop a professional environment for teachers.

right of protection The right of children to protection from abuse.

rights of provision The rights of children to have physical, social, economic, and cultural well-being.

TEACHERS AS PROFESSIONALS AND LEADERS

Three fictional teachers have been introduced in this text; in his or her own way, each is considered an expert teacher. Mary Hogan, Greg Thomas, and Karen Adazzio have demonstrated that they care about their students. They have demonstrated their skills in planning and implementing lessons and their ability to assess students' needs, interests, and accomplishments. We will now explore how they demonstrate leadership skills, how they work with colleagues, and how they feel about teaching as a profession.

MARY HOGAN

"Sometimes I get really tired of teaching. Particularly after what feels like a bad day—when there's too much noise and commotion, nobody is listening to me, and time gets away from me. But then after school I talk to a friend who is also a teacher, and she helps me think back about the day and figure out what went wrong. I know I do like teaching; I like being able to think about what to teach and how to teach it, and anticipating stu-

dents' reactions. I really like it when I see that special look in students' eyes that says, 'Hey, that's neat!' and 'I got it!' and then they begin to talk about their own experiences that make it all fit together.

"Because so much of the day is spent talking to children, I really was excited when I was asked to demonstrate teaching models for other teachers. It's fun talking to colleagues about the decisions involved in choosing one model over another. We are going to set up a peer coaching plan, and I look forward to the opportunity to work with other teachers at my school."

GREG THOMAS

"What I like best about teaching is thinking about what will involve the students in real problem solving. I like arranging stuff to create a situation or event for students to explore—and then listening to them wonder. I've never had to worry about students getting out of hand. I like listening to students talk about their ideas together. I don't think you need to set up artificial means so that every student participates; all you need to do is plan challenging experiences. I guess one of the first things I learned as a beginning teacher was to throw out the teacher's manual, look at and listen to the kids, and then reflect on my goals and how to achieve them.

"Two days per month I work with new teachers, helping them with classroom management and instructional problems. I am involved in developing a new resource guide for the district for teaching social studies. These activities are very rewarding professionally. I think these activities with other teachers help me, personally, to be a better teacher."

KAREN ADAZZIO

"The other day I was teaching a lesson within a lesson—using Roger Green's story of *King Arthur and the Knights of the Round Table*. The class had recently read the book, so it was perfect to use as an advance organizer for a historical timeline to study the Middle Ages, the High Middle Ages, and the Renaissance Reformation. I really had fun with it, but it took a little bit before the kids caught on that the story was a means to study feudalism, help us connect the historical time period, and study geography. I told my teacher friend Jan about it, and she shared a similar experience where she was 'nesting' lessons together and integrating several subject fields. When Jan and I start talking about teaching, we tend to lose track of time. I really learn so much from her during these sessions, and it always makes me realize how fortunate I am to be a teacher. No two days are ever the same. Teaching is constantly challenging.

"When I began talking with several other teachers about teaming and grouping our students, I really felt like I was on a high. Pretty soon we realized that we needed to figure our block scheduling to lock in our students so that the teaming would work. The other teachers asked me to serve as the group leader; I think that really made me feel good—that they would choose me—and I work hard to keep the team on track. We are really committed to improving the instructional program for students, and it's great sharing decisions and designing a new program."

ACCOUNTABILITY AND ASSESSMENT

Most teachers recognize that teaching is not just about focusing on state testing systems and state standards. It is about teaching significant concepts in subject fields, meeting students' needs, and preparing students for successful lives. Plitt (2004) shares his perspective of the teaching challenge by asking himself three questions:

1. Who are my students and what are their needs and strengths?
2. What is it that I believe my students need to know and be able to do?
3. How will I know that my students are different as a result of the learning experience? (p. 746)

Teaching to the tests may be attractive if one considers the consequences for teachers, schools, and districts. Teachers' performance is measured by students' achievement schoolwide. In schools where test scores do not improve, the school is subjected to publicity and ultimately may be closed. The teachers are branded as inadequate and will have difficulty obtaining another position. But as Posner (2004) points out, students whose curriculum is limited to the ability to answer standardized test problems also will be limited to solving simplistic and routine questions that will not prepare them for dealing with complex situations and analysis of real-life problems.

For teachers the dilemma causes many professional questions. For example, how do you deal with reading programs or social studies programs that your school district has bought where the format is structured with precise questions and, as Posner notes, exact material, timing, and wording for instruction? Would Plitt be able to address his three questions? Would you really need a teaching credential to mimic and follow the directions in the teaching manual? What should teachers do? The balance of the chapter will provide suggestions for improving practice.

TEACHER DECISION MAKING

Many Hogan, Greg Thomas, and Karen Adazzio demonstrated that they are constantly engaged in making judgments because what they do in their classrooms cannot be routinized. They need to be involved in problem solving about teaching. Through advance planning and throughout the school day, teachers need to decide what to teach, how best to teach it, how to accommodate diverse learners, how to utilize both theory and pedagogy, and how to meld subject-field academic concepts into concepts appropriate for teaching. All three of the teachers called attention to *time* as a critical constraint on their professional activities.

TIME AND TEACHING

One of the biggest constraints on improving teaching, student achievement, and reforming schools is the lack of time for teachers to plan, reflect on teaching with colleagues, and interact with students, parents, and other professionals (Lemlech, Hertzog, & Hackl, 1994). The U.S. Department of Education's report titled "Trying to Beat the Clock" (1998) verifies that teachers have very little time to plan lessons and very few opportunities to interact with colleagues. Stevenson (1998) compares U.S. teachers with German and Japanese teachers and notes that only in our country are teachers expected to provide instruction for almost the entire day. In Germany, teachers provide instruction until noon and have the rest of the day for planning and professional activity. In Japan, teachers provide instruction for only half of their day.

Still another problem for teachers in the United States is that they are paid for only 9 months of teaching. As a consequence, many teachers need to find employment for the remaining 3 months. In other countries, teachers are paid a 12-month salary and are provided time for professional and curriculum development. Clearly, we need to invest in our teachers and

provide time for professional learning. Some teacher responsibilities beyond the classroom are listed next.

Teachers' Professional Responsibilities (Outside the Classroom)

- Consideration of school organizational structures (Adazzio's block scheduling)
- Teacher teaming for instruction
- Collaboration to develop new curricula
- Uses for technology
- Self-assessment and peer coaching
- Responsibility for continuing education for self and with colleagues

IMPROVING TEACHING AND REFORMING SCHOOLS

A great deal of research points to several strategies for improving teaching and reforming schools. Some of what has been learned includes the following:

- *Teachers talking together about teaching:* providing ideas for what works (and what doesn't), sharing problems, reflecting on lessons
- *Participation in professional communities:* may be within the school or participation in a professional association; the important aspect is that teachers are sharing learning and expertise, engaging in collaborative teacher research, and supporting each other with knowledge and assistance
- *Sharing in school governance:* involvement in decision making that affects the school culture and the school community (an example follows in the next section)

School Organization

At Karen Adazzio's school, students are now group clusters that are assigned to several teachers for ing and guidance. In addition, class periods ha changed to provide larger blocks of time so th ers can implement thematic units and inter instruction. To accomplish this, the teach work together planning instruction and ing during instruction. The teacher responsibility for counseling the stud of restructuring affected teacher re of instruction, how students are g is structured, and schoolwide d

The small-school concept middle and high schools th

Teaching Hints: Professional Development

Paez (2003) teaches in a school committed to professional development: (1) Teachers are expected to make time for teacher collaboration. This occurs in a weekly meeting. (2) School time is used for teacher demonstrations to observe each other teach. (3) Literacy training focuses on what students need to learn to be successful readers and writers. (They do not use scripted lessons.) (4) Professional-development consultants work collaboratively with teachers, sharing ideas, information, and opinions.

Planning together, these teachers are sharing ideas for a thematic unit to be taught in their three classrooms.

New York City, 15 small schools serve grades 6–12, 41 more serving grades 9–12. The small schools within the walls of huge comprehensive high major purpose of the small school is to e low and achievement high. Help ols comes from community organizations, higher-ncies). Aside from of these small mplement rials,

ed in
teach-
ve been
at teach-
disciplinary
ers began to
at times team-
ents. The process
lationships, content
ouped, the way time
cision making.
s being shared at many
roughout the nation. In

329

Teaching Processes

Restructuring should affect the ways in which students are taught. Thematic teaching emphasizes the relationships of the different disciplines. Factual information is deemphasized; instead, deeper meanings are sought. Use of students' prior knowledge becomes integral to the process because the focus of teaching is on student engagement and participation.

The Teachers

The "egg-crate" structure of the classroom and the isolation of teachers disappears in the small-school setting. Teachers have access to each other for planning, collaboration, consultation, and coaching (Lemlech, 1995). Teachers are actively engaged in developing curriculum, selecting resources, and defining assessment processes. Teachers "teach" differently. They encourage self-directed learning. They guide and facilitate through creating appropriate environments for learning. They question instead of telling.

The Students

Students are engaged in active learning, which means that students interact frequently in small groups—not just in skill activities—for the purpose of raising questions, experimenting, sharing knowledge, discussing, and using technological resources. Students manipulate objects and data to construct their own understanding. They are expected to explain and demonstrate what they are learning through the products they create (stories, reports, pictures, programs, and projects).

Schoolwide Decision Making

The involvement of teachers in decision-making and problem-solving teams, teacher networks, learning communities, and school-to-school networks affects the structural organization of the school. Traditional hierarchical relations fade and the school's organizational structure becomes flat. Faculty dialogue and support for risk taking affect policy decisions and professional development.

Teacher Reflection

All three of the teachers featured in this text think about teaching. They are active learners and they attempt to understand the following:

- What their students know and are learning
- What worked and why, and what didn't work and why

The reflective teacher constantly wonders: "If I had tried this or that, would it be better?" "What else would work?" "How could I have . . . ?" "What would have happened if . . . ?" "This reminds me of the time when . . . ."

Researchers have long been aware of the value of reflection on practice. Changes in practice depend on thinking about tradition (routines you are accustomed to enacting) and consideration of alternatives. Interaction with others and collaboration stimulate the process of reflection. The process of reflection requires that the reflector detach self from the situation or event and reconsider it for the purpose of perceiving alternative actions and interpretations. Talking to others about

actual teaching happenings stimulates the reflective process. Making reflection a habit of professional practice has the potential to improve our thinking about teaching and improve our instructional practices.

Assessment Informs Instruction

Many researchers have concluded that professional development must focus on using student achievement data to guide instructional decisions. Too often, students' tests are forgotten after scores are recorded. Instead teachers need to (1) analyze their teaching goal, (2) verify that students were tested on what was taught, (3) check what students achieved, and (4) target what they failed to learn. The gap between what students know and what they failed to learn needs to guide immediate instructional lessons.

 Teaching Hints:
Meeting the Needs of English
Language Learners

Miller and Endo (2004) describe the language shock experienced by new students who enter an English-speaking environment and suffer anxiety and stress because they do not understand anything that is said. As a consequence, their motivation to learn is nil and self-esteem is destroyed. What should teachers do?

1. Know your students' schooling history so that lessons can be planned that fit prior knowledge, interests, and needs.
2. Select learning activities that allow the ELL student a variety of ways to respond (verbal, written, project).
3. Do not be afraid to meet with parents to learn about the student and discuss the needs of the child. Team up with the parents.
4. Demonstrate respect for the culture of each ELL student. Include pieces of the child's culture in the lesson and the environment of the classroom. Treat the student as an "expert" about his or her culture.
5. Reduce concept load when teaching by using simpler sentences and words to convey meaning.
6. Encourage second-language learners to keep their native language intact through either home and community or in school at appropriate times.

Research Findings

Cox-Petersen (2001) asked 44 science teachers participating in an advanced science methods class to perform action research in their own classrooms. Teachers were to report the problem, rationale, literature review, method for collecting data, findings, and instructional decisions made as a result of their research.

Findings indicated that, as a consequence of the study, teachers planned changes in their practice, and critically reflected on tactics that impeded or enhanced science learning and teaching. The teachers found that their own action research was more effective for their personal development than reading and applying the research findings of others.

TEACHERS AS RESEARCHERS

Action research is another way in which teachers work individually and collaboratively to solve school-based problems. Action research is the name given to research conducted by teachers in their own classrooms or on school grounds. Research planned and carried out by teachers tends to be *authentic*—meaning it is genuinely needed to improve instruction and provide professional learning.

In a collaborative mode, teachers jointly identify a problem that they feel can be solved by school-based research. They develop the research process together and then conduct the research in their own classrooms. They report their results to each other and modify instructional procedures as needed or design an intervention strategy.

Although many teachers involve themselves in short action research projects in their own classrooms, others seek peer collaboration on an action research agenda. An example of action research that began as an individual project and ultimately became a collaborative project was told to me by an inner-city fifth-grade teacher. She was curious about the effect on school attendance if she initiated active learning experiences that would be introduced on Monday and concluded on Friday, so that students would recognize that if they were absent, they would miss out on constructing and

experimenting. She found that her students' attendance improved as a consequence. Teachers need to be active researchers and reflect on practices in their schools and classrooms. Many such studies have been extremely valuable and have contributed to knowledge about teaching and to the dialogue about teaching.

PREPARATION FOR LEADERSHIP: COLLEGIAL RELATIONSHIPS

Preservice Preparation

Beginning in 1987, the University of Southern California experimented with a collegial teacher preparation program for student teaching. Student teachers were paired for their classroom practice experience. The purpose of the program was to create a bond between partner student teachers to enhance their ability to become professionals and teacher-leaders. The authors defined **collegiality** as "the establishment of a professional relationship for the purpose of service and accommodation through the mutual exchange of perceptions and expertise" (Lemlech & Kaplan, 1990).

Lemlech and Kaplan (1990, 1991) studied the developmental pattern and sequence of collegial relationships among the student teachers (Figure 14.1). They found that collegial relationships progress from a friendly and helping relationship to the exchange of ideas and to dialogue about beliefs and knowledge, appreciation of each other's strengths, and ultimately to trust and commitment to each other based on a feeling of proficiency and equality.

As colleagues, the partner student teachers established their own identity, recognized each other's expertise, and accepted responsibility to provide each other with consultant services. In essence, colleagues become co-problem-solvers. The collegial relationship generates reflective thinking about teaching processes, enhances the individual's own learning, and promotes problem solving and insight. Lemlech and Kaplan (1991) theorized that the professionalization of teaching depends on the development of expertise in the knowledge base of teaching, teacher empowerment, teacher leadership, and collegial relationships.

Just as the collegial teacher preparation program changed the student teaching program from an apprenticeship model to a collegial model, the program also

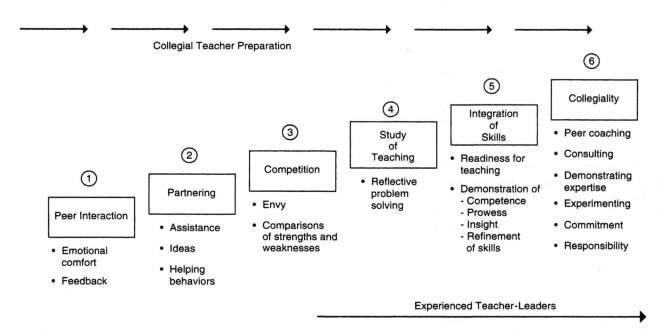

Figure 14.1 Figure   Collegial Development Stages and Characteristics

Source: From *Collegial Preparation, Reflective Practice, and Social Studies Teaching*, by J. K. Lemlech and S. N Kaplan, 1991.

necessitated changes in the roles and responsibilities of the public school supervising teachers. Hertzog-Foliart and Lemlech (1993) compared traditional supervision with collegial supervision of preservice teachers. They found role changes in three teaching components: planning, lesson enactment, and feedback. Traditionally, the supervising teacher directs what the preservice teacher should teach, and then during the lesson, watches to see that it is enacted; for feedback, the supervising teacher traditionally "tells and critiques." But in collegial supervision, the supervising teacher becomes part of the planning team as the partners and the supervisor engage in the process of planning. During the lesson, the supervising teacher guides partner observation. During feedback time, the supervising teacher guides the reflective thinking of the colleagues, models professional dialogue, and facilitates the collegial relationship of the preservice teachers.

CONTINUING EDUCATION—PERSONAL DEVELOPMENT

All professionals need to be concerned about keeping abreast of current knowledge and skills in their field of endeavor. For many years, medical and dental professionals have been required by state law to attend professional-development classes. Accountants and attorneys are also required to obtain continuing education credits each year. Thus, it is not surprising that the public expects public school teachers to attend continuing-education classes in their school districts or on college campuses.

Personal/independent continuing education can be accomplished in a variety of ways. For example, with membership in one or more professional organizations, you receive monthly professional journals. Articles in these journals help you keep abreast of new ideas, research, and current problems affecting public education.

Another form of continuing education is attendance at state and national conferences sponsored by professional organizations. Membership is not required to attend these conferences, where you will hear leaders in the field discuss current happenings in the field. You will also be invited to join subcommittees focused on specific areas of interest.

Listening to audiotapes from the conferences provides another means of tuning in on significant issues that were recorded at national conferences. These can be purchased soon after the conferences and can be listened to in your car on the way to work.

Accepting Personal Responsibility for Professional Development

National Board Certification

The National Board for Professional Teaching Standards (NBPTS), created in 1987, developed a set of national standards to certify highly accomplished teachers. National Board Certification requires that teachers demonstrate specific knowledge and skills appropriate to the level they are teaching (early childhood, middle childhood, and so on) and appropriate to what they teach (generalist, social studies/history, art, mathematics, and so on).

Research Findings

Lemlech and Hertzog (1999) studied the reciprocal relationship between student teacher partners and their master teachers. They questioned: What do master teachers and student teachers learn from each other? They learned that the value of pairing student teachers to develop collegial relationships affected the professional relations of prospective teachers and their master teacher because the master teachers assumed the roles of coaches, mentors, and team leaders. Dialogue among partners and master teachers encouraged professional reflection and motivated risk taking by master teachers with new teaching approaches. Similar benefits are possible between beginning teachers and mentors if collegial relationships are developed.

Research Findings

A four-year study of test scores in Florida and North Carolina questioned whether nationally certified teachers actually raised students' test scores. The answer was yes. The study confirmed that teachers who have earned National Board certification "are more effectively producing learning goals and raising test scores" (Viadero & Honawar, 2008).

Quality Teaching

School districts, schools of education, and the public all want and expect a connection between teacher competence (quality of teaching) and student achievement. In every chapter of this text, attention has been directed to the Interstate New Teacher Assessment and Support Consortium (INTASC) standards. The certification process in most states requires that teachers pass an examination in which beginning teachers' performance is assessed by their responses to aspects of teaching. Performance expectations relate to teachers' knowledge of students' development and what students know and do not know, content/subject matter knowledge, and instructional processes (review Figure 6.1). In addition, teachers are expected to know how to develop and maintain an appropriate environment for learning, and understand personal legal and ethical responsibilities as an educator. Table 14.1 uses the INTASC standards as a performance checklist to assist your planning for professional growth.

Set Personal Goals

To improve personal performance, it is important to set goals that focus on your own planning and teaching behavior, rather than on students' behavior or on the improvement of the school's educational program. The following goals are recognized as important to instructional improvement:

- Base learning experiences on significant conceptual content rather than on "fun" activities.
- Select learning experiences that are consonant with personal goals. (If critical thinking is a goal, then the activity should engage students in practicing critical-thinking skills.)

- Increase student-to-student interaction versus student-to-teacher-to-student interaction.
- Encourage constructivist thinking.
- Differentiate instruction based on students' needs, interests, and learning styles.
- Improve organizational skills to decrease nonteaching time.
- Integrate subject fields to unify learning.
- Utilize academic fields to teach reading comprehension skills.
- Increase teacher feedback to students during direct instruction.
- Increase flexible grouping of students throughout the school day.
- Increase output activities for students.
- Increase professional reading.
- Apply research findings in the classroom.

Analyze Your Own Performance

It is possible to analyze your own performance to verify what you need to improve. Using a recorder in the classroom, small episodes of instruction can be recorded for later analysis, or you may want to ask a student or another teacher to videotape a teaching episode. Before listening to or viewing the episode, decide on the purpose of your evaluation:

- Do you want to listen to the questions you asked?
- Are you listening for the number of responses and degree of interaction?
- Are you concerned about management skills?
- Is enthusiasm or clarity of instructions what interests you?

Research Findings

Viadero (2004) reports that research studies of kindergarten, elementary, and middle school students from a national sample and in Texas confirmed that math scores were higher when students were taught by qualified teachers. Studies were controlled for students' differences in socioeconomic status, previous achievement, and teachers' experience. Qualified teachers were those who were credentialed and state certified and had had pedagogical instruction in teacher preparation. The studies also revealed that poor students were less likely to have qualified teachers.

Table 14.1   Teaching Competencies

Rate yourself using a scale from 1 to 5, with 5 as the highest level.

1. I am comfortable with my conceptual knowledge of the subject matter I am required to teach.	1	2	3	4	5
2. I am able to translate subject-matter concepts into meaningful experiences for students.	1	2	3	4	5
3. I am able to use my knowledge of child/adolescent growth and development to create appropriate intellectual, social, and personal learning experiences.	1	2	3	4	5
4. I am able to identify ways in which my students differ in learning preferences and adapt learning activities to address their needs to achieve content standards.	1	2	3	4	5
5. I am able to implement teaching strategies to assist English language learners' progress in achieving content standards.	1	2	3	4	5
6. I am able to implement a variety of teaching strategies to encourage students' skill development, critical thinking, and problem solving.	1	2	3	4	5
7. I can create a motivating learning environment that encourages students' interactions and active engagement in learning experiences.	1	2	3	4	5
8. I am able to communicate effectively with the whole class and with individuals to stimulate inquiry and collaborative endeavors.	1	2	3	4	5
9. I am able to engage in both short- and long-range planning in the subjects I teach to meet the needs of my students.	1	2	3	4	5
10. I am able to use a variety of assessment techniques to inform teaching and determine what students learned and what they need to know.	1	2	3	4	5
11. I engage in reflective inquiry to determine what works and what doesn't and to evaluate my decisions' effects on others in the learning community.	1	2	3	4	5
12. I have developed relationships with other teachers, collaborate with them, and recognize the significance of collegial interactions to support the learning of students.	1	2	3	4	5
13. I interact with parents and community representatives to foster the well-being of students.	1	2	3	4	5

• When students work in groups, do you encourage them to ask for and give each other help?

Do not attempt to critique everything. Focus on one or two elements of your teaching style and develop a checklist that will enable you to listen in a purposeful manner.

Another way to help you analyze your performance is to invite a trusted colleague to observe. You and your colleague should develop an observation chart to enable your friend to observe specific elements of instruction.

Design a Self-Help Program

After analyzing your performance, decide on your goal and arrange a timeline to accomplish your objectives. Use Table 14.1 to help you in your analysis. Consider what you have learned about successful staff development programs and, using that information, model your personal program. For example, to increase your awareness and knowledge about your goal, you could decide to do the following:

• Read professional literature.
• Attend a professional class.
• Talk to a knowledgeable expert.

Your next task may be to find another teacher who is an expert in the technique you want to master. Ask your colleague if you may visit his or her classroom during a particular session so you will have an appropriate model. You may need to share your goal and your plan with your principal so provisions can be made to allow you to visit other teachers.

Your third task is to develop a plan for practicing the skill. You will probably have to arrange to have someone observe your performance so you can receive feedback.

Finally, after appropriate practice and feedback, work out a system whereby you utilize the technique consistently in your teaching. Once again, you may want the assistance of a colleague to help you plan instruction implementing the new skill.

COOPERATIVE/COLLEGIAL DEVELOPMENT

Many teachers, including me, find it rewarding to work with one or more colleagues for the purpose of professional growth. Speaking with others about what works and what doesn't helps to clarify teaching theory, per-

Research Findings

Strahan (2003) described a three-year study of three elementary schools in North Carolina engaged in promoting a collaborative culture among teachers and administrators and improving low-income and minority student achievement. Each school began the process of change in slightly different ways, but all accomplished reform. The process at each school followed a general framework:

1. Faculty members identified priorities for professionalism.
2. Teachers targeted curriculum areas to work on that addressed students' needs.
3. Faculty members developed a supportive climate for students.
4. Regular grade-level meetings among teachers were held to talk about teaching and focus on teacher efficacy.

sonal beliefs, planning, and decision making. It is particularly helpful when colleagues who disagree with each other about methodology work to prove what is appropriate or optimal. Personal experience some years ago with several colleagues emphasized how much fun and interest in the teaching process is generated when you discuss (argue!) with good friends about when to introduce a particular concept, what should come first, appropriate activities and materials, and motivation. Discussions such as these are good medicine for instructional improvement in the classroom.

PEER COACHING

The concept and purpose of peer coaching is often misunderstood. It is not intended as a means to remediate poor instructional practices, nor is it intended as a mentoring strategy.

Characteristics of Coaching

Colleague teachers choose to coach each other because they want to master a new instructional strategy (new to them); they want to master the use of new instructional materials/resources; or they are experimenting with new ideas, grouping, or content. The major purpose for coaching is the implementation of an innovative method of teaching to determine its effect on various groups of students. Suppose a group of teachers are learning the group investigation model of teaching. One of the teachers demonstrates the model and introduces the theory and research about the model. Next, the teachers practice the model with each other. Then several of the teachers decide to try it out in their classrooms. By utilizing a peer-coaching process, teachers can work with a partner to observe the implementation of the model. The peer partners observe each other and verify whether the syntax of the model was utilized precisely and accurately. The observer notes how well students worked with the model. Suggestions by the observer to the partner teacher support and provide insight to supplement the teacher's self-appraisal.

Based on staff development experiences, Hillary Hertzog, Margo Pensavalle, and I recommended the following format for peer coaching:

1. Peer partners share a concern or teaching problem.
2. The concern or problem is delimited so that the consulting partner can focus specifically on the teaching behavior or problem during an observation.
3. The partner consultant observes and takes notes.
4. The notes are shared, and both teachers take part in the analysis.
5. The consulting partner provides feedback only on what was specified. If additional information about teaching is sought, the partner who was observed must ask for it. It is not volunteered.

TEACHERS AS STAFF DEVELOPERS

Staff development is one of the new role responsibilities that teachers are assuming. Collegial relationships free teachers to both acknowledge and accept personal strengths and weaknesses. Teachers should not be ashamed to acknowledge areas in which they are not, and perhaps do not want to be, expert. But many teachers do have areas of expertise, and in these areas they must assume responsibility for leadership.

Teachers are uniquely qualified to lead staff development programs because of their intimate knowledge of the classroom population, the community context, and essential skills. Many of the same skills needed for motivating children are important in staff development programs. For example, the teacher-leader needs to be enthusiastic, be clear about the staff development purposes, keep the program participants engaged in the task at hand, select activities appropriate to the goal,

Teaching Hints: Peer Coaching

- Coaching is situation-specific to colleague teachers.
- Colleagues are learning/practicing new skills, knowledge, and/or strategies.
- Colleagues are experimenting.
- Coaching is ongoing and continuous.
- Teachers have a collegial relationship, and coaching is a means for self-help.

and relate the program to classroom implementation. The teacher-leader should also be skillful in human relations.

Staff Development Programs

Successful staff development programs typically focus on the following:

- Improvement of specific skills
- Demonstrations and opportunities for practicing new skills and receiving feedback
- Relationship to local school problems
- Curriculum development needs and processes and new programs
- Support services

Good teaching is contagious. Successful teachers attract other teachers who want to learn new ideas and techniques. Schoolwide improvement occurs simultaneously as teachers improve. Improvement of teaching performance happens slowly and developmentally. Most teachers are motivated to improve their instructional performance because they care about their students. Research indicates that paying teachers to participate in staff development programs is not as effective as appealing to teachers' natural motivation to improve their abilities and become better at what they do.

Improvement at the school level depends on individual teachers. Concerned teachers must be involved in the planning of the improvement process. For schools to improve, teachers must meet together, be aware of the scope of the problem, and be committed to improvement. Teachers are professional experts and must make the decisions about the change process.

As teachers take on the role and responsibility for their own staff development, consideration must be given to the following questions:

- *Who* needs to learn what? (Who else, other than the teachers, need to "know"—students, parents, library personnel, principal, district personnel?)
- *How* is the new different from the old?
- *What* needs to be learned to implement the new?
- *What* support services and resources are affected by the "new"?

Teacher Leadership

There is considerable evidence that teachers are performing a variety of roles and assuming responsibilities beyond the classroom, unlike those performed in the past by traditional classroom teachers. Classroom teachers have become researchers, mentors, peer coaches, curriculum developers, and staff developers. The new teacher-leader is involved structurally in the school, participating in decision-making teams and problem-solving groups, creating standards, writing grants, and serving on personnel committees to screen new teachers.

Teachers are engaged in the study of their profession and are involved in experiences as learners, teachers, and leaders. Their activities are full-time, continuous, and interactive. Roles and responsibilities nurture inquiry processes and make teachers more thoughtful and reflective personally and professionally.

PARTNERSHIP MODELS: UNIVERSITY AND SCHOOL DISTRICT

The university–school district partnership model offers teachers another approach to continuing education and teacher leadership. There are a remarkable number of partnership models in existence. Some have informal arrangements; others have formalized the association and may call themselves *professional development schools* (PDSs).

Informal models may be "favored" schools or cooperating network schools that work with one university teacher-education program. The university assigns a cluster of student teachers and a university coordinator to the school. The close relationship and favored status evolves as teachers and university personnel become accustomed to each other and both develop expectations about the relationship, which includes relinquishing traditional controls. The teachers participate and lead school-site seminars for the student teachers and interested university faculty, and the university coordinator may help arrange staff development programs for the participating teachers.

The PDS may be a formalized partnership funded by an outside agency. The funds are often used to release teachers by paying for substitutes to enable the partner teachers to engage in staff development. PDSs are usually involved in restructuring activities. The expert teachers at the PDS and the university share responsibility for providing appropriate experiences for the student teachers.

Partnership schools are characterized by the following:

- The continuing education of teachers
- Reflective teachers engaged in site-specific inquiry
- A democratic community with shared school governance
- Collegial relationships among school faculty and between university and school faculty
- A cohort of student teachers educated jointly by the university and the expert teachers
- An environment that supports and nurtures the sharing of expertise

CHARTER SCHOOLS

A charter school provides an alternative to the traditional school system. It is an alternative for students and their parents, teachers, and administrators. Charter schools are funded with public money and may be designed by parents, teachers, or community groups. The charter must be approved by a school district or by the state government. The purpose of the charter should be:

Innovation
Freedom from school district rules
Unique means in curriculum, instruction, or
    environment

Generally the charter is set for three to five years; however, the charter may be revoked if the school's academic performance lags behind district schools with similar populations. Though publicly funded, money is not given for the use of facilities. As a consequence, charter schools beg for places within other schools or in the community to conduct classes. The charter school is a free-choice school. Teachers choose the school because they believe in the goals of the charter and because they choose to teach in a particular way. Administrators also choose the charter because of philosophic beliefs, and students attend because their parents believe that the charter is superior to the traditional school.

HOME SCHOOLING

Home schooling is for children who are unable to attend regular school classes because of illness, autism, giftedness, working responsibilities, and/or parental philosophic beliefs. There are laws that protect the parent (and the child) so that schooling can occur in the home environment. School districts are responsible for employing a credentialed teacher(s) who will supervise the home-schooling program.

The teacher's responsibilities include holding periodic classes for home-schooled children, verifying that the child is learning appropriate subject matter, testing the child, helping the parent as needed, assessing progress, and counseling both child and parent. Home-schooled children may be a very diverse group: different needs, varied ages and grades. As a consequence, the teacher has a difficult assignment, particularly when it comes to holding classes for the students.

PROFESSIONAL ASSOCIATIONS CONTRIBUTE TO PROFESSIONAL DEVELOPMENT

Teachers have a wide range of professional-group choices available to them for membership. There are professional associations related to almost every subject field. The following organizations provide services to elementary and middle school teachers; most have web sites, which can be found in Appendix A.

- American Alliance for Health, Physical Education, Recreation, and Dance
- Council for Exceptional Children
- International Reading Association
- National Art Education Association
- National Association for Bilingual Education
- National Association for Gifted Children
- National Association for Research in Science Teaching
- National Association of Music Educators
- National Council for Geographic Education
- National Council for History Education
- National Council for the Social Studies
- National Council of Teachers of English
- National Council of Teachers of Mathematics
- National Science Teachers Association

Professional development is enhanced by membership in these national groups. Each of the associations offers members periodic journals, newsletters, bulletins, and research information. In addition, they typically hold a national conference that meets over a long weekend. The conference location shifts each year to vary both the local perspective and the travel time. At the conferences, teachers take part in committee work, workshops, and discussion groups. Each association brings in noted scholars in the subject field who report on noteworthy curriculum development, research, and socially significant issues. The association, in cooperation with a local university, frequently manages compressed classes for teachers interested in unit credit. Publishers' exhibits at these conferences provide teachers with the opportunity to view and critique the latest instructional materials and media related to the subject field.

In recent years, professional associations have assumed the responsibility of providing their members with continuing education. The conference enhances professional life and provides teachers with an enjoyable way to engage in dialogue with other professionals.

Two other national groups need to be recognized for their contribution to the professional advancement of teachers: the National Education Association (NEA) and the American Federation of Teachers (AFT). Both provide members with ethical, legal, and political leadership and services. The NEA primarily serves members who live in suburban and rural areas; AFT members typically live in the large urban areas. The NEA publishes *Today's Education* and the *NEA Reporter*. The AFT publishes *Changing Education* and *The American Teacher*. Both groups furnish members with congressional and political information important for the profession, as well as curriculum and instruction articles, through their journals and newsletters.

Local and State Associations

Many of the national professional associations have local and state chapters. These smaller groups often have their own newsletter or journal and regional conferences. The local meetings focus on classroom and community problems and function as a collegial support system. Committee and task force participation is encouraged by these groups. Frequently state legislative information on problems is handled by these state associations, and state departments of education turn to the local chapters for assistance and information about educational problems and priorities.

PERSONAL DEVELOPMENT THROUGH EXTRACURRICULAR ACTIVITIES

It is as important to grow as a mature and cultured adult as it is to develop as a professional person. It is commonly recognized that "all work and no play" can truly make one a very dull person. The all-work syndrome also contributes to the phenomenon known as teacher burnout. Outside interests, activities, and friendships, distinct from professional associations and activities, help the professional person achieve balance.

Teachers join drama groups, political party groups, book clubs, and recreational organizations in order to get away from school and gain a different perspective about community life. Involvement in community affairs and in the cultural life of the community helps teachers develop vital intellectual, social, and emotional capacities. Continuing education encompasses all aspects of human development. Adult growth depends on positive relationships with others as well as interaction with one's life work.

TEAM TEACHING: CONTRIBUTION TO PROFESSIONALISM

Team teaching is a way of combining the instructional efforts of two or more teachers to use their abilities to the best advantage. Teacher aides or assistants may also be included in the teaming arrangement. Teaming can be particularly advantageous at the elementary school level because of the diversity of subjects that are taught. For example, if several fourth-grade teachers at a school teamed, each might be a team leader for a different subject of the curriculum. The team leader would accept greater responsibility for planning and teaching in the area of his or her expertise. The other members of the team would serve as assistants during instruction and would help with reinforcement.

Group planning time is critical when working in a team situation. Members of the team need to share plans and objectives and receive feedback about whether a lesson accomplished its purpose. Team teaching provides a system whereby new and inexperienced teachers can learn teaching methodologies from more experienced colleagues and receive feedback about their own teaching performance.

Implementation of teaming is different in each situation. In some schools, an experienced teacher is called the *lead teacher* and is responsible for most of the planning. However, the professional reason for teaming should be to refine instructional techniques and provide students with instruction from teachers who are motivated and superior in each subject field. Teaming provides a built-in system for staff development.

Because teachers pool their respective classes in team teaching, this organizational system allows students to be grouped by need rather than by grade. Students move from one group to another depending on the subject and the student's ability. Nongraded teaching teams from primary grades, middle grades, or upper grades are popular in many schools.

In Karen Adazzio's middle school, the students are clustered in what have been called *houses*. Teachers do team teaching in this arrangement for integrating the core subjects. At Adazzio's school, the teachers bank time in order to have extra planning time together. Banking time is a means to teach longer several days a week so that school can be dismissed earlier on another day to accommodate teachers' planning needs.

LEGAL ISSUES AFFECTING TEACHERS

Teacher Tenure

Most states have tenure laws to protect teachers from irresponsible and arbitrary dismissal. Tenure laws specify how teachers gain tenure and under what conditions or circumstances tenured teachers can be dismissed. The purpose of tenure is to provide capable teachers with security so that changes in school boards or public reaction to educational issues will not result in teacher dismissal without just cause. Generally, grounds for dismissal are described in the state's tenure statute. Most states will dismiss a teacher for immorality, unprofessional conduct, insubordination, and incompetency. Teachers must be dismissed for cause.

Dismissal of tenured teachers cannot occur without specific procedures being followed. These procedures vary from state to state. In most states, the teacher needs to be informed in writing of the charges filed against him or her prior to the dismissal hearing. After written notice, the teacher is usually given a specified amount of time to prepare for a hearing before the school board. The teacher has the right to have counsel at the hearing. If a teacher is dissatisfied with the results of the hearing, he or she may take the case before the courts.

Teachers can also lose tenure status by resigning from their school district position. Unless the school board grants a leave of absence, teachers will lose tenure status if they voluntarily absent themselves from their position. Teachers moving from one school district to another within their own state can also lose tenure unless the new school board agrees to tenure status.

Teachers gain tenure by teaching in a school district for a predetermined number of years and following the requirements of the state. Teachers are typically considered probationary teachers during the nontenured period. The probationary period varies between two and four years among the states. In some school districts, teachers must be evaluated a specified number of times during the probationary period to verify satisfactory performance. In some states, the teacher applies to the state for tenure status after serving satisfactorily in a school district; in other states, the teacher must be recognized by formal action of the school board before tenure rights are granted.

Some states have **continuing contract** laws. For teachers who have not yet gained tenure, they may expect that a school board will notify them of the expiration of their contract, usually by May 1. If they are not notified of dismissal by that date, they may assume that they have a continuing contract. The continuing contract protects nontenured teachers from summer dismissal, when it would be difficult to obtain another position.

Tenured teachers have what is called an **indefinite contract.** This means that the contract is renewed automatically each year without mutual action by teacher and school board.

Salaries

Most school districts have a single salary schedule for all teachers. Salaries are differentiated by experience and education. Salaries are adjusted both vertically (for experience) and horizontally (for education). Thus, a teacher with an advanced degree and/or special training will be placed higher on the salary schedule than a teacher without special education. Currently, however, there are controversial proposals to pay some teachers more than others based on their subject expertise—for example, teachers who are able to teach bilingually or who specialize in mathematics or science.

Some states have a minimum-salary law that affects public school teachers. In such cases, the school board may pay teachers higher than the minimum salary, but not lower.

Many states have collective bargaining laws, which identify the procedures for school boards to negotiate with teacher organizations. The teacher organization with the greatest membership in the school district is typically given the right to represent the teachers of the district for salary and benefit negotiations.

The First Amendment

The Association for Supervision and Curriculum Development (ASCD) and the First Amendment Center are working to educate school leaders, teachers, and others about the meaning and significance of the First Amendment. The First Amendment guarantees expressive and religious freedom, and one of the joint project's goals is to encourage curriculum developers and teachers to educate for freedom and responsibility. Their publication *The First Amendment in Schools* (Haynes, Chaltain, Ferguson, Hudson, & Thomas, 2003) provides guidance on many issues that affect teachers, administrators, students, parents, and board members. The authors include a special section on teacher and administrator rights and responsibilities (pp. 92–103), and I will refer to several of the questions they pose in this segment.

1. *What protection do teachers have if they feel they have been treated unfairly?* Teachers are protected by (1) teacher tenure laws, (2) collective bargaining agreement contracts between the school district and the local teacher union, and (3) the U.S. Constitution (Bill of Rights and the Fourteenth Amendment).
2. *Are teachers required to salute the flag when the Pledge of Allegiance is recited?* The authors answered, "Probably not." Citing related cases, the authors believe that teachers may refuse to salute the flag.

3. *May teachers dress as they please?* Again the response was, "Probably not." Though there have been few court cases related to this question, the authors believe that teacher dress codes can be enforced.

4. *May teachers wear religious symbols when teaching?* The experts seem to agree that symbols (cross, Star of David) may be worn, but "proselytizing" messages cannot be displayed on clothing.

5. *May teachers teach whatever they believe is appropriate?* "Probably not." Subjects considered unsuitable by the school district or parents may not be taught in the classroom, and the teacher may be fired for doing so.

6. *Do students have complete artistic freedom of expression?* Teachers may set standards and requirements for assignments. However, if the student has fulfilled the requirements and the teacher just dislikes the message communicated by the student, the student should not be "marked down." The authors note that if the student's work is "vulgar, profane, or obscene, then a teacher has the authority to remove the work or restrict its presence on school grounds" (p. 103).

Immoral Behavior

A school district learns that a young female teacher is living with her boyfriend and gives her notice of dismissal. After receiving the notice, the teacher marries her boyfriend, but the school district goes ahead with the case, claiming that she is guilty of immoral behavior. The teacher challenges the charge in court. The court finds no evidence that her behavior affected her classroom behavior and upholds the rights of the teacher. Lifestyle issues are a problem only if it can be proved that they interfere with teaching effectiveness.

Other Benefits

Most school districts allow teachers 10 full days of sick leave. Some districts allow half days. Generally, unused sick days may be accumulated from year to year, and in some districts the unused time may be part of a retirement package.

Most districts provide health care benefits for teachers and their families. Other benefits include maternity leave, child care leave, personal business leave, and sabbatical leave. Districts differ in terms of benefits paid to teachers for sabbatical leave.

Professional Liability and Malpractice

Professional liability occurs as a result of **negligence**, that is, because the teacher did not exercise due care or did not foresee harm. Fischer, Schimmel, and Kelly (1987, p. 57) identify the four conditions necessary for a teacher to be held for damages when a student is injured:

1. The teacher was required to be on duty and protect the student from injury.
2. The teacher failed to exercise due care.
3. The student was injured as a result of the teacher's failure to exercise due care.
4. The student can prove injury as a consequence.

Professional liability increases if the students are young and the teacher is expected to be on duty. Negligence charges need to be proved based on lack of supervision and foresight of foreseeable danger. Close supervision is necessary during physical education and when students use special equipment that is dangerous. Whenever students can harm each other during activities and through use of equipment, teachers can be held liable for negligence.

If the injured student failed to exercise reasonable care of him- or herself, then the student may be guilty of **contributory negligence.** This can occur only if the student is old enough and has the mental maturity to exercise reasonable care.

Comparative negligence arises in situations in which both the teacher and student are at fault. This typically means that the teacher will be held accountable for some proportion of damages to the extent that the teacher contributed to the injury (McNergney & Herbert, 1995).

Teachers can protect themselves by purchasing insurance. Insurance programs are often sponsored through professional organizations; both the NEA and AFT have liability insurance programs.

Public pressure groups seek to charge school districts with educational malpractice when a student is injured intellectually or psychologically. Such cases are often based on a student's failure to learn. Cases involving student failure to learn would involve many teachers and the school district. There does not appear to be a way for parents to prove the liability of a given teacher or school district in such a case.

Copying Materials for the Classroom

Several years ago, an instructional specialist from a small school district proudly told me how she had copied a whole chapter out of one of my textbooks for the teachers in her school district. She anticipated that I would be flattered and pleased. Imagine her surprise when I countered with, "Don't you know that you violated copyright law?"

Copyright law protects materials from being copied by others either before publication or afterward. Fischer, Schimmel, and Kelly (1987) relate the case of the UCLA professor whose lecture notes were recorded by a student in class, sold to an entrepreneur, copied, and sold to other students. The professor sued the entrepreneur, claiming that his lecture notes were protected by common-law copyright. The court agreed. Common-law copyright protects an author's or artist's creative endeavor before publication; after publication, federal law protects the author or artist.

Teachers often want to use published pictures, articles, or poems in their classrooms. In general, teachers may make a single copy for use in the classroom. Copies for each student can be made under certain conditions. Conditions include tests of brevity, spontaneity, and cumulative effect (Fischer, Schimmel, & Kelly, 1987). Most school districts have guidelines available for teachers to verify what is fair use of an author's work.

In Loco Parentis

The idea of schools operating **in loco parentis** (in place of parents) means that schools have the power to act as if they were parents from the time students leave home to the time they return home. In recent years, this doctrine has been weakened, and courts often rule in favor of First Amendment rights for students versus school rights and authority. The doctrine has also been weakened in the instance of corporal punishment; in some states, parents have the right to forbid the use of corporal punishment. In general, decisions about punishment of students fall to the local school board.

In elementary schools, in loco parentis often means that teachers perform tasks that a parent would perform. For example, primary school teachers may have to tie shoes, button sweaters, or verify that students eat their lunches. The teacher listens and sympathizes.

Students' Rights

On November 20, 1989, the United Nations General Assembly adopted the Convention on the Rights of the Child. The convention deals with three kinds of rights: participation rights, provision rights, and protection rights. Edmonds (1992) defines these rights as follows:

- **Participation rights** mean that children have the right to participate in decisions that affect their lives and futures; they have freedom of expression; freedom of conscience, thought, and religion; freedom of association and assembly; and freedom from government interference in their privacy.
- **Rights of provision** deal with the economic, social, and cultural rights of the individual. For example, rights of provision include the rights to have adequate food, shelter, health care, and conditions that do not foster conflict or abuse.
- The **right of protection** means that the convention protects children from potential abuse or harm. For example, in Guatemala, a 13-year-old youth was kicked to death by the Guatemalan police in March 1990. Amnesty International pressured the director of the national police force and, ultimately, the police officers were sentenced to 15 years in prison. This was, of course, a hollow victory, but it emphasizes the nature of the covenant.

The challenge for teachers, according to Edmonds (1992, p. 205), is to do the following:

- Learn what human rights are.
- Help young people understand their rights.
- Examine the problem of universality and global multiculturalism.
- Create a classroom and school in which children's rights are achieved.

SUMMARY

Teachers' knowledge encompasses subject-field content, pedagogical strategies, and knowledge about students. To engage in appropriate lesson planning, teachers need to know what students know and do not know. Teachers make decisions about use of resources, setting standards, organization, and management of the school environment.

Teachers improve teaching and schools by participating in professional communities and teacher networks, sharing learning and expertise, and engaging in collaborative research. Teachers share in school governance by making decisions about school culture, school organization, and the school community.

Teachers are actively engaged in classroom research to change teaching practices and the classroom environment. Peer coaching helps teachers study teaching and develop shared professional language and provides a structure for the follow-up of professional learning. Teacher-leaders participate in a variety of school-based activities: faculty committees, grade-level and subject-field leadership, collaborative sharing, curriculum development, and mentoring.

A number of legal issues affect teachers' work. Tenure laws protect teachers from irresponsible and arbitrary dismissal. Most states grant tenure after a predetermined number of years and satisfactory evaluations during the probationary period. Because schools operate in loco parentis, teachers of young children often perform tasks that a parent would perform. Students are covered by the right of protection, which guards them from harm and potential abuse.

PORTFOLIO ACTIVITY

Teachers contribute to school effectiveness by collaborating with other professionals. Identify ways that you are involved in nonteaching professional activities. These activities may include curriculum development, sharing responsibility with colleagues for decisions about instructional strategies, peer coaching, improving the school culture, relationships with parents, service learning, and demonstrating new models of teaching. Describe your activity and your relationship with others. Identify the purpose (goal) of your work and your means for accomplishing it. Analyze your progress and provide some form of evidence.

 ## DISCUSSION QUESTIONS AND APPLICATION EXERCISES

1. You are initiating the use of cooperative learning groups in your classroom. How can you model cooperative collegial development for your students to demonstrate adult cooperative learning?

2. You are teaching primary-age children, most of whom are learning to read successfully; however, some are lagging behind. The students enjoy listening to stories, drawing pictures, and writing their own stories about the pictures. Using your knowledge of growth and development, describe several lessons you would emphasize with the students and the activities in which they would participate.

3. Identify some instructional areas for improvement. What are some activities that will help you improve your performance?

4. You are teaching middle school students. The students have been discussing mad cow disease. Identify subject fields appropriate for the topic and explain how you will incorporate the students' interest and concern into your lesson plan. Describe your students, their needs, and the activities they will participate in.

5. Using the information about successful staff development programs discussed in this chapter, suggest some questions to evaluate a staff development workshop.

6. Write a content outline and suggested activities to teach your students about human rights and, in particular, children's rights.

7. Name one or more books on the current best-seller list.

8. List the cultural events you have attended in the last month. (Delete movies from your list!)

9. Identify a teaching/learning problem in your classroom. Describe how you could gather research data to provide insight concerning the problem.

10. Describe several successful means you use to grab students' interest and participation.

11. Design a self-evaluation checklist similar to Figure 14.2.

12. Design a rubric for you and your students to assess how well students work in cooperative groups.

READER RESEARCH

You have been asked to judge another teacher's portfolio. Discuss the research on teachers' portfolios and what you will be looking for when you examine the teacher's work.

Figure 14.2 Self-Evaluation Checklist

Develop your own self-evaluation checklist similar to this one.

	Yes	No
I plan my lessons before presenting them.	_____	_____
I choose instructional materials that are relevant and appropriate for my students.	_____	_____
My directions are clear and concise.	_____	_____
My follow-up materials reinforce my lessons. (They are not busy work.)	_____	_____
I edit my handouts to see that they are grammatical and legible.	_____	_____
I pace my lessons to keep students interested.	_____	_____
I encourage students to participate.	_____	_____
I try to talk to each student individually.	_____	_____
I listen when students want to talk to me.	_____	_____

The "scripted" lesson plan is closely related to painting by the numbers!

TECHNOLOGY APPLICATIONS

Devise a rubric in table format to self-assess your skill in facilitating students' discussion. If students are mature enough (ages 8 to 12), ask them to evaluate your skills. Read about rubrics in this text and use other resources available on the Internet. Read about facilitating class discussions in this text (Chapter 4) and use other resources.

Credits from Johanna Kasin Lemlech. *Curriculum and Instructional Methods for the Elementary and Middle School*, 7/e

Photo credits: Photos on pages 241 and 334 by Johanna Kasin Lemlech. All other photos by Paula Goldman.

Index